A HANDBOOK
OF GREEK MYTHOLOGY

A Handbook
of Greek Mythology

INCLUDING ITS EXTENSION TO ROME

H. J. ROSE

METHUEN & CO. LTD

First published 1928 by Methuen & Co. Ltd
11 New Fetter Lane, London EC4P 4EE
Sixth edition 1958

First published as a University Paperback in 1964
Reprinted four times
Reprinted 1983

ISBN 0 416 68200 6

Printed and bound in Great Britain
by J. W. Arrowsmith Ltd, Bristol

VIRO DOCTISSIMO

DEQVE HIS STVDIIS OPTIME MERITO

L. R. FARNELL, D.LITT

COLLEGII EXONIENSIS APVD OXONIENSES

RECTORI

AMICITIAE ERGO

PREFACE

AS a teacher of Classics I have often felt handicapped by
the lack of a book of moderate length, containing an
accurate account of Greek mythology, in accordance
with the results of modern research. This work is an attempt
to supply that want. It claims no originality, being frankly
a compilation from such standard works as Roscher's *Lexikon*,
Preller-Robert, and others named in the Bibliography. I have,
however, in all cases examined the original authorities and hope
that the references given will be found accurate and to the point ;
experience of the shortcomings of others in these respects forbids
me to hope that they are faultless.

I have had in mind three classes of readers. Firstly, the
student, whether of ancient or of modern literature, who wants
an outline knowledge of the subject, may content himself with
reading the matter set out in large print ; he will thus acquaint
himself with those stories of gods and heroes which were commonly known and more or less believed in the classical epoch by
Greeks. Secondly, those who want more detail will find, in the
paragraphs in smaller type, a number of obscure, late, or purely
local stories, told perhaps in a single Greek city or district. or
appearing for the first time in some Roman author. Thirdly,
the notes at the ends of the chapters will give the reader who
wishes to embark on a thorough study of mythology a clue to
further researches.

The great problem in such a work as this is one of omission.
I have tried to solve it by leaving out all those persons who
have no story worth telling,—warriors who appear in an epic
only to be killed; gods worshipped in some obscure corner, whose
myth, if ever they had one, is now lost; heroes who exist but to
provide a legendary founder for some city, and the like. Whether
I have chosen judiciously is for those versed in the subject to
decide, or perhaps rather for those who use this book as a source
of information. Criticisms will be welcomed from either.

Finally I must thank, not only those friends who have personally helped me, but the numerous scholars, known to me only through their writings, without whose works a book of this sort would be impossible for anyone not a miracle of patience and erudition to compose.

In the Second Edition some slips of author or printer have been corrected and the Addenda on page 340 enlarged.

H. J. R.

St. Andrews

NOTE TO THIRD EDITION

IN this edition, such limited correction as seemed possible in wartime has been done.

H. J. R.

St. Andrews

NOTE TO FOURTH EDITION

THIS is substantially identical with the third, a few minor corrections having been made.

H. J. R.

St. Andrews

NOTE TO FIFTH EDITION

IT has been found possible in this edition to make somewhat more extensive changes than before ; it is hoped that they will be found improvements.

H. J. R.

St. Andrews

NOTE TO SIXTH EDITION

I HAVE tried, so far as was practicable, to get rid of residual errors and to bring the notes and bibliography up to date.

H. J. R.

CONTENTS

A HANDBOOK OF GREEK MYTHOLOGY

CHAPTER I

INTRODUCTION : HISTORY OF MYTHOLOGY

WE use the word mythology to signify the study of certain products of the imagination of a people, which take the form of tales. These tales the Greeks called μῦθοι, or myths, an expression which originally meant simply ' words '. The purpose of this book is to set forth what stories were produced by the active imagination of those peoples whom we collectively know as Greek, and by the narrow and sluggish imagination of the ancient inhabitants of Italy. It is well to begin by inquiring what manner of tales they were ; for it is very clear that we cannot take them, as they stand, as historically true, or even as slightly idealized or exaggerated history. Full as they are of impossible events, it needs no argument to prove that they differ widely from Thucydides' account of the Peloponnesian War, or Hippokrates' discussions of the effect of diet on a patient. We may disbelieve some of Thucydides' statements, and we have come to consider many of Hippokrates' methods erroneous ; but obviously both are trying to state facts and draw reasonable conclusions therefrom. What are we to say of the tellers of these quite unbelievable, although picturesque legends, and of those who heard and more or less credited them ? It is here that opinions differ most widely, and have differed in the past.[1]

1. *The Allegorical Theory.* One of the most ancient explanations is that these tales of wonder are allegories, concealing some deep and edifying meaning, which the wisdom of primeval sages prompted them to hide in this manner, either to prevent great truths passing into the hands of persons too ignorant or too impious to use them aright, or to attract by stories those who

1

would not listen to a dry and formal discussion. As an example, I will cite the interpretation given of a well-known myth, the Judgment of Paris, by the so-called Sallustius.[2] As he tells the story, the gods were at a banquet, when Eris (Strife, Emulation) cast among them a golden apple, inscribed ' For the Fairest '. Three goddesses, Hera, Athena and Aphrodite, having all claimed it, the decision was referred by Zeus to Paris, son of Priam of Troy. Aphrodite having bribed him with the promise of the loveliest of mortal women as his wife, he decided in her favour. ' Here,' says our author, ' the banquet signifies the supramundane powers of the gods, and that is why they are together; the golden apple signifies the universe, which, as it is made of opposites, is rightly said to be thrown by Strife, and as the various gods give various gifts to the universe they are thought to vie with one another for the possession of the apple; further, the soul that lives in accordance with sense-perception (for that is Paris), seeing beauty alone and not the other powers in the universe, says that the apple is Aphrodite's.'

It needs no great amount of argument to show that such a view as this is wrong. It assumes that these early Greeks among whom the story of Paris originated possessed a systematic philosophy concerning the powers, both visible and invisible, of the universe, and also the moral duties of man. Now we know enough of their early history to be able to say that neither they nor any other people in a similar stage of development ever had any such philosophy, which is the product of ages of civilized thought. Had any system of the kind existed in the days before Homer, we may be very certain that the long series of brilliant intellects to whom the organized thought of Greece, and ultimately of modern Europe, is due, would not have had to begin at the very beginning and discover for themselves the elements of physics, of ethics, and of logic. The myth cannot be an allegory, because its originators had little or nothing to allegorize.

Still, we can see how the idea originated. In the first place, the Greeks, like most peoples, had great respect for their ancestors, and were apt to credit them with much that later generations had produced. Hence came a tendency to try to find deep wisdom in anything they were reported to have said or done. Secondly, allegory is really very old in Greece; we shall find examples in Homer and Hesiod, for instance.[3] Moreover, one of the oldest forms of religious composition, the metrical answers given at oracular shrines, affected a dark and allegorical language. Hence it is no wonder that this theory, although false, gained popularity, was widely used by orthodox pagans to explain away certain features in the stories told of their gods and heroes which seemed inconsistent with a divine or exalted nature, and was in turn eagerly adopted by Jewish and Christian commentators to read sublime meanings into puzzling passages of the Old Testament.

2. *The Symbolic Theory.* After lasting in various forms through the Middle Ages, this view appeared in a modified form as late as the nineteenth century. Friedrich Creuzer (1771–1858), in a very learned but very cloudy and uncritical work,[4] set forth a theory which may be interpreted as follows. The ancestors of the ancient nations whose history we know, —Egyptians, Indians, Greeks, Romans and others,—possessed, not indeed a complete philosophy, but a dim and at the same time grandiose conception of certain fundamental religious truths, and in particular of monotheism. These truths their priests set forth in a series of symbols, which remained much the same for all peoples, but were hopelessly misunderstood in later times. To recover the oldest ideas, according to him, we shall do well to take those myths which seem absurdest, and try to interpret them. For myths are not the result of the artistic activity of poets, but something far older. One specimen of his methods will be enough.[5] Thus, it is stated that Talos' name meant ' sun ' in Cretan. His legend, says Creuzer, signifies that the Cretans set forth the beneficent powers of the sunlight under the form of a divine guardian of their island ; they also, like the Phoenicians with their Moloch, symbolized his destructive power, perhaps by a human sacrifice by burning ; but also they gave a moral aspect to his nature, for is it not stated that Talos was in reality a man, who went about with bronze tablets containing the laws of Minos, whose observance he enforced ?

All this is very ingenious, but falls to pieces at a touch of criticism. To begin with, there is the old difficulty which beset the allegorical theory in its cruder form ; we have no right to suppose either that the early Cretans had an elaborate solar philosophy or that, if they had had one, they would have expressed it in allegories. Moreover, his account of Talos is a mere jumble, made up of tags from various late or lateish authors, which Creuzer has put together into a composite picture of what never existed in the Cretan imagination or any other, save his own. He goes on to make the jumble worse by adducing further supposed parallels with which the story of Talos has in reality nothing to do. And if we look at other interpretations of myths scattered up and down his work, or similar works by his followers and predecessors, we shall find many instances of just this uncritical handling of a myth, *i.e.*, this mixture of older and newer forms, combined with absence of any clear recognition of how stories of this sort really do originate.

But for all his absurdities, Creuzer was right on one point. Schiller, to whom he owed much, had said that Art breaks up the white light of Truth into the prismatic colours; and the imagination works in a somewhat similar way, not setting forth facts clearly and sharply, as the reason does, but dealing in pictures. In a sense, myths are symbolic, though not as Creuzer supposed them to be.

Besides this truth which he recognized, and which entitles him to a not dishonourable place in the history of Mythology, there is another and a worse reason why symbolism continues here and there to have a certain popularity, and that is the childish fascination which anything mysterious has for certain minds. A story, or anything else, which is supposed to have a hidden meaning attracts some adults, just as a secret society with pass-words and so forth attracts children ; and so there are to this day half-educated persons who read all manner of extraordinary meanings of their own invention into details of pictures by great artists, obscure passages in such documents as the Book of Daniel, or the measurements of ancient monuments, particularly, for some reason, the Great Pyramid of Gizeh. I have even come across one ingenious theorist who had found abstruse secrets hidden in the letter H and in one or two buildings the ground plan of which suggested that letter.

3. *Rationalism.* There is a type of mind, which also existed in antiquity, which is utterly incapable of realizing how simple people think. To such a mind, certain facts of experience are so self-evident that every one except a fool must always have recognized them. It follows therefore that no one who thought at all can ever have believed, for instance, that a monster half-horse and half-man could exist, or that a woman was turned into a stone or a tree. If therefore stories of this sort are told, they must be the result of misunderstanding or trickery. There have come to us from antiquity several treatises which put this theory into operation, for instance a little work *On incredible tales*[6], which bears the name of Palaiphatos. The author, after proving elaborately that there are no such things as Centaurs, gives the following reconstruction of the legend. When Ixion was King of Thessaly, the country was much plagued by herds of wild cattle. On his offering a reward for their destruction, certain enterprising archers from a village called Nephele went out on horseback and shot them down. Hence arose the tale

that Ixion was the father by Nephele (the Cloud) of a race of beings called Kentauroi (prickers of bulls) who were a mixture of man and horse.

One example is enough of this sort of nonsense, which hardly needs to be refuted. It supposes such a state of mind as never existed or will exist in this world. People so blind to facts as to make a tale of wonder out of a commonplace event like the shooting by mounted archers of some wild cattle would have believed easily enough in all sorts of marvels, and freely invented them without any motor to set their imaginations at work. For savages and barbarians (and it is to be remembered that the origins of Greek and other myths go back to barbarism or savagery)[7] have but a small range of experience, and therefore have generally no standard by which to try whether a tale is incredible or not ; and even among civilized men there are to be found plenty who will believe almost any wonder if only it is far enough off in space or in time. But even the lowest savages are not as a rule so densely stupid as to misunderstand what is clearly visible to them, or simple statements in their own tongue about things happening to their neighbours ; and Palaiphatos supposes the tale of the shape and parentage of the Centaurs to have arisen from a remark that ' the Bull-stickers from Nephele (ἐκ Νεφέλης ; the phrase might be taken to mean " born of the Cloud ") are raiding ', and the supposedly novel sight of horses with men on their backs. Nevertheless, this feeble and irrational ' rationalism ' still persists.

I have seen a children's book containing the story of Dick Whittington, which solemnly stated in its introduction that Whittington really laid the foundation of his fortune by a successful venture in a ship called *The Cat*. Among other things, this explanation neglects the fact that in Whittington's own day the story of the cat was at least two centuries old, for he died in 1423 and the story is to be found in the *Annals* of Albert von Stade, who died in 1264. Who first told it we do not know. Naturally the old story had been attached to the historical Whittington, as such tales often are to a well-known and popular man.

This miserable theory has not even the grain of truth which is to be found in the first two. Such origins of stories as it imagines simply do not exist. The nearest approach to the supposed process is that, as we shall see presently, legendary details are often enough added to historical facts.

4. *Euhemerism.* Somewhat less absurd is the theory called after Euhemeros, a writer who lived not long after Alexander the Great,[8] although it existed in a less systematic form before

him. His ideas were couched in the shape of a romance, in which he claimed to have discovered evidence that the gods of popular tradition were simply men deified by those whom they had ruled or benefited. Thus Zeus became an ancient king of Crete, who rebelled against and overthrew his father Kronos, the former king, and similar biographies of the remaining deities were offered. Omitting the absurdities in detail,—for the events in these alleged lives of the gods were arrived at simply by rationalizing the current legends,—we may look for a moment at the kernel of the theory, namely that popular gods are nothing but deified men. Here at least we have a fact alleged as a cause, for there is abundant evidence that some men have been deified, from flattery or gratitude, in Greece and out of it. But to make a dead man into a god, one must believe already in gods of some sort ; hence this theory will not do as an explanation of the origin of either religion or mythology. Even in its modified form, that the cult of gods arose from fear of ghosts, a view put forward by Herbert Spencer and others, it is unsatisfactory. However, in a book of this sort we are chiefly concerned to note, first, that it will not explain more than a small fraction of the existing mythical tales ; second, that there is an element of truth in it, since no very sharp line of cleavage can be drawn between legends of heroes and myths concerning gods.

In antiquity the theory of Euhemeros had a great vogue. In particular, Christian apologists seized joyfully on a statement coming from pagan sources that the best-known pagan gods were nothing but men, for by that time the sense of historical reality was grown too faint for the absurdities of Euhemeros to be noticed, and apart from this particular development, numerous writers tried to discover in these venerable tales some reminiscence of early history, a proceeding which, however mistaken in its methods, was not irrational in itself.

5. *Theory of Nature-myths.* We may distinguish here an older and simpler form of the theory from a later and more sophisticated one ; but they are fundamentally the same, and both alike possess both truth and falsehood. It is admitted on all sides that the gods of Greek religion and of most if not all others are supposed to be able to control the forces of nature. It seems therefore a suggestion at least worth considering that the gods are these natural forces and nothing else, at least originally. Thus Zeus would be the sky, or the celestial phenomena ; Hera, the ancients suggested, using an etymology which was hardly

more than a bad pun, was the air, *aēr* ; Aphrodite was the moist
principle in nature, Hephaistos the element of fire, and so forth,
while in later times there was a decided tendency to make all
gods into personifications of the sun[9]. Into these supposed
personifications were read, of course, whatever physical theory
the interpreter might happen to hold.

Obviously, the idea that gods are personifications cannot
stand, for a personification is a kind of allegory, and therefore
open to all the objections urged against the allegorical and
symbolic theories. When Spenser personifies the virtue of
chastity under the lovely figure of Una, or holiness as the Red-
Cross Knight, he is merely putting into poetical form what he
could have expressed in prose, namely a current theory, derived
from Aristotle, of the virtues and vices, and adorning it with the
flowers of his inexhaustible fancy. Had no ethical doctrine
then existed, the *Faerie Queene* could never have been written ;
and in like manner, personified physical forces are unthink-
able among a people who were not to learn for centuries that
any such forces existed.

But it remains possible to suppose the gods, or some of them,
to be the result, not of allegorizing known and understood physical forces, but of a sort of imaginative speculation about
unknown ones. In this sense we may say, for instance, that a
river-god (usually imagined, in Greece, under the form of a
bull-headed man) is simply the river itself, the noise of whose
waters is naïvely accounted for by envisaging it as a powerful,
noisy beast. The early Greeks, we might conjecture, observed
the apparent daily motion of the sun and were sharp-witted
enough to see that it must move very fast, in order to get over
so much ground in a day. They therefore fancied it as a charioteer, since a chariot drawn by swift horses was the fastest mode
of locomotion they knew. The difficulty is, that there seems
no very cogent reason why they should worship forces thus
explained, and especially why, as appears on careful investiga-
tion of their religion, they gave so little worship to the most
impressive of them, as the sun, the moon, earthquakes, thunder
and lightning, and so forth. It is far more consistent with what
we can see of their thoughts and what we know of the ideas of
peoples still in the myth-making stage or very near it to suppose
that they worshipped the gods whom they supposed to control
these forces,—Zeus, who lived in the sky, and not the sky or
its thunder and lightning ; Poseidon, who lived in the sea, and
not the actual sea-water, and so forth. The problem of how
the idea of divine beings really originated is very complex and

far from being fully solved as yet ; fortunately it is not necessary
to solve it in order to discuss the myths concerning them.

The most famous exponent of the doctrine that mythology
springs from imaginative treatment of physical forces is in modern
times the great Sanskritist F. Max Müller. His theory was
briefly this. Primitive man was filled with a vague feeling of
awe and reverence, leading to ideas of divinity, to which, in his
hesitating and imperfect speech, he tried to give expression.
Of course, his effort to voice the ineffable was hopeless from the
first, and the words he used were sadly lacking in precision,
ambiguous and metaphorical. Thus, trying to find a name for
the divine Being whose existence he dimly conjectured, he hit
upon the word ' sky ' as the least inadequate he could think of ;
but some at least of those who heard him could not understand
his metaphor, and hence imagined that the literal sky was either
the abode of God or God Himself.

Müller further imagined that he had come fairly near to this
primitive stage of religion by studying the earliest Sanskrit
documents, the Vedas, which undoubtedly are of venerable
antiquity. Analysing these and comparing them with what
he knew of the mythology of other peoples, he believed that he
could trace back a number of names, and consequently the
legends containing them, to the sort of primeval metaphors
which he postulated. In particular, he held that numerous
deities, indeed almost all of them, owed their being originally to
the metaphorical use of language concerning the sun. Thus to
him Athena, born from the head of Zeus, is the sky's daughter,
Dawn, whose birth is helped by the young Sun (Hephaistos).
She is called virgin, because her light is pure ; golden from its
colour ; Promachos (Champion) because she does battle with the
darkness, and so forth.[10]

It is not necessary to dwell nowadays on the many weak
links in this chain, such as the true character of the Indian literature, which although old is very far from primitive, the badness
of many of Max Müller's etymologies, his imperfect knowledge
of Greek religion and mythology, and so forth. It is enough to
remind ourselves that, firstly, Müller's picture of the primitive
theologian is about as unlike that practical person, the savage,
as possible ; that examination of savage traditions and beliefs
indicates that savages are but little impressed by such regular
phenomena as sunrise, seldom worship the sun, and have not
many legends about it ; further, that their tales seem to deal
with a very wide variety of subjects, which makes it highly unlikely
that the ancestors of the Greeks confined themselves to imagina-

tive and metaphorical talk about the weather ; and also that the earliest and most primitive languages we know have a large vocabulary but are extremely poor in general terms capable of a confusing variety of senses, which makes it unlikely that the ' disease of language ', as it has been unkindly called, postulated by Müller, was ever a reality. In particular, the more we study the different Wiro languages[11], the more evident it becomes, firstly, that the peoples who speak them have many legends and beliefs which they share with their non-Wiro neighbours, and secondly, that the number of traditions provably common to all Wiros is very small ; so that even if Müller's theories were proved up to the hilt for India, they would throw but little light on the state of things in early Greece. Incidentally, it seems now to be recognized by the best students of the subject that the supposed preponderance of sun-myths in the Vedic literature is the result rather of the theories of later commentators than of the true nature of the legends themselves.[12]

6. *Modern methods.* The failure of so many theories may well make us hesitate before adopting another ; and indeed, the best modern mythologists are as a rule none too eager to put forward a complete theory of the origin and primary meaning of any myth. There are, however, four things which we may do :

(*a*) We begin by carefully examining the source of the tale, and determining its date. This is not so easy as it sounds, for it is not enough to discover, for example, that one form of a story is found in Sophokles and another in Plutarch. We must find out, if we can, where Sophokles and Plutarch got the story, and it may turn out that the earlier writer invented a good deal of what he says, while the later one drew upon some very early source now lost. The first modern writer to lay emphasis, consistently and thoroughly, on this point was the most notable of the opponents of Creuzer, C. A. Lobeck (1781–1860 ; principal work, *Aglaophamus*, 1829).

(*b*) We may now try to determine, if we can, to what section of the very mixed population of Greece the story is due, *i.e.*, whether it is Achaian, Dorian, Ionian, or belongs to some other Greek people, or whether it is pre-Greek, or a later importation from Asia or Thrace. A great pioneer in this work was K. O. Müller (1797–1840).

(*c*) Next we may ask to what class the legend in question belongs, *i.e.*, whether it is myth proper, saga, or *märchen*. This, as will be explained presently, may throw light on its ultimate origin. The distinction cannot be attributed to any one researcher, but its existence has become recognized largely through the work of the folklorists and investigators of medieval European and other non-classical legends during the nineteenth century, prominent among whom were the indefatigable brothers, Jakob and Wilhelm Grimm (1785–1863 and 1786–1859).

(d) Lastly, when we have constructed a theory of the origin and continuance of a story, we shall do well to compare it with those tales which we can study in an early and undeveloped form,—the legends of savages and, to a less degree, of peasants. In a word, we may apply the Comparative Method, but with due caution, for nothing is more misleading than a false but plausible analogy. That this method is now part of the equipment of most scholars is due above all (if we leave out of account men still living) to one of the most learned and honest researchers Germany ever produced, J. W. E. Mannhardt, 1831–80, and one of the most brilliant and versatile of British writers, the late Andrew Lang.

7 *Psychological analysis.* Since legends are the work, not of memory (as historical traditions largely are) or of the reason, but of the imagination, it is obvious that all mythologists must wish well to those who study the imagination, that is, to psychologists. Hence it is interesting to note that the school of psychological thought now most in fashion, that associated with the names of Freud and Jung, devotes considerable attention to myths and tries to explain their genesis. Thus far one can approve ; but beyond general approval of endeavour in what may be a fruitful field I for one cannot go. Hitherto, even allowing the truth of the main positions taken up by the psycho-analytic school with regard to the composition of the human mind, I have failed to find in its writings a single explanation of any myth, or any detail of any myth, which seemed even remotely possible or capable of accounting for the development of the story as we have it. I therefore content myself with mentioning their methods, without going into a full account of them.[13]

We may divide legends, in a fashion which by now is almost traditional, into three classes. We have first the myth proper, concerning which a word of explanation is necessary. Man, brought face to face with the world about him, cannot help reacting to his environment in some way. Besides bodily actions, whether practically useful, such as chipping flints, ploughing fields, and making locomotives, or those meant to be practically useful, such as the various operations of magic, he has two mental processes open to him ; he may reason about the world and the objects in it, or he may let his imagination play upon them. Speaking very roughly and very broadly, the more civilized he is, the more apt he is either to reason or, if not, at least to realize when he is not reasoning but imagining. Let us take as an example the phenomenon of rain. A man may busy himself collecting rain-water in a cistern or tank : he may construct a rain-gauge and observe the amount of rain that has fallen, and the season of year at which it falls most abundantly, and from these and other observations theorize about the cause of rain. These proceedings we may call applied and pure science respectively. Also, especially if he is a savage, he may work magic intended to make the rain fall abundantly, or to stop altogether. This, being in intention practical, is a sort of bastard sister of applied science. But there is a third set of activities possible. A poet or other artist may let the rain inspire him to production, and so give the world an ode, good or bad, to the rain, a picture such as Turner's *Rain, Steam and Speed*, or a pretty fantasy concerning the refreshment brought to the earth by a shower. But the imagination of the artist has also a half-sister, namely the less controlled but equally lively imagination of the myth-maker. He does not try to reason out the causes of rain, nor is he particularly concerned to make an artistic picture of it ; he attempts rather to visualize the whole process, for the imagination of course works in pictures, or, if we like to use a favourite word of psychologists, in symbols. The result of this visualizing may be some such mental picture as of a being, or beings, who pour water out of a reservoir upon the earth. The nature of these beings and of their reservoir will vary enormously, and the myth may be anything from very grotesque and absurd to very beautiful, just as the picture made by the civilized painter might be good or bad ; but an imaginative picture of some kind it will certainly be.

But now the myth touches upon science, for it offers a sort of cause for the rain-shower. Asked why it rains, scientist and myth-maker alike can give an answer. The former answers ' Because of such-and-such atmospheric conditions ', and can give proofs of his statements, more or less cogent according as he is a better or a worse scientist. The myth-maker can reply, ' Because Zeus is pouring down water out of heaven ', ' because Yahweh has opened the windows in the firmament ', ' because the angels have poured water into a great tub in the sky which has holes in its bottom '. To any one who has dealt with inquisitive children it must be obvious that in many cases this kind of answer would be satisfactory ; it gives *a* reason, and the hearers' minds are not developed enough for them to inquire whether it is *the* reason.

We see therefore that myths, in the proper sense, are a some-what primitive form of those mental processes which, further developed, give us both art and science. Of the two sides, the more active is what we may term the artistic or imaginative and visualizing process. This consideration enables us largely to dispose of a question which often arises, namely, Did the myth-makers, in Greece for instance, believe in their myths? The absurdity of this will be evident if we transfer it to a higher sphere and ask, Did Michael Angelo believe in his Moses, or Swinburne in his *Atalanta in Calydon*? No doubt Michael Angelo believed that there had been a man called Moses, who had done the things recorded of him in the Pentateuch ; Swinburne doubtless believed that one of the districts of classical Greece was called Kalydon, and probably did not believe that there had ever been a virgin huntress called Atalanta ; but these are intellectual processes, and had nothing to do with the statue or the poem. So with the man who first thought of thunder and lightning as caused by Zeus hurling a celestial dart ; it probably would be far truer to say that he imagined it than that he either believed or disbelieved it. It is, however, no doubt true that many people accepted his imagination as a sufficient reason for thunder-storms, while others in time grew doubtful, that is, set their reason, as well as their imagination, to work, perceived that there were other possible causes, and found grounds for preferring one or another of them.[14]

We may then define a myth proper as *the result of the working of naïve imagination upon the facts of experience.* As a large proportion of these facts are natural phenomena, it follows that the nature-myth is a common kind ; and as the imagination is commonly set going by an object which appears wonderful or puzzling, it follows that a very large proportion indeed of myths is of the kind known as *aetiological,* concerned, that is, with the causes of all manner of things from the apparent movement of the heavenly bodies to the shape of a neighbouring hill or the origin of a local custom. In the last case, the myth often tells what purports to be a history, and this brings us to the next form of legend.

The name *saga* (in origin, simply the Scandinavian word for ' tale, story ') is commonly given to those legends which deal with historical events. To take common instances from the modern countryside : if a folk-tale attributes the formation of a peculiarly-shaped hill to the devil, that is myth pure and simple ; but if an ancient earthwork is said to have been built by Julius Caesar, that, if not due to some local antiquary, is rather saga.

and may contain a germ of historical fact.   That is, the earthwork may really be part of a Roman camp, and we have but to
substitute for 'Julius Caesar' the words 'some unknown Roman
officer'.   Excavation may enable us to find, if not the name of
the officer and his force, at least their date, and so we pass from
saga into history.   There are instances of fragments of real
history being preserved for an extraordinary length of time in
legends of the peasantry.[15]

Few are so well-trained as to be able to see any event quite
as it is without reading into it something which exists only
in their own fancy ; and this applies much more strongly to
events which are not seen but remembered, and most strongly
of all to those which are not remembered but told by another.
A story handed down from father to son is rapidly altered in two
ways ; real details are forgotten and unreal ones are added.
These additions, being imaginary, are almost invariably of a
picturesque kind, attractive to the teller or the hearer, or both ;
and the omissions are especially of details which teller and hearer
alike find dry, such as dates, geographical minutiae (except
those of a well-known locality, which are generally found interesting), exact figures of all kinds, economic facts, and the doings
and sayings of commonplace people.   The Homeric account of
the Trojan War is one of the best possible examples.   The war
was a perfectly real one, very likely caused by trade rivalries ; it
seems to have consisted in a blockade by the Achaians of the
fortress of Ilion, be it Hissarlik or not, interrupting the Trojan
communications with the neighbouring country ; and it was
apparently decided by the exhaustion, economic and military,
of the Trojans, which led to the subjugation of the cities allied
with them and at last to the fall of Ilion itself.   In Homer, the
cause of the war is the abduction of Helen by Paris, and the deci-
sive factors are the personal intervention of various gods, together
with the surpassing prowess of numerous heroic chieftains, the
most prominent of whom is Achilles.   Of trade jealousy we hear
nothing at all, of the wearing down of the Trojan resources
only a few casual remarks, and of the details of the tactics
and strategy of both armies practically nothing whatsoever.
The result is, at some cost to history, the greatest and most
fascinating epic poem ever written, the *Iliad*, which is the
product of a first-class genius finding a good saga ready to his
hand.

There remains one form of legend, the *märchen*. This German
word fits it better than the nearest English equivalent, 'fairy-
tale ', because it does not always deal with fairies or supernatural

beings of any kind. It differs from the last two in an important particular. They both are intended to command, if not exactly belief, at least imaginative assent, and their aim is often to find or record a truth : but the *märchen* aims rather at amusement. It accounts for the cause of nothing, it records no historical or semi-historical event, it need not fit the hearers' notions of probability. It is a story pure and simple, and makes no pre- tence to being anything else.

This brief outline of the classification of legends must suffice. It is, however, to be noted that any given story may well combine two of these forms, or even all three. For instance, the tale of Herakles probably started as a saga, an imaginative telling of the adventures of a real man. But it combined at an early date with elements of aetiological myth ; thus, the presence of cer- tain hot springs was explained by the myth that they had sprung from the ground to provide Herakles with a hot bath after some of his labours, and a certain ancient sacrifice on Mt. Oite was declared to commemorate the death of the hero. Also, an ele- ment of *märchen* intruded here and there ; for instance Herakles, like many other adventurers, goes forth to look for the pot of gold at the end of the rainbow, represented in his case by the golden apples of the Hesperides.

Another and a more important point to be remembered in the case of Greek myths is the way in which they reflect the national character. The Greeks at their best were sane, high-spirited, clear-headed, beauty-loving optimists, and not in the least other-worldly. Hence their legends are almost without excep- tion free from the cloudiness, the wild grotesques, and the hor- rible features which beset the popular traditions of less gifted and happy peoples. Even their monsters are not very ugly or uncouth, nor their ghosts and demons paralysingly dreadful. Their heroes, as a rule, may sorrow, but are not broken-hearted ; on occasion they are struck down by adverse fate, but not weakly overwhelmed ; they meet with extraordinary adventures, but there is a certain tone of reasonableness running through their most improbable exploits. As for the gods and other super- natural characters, they are glorified men and women, who remain extremely human, and on the whole neither irrational nor grossly unfair in their dealings. Such tales as contain savage and repulsive elements tend to drop into the background or be modified. In short, the handling of the myths, even, it would appear, by unlettered Greeks, shows the spirit expressed in two famous sayings of famous poets :

' Winsomeness, by which are wrought all lovely things for

mankind, lends its lustre to make even the incredible seem credible full often.'

' If I deal in falsehood, let it be such as may persuade the ears of the listener.'[16]

NOTES ON CHAPTER I

(For the full titles of books cited, see General Bibliography.)

[1] See, for a history of the subject from the end of antiquity to the year 1913, Gruppe 1921, and Nilsson, *GgR*, i[2], 3 *sqq.*

[2] Nock 1926, pp. 6, 7 ; Murray 1925, p. 245. See Chapter V, p. 106.

[3] *Iliad*, XIX, 91 foll.—a passage very likely interpolated into the original poem by a later hand, but nevertheless old—may serve as an example.

[4] See General Bibliography.

[5] *Symbolik*, I, p. 37 foll. For Talos, see Chapter VIII, p. 204.

[6] *De incredibilibus*, I. The work we have is not that of Palaiphatos himself, who lived in the time of Aristotle, but a later epitome.

[7] I have discussed the problem how much of their savage ancestry the historical Greeks retained in *Primitive Culture in Greece*.

[8] For Euhemeros, see Jacoby in Pauly-Wissowa VI, col. 952 foll.

[9] The Stoics were particularly fond of explanations of this kind, see, for instance, *R.P.*[8], 503, but it was by no means confined to them, see, for example, Plato, *Cratylus*, 397 C, and for many such explanations, Athenagoras, *legat. pro Christ.* 22. For the theory that all gods were in some way the sun, see Macrobius, *Saturn.*, I, 17, 2 foll. See, in general, Frazer, *W.N.*, J. Tate in *C.Q.*, xxiii, 41–5 ; 142-54 ; xxviii, 105–14.

[10] See *Lectures on the Origin of Religion* (1882), Lecture IV ; *Introduction to the Science of Religion* (new edition, 1882), pp. 49, 197.

[11] By Wiro I mean the group of languages otherwise called **Aryan,** Indo-European, or Indo-Germanic, to which Latin, Greek, Sanskrit, etc., belong. By Wiros I mean the people or peoples who spoke the language from which all these tongues are supposedly derived. The word in the latter sense is due to Dr. P. Giles.

[12] See Sten Konow in Chantepie de la Saussaye,[4] II, p. 23 foll.

[13] See, for instance, Jung, *Psychology of the Unconscious* (trans. B. M. Hinkle, London, 1922), Chapter VI.

[14] For a deliciously funny sketch of the type of mind which is hungry for a reason and content with whatever is offered it, see Aristophanes, *Clouds*, 366 foll.

[15] Excellent examples are given by van Gennep, 1910, p. 155 foll.

[16] Pindar, *Olymp.*, I, 32 ; Kallimachos, *Hymn.*, I, 65.

ADDITIONAL NOTE

For full accounts of the ancient authors quoted, the reader is referred to the many good manuals of Greek literature in English, French and German. It may, however, be mentioned that our sources in Greek are firstly the poets, of all dates from Homer and Hesiod down ; and of these, especially those up to and including the great Attic dramatists of the fifth century B.C. Next in importance to these are the Alexandrian poets, such as Kallimachos, from the fourth century onwards, who often give us curious information not to be had elsewhere, but who must be used with caution, as they often of set purpose confine themselves to very out-of-the-way stories, not forming part of what may be called the normal mythology of Greece; moreover, they not infrequently re-shape the legends or invent new ones, to suit their own purposes, a fault, from the modern mythologist's point of view, of which the older writers also are sometimes guilty. Next come the earlier historical writers, such as Pherekydes, who unfortunately are known to us only in fragments and excerpts; these, in dealing with early history, treated also of legends, which were indeed often their only source for events of other than recent date, and later compilers, such as Diodoros of Sicily, drew freely upon them. Finally, a great deal is due to the mythological handbooks, for these contain much of the learning of the Alexandrian critics, although in an epitomized form. Of these, one of the best is the so-called Apollodoros, whose work (first century A.D. ?) contains much good old material. With these may be reckoned the scholiasts, or ancient commentators on classical authors, such as Pindar and above all Homer, and on Alexandrian poets such as Apollonios of Rhodes. As regards the Latins, even their earliest poets draw upon the Alexandrians, and may for our purposes be counted as late Greek authors. Here again, notably in the case of Ovid, the writers' own fancy is the source of not a little. Roman scholarship also is often of value; we have, for example, the so-called Hyginus, whose *fabulae*, although but an epitomized, mutilated, and very ill-copied treatise, yet often preserves in a not too garbled form some story otherwise lost, as told in a vanished work of Euripides or some other classical writer. Much can also be gleaned from Latin scholiasts, notably that commentator on Vergil who is conventionally called Servius. But there is hardly a writer in either language who does not somewhere mention a myth or saga, and on whom therefore we cannot now and then draw for information. This applies to the Christian writers, for they often, in order to show what absurd and immoral stories the pagans told, relate these stories at considerable length, thus preserving for us the erudition of sundry mythologists whose works have not come down, or of poets now lost.

CHAPTER II

THE BEGINNINGS OF THINGS

In the beginning, how the heavens and earth
Rose out of Chaos.
—Milton, *P.L.*, I, 9.

IN order to understand the cosmological myths of the Greeks, it is necessary to realize what they, in early times, supposed the shape of the world to be. They began with much the same notion as all early peoples appear to possess, namely, that its real shape is that which as much of it as can be seen at once appears to have. Now this, unless the observer be shut in between long lines of hills, like an Egyptian, or confined to an island, or a group of islands, like the peoples of the southern Pacific, is a circle, more or less flat except where mountains or hills rise from it, and capped by the immense dome of the sky, which touches it at the horizon. On the one side the sun and stars can be seen rising above the horizon, while on the other they disappear at their setting. As they always rise on the same side, presumably they make their way back again, either under the ground or by some other hidden route.

This and no other is the earliest Greek picture of the earth, presupposed by all the earliest legends, and surviving inconsistently into later ones. In particular, the Greeks supposed that the boundary of this plain of earth was formed by the stream of Ocean (Okeanos), which is not the sea, but a great river, flowing in a circle. The sky is a substantial dome, sometimes said to be made of bronze or iron[1]; it is at a considerable height above the earth, but not an immeasurable distance ; the residence of the gods is now the sky itself, now the summit of Mount Olympos. At most, if one could pile three large mountains one above another, they would form a ladder to heaven.[2] The tale of Phaethon, to take but one instance, implies that if one goes far enough east, he will come to the very place where the sky touches the earth and the sun begins his ascent. Far tc

17

the west, on the other hand, where the sun goes down, is a land
of darkness, near which is the entrance to Hades, as will be
clearly seen in the story of Odysseus.   At the same time, Hades
is often conceived as being underground, to be reached through
one of the many deep rifts in the strata of the Greek rocks,
katavóthra as they are called in the modern tongue, such as the
famous one at Tainaron near Sparta.   Of this idea we have
abundant evidence in the tales of Amphiaraos, Orpheus, and
especially of Herakles.   Such double beliefs are common enough ;
it is noteworthy that we find them blended together in at least
one passage of Hesiod,[3] where certain monsters are for a while
confined by Zeus ' under the earth ' but at the same time ' on
the farthest verge, at the boundary of the mighty world '.

Of the actual geography of the world, a varying amount was
known, as might be expected, in different ages.   In Homer,
Greece proper and part of the coast of Asia Minor are familiar
ground for the most part, but beyond that, fairyland begins.
The adventures of Odysseus in particular seem to take place in
a vague region west of Greece, traditionally somewhere in and
around Southern Italy.[4]   To Aeschylus, Southern Italy is familiar territory enough, but the interior of Asia Minor begins to
fade into the unknown and marvellous.[5]   After the conquests
of Alexander, those who wanted a land of wonders must go farther
afield yet, to India or Northern Europe.

Having this conception of the world in which they lived,
the Greeks from quite early times were interested in the question
of its genesis.   Their imagination had peopled every part of it
with divine inhabitants who were not all of one origin.   Some
few had been brought with them by the Greek-speaking peoples
when they entered the countries they occupied in historical
times ;   some no doubt belonged to the Minoan-Mycenaean
civilization which they found there on arrival, or more likely
created ;   others again, especially little local deities, had been
there since the days of savagery, many centuries in the past.[6]
Moreover, the invading Hellenes were not all one political
unit, and never attained unity, and it is highly likely that
various divisions of them were variously blended with the pre-
Greek population.   Hence almost from the time when first the
Greek speech was heard in Greece, there was a vast assemblage
of all manner of cults and all sorts of deities, great and small,
savage and civilized, credited with functions connected in various
ways with the processes of nature and the life of man.   No
people of lively imagination, least of all the ancestors of European philosophy, could have refrained from asking what con-

nexion there was between these different gods, and also between them and the world in which they and their worshippers lived. Thus it is that we find, not indeed a single orthodox account of how the universe and its divine and human inhabitants came into being, but a general agreement in outline, the fruit of early and imaginative speculation, as regards these matters. In Homer the gods are already organized on the model of a human clan, with Zeus at its head ; Hesiod preserves the earliest account of how this state of things came about.

Before all things, he tells us, came Chaos.[7] This word, which seems literally to mean ' gaping void ', apparently does not signify mere empty space ; even at that time the Greeks were unlikely to conceive of anything as coming into being out of nothing. Nor does Hesiod say that even Chaos had existed from all eternity, for he uses the word γένετο, ' came into being ', rather than ' was,' a term with which philosophers in later ages made great play. It is his starting-point rather than an absolute beginning. Next, sprung apparently from Chaos, came Earth, Tartaros (which he explains as a dark place ' in the depths of the ground '), Love (Eros), Darkness (Erebos), and finally Night. From Night and Erebos were born Aither (Sky, upper air) and Day ; while Earth produced unaided Heaven, the Mountains, and Pontos (the sea).

Thus far, we are dealing with theology or philosophy rather than mythology. The terminology is fairly elaborate, a distinction being made between Γαῖα, the Earth, and χθών, ground, also between Οὐρανός, the heaven (conceived as quasi-anthropomorphic) and αἰθήρ, the upper air or sky, and between darkness and night. A still more elaborate attempt to bridge the gap between nothingness and the visible world is the Orphic cosmology, according to which Chaos, Night, and Erebos were in the beginning ; Night laid an egg, and from that sprang Eros, also known as Phanes, Metis, and Erikapaios or Erikepaios. He appears to have been the father (or mother, since in some accounts at least he was bisexual) of a series of generations of gods, which need not be detailed here, as they have absolutely nothing to do with popular Greek belief, and in any case their order varies in different accounts.[8] A good instance of the influence of later speculation on the traditional Hesiodic tale will be found in Ovid's *Metamorphoses*, where Chaos becomes a formless mixture of the elements or principles of matter, hard and soft, heavy and light, and so forth.[9] Much later, we still find traces of the classical cosmogony mingling with accounts derived from the Hebrew creation-myth ; thus in a paraphrase of Genesis, falsely ascribed to St. Cyprian and written in very indifferent Latin hexameters,[10] the traditional chaos replaces the ' deep ' of the original.

'Next', the Hesiodic account goes on, 'Earth mated with Heaven and brought forth Okeanos with his deep eddies, Koios also and Krios, Hyperion and Iapetos, Theia and Rhea, Themis and Mnemosyne, Phoibe golden-crowned and lovely Tethys. Last of all, after these, was born Kronos of the crooked counsel, most dread of children, for he hated his lusty sire.'

Here we enter the region of genuine, and obviously early, myth. The primeval pair, Heaven and Earth, are in no wise peculiar to Greek legend, but are to be found, for example, as far off as New Zealand, where they appear respectively as Rangi and Papa, and the myth continues on much the same general lines as in Hesiod. The enormous gap between Greece and New Zealand is being gradually filled up as our knowledge, especially of the Near East, increases. In particular, the Hittite-Hurrite myth of Kumbarbi (see p. 340B) bears such resemblance to that of Uranos and Kronos as to suggest that it, or one like it, was known to Hesiod.

Heaven (Uranos) is hardly a god, *i.e.*, it does not appear that the Greeks at any time or place worshipped him. His place was taken by Zeus, whom we shall consider later. Not being the object of any cult, he naturally has no fixed type in art, it being seldom desired to represent him. For a like reason we find that his parentage and relationships vary. He is not infrequently called Akmonides, *i.e.*, son of Akmon, the latter name being of somewhat uncertain meaning. It seems possible to take it as signifying 'unwearied', but it has been ingeniously suggested that it is connected with Old Persian and Sanskrit *açman*, in which case it would mean 'stone'; we have already seen that Heaven is elsewhere spoken of as being of bronze or iron. It seems very likely that this deity is no other than Uranos himself; in like manner Hyperion is sometimes the Sun, sometimes the Sun's father.[11] Sometimes, again, Uranos is the son of Aither,[12] in other words, Heaven is begotten of Sky.

Earth (Gaia, Ge), on the other hand, is a genuine goddess, having a fairly widespread and well-known cult.[13] It is unlikely that she was, to begin with at least, anything so huge as the planet Earth in general; rather was she the particular piece of earth (farm, group of farms, or territory of a petty state) with which the particular worshipper or worshippers were acquainted; or, still more likely, the power residing in that patch of ground which made it produce all manner of plants. Hence it is that we not infrequently see Earth represented in art as rising out of the earth, precisely as Zeus is shown descending from heaven, or Poseidon riding upon the sea. She remains, however, a vague figure, largely displaced in cult and in mythology by goddesses more completely humanized but having the same or a similar origin.

The children of this primeval couple thus far enumerated are known collectively as the Titans, a word of uncertain meaning.[14] Still more uncertain are their origin, their significance to those who first believed in them, and the place or places where they originated. The long and highly controversial articles of Bapp and Mayer in Roscher under *Titanen* are enough to show how very large a part of our ideas concerning them is the result of deduction, often most ingenious and learned, from scanty and doubtful facts. This much may be taken as fairly certain, that the Titans are very ancient figures, little worshipped anywhere in historical Greece, and belonging to a past so remote that the earliest Greeks of whose opinions we have any certain knowledge saw them surrounded with a haze of extreme antiquity. From the list which Hesiod gives, and which can be extended from other authors, six names form a separate group : Kronos, Okeanos and Iapetos, with their consorts Rhea, Tethys, and Themis. Of these, Kronos and Rhea will be considered presently ; Okeanos and Tethys are spoken of in a famous passage of the *Iliad*[15] as the progenitors of the gods ; Iapetos is mentioned along with Kronos by Homer,[16] and Themis is positively stated by Aeschylus to be the same as Gaia herself.[17] The names Kronos, Iapetos, Okeanos, Tethys are in all probability not Greek ; Themis is a word of doubtful origin, but probably from a Greek root[18] ; Rhea or Rheia is again of doubtful etymology.

It is generally agreed that the Titans are nature-powers of some sort. Hyperion is apparently that rather rare thing, a sun-god ; Themis, as already mentioned, is an earth-goddess, Okeanos' name shows his connexion with the mythical stream which encircles the world. The names and natures of Koios and Krios are uncertain ; Theia and Phoibe are ' the divine ' and ' the bright ' respectively, and the latter is connected with the moon, but only in later writers, and, it would appear, by way of an identification with her own granddaughter, Artemis. The far weightier testimony of Aeschylus[19] says that she was the third possessor of the Delphic oracle, before Apollo, to whom she gave it. Mnemosyne is a pure abstraction, Memory personified, and clearly has no business among the Titans proper. We find, then, a group of deities, mostly not Greek, connected possibly with the heavens, pretty certainly with the earth, of whom it seems reasonable to conclude that they were once worshipped in Greece, before the Greeks came, and that some memory of them lingered on, with here and there a remnant of worship. The legend of the Titans consists chiefly in the tale of their battle with the Olympian gods, in itself very possibly a reminiscence of ancient strife between invaders and invaded, with the natural corollary that the gods worshipped by either party shared its struggle and its victory or defeat.

In addition, there were born the three Kyklopes,[20] Brontes, Steropes, and Arges (i.e., Thunder-man, Lightning-man, and Shiner), and the three Hekatoncheires, hundred-handed giants, Kottos, Briareos (or Obriareos ; according to Homer,[21] men called him Aigaion), and Gyes. The former, an early interpolator of the poem explains, were called Kyklopes (' Round-eyes ') because they had but one eye each, in the middle of their foreheads ; they were a sort of divine smiths, makers of the thunderbolts of Zeus. But Homer gives us a wholly different account of them.[22] For him, they are a race of savage giants, living on an island (possibly Sicily, certainly supposed to be Sicily in later times), in a stage of rude pastoral culture. Having no illusions about the ' noble savage', he represents the Kyklops Polyphemos, whom Odysseus meets, as a coarse and brutal monster, quite insensible to the most elementary moral obligations, and easily tricked by the superior wits of the civilized Achaian. More will be said of both kinds of Kyklopes in dealing with Hephaistos, Odysseus and Galateia. The Hundred-handed trio are very vague figures. Aigaion-Briareos seems to be connected somehow with the Aegean Sea ; a possible suggestion as to his origin is that the octopus, a favourite subject of Cretan art, has contributed to his monstrous shape.[23]

Strife soon broke out in this strange family of primeval deities and monsters. Uranos was jealous of his children, and hid them all in the huge body of Gaia, till she could no longer endure the strain and begged them to take vengeance on their terrible father.[24] Kronos listened to his mother's plea, when the others were afraid, and was given a curved sword or sickle ' of grey adamant ' (presumably iron or steel), with which he castrated Uranos as he approached his consort, and flung the severed member away into the sea. From the drops that fell from it upon the earth were born the Erinyes, the Giants, and the Meliai, guardian nymphs of manna-ashes.[25] But from the member itself, as it floated in the sea and gathered foam ($\mathring{\alpha}\varphi\varrho\acute{o}\varsigma$) about it, sprung the goddess Aphrodite, who will be more fully dealt with in Chapter ·V. She landed at Kythera, an island off the coast of Sparta, which afterwards became a famous place of her worship, and Love straightway attached himself to her, together with Desire (Himeros).

Hesiod gives also a whole list of abstractions mostly unconnected with myth and cult alike, and their relations to one another, as follows : Night bore Fate and Doom (Moros and Ker, the latter a vague name for a kind of spirit or demon, a sort of death-angel), Death (Thanatos), Sleep (Hypnos, a figure common in literature and art, and not wholly foreign to religious beliefs, for there was an altar of Hypnos at Trozen; [26] possibly the statement that he loved Endymion and caused him to sleep with his beautiful eyes always open is something more than the pretty fancy of a littérateur [27]), Dreams, Momos (a personification of fault-finding, who occurs in fables and the like as a sort of licensed grumbler, objecting to everything that the gods do, in a manner reminiscent of the Accuser in the Book of Job [28]), Pain (Oïzys), Nemesis (generally an abstraction, Retribution for or Resentment at ill deeds ; she had a cult at Rhamnus in Attica and seems there to have had some existence in popular belief as a goddess [29]), Deceit, Philotes (pleasure of love), Old Age (Geras), and Strife (Eris). Eris in turn bore Labour (Ponos), Forgetfulness (Lethe, which we shall come across again as the name of a water in the underworld), Famine, Woes, Strifes, Battles, Slaughters, Manslayings, Quarrels, False Words, Disputes, Lawlessness, Infatuation, and Horkos, literally Oath, but rather less of a mere abstraction than the rest of his kind. He is mentioned as an infernal deity, the fact of whose birth on the fifth day of the month makes that an unlucky day. He would appear to be a spirit that punishes perjury. Some hold that the Roman god of the underworld Orcus is nothing but this Horkos, but the matter is uncertain. [30]

Hesiod, or some early interpolator of him, [31] declares Night to have been the mother of the Hesperides. As their name (' Daughters of Evening ') implies, they are thought of as living far to the west, their occupation being to guard a wonderful tree, growing golden fruit, which was given by Ge to Hera at her marriage with Zeus. Their recreation was singing, and they were aided in their watch by a formidable dragon, the offspring of Phorkys and Keto. Their names are given by some authors as Aigle, Erytheia, Arethusa and Hespere, Hesperia, or Hesperethusa. Generally their garden is located in northwestern Africa, somewhere near the Atlas mountains ; as the name Atlas is found also applied to an Arkadian mountain, it has been conjectured, not without plausibility, that Arkadia was their original home, before the western end of the Mediterranean became known, even vaguely, to the Greeks. This would explain why their dragon is called Ladon, which is also the name of an Arkadian river.

2

Night was also the mother of the Moirai, better known to modern readers under their Latin name of Fates.[32] It is not improbable, indeed it is highly likely, that these were originally not abstract powers of destiny, but birth-spirits, such as those which, in modern Greek belief and in other folklore of that region, visit a new-born child and determine what his portion in life shall be. So at least the Moirai do in the tale of Meleagros, to be told later. In this capacity they were objects of cult in many parts of the Greek world, as inscriptions and other monuments abundantly testify. We may be reasonably certain that the singular Moira, Fate or Necessity, developed out of the plural Moirai, ' the Allotters ', and not the other way about. Early and interesting as the development is (we find it complete in Homer), it does not concern a mythologist, but rather a historian of Greek philosophy. In Latin, the plural Fata seems to be little more than an adaptation of the singular *fatum*, ' that which is spoken ', ' the decree (of the gods) ', to the plural number of the Greek goddesses, although it does occur once or twice without a mythological reference, meaning ' the decrees ', much as we say indifferently ' the commandment ' or ' the commandments of God '. Later, the neuter plural *Fata* gave rise to a feminine singular, quite foreign to classical Latin, which still exists in the Italian and French words for ' fairy ' (*fata, fée*). A surer instinct led the Romans to identify their own spirits of birth, the Parcae (Paricae, from *parere*, to bring forth) with the Moirai, although probably a false etymology helped.[33]

The Moirai are regularly represented, from Homer down, as spinners, and from Hesiod down as three in number, called Klotho (the Spinner), Lachesis (the Apportioner) and Atropos (the Inflexible). In art they appear as women, in literature often as very old women,—naturally, for, on the one hand, deities of this very ancient stratum appeared to popular fancy as showing the signs of old age, and on the other, old women were above all others the traditional spinners of the Greek household. The thread they spin is, or carries on it, the destiny of each individual in turn, and when it is broken, a life ends.

Later poetical imagination elaborated this in various ways, making them for example spin a gold thread for the lifetime of a particularly fortunate individual, or take up again an abandoned task when some one is recalled to life.[34] Their functions, again, are in later times specialized, Atropos spinning,[35] or singing,[36] the past, Klotho the present and Lachesis the future ; or Klotho holding the distaff, Lachesis spinning off the thread, and Atropos cutting it short, or the like.[37] Often they, or one of them, are represented in art as reading or writing the book of fate, hence presumably the quaint statement in Hyginus that they invented some letters of the Greek alphabet.[38] As might be expected, they are often associated on the one hand with Eileithyia, on the other with Ananke, Tyche, and other such abstractions.

Pontos (the Sea) begat Nereus, who although almost eclipsed in classical times by Poseidon, apparently was once a sea-god of considerable importance. Hesiod [39] declares that he is ' unlying and a teller of truth ', and that he is called the Old One, a statement in agreement with Homer,[40] who speaks of him as ' the Old One ' (γέρων), in more than one passage, although he nowhere uses his name. Unlike many deities of the sea he is hardly ever formidable, but a kindly, wise and helpful figure. Herakles, in one version of his adventure with the Hesperides, gets from him by violence the secret of the way to their garden ;[41] once, in Vergil, he appears as raising a storm ;[42] but in the majority of instances he is introduced as giving prophecies,[43] retailing wise saws,[44] voluntarily helping and befriending younger gods or heroes. Thus he brings up Aphrodite[45] (who, despite her ancientry in the Hesiodic account already quoted, is always thought of as a young goddess), and gives Herakles the cup of the sun.[46]

But by far his most important rôle is that of father to the Nereids. He and his consort Doris are represented as having a son only in a late and unimportant tale[47] ; in Greek as in modern European fancy, the most prominent inhabitants of the sea were the mermaids ; and in Greek, as in modern fancy, they remained lovely, but vague figures. Poets exercised their ingenuity in giving them pretty names, mostly referring to the sea and seafaring, such as Neso or Nesaie, ' island-girl '; Eulimine, ' good-harbour-woman '; Pontoporeia, ' sea-farer '. One or two of them were worshipped individually here and there,[48] and clearly most people believed in them firmly, for they not only are still believed in, but have given their name (in the form Νεράϊδες) to nymphs and fairies in general, in modern Greece, quite displacing the Dryads, Meliai, and so forth.[49] But only two emerge as clear separate personalities, one in an early and important myth, one in a later but exceedingly pretty tale.

Thetis the Nereid was fated to bear a son mightier than his sire. Zeus knew that, like his father Kronos and his grandfather Uranos, he was in danger from his own offspring, but he did not know who the mother of the formidable son was to be Prometheus knew, for it had been revealed to him by his allwise mother, Themis ; but he was at feud with Zeus, and would not tell the secret, despite the torments inflicted upon him by the enraged god, and the promise made to him of release if he revealed it. Now both Zeus and Poseidon loved Thetis, and so a disaster to the Olympians seemed imminent. But the secret finally came out, being revealed either by Themis herself or by Prometheus, as the price of his freedom ; and Thetis was wedded to Peleus, who being a mortal could not beget an immortal son.[50]

There is another version, as old as the Epic Cycle,[51] that it was Thetis herself who refused the attentions of Zeus, out of love and gratitude to Hera, who had brought her up. As Homer knows of the relations between Hera and Thetis, and nowhere mentions the prophecy of Themis, or Prometheus, it may well be that this version is very old, and the episodes now to be described a later addition.

But Peleus had, at least in the later versions of the story, first to catch her, which, as she was a sea-goddess, was not easy. His subsequent fortunes have all the flavour of a fairy-tale. He had first of all, like Herakles with Nereus, to win his bride by wrestling, for she had no inclination to mate with anyone so inferior to her in rank. Contriving to meet her somewhere (according to Ovid, he caught her asleep on the shore), he at once assailed her ; she tried to shake him off by turning into all manner of forms, as fire, a lion, a serpent, and so forth, but all to no purpose ; so the marriage was duly celebrated, all the gods attending in great state.[52]

But, as usual with a man who weds a fairy bride in the folk-lore of any country, his troubles were not at an end. Thetis was determined to have an immortal child, and used an expedient very like that which we shall find Demeter employing with her nursling Demophon. Seven children were born, and one after another their mother threw them into fire, or according to others a boiling cauldron, either to test their powers or to burn away the mortal part that they had inherited from their father. At last Peleus interfered, and the baby Achilles was either saved from destruction or prevented from becoming fully immortal. Thetis then, in high dudgeon, left her husband, exactly after the manner of fairy brides when crossed.[53] The rest of her legend cannot well be separated from that of her son, and will be discussed in connexion with him. It is to be noticed that although the story of the burning or boiling of the children is fairly early, it is not the earliest, for neither Homer nor Hesiod seems ever to have heard of it, or of any child of the marriage except Achilles.

A number of late and obscure authors name Cheiron instead of

Nereus as the father of Thetis. To what this variant is due, we do not know ; but her name, derived probably, like that of Themis, from the root θε, has no obvious connexion with the sea, rather suggesting the idea of fixity or stability, although the exact sense is quite obscure. She was worshipped, alone or with the Nereids or Achilles, in several places in the Greek world.[54]

According to a Sicilian legend, of unknown date and probably popular origin, the Kyklops Polyphemos was a less formidable and savage creature than Homer makes him out. At all events, the story represented him as falling violently in love with Galateia, and trying to win her favour with such untutored love-songs and other methods of wooing as his not very abundant wits could suggest. The piquant contrast between the clumsy, boorish giant and the delicate sea-nymph caught the fancy of poets from Philoxenos, in the fourth century, onwards, and from them has been taken up into English literature, as in Gay's famous libretto to *Acis and Galatea*. There were two versions : according to one, Galateia would have nothing to do with her uncouth lover ; in one variant (Ovid and, after him, Silius Italicus and Servius) she loved a youth named Akis, son of a nymph. Polyphemos finally crushed him under a stone ; in response to his cries for help, Galateia turned him into a river, which afterwards bore his name. In the other version, however, she was more compliant, and apparently the two were happily married and had several sons, or at least a son, Galates or Galas.[55]

To return to Pontos, he had by Ge two more sons, Thaumas and Phorkys, and two daughters, Keto and Eurybie (*i.e.*, Sea-monster-woman and Mighty One).

Thaumas is of little importance. His name perhaps means ' the wondrous ', or may conceivably be connected with the name of a Thessalian tribe, the Thaumakoi. He is noteworthy chiefly as the father, by Elektra daughter of Ocean, of Iris and the Harpies ("Αρπυιαι)[56].

Of these, the former is the goddess or spirit of the rainbow, whose name still finds a place in modern languages in the technical name for part of the eye and in the adjective ' iridiscent '. As the rainbow is throughout classical literature spoken of primarily as a sign of rain, Iris not unnaturally is represented here and there as the wife of the rainy west wind, Zephyros.[57] In this capacity she is once or twice said to be the mother of Eros, which amounts to little more than a physical allegory ; the love-god is connected with those powers which make for moisture and therefore for fertility. That she had a place in cult is asserted by a single witness, the almost unknown writer Semos, who says[58] that she was worshipped on Hekate's Island, near Delos. Her chief importance, where she is not simply the rainbow itself personified, is as the messenger of the gods ; from Euripides on she tends more and more to be specifically the servant of Hera, as Hermes is of Zeus ; Kallimachos even shows her crouching like a dog under the throne of the great goddess, ready to run on her errands at any moment. In art she constantly appears as a subordinate figure, in the train of the greater deities. Altogether, she is a good example of the small importance in Greek belief and even fancy of personifications of natural phenomena.[59]

We find in the Harpies two quite distinct ideas. The earlier, so far as we can judge, represents them as being simply what their name implies, ' snatchers '. In this capacity, for instance, they appear in the *Odyssey*, in the curious episode of the daughters of Pandareos.[60] These girls, left orphans, were for some reason especially favoured of the goddesses Hera, Artemis, and Aphrodite, who nurtured and taught them. But when they reached maturity, being left alone by their protectress Aphrodite while she went to ask Zeus to provide husbands for them, they were snatched away by the Harpyiai, or by storm-winds,—obviously the two are identical in this passage,—and given as servants to the Erinyes. The Harpies, then, in this context are clearly powers of nature, strong winds which can blow some one away , and this suits their names very well, viz., Aello (Stormwind), Okypete (Swiftwing) and Kelaino (Dark).[61] But because Homer and Hesiod in all probability thought the Harpies were windspirits, it does not necessarily follow that they originally were such. They are described, and represented in art, notably on the frieze of the famous Harpy tomb from Xanthos in Lydia, now in the British Museum, as a sort of birds with the faces of women ; and it has been pointed out by Weicker[62] that this is a well-known form of the soul in popular belief. But that the souls of the dead snatch away those of the living is an idea found in the beliefs of almost all ages and lands, and lies behind a great number of funeral customs, ancient and modern. In this connexion we cannot separate the Harpies sharply from the Seirenes (see p. 245), who also are represented as bird-like creatures with the faces of women, and also are highly dangerous to those they meet. We cannot therefore refuse to allow that the conception of a ghost has played its part in the creation of the weird figure of the Harpy, and it should be remembered that by the evidence of language and custom alike, the ideas of soul, ghost, breath, and wind are closely allied, in Greece and elsewhere.[63] It points, however, rather to the idea of wind-spirits than to ghosts that they were once at any rate thought of as capable of producing, not a human- or bird-like child, but a horse ; Achilles' immortal steeds, Xanthos and Balios (Chestnut and Dapple) are the children of Zephyros and the Harpy Podarge (Fleet-foot). Greek ghosts do not enter into or become the mothers of horses ; but apart from the poetical appropriateness of a swift horse being called the offspring of two winds, it is to be remembered that there was an ancient belief, that mares could be impregnated by the wind, which is not unlike Homer's story.[64]

Thus far we have dealt with Harpies which, although terrible enough, have nothing disgusting about them. A different picture is given, however, in connexion with the punishment of Phineus.[65] The Harpies that plagued him seem to be modelled on carrion-feeding birds, for they are represented as not only hideous and ravenous, but as so disgustingly filthy that such food as they did not carry off was left totally uneatable.

Phorkys married his sister, Keto, and begat a weird offspring enough, the Graiai, Pemphredo, Enyo and Deino, who were grey-haired from birth, and the three Gorgons, Sthenno, Euryale, and Medusa ; these strange figures will meet us again in the legend of Perseus. The former are apparently nothing else than old age personified, the spirits of Eld. Their name seems to connect itself with the root of $\gamma \acute{\epsilon} \rho \omega \nu$ (old man) and $\gamma \rho a \widetilde{\upsilon} \varsigma$ (old woman). It is most characteristic of the Greek hatred for all uncomeliness that in the text of Hesiod they are called ' fair-cheeked ', an epithet suggesting young and beautiful women, and in art they are shown accordingly with none of the deformities of age. But all accounts agree in making them blind and toothless, or to be exact, as having but one eye and one tooth between the two, or three, of them. Perseus contrived to steal their eye and tooth, and would not give them back until they gave him in exchange the magic shoes, wallet and cap which he needed ; or, according to another version, followed by Aeschylus, he stole the eye only, threw it into Lake Tritonis, and thus left the Gorgons, whose sentries the Graiai were, unguarded, and was able to surprise them.[66]

With regard to the Gorgons, it has been rightly pointed out, for instance by Miss Harrison,[67] that we hear of the head of the Gorgon before anything is told us of the Gorgon herself. The kernel of the myth is, that there existed sometime and somewhere a creature of aspect so terrible that those who saw her turned at once into stone. I am much inclined to think that this tale has a very simple explanation, namely, certain phenomena of dreams. To see, in a nightmare, a face so horrible that the dreamer is reduced to helpless, stony terror, is not a peculiarity of any age or race ; something of the kind, for example, gives the final touch of gruesomeness to Kipling's story, *At the End of the Passage*. Once started on its way, this idea would naturally blend with the widespread superstition, common in both ancient and modern Greece, of the evil eye. Finally, the name of one of the Gorgons, Euryale (Wide-leaping) and the running or striding attitude of the monster in early art comport well with a pursuing nightmare-phantom.

Homer speaks of the Gorgon most commonly as a decoration and only once as an actual living monster.[68] The older Greek art tallies well with the Homeric passages, for it shows a horrible, grinning head, with flat nose, lolling tongue, and staring eyes, sometimes adding a striding, winged body. With this the descriptions of the poets later than Homer correspond. In particular several passages give the Gorgons serpents in their hair or girdles, with other monstrous features. This hideous bogey is expanded into the trio, Sthenno (Stheno, Sthenusa ; the ' Mighty One '), Euryale, and Medusa (' Queen '), of whom the last was mortal. Poseidon was her lover, and when killed by Perseus she was pregnant by him. From her trunk sprang the winged horse Pegasos (it is to be remembered that Poseidon was among other functions a horse-god) and Chrysaor, ' he of the golden sword '.[69]

There is another tale of her death which seems purely Attic. As the armed Athena had a Gorgon-head or *gorgoneion* on her shield, she was credited with having killed the Gorgon herself, in the battle with the Giants ; the two traditions were reconciled by making Perseus slay the Gorgon at Athena's bidding, and give her the head. A reason was invented for the enmity—Medusa had preferred her beauty above Athena's. It was supposed that the head was buried under the market-place (Agora) at Athens, and that one lock of it had been given to the city of Tegea, in Arkadia, to protect it. As a result of the Greek hatred of ugliness, or possibly to avoid representing Poseidon as being in love with anything so misshapen as the traditional Gorgon, later art [70] shows Medusa as a beautiful woman, from about 300 B.C. on with a look of terror or pain about the eyes. This last detail is quite late, being part of the realistic art of the third century B.C. ; between that time and about the year 400 B.C. or so, Medusa is shown coldly and calmly beautiful.

Chrysaor became, by Kallirhoe (' Fair-flowing ') the Okeanid, father of Geryoneus, Geryones or Geryon, a three-headed or, in some accounts, three-bodied monster, of whom we shall hear more in connexion with the adventures of Herakles.[71] He lived, with his herdsman Eurytion and his dog, Orthros, the child of Typhon and Echidna, on the island of Erytheie (' Red Island ') in the stream of Ocean, and was rich in cattle, until Herakles came to slay him and reive them.

' Red Island ' is probably nowhere in the known world, but, as the name would imply, a fairy-land place lost in the glow of the sunset. Later, when the Greeks came to know of Spain, they located Geryon there, although there is a tradition, probably earlier in origin, which puts his home some place in Ambrakia, which being on the west coast of Greece was doubtless once the region of the sunset for the Hellenes.[72]

Geryon had a sister, the monster Echidna, half woman and half serpent. To her the gods assigned a dwelling underground, beneath Arima, where she mated with Typhon, and bore him a yet more monstrous progeny : Orthros, already mentioned ; Kerberos, the hell-hound, ' with voice of bronze and fifty heads ', according to Hesiod, who became the watch-dog of the under-world ; the Lernaian Hydra, the Chimaira, and finally the Theban Sphinx or Phix and the Nemean lion.[73]

In all this hideous brood we may safely recognize the influence of non-Greek fancy, chiefly Anatolian, on the Greek mind. The many-membered creatures, Geryon, Kerberos, and the Hydra, all remind us of the many-armed and many-headed deities of Indian and other Oriental religion. The Chimaira, a composite of lion, goat ($\chi i\mu\alpha\iota\rho\alpha$) and dragon, also the twy-formed Echidna herself, suggest the winged, human-headed bulls and other monsters of Assyrian and Babylonian art and legend. The Sphinx is regularly represented as a creature with a lion's body, woman's face, and wings, a well-known figure in Levantine art, which was early taken over by the Greeks. She will be discussed in connexion with the legend of Oidipus.

It is not surprising, considering how little the Greeks liked monstrosities, that these products of an imagination not their own are represented as living in the lower world. Kerberos is regularly, although not always, doorkeeper of Hades ;[74] Hesiod elsewhere[75] declares that he lets new-comers in, fawning upon them, but devours them as they try to go out. Here we probably have a definitely savage figure, the devourer of the dead, not unfamiliar in Pacific mythology. Not dissimilar is the horrible monster Eurynomos, whom Pausanias saw[76] in the famous picture of Hades by Polygnotes, at Delphi. The local interpreters told him that he was a daimon of the lower world, who devoured the flesh of the dead, leaving only their bones. The painter had represented him with grinning teeth and a body the

colour of a blue-black carrion-fly. Vergil's Aeneas[77] sees at
the very entrance to Hades 'the beast of Lerna, screeching
horribly, and the Chimaira armed with flame, Gorgons also and
Harpies and a triple-bodied shade' (*i.e.*, Geryon), and numerous
other passages point the same way. They are rather horrors
lurking in the background than clear-cut figures of the generally
sunny Hellenic mythology. We may be sure that the Nemean
lion would not have figured in this group but for the fact that
he, like Kerberos and the Hydra, was associated with Herakles.

The dragon of the Hesperides, as already mentioned, was
the offspring of Phorkys and Keto.[78]

Okeanos and his wife Tethys had a very numerous progeny,
namely all the rivers of the world and also the Ocean-nymphs
(Okeanides, Okeaninai), three thousand in number, *i.e.*, innumerable, whose functions are in no way confined to the water,
for they are active on land also, guarding men in their youth.
They are, among other things, river-spirits, the most famous
among them being Styx (' the abhorrent '), the river of the underworld by which the gods dare not swear falsely. The reason
for her pre-eminence will be clear later.[79] As is the case with
not a few of these figures of early mythology, Styx is connected
with Arkadia, where her name was given to a little stream which
trickles over a cliff near the village of Nonakris.[80] The reason
for this and similar identifications is very simple ; every people
loves to localize in its own territory the sites of famous events
in tradition and places in any way connected with its religion
and mythology ; now the population of Arkadia had occupied
the country for a very long while, and claimed to have been there
since before the moon was created or corn discovered ; therefore, even if a myth did not originate there, it had very good
chances to be localized there and to have its claim recognized
by a sort of prescriptive right, no other place having so old-established a title to it.

The Titaness Thea or Theia became, by the Titan Hyperion,
mother of the Sun (Helios, Latin Sol) and Moon (Selene, Latin
Luna).[81] These deities were but little worshipped in Greece,
although Helios is commonly invoked in oaths, from Homer
down,[82] in his capacity as an all-seeing god. He was worshipped
in Rhodes, but elsewhere is of little importance ; the attempts
to identify him with some other deity, as Apollo or Herakles,
which have been frequently made in ancient and modern times,
prove little save the credulity of their learned originators.[83]

In art and in literature he is normally represented as a charioteer ; exceptionally, however, he rides on horseback, and he is

not infrequently winged. His head is commonly surrounded by
the radiate disk of the sun, and his team consists of four horses,
to which the poets give appropriate names, as Pyroeis (Fiery),
Eoös (Orient), Aithon or Aithops (Blazing), Phlegon (Flaming),
or the like. His palace is in the East ; at night, he plunges
into the western sea, or the stream of Ocean, there rests and bathes,
and so returns to the East, floating along the stream of Ocean in
a huge cup.[84]

Apart from this imaginative description of his daily activities,
mythology has but little to say concerning the Sun. He is
represented, in the *Odyssey*, as the owner of certain herds of
cattle, seven in number, and as many flocks of sheep, fifty head
in each, on the island of Thrinakie, vaguely situated somewhere
in the West. In wrath at the action of Odysseus' men, who kill
some of these to stay their hunger after being long imprisoned
by bad weather on the island, he appeals to Zeus, who takes
vengeance on his behalf by sinking their ship and drowning them
all, save Odysseus himself, who had taken no part in the killing.[85]

It is commonly supposed, from Aristotle onwards, that these cattle
and sheep, 350 of each, are an allegory of the days and nights of
the year, since 350 is not far off the number of days in twelve lunar
months (354). I can see no reason for this. There are seven herds
of each, and seven is a very old Oriental sacred number which early
reached Greece ; in each herd there are fifty beasts, and that is a
common Greek round figure for all manner of companies and assemblies.[86] The approximate agreement with the number of days in the
year is a mere accident.

Helios also plays a part in the tale (probably an interpolation into the *Odyssey*) of the loves of Ares and Aphrodite, for it
is he who tells Hephaistos of his wife's misconduct.[87] The rest
of his mythology consists principally of his love affairs. These
are far less numerous than those of Zeus, which is not surprising,
for in a warm climate it is rather the rain than the sun that is
thought of as fertilizing, and therefore rather the rain-god than
the sun-god who is regarded as married.

His official consort, so to call her, was Perse or Perseis, daughter of Krios and Eurybie ; she became the mother of Aietes and
Kirke, whose legend will be told later.[88] His mistresses, Klymene, Klytie, Leukothoe and Rhode, will be discussed in connexion with the heroes and heroines.

About the middle of the fifth century B.C. a theory arose to the
effect that Helios was the same as Apollo. This causes a certain
slight confusion between the mythologies of the two deities in later

times.[89] The fact that both gods are archers (the sun's rays being, by a common and natural metaphor, called his arrows) probably helped to start the identification.

Being one of the most prominent of the Titans, the sun is commonly, especially in Latin, called Titan simply.[90]

The Moon (Selene, Selenaie, Selenaia, often Mene) is of great importance in magic, and also in many ancient and modern theories as to the nature of other goddesses : in particular, she has again and again been identified with Artemis, with whom she has nothing in reality to do. But for mythology proper she is of even less importance than Helios. Like her brother the Sun, she is conceived as a charioteer ; no one who has ever seen the Elgin Marbles is likely to forget the marvellous head of one of her team which survives among them. But unlike him, she drives a pair, not a four, and sometimes her beasts are oxen ; now and then she rides, generally on a horse, sometimes on a steer, once or twice on a mule.

In regard to the last two beasts, it is not to be forgotten that the exaltation ($\H{v}\psi\omega\mu\alpha$) of the Moon in astrology is in the constellation Taurus, and that a fanciful connexion was traced between the sterile animal and the sterile luminary [91]; this is therefore more pseudo-philosophy than mythology.

Her genealogy varies ; the author of the 'Homeric' Hymn to Hermes calls her daughter of Pallas (the Titan, not the goddess) ; both she and her brother are elsewhere said to have Euryphaessa ('She who shines far and wide') for their mother instead of Theia ; one or two passages of tragedy call her daughter, not sister, of the Sun.[92] I doubt if this latter be anything but allegory, and therefore late and literary in origin ; she gets her light from the Sun, therefore may be called his daughter. Finally, she is identified with Artemis. This seems to be as old as Aeschylus, who calls her [93] daughter of Zeus and Leto. It is very common in later times, and is in the last degree unlikely, although very popular in the last generation with mythologists.

The one story of any consequence concerning her is her love for Endymion, which will be more conveniently dealt with later.

No time need be wasted over transparent allegories such as that of Alkman, frag. 39 Bergk, which makes Herse (Dew) daughter of Zeus and Selene, i.e., dew falls from the moonlit night sky, or over a few late mentions of this union and its fruits.[94] Another myth, natural enough, but late, represents her as wedded to the Sun.[95] There is also a curious and obscure tale which Vergil alludes to, borrowing from Nikandros, according to which Pan loved Selene and allured her to follow him into the woods. He somehow attracted her attention with a particularly fine fleece of wool, behind or in which he hid. The rusticity of the tale suggests that it is a local Arkadian legend.[96]

A third child of the union between Hyperion and Theia was Eos (the Dawn, Latin Aurora). Like her brother and sister, she is imagined as driving a chariot ; like Selene, she drives a pair, not a four. In poetry from Homer down she is described by epithets suitable to the colours of the sky at dawn, as rosy-fingered, saffron-robed, and so on.[97] She has a comparatively well-marked personality and appears as the heroine of three love-stories, in all of which she appears, not as pursued, but as pursuer. The most famous of these represents her as mated to Tithonos. Homer already knows him as her husband, and gives Tithonos' genealogy (he is son of Laomedon and brother of Priam).[98] The author of the ' Homeric ' Hymn to Aphrodite tells his story in full ; Eos loved him for his beauty, and carried him off ; she then begged Zeus to make him immortal, which he did, but forgot to ask that he might be ageless also. So he grew older and older, until at last he shrank away to a shrivelled thing which she kept hidden away in a shut chamber, only his voice remaining active.[99] He was the father of the Ethiopian hero Memnon.

One or two later writers make Tithonos the son of Laomedon, not by his wife, but by Strymo, daughter of the river Skamandros, or move him a generation back, calling him brother, not son, of Laomedon.[100] His aged body was according to some changed into a cicada, probably a mere corollary to what ' Homer ' says of his voice.[101]

One passage in Homer informs us that Eos also loved and carried off Orion. The gods, however, were jealous, and Artemis slew Orion with her arrows, ' in Ortygia ', which according to the later identifications is Delos.[102] An obscurer story, mentioned apparently nowhere save in a passing reference in the Odyssey, tells of a certain Kleitos, a member of the great prophetic family of the Melampodidai and uncle of Amphiaraos, who likewise was carried off by Eos.[103] It has been suggested that the phrase is no more than a periphrasis, in this case at any rate, for sudden and early death. As Rohde has well pointed out,[104] a certain number of legends are to be found in Greek telling how some one was carried off, to the Islands of the Blessed or elsewhere, in a manner reminiscent of the translation of Enoch in the Hebrew tradition. It is obvious that euphemism, flattery, and so forth might well lead to the extension of this belief to cases of mysterious death or disappearance.

The third important love-affair of Eos, for the carrying off
of Kleitos hardly counts, was with Kephalos. Hesiod is the
first to mention this.[105]   Eos bore him a son, Phaethon (not the
same as the Phaethon of whom we shall hear later, the son
of Helios and Klymene), who was carried away in his young
manhood by Aphrodite, who ' made him a servant in her holy
temples by night, a divine daimon '.   The story is mentioned
in several later authors, as Euripides,[106] and finally is combined,
very prettily, with the romantic tale of Kephalos and Prokris.

There was an Attic form of the story in which the son of Kephalos
was Tithonos, who in turn became the father of Phaethon.[107]

Another pair of Titans, Krios and Eurybie, had three children, Astraios, Pallas, and Perses.[108]   None of these is particularly important.   Astraios (' Starry ') is, in Hesiod,[109] yet
another mate of Eos, who bore him the Winds and the Morning
Star, and also all the other stars.   Pallas (genitive *Pallantis*;
not the same name as Pallas, gen. *Palladis*, the well-known title
of Athena) in Hesiod, is the husband of Styx, by whom he has
a whole family of abstractions, Zelos (Emulation), Nike (Victory),
Kratos and Bia (*i.e.*, Strength and Might).   When the quarrel
between Zeus and the Titans was imminent (see next chapter),
and the former was seeking allies, Styx brought her children
to his aid, for which the god greatly honoured them all, in particular granting Styx the privilege of furnishing the one inviolable oath of the gods.   If any do swear falsely by her terrible
waters, the penalty is a year of unconsciousness followed by
nine years' banishment from heaven.   Her children dwell forever in the house of Zeus,—a transparent allegory, not improbably
of Hesiod's own invention, but taken up by Aeschylus and other
authors.[110]

Astraios and Pallas have namesakes who may conveniently be
listed here.   ' Hyginus ' mentions an Astraeus among the Giants,[111]
and the rubbishy author of the treatise *On Rivers* falsely ascribed to
Plutarch asserts that another Astraios, having in ignorance violated
his own sister, drowned himself in the river afterwards known as the
Kaïkos.[112]   An Arkadian hero called Pallas is mentioned in Apollodoros and other late writers ; he is said to be a son of Lykaon, but
as he also is called father of Nike, it would seem that either he was
originally the same person as the Titan, or else their legends have been
confused.   He founded the city called after him Pallantion, and is the
grandfather of that Euandros who plays so prominent a part in the
foundation-legend of Rome (see Chapter XI).[113]   Euandros' son, in
the eighth and following books of Vergil's *Aeneid*, is also called Pallas ;
that his character is interesting is due wholly to the poet's genius,

for tradition gave him no help ; there was nothing, apparently, but
a dull tale that Euandros' daughter Launa (probably Lavinia) had by
Herakles a son called Pallas, who died young and after whom the
Palatine was named.[114]   Athena is said to have got her title Παλλάς
from a giant Πάλλας whom she killed either in the battle with the
giants or because he offered her violence ; according to this form of
the story he, and not Zeus, was her father.[115]   Finally there is the
Attic hero Pallas, father of the Pallantidai.

Perses, ' who also excelled them all in wisdom ', says Hesiod,
wedded Asterie, daughter of Koios and Phoibe, and thus became
the father of the goddess Hekate.   He is also called Persaios
and Perseus,[116] and must be differentiated from the hero Perseus.

Another Perses, a mortal, is mentioned by a few authors ; he was
a brother of Aietes king of Kolchis, seized the kingdom, and was
afterwards killed either by Medeia or by her son Medos.[117]   Yet a
third Perses was the son, according to one story, of Perseus and
Andromeda, and became the eponymous ancestor of the Persian
nation.[118]

Koios and Phoibe had, besides Asterie, another daughter,
Leto.[119]

NOTES ON CHAPTER II

[1] Bronze, Homer, *Il.*, XVII, 425 ; cf. *Od.*, III, 2 ; iron, *Od.*, XV, 329.
See further, Cook, *Zeus*, I, p. 632, n. 3 ; II, p. 358, n. 6.
[2] Hom., *Od.*, xi, 315. See Cook, *op. cit.*, II, p. 114 foll., for many
parallels to the idea that the sky can be climbed by a ladder of some sort
(as in the Hebrew legend of the Tower of Babel).   With his deductions, so
far as they concern Greek religion, I do not agree.
[3] *Theog.*, 620 foll.
[4] For the most thorough-going modern support of this view, see Bérard,
Phéniciens, and the introductions and notes to his edition of the *Odyssey*,
passim.
[5] See Aesch., *P.V.*, 788 foll.
[6] For the early population of Greece see any recent history of the
country, *e.g.*, the relevant chapters of the *Cambridge Ancient History*.
A short sketch will be found in *P.C.G.*, chapter II
[7] Hesiod, *Theog.*, 116 foll.
[8] See Kern 1922, frags. 1, 54 foll.
[9] Ovid, *Metam.*, I, 5 foll.
[10] Pseudo-Cyprian, *Genesis* (Vol. II, p. 283, Hartel), 3.
[11] See Roscher, arts. HYPERION, AKMON, also URANOS, col. 107, 1, 17.
The first mention of Akmon seems to be in Alkman, fr. 111 Bergk.
[12] *Titanomachia*, fr. 1, Kinkel ; cf. the references given by Bergk on
the fragment of Alkman above quoted. Aither and Ouranos are occasionally identified, as by Euripides, fr. 1023 (the other references to
Euripides in Roscher, VI, 108, 6, are off the point).
[13] See Farnell, *C.G.S.*, III, 1 foll.

[14] The least unlikely meaning is ' honoured ones ', from rt. of τίω. For the Titans in general, see Roscher, art. TITANEN, and under names of particular Titans.

[15] *Iliad*, XIV, 201 foll.

[16] *Iliad*, VIII, 479, where both are mentioned as living in Tartaros.

[17] *P.V.*, 209–10 ; but *Eumen.*, 2, distinguishes them.

[18] The root θε, *put, make fast* ; but the exact meaning is very uncertain.

[19] *Eumen.*, 4. For Phoibe=Selene, see Roscher II, col. 3129, 41.

[20] Hesiod, *Theog.*, 139.

[21] *Iliad*, I, 401 : a plot of Hera, Poseidon, and Athena to bind Zeus is stopped by the intervention of Thetis, who brings Briareos to the rescue.

[22] See *Odyssey*, IX, 116 foll.

[23] See Roscher, *Lex.*, I, 142, 2. Dr. G. H. Green suggests that the octopus with its tentacles and staring eyes may have helped to form the snaky-haired Gorgon.

[24] Hesiod, *Theog.*, 154 foll. Apollodoros, I, 3, says that Ge was angry with Uranos for hurling her children, the Kyklopes and Hekatoncheires, into Tartaros. See p. 340B.

[25] The Erinyes will be discussed later. Apollod., *ibid.*, and a score of other authors, none pre-Alexandrian, give their names as Alekto, Megaira, and Tisiphone, *i.e.*, Never-ceasing, Grudger, and Avenger of Blood. The Meliai are similar to the Dryads ; powers inhabiting or protecting some one particular species of tree are found in several mythologies.

[26] Pausanias, II, 31, 3.

[27] Likymnios of Chios *ap.* Athenaios, XIII, 17, 364 C ; hence, probably, the mention of the story in Suidas *s.u.* 'Ενδυμίωνος ὕπνον καθεύδεις and the *paroimiographoi* in explaining the same proverb (II, p. 25, Leutsch).

[28] See, *e.g.*, Aristotle, *de part. anim.*, III, 663a, 35, and often in later authors ; Momos finds fault with Zeus for not making a bull's horns grow out of its shoulders, where it is strongest ; for full citations, see Tümpel in Roscher, II, 3117 foll. Some readers may perhaps need to be reminded that the Satan of the Book of Job is a cantankerous angel, not the devil of later theology.

[29] See for the cult and legend of Nemesis, Farnell, *C.G.S.*, II, 488 ff.

[30] For Horkos, see Hesiod, *Theog.*, 231, *Op. et di.*, 802, whence Verg., *Georg.*, I, 277 ; see Wissowa, *R.K.R.*, p. 310, for Orcus.

[31] Hesiod, *Theog.*, 215, 275, 518 ; the dragon, *ibid.*, 334 ; called Ladon, Apoll. Rhod., IV, 1396 ; names of Hesperides, Apollod., II, 114, SdA IV, 484, schol. on Clem. Alex., Vol. I, p. 420, 26 Dindorf (both these last are Hesiod, frag. 270 Rzach, but the ascription is doubtful) ; apples, Pherekydes *ap.* schol. Apoll. Rhod. IV, 1396. For fuller references, see Roscher *s.u.* HESPERIDEN.

[32] Hes., *Theog.*, 217, 904. In the latter passage, they are the daughters of Zeus and Themis (= Righteousness), a transparent allegory. For their worship, see Farnell, *C.G.S.*, V, p. 447, Weizsäcker in Roscher, II, 3089 foll. A few typical mentions of the Moirai are Homer, *Il.*, XXIV, 210, ὥς ποθι Μοῖρα κραταιὴ | γιγνομένῳ ἐπένησε λίνῳ, ὅτε μιν τέκον αἰτή, cf. XX, 127, *Od.*, VII, 197 (in these passages Moira is replaced by Aisa, Fate, and Klothes, the Spinners), Eurip., *Alkestis*, 32 (Apollo deludes the Moirai), Catullus, LXIV, 305 foll. Modern Greece, see Lawson, p. 121 foll., Politis, p. 559 foll. ; Argenti and Rose, *Folklore of Chios* (Cambridge 1949), index under *Moirai*.

33 Wissowa, *R.K.R.*, p. 264. *Parca* was falsely derived from *pars* = μέρος, μοῖρα. Fata Scribunda, the Fates or birth-fairies who write (?), visit a child on the seventh day from birth, Tertullian, *de anima*, 39.

34 For instance, Seneca, *Apocolocyntosis*, 4 (thread turns to gold as Nero's fate is being spun), Stat., *Theb.*, VIII, 59, iterataque pensa Sororum (on Eurydike being restored to Orpheus).

35 Pseudo-Aristotle, *de caelo*, 401*b* 18.

36 Plato, *Rep.*, X, 617 C.

37 Isidorus, *Etymologiae*, VIII, 11, 93. Cf. *Anthol. Latina*, 792 Riese ; tres sunt fatales quae ducunt fila sorores ; | Clotho colum baiulat, Lachesis trahit, Atropos occat. The second line is also in M1, 109. See also Egbert von Lüttich, *Fecunda Ratis*, p. 170, ed. Voigt (Halle, 1889).

38 Hyg., *Fab.*, 277, 1 ; the corrupt state of the text does not allow us to say which letters they are supposed to have invented.

39 *Theog.*, 233.

40 *Iliad*, I, 358, XVIII, 36 ; *Od.*, IV, 365 and elsewhere, ἅλιος γέρων is used of Proteus, not Nereus. The mother of Nereus is not named in any early account ; a few late writers assume that it was Ge, the mother of Pontos' other children, but Hesiod does not say so.

41 Pherekydes *ap.* schol. Apoll. Rhod., IV, 1396 ; Nereus, after the manner of sea-creatures in mythology, tried to avoid Herakles by taking all manner of shapes, but at last had to yield. Cf. Apollod., II, 114–15, obviously from the same source.

42 Verg., *Aen.*, II, 417 (a mere passing mention in a simile).

43 See Horace, *Odes*, I, 15, 1 foll.

44 Pindar, *Pyth.*, IX, 94.

45 Lucian, *Tragoedopodagra*, 87 foll.

46 Panyasis *ap.* Athenaios, XI, 38, 469 D.

47 Aelian, *Hist. anim.*, XIV, 28 ; a certain pretty shell-fish is called *nerites*, and said to have been a remarkably handsome son of Nereus and Doris, who somehow offended either Aphrodite or Helios, and so was metamorphosed.

48 Doto at Gabala, Pausanias, II, 1, 8 ; Nereids collectively in several places, references in Roscher, III, 236.

49 See Lawson, p. 130 foll. ; Politis, p. 387 foll. Lists of Nereids, Homer, *Il.*, XVIII, 38 foll. ; Hes., *Theog.*, 243 foll. ; Hygin., *praef.* 8 ; Apollod., I, 11 ; Verg., *Georg.*, IV, 336 foll.

50 See Aeschylus, *P.V.*, 757 foll., 907 foll ; and the fragments of the *Prometheus Solutus* (p. 63 foll., Nauck²) ; Apollod., III, 168 ; Hygin., 54 ; Ovid, *Met.*, XI, 221 foll.

51 Hes., fr. 80 ; Apollod., III, 169 ; cf. Hom., *Il.*, XXIV, 59.

52 For the wrestling, see Pausanias, V, 18, 5 and Frazer on the passage ; Bloch in Roscher, III, 1834, 39 foll. ; Pindar, *Nemeans*, III, 35 (earliest literary evidence). For the shape-changing of Thetis during the wrestling, see especially, apart from artistic evidence, Pind., *Nem.*, IV, 62, and schol. on both passages of Pindar ; Sophokles, fr. 561 N², 618 P. ; Euripides, fr. 1093 N² ; Ovid, *Met.*, XI, 229 foll. ; Apollod., III, 170, besides numerous later or more obscure passages. For the wedding, besides the passages quoted in this and the last note, see Catullus, LXIV, *passim*.

53 See Chapter X, note 3.

54 See Roscher, III, 785, 33 foll., 792–4.

55 See Philoxenos, Κύκλωψ (frags. in Bergk, *P.L.G.*) ; Kallimachos *ap.* Athenaios, VII, p. 284 C (fr. 378 Pfeiffer) ; Theokritos, *Idyl.*, XI ;

Ovid, *Metam.*, XIII, 750 foll. ; Sil. Ital., *Punica*, XIV, 221 foll. ; SB., IX, 39 ; also numerous passages in other authors, notably in the *Eclogues* of Vergil. Other versions of the legend, Propertius, III (IV), 2, 7 ; Appian, *de reb. Illyricis*, 2 ; Nonnos, *Dionysiaca*, VI, 360 foll. ; for more references (mostly to very obscure authors) see Roscher, I, 1588, 4, 1589, 31.

⁵⁶ Hes., *Theog.*, 265, and very numerous later passages. In Hyginus 14, 18, the mother of the Harpies is apparently called Ozomene (*i.e.*, Stinker) if the text is not corrupt.

⁵⁷ Alkman, fr. 13B Bergk (*P.L.G.*⁴), 'Eurytos the Lakedaimonian lyric poet' (otherwise unknown, name very possibly corrupt, perhaps Alkman, see Mayer in Roscher, II, 323, 24), *ap.* Lydus *de mensib.*, p. 172, 8 Wuensch ; Plutarch, *Amatorius*, 765 E foll., and a few later passages.

⁵⁸ Cited by Athenaios, XIV, 53, 645B.

⁵⁹ Generally the messenger of Zeus in the *Iliad*, but sometimes of Hera (XVIII, 168) ; servant of Hera, Eurip., *H.F.*, 829 ; Kallimach., *Hymn.*, IV, 228, and so often later, *e.g.*, Verg., *Aen.*, IV, 693, IX, 2.

⁶⁰ Homer, *Od.*, XX, 66 foll. ; cf. I, 241, XIV, 371, in both of which ἅρπυιαι plainly means 'storm-winds'.

⁶¹ Aello and Okypete, Hes., *Theog.*, 267 ; Kelaino, Verg., *Aen.*, III, 211, 245 ; Hygin., 14, 18.

⁶² Weicker 1902, see his index under *Harpyien* and *Harpyien-monument*.

⁶³ See any good etymological dictionary under the words *animus, anima*, in Latin, ψυχή and πνεῦμα in Greek.

⁶⁴ *Iliad*, XVI, 149 ; Arist., *Hist. anim.* Z, 572ᵃ 10, whence Verg., *Georg.*, III, 271 foll., see Varro *ap.* Servius *ad loc.*, and *de re rustica*, II, 1, 19 ; Pliny, N.H., VIII, 166.

⁶⁵ See Apoll. Rhod., II, 188 foll., cf. Vergil, *Aen.*, III, 210 foll. ; Hyginus, *fab.*, 14, 18. See further Chapter VIII, p. 254. In this capacity they are confused with the Erinyes, see, for instance, Verg., *Aen.*, III, 252.

⁶⁶ Hes., *Theog.*, 270 foll. (names Pemphredo and Enyo only ; the name Deino is from Pherekydes) ; Pherekydes *ap.* schol. Apoll. Rhod., IV, 1515, whence Apollod., II, 37 ; other version in Aeschylus, *Phorkides* (frags., p. 83 N²), whence [Eratosthenes] *catast.*, 22 ; Hyginus, *Astron.*, 2, 12, cf. Palaiphatos *de incred.*, 32. See also Aesch., *P.V.*, 794 ; representations in art, see Harrison, *Proleg.*, p. 195, Rapp in Roscher, I, 1737, 48 foll.

⁶⁷ Harrison, *Proleg.*, p. 187.

⁶⁸ Homer, *Iliad*, V, 741, XI, 36 (gorgoneion as ornament of armour), VIII, 349 (Hektor glares like a Gorgon) ; *Od.*, XI, 634 (Odysseus fears to see a Gorgon-head come up from Hades).

⁶⁹ See Hesiod, *Theog.*, 274 foll. (names and number ; Medusa a mortal, cf. Pherekydes *ap.* schol. Apoll. Rhod., IV, 1515, p. 526, 20 Keil) ; Hesiod, *Scutum Herculis*, 233 ; Pind. *Olymp.*, XIII, 63, *Pyth.*, X, 47 ; Aesch., *P.V.*, 798–800 (deadly look of the Gorgons), *Choeph.*, 1048 foll. (Gorgons compared to Erinyes) ; Hesiod, *Theog.*, 280 (death of Medusa, birth of Pegasos and Chrysaor). For fuller references, see Roscher, art. GORGONES ; with the explanations given there I entirely disagree. My colleague, Dr. G. H. Green, tells me that from the psychological standpoint the dream-explanation is probable.

⁷⁰ Athena slays the Gorgon, Eurip., *Ion.*, 989 foll. The Gorgon is here represented as brought forth by Ge to attack the gods. Paus., II, 21, 5 ; Apollod., II, 144. Cf. *SA* VI, 289.

⁷¹ Hesiod, *Theog.*, 287 foll. ; see Chapter VIII, 1, p. 214. Geryon is three-headed in Hesiod ; winged and had six hands and six feet, schol.

on Hesiod, *loc. cit.*, quoting Stesichoros ; triple-bodied, Aesch., *Agam.*, 870, and commonly.

[72] Hekataios *ap.* Arrian, *Anab.*, II, 16, 5 (Ambrakia) ; Stesichoros *ap.* Strabo, III, 2, 11 (off the ' river Tartessos ', *i.e.*, the Guadalquivir ; near Cadiz therefore).

[73] Hesiod, *ibid.*, 295 foll. For Typhon, see below. Echidna is possibly the child of Phorkys and Keto, not of Chrysaor and Kallirhoe, the text of Hesiod being ambiguous (ἣ δ᾽ ἔτεκ᾽ ἄλλο πέλωρον, where it is not certain whether ἣ refers to Kallirhoe or Keto). She appears in Pausanias, VIII, 18, 2, on the authority of Epimenides of Crete, as daughter of Styx and Peiras, ' whoever Peiras may be ' ; in Apollodoros, II, 4, she is child of Earth and Tartaros, lives somewhere in the Peloponnesos and seizes on all passers-by, and is finally caught asleep and killed by Argos. Kerberos has fifty heads in Hesiod here, but apparently only one in 771, and in the very doubtful passage of Horace, *Carm.*, III, 11, 16 foll. ; a hundred in Pindar, frag. 249 (Bergk), and in Horace, *Carm.*, II, 13. 34 ; three commonly, as Verg., *Aen.*, VI, 417 foll., Hygin., *fab.*, 151, and in art.

[74] Besides the burlesque description in Aristophanes, *Frogs*, 464 foll. (cf. Lucian, *Dial. Mort.*, 20, 1, where Aiakos is Pluto's doorkeeper), and one or two references in classical authors to foreign mythology, as Statius, *Siluae*, III, 2, 112, there is at least one passage in literature, Lucan, *Phars.*, VI, 702, which speaks of a *ianitor* of Hades other than Kerberos, and a tomb-painting from Ostia (Roscher, III, col. 1175) shows a person labelled IANITOR sitting behind him.

[75] *Theog.*, 769 foll. ; sundry later poets have fanciful variants on this.

[76] Paus., X, 28, 7, where see Frazer ; cf. *P.C.G.*, p. 132.

[77] Verg., *Aen.*, 286 foll. ; and so in many descriptions, serious and burlesque, as for instance Lucian's *Dialogues of the Dead*.

[78] Hesiod, *Theog.*, 333 foll.

[79] *Ibid.*, 337 foll.

[80] Pausanias, VIII, 17, 6 ; 18, 4 foll. See Frazer, *ad loc.*

[81] Hes., *op. cit.*, 371 foll. Hyperion is in reality an old name or title of the Sun, see, *e.g.*, Hom., *Od.*, XII, 346, 374.

[82] As *Iliad*, III, 277 ; Euripides, *Medea*, 746 ; and scores of other passages.

[83] The least absurd ones are disposed of by Farnell, *C.G.S.*, IV, 136 foll.

[84] For art representations, see Roscher, I, 1995 foll. ; see, for a few literary references out of many, Eurip., *Ion*, 82 (four-horse chariot), 122 (wings) ; Ovid, *Metam.*, II, 153, Hyginus, *fab.*, 183 (names of horses ; more in Roscher, *l.c.*, 2006–7) ; Helios riding, Eurip., frag. 779, 8, N² ; palace, Ovid, *Metam.*, II, 1 foll. Plunges into ocean, Hom., *Il.*, VIII, 485, and many later passages ; fanciful description, Statius, *Theb.*, III, 467 foll. Sun's cup, see Athenaios, XI, 469D foll., who cites a string of poets from Stesichoros on.

[85] *Od.*, XII, 127, etc.

[86] Fifty oars and hence fifty oarsmen in an ancient type of ship, the pentekonter ; fifty daughters of Danaos ; fifty sons and fifty daughters of Priam ; Kerberos' fifty heads ; fifty Trojans at each camp fire, *Iliad*, VIII, 563 ; fifty, or approximately fifty, Nereids and the same number of Argonauts, and so forth. Cf. Roscher, *Die Zahl 50 in Mythus . . . d. Hellenen etc.*, Teubner, Leipzig, 1917. See for the theory, Arist. *ap.* Schol., *Odyssey*, XII, 129 (fr. 167 Rose) ; for criticism, Frazer, *W.N.*, I, p. 468 foll.

[87] *Od.*, VIII, 392.

[88] Perse, Hesiod, *Theog.*, 377, 957 (the latter passage calls her Perseis).
[89] Eurip., frag. 781, 11, N².
[90] As, for example, Lucan, VII, 2 ; Statius, *Theb.*, I, 501. So the moon is called Titanis, as by Statius, *op. cit.*, I, 337.
[91] Chariot, Pindar, *Olymp.*, III, 19, and countless other passages ; two-horse, apparently only in later authors, as ps.-Verg., *Ciris*, 38, but common in classical art of the best period ; steer, or bull, only in very late works, as *hymn. magic.* in Abel, *Orphica*, p. 292, line 4 ; Nonnus, *Dionys.*, I, 97, 217 ; mule, Pausan., V, 11, 8, Festus, pp. 134, 135, Lindsay. Evidence from art and fuller references, Roscher, II, col. 3139 foll.
[92] *Hymn. Homer.*, IV, 99–100, XXXI, 4 foll. ; Eurip., *Phoeniss.*, 175, where, however, see Powell's note.
[93] Aesch., frag. 170 N², and numerous later passages.
[94] *Hymn. Homer.*, XXXII., 14 (a palpably late work), schol. Pind. *Nemeans*, ὑπόθ. 3.
[95] Quintus Smyrnaeus, X, 337 ; the Horai were their children.
[96] Verg., *Georg.*, III, 391, where see Servius ; cf. Macrobius, *Sat.*, V, 22, 9. In the Orphic tradition Selene is mother of Musaios, see Plat., *Repub.*, II, 364 E ; Orpheus, frag., 4, 2 (Abel), 245, 2 (Kern).
[97] Hesiod, *Theog.*, 372 (birth and parentage) ; Homer, *Od.*, XXIII, 243 foll. (chariot), and many later passages. For her epithets, see any large Greek dictionary, or lexicon to Homer, under ῥοδοδάκτυλος, κροκόπεπλος, and any good Latin dictionary under *roseus, luteus ;* add Roscher, I, 1258.
[98] *Od.*, V, 1 ; *Iliad*, XX, 237.
[99] *Hymn. Homer*, V, 218 foll.
[100] Schol., *Iliad*, XI, 5, cf. Lykophron, 19, with the scholium of Tzetzes ; Servius on *Aen.*, I, 489.
[101] Schol., *Il.*, ibid. ; Servius on *Georg.*, III, 328 ; *Aen.*, IV, 585.
[102] Homer, *Od.*, V, 121 foll.; cf. XI, 572 foll., Apollod., I, 27.
[103] *Od.*, XV, 250.
[104] See Rohde⁴, index under *Entrückung*.
[105] Hes., *Theog.*, 986.
[106] Eurip., *Hippol.*, 454 foll. ; more references in Roscher, I, 1268, 30 foll.
[107] Apollod., III, 181.
[108] Hes., *Theog.*, 375 foll.
[109] *Ibid.*, 378 foll.
[110] *Ibid.*, 383 foll., 775 foll. ; Aesch., *P.V.*, 1 foll.
[111] *Praefatio*, 4.
[112] Pseudo-Plutarch, *de fluuiis*, 21, 1.
[113] Apollod., III, 97 ; Dion. Hal., *antiquit. Rom.*, I, 33, 1 foll. ; Pausanias, VIII, 3, 1 ; 44, 5 ; SA VIII, 51, 54.
[114] Dion. Hal., *op. cit.*, I, 43, 1 ; SA VIII, 51.
[115] Apollod., I, 37 ; Festus, p. 246, Lindsay ; Clem. Alexand., *Protrept.*, 28 (p. 24, Potter) ; Cicero, *de nat. deor.*, III, 59 ; for other passages (from late writers), see Roscher, III, 1338, 46 foll.
[116] Hesiod, *Theog.*, 377, 409 ; *Hymn. Homer.*, II, 24 ; Lykophron, 1175.
[117] Apollod., I, 147 ; Hyginus, *fab.*, 27, 5.
[118] Herodotos, VII, 61, 3.
[119] Hesiod, *op. cit.*, 404 foll. In Hyginus, *fab., praefat.*, 10 and 140, 2, Leto's father is called Polos (Heaven or Pole) ; a genealogy found nowhere else.

CHAPTER III

THE CHILDREN OF KRONOS—I

ἄναξ ἀνάκτων, μακάρων
μακάρτατε καὶ τελέων
τελειότατον κράτος, ὄλβιε Ζεῦ.

—ÆSCHYLUS, *Supplices*, 524–6.

King of Kings, most blessed of the Blessed Ones, most perfect might among the Perfect, blissful Zeus.

OF the Titans described in the last chapter, by far the most important are KRONOS and his consort Rhea or Rheia. The former of these venerable figures is in all probability a pre-Greek god, for attempts to give his name a Greek etymology have so far failed.[1] He was but little worshipped in classical times ; the one festival of any importance connected with him, the Kronia, is known to have existed in three places only, Athens, Rhodes and Thebes. It was a harvest-festival, and we know that at it all social distinctions were for the time being abolished, and master and man feasted together,—a rite not uncommon in festivals of this sort. We have some reason to suppose that human sacrifice was occasionally offered to him, which in Greece at any rate marks an early rite. The rare representations of him in art show him as a majestic but sorrowful old man, holding a curved object traditionally interpreted as the knife wherewith he wounded Uranos, but which is quite as likely, considering the time of his festival, to be a reaping-hook. The Greeks frequently identified him with unlovely foreign deities such as Moloch. To the Roman theorists, he was identical with Saturn (Saturnus or Saeturnus), a deity whose name and functions are alike obscure, and quite possibly foreign, although early.

Under his rule, according to a legend as old as Hesiod,[2] all was innocent happiness. Men lived long and virtuous lives, without labour, strife, or the need of law, having all things in common and dwelling safely amid the great abundance of all

43

manner of produce which the earth brought forth of her own
accord. In short, it was the Golden Age, ὁ ἐπὶ Κρόνου βίος,
Saturnia regna. But another and certainly very old group of
legends shows Kronos in a much less pleasant light.[3] Ge and
Uranos had warned him that he should be overthrown by one
of his own children ; he therefore swallowed them as fast as they
were born. But Rhea, when she bore her youngest child, Zeus,
hid him away, and gave his father a stone wrapped in swaddling-
clothes instead. Thus Zeus grew to maturity, and soon raised
a power against his father. Rhea contrived to beguile her
lord into vomiting up the elder children ; Zeus set free certain
of his father's brethren who had been imprisoned in Tartaros,
including the Kyklopes, who armed him with thunder and lightning in return for their freedom,[4] and the Hekatoncheires,
Briareos and the rest, who proved formidable allies in the battle
which ensued.[5] Moreover, as already narrated,[6] Styx with her
brood rallied to his side. For ten years the battle raged, Zeus
and his allies fighting from Mt. Olympos, the Titans under
Kronos (except Prometheus and Themis) from Mt. Orthrys.
The earth, and even Tartaros, was shaken with the trampling
and noise of the immortal warriors ; but at last the Titans
gave way before the thunderbolts of Zeus and the showers of
huge stones hurled by the Hekatoncheires. They were then
imprisoned in Tartaros, save those who had taken Zeus' part,
and Atlas, whose prodigious strength was employed to hold up
the sky. The prison was guarded by the Hekatoncheires.

So, it would appear, the original story ran. But, perhaps
because the Titans did not wholly disappear from cult, it seems
to have been felt that their punishment and imprisonment was
not endless. Pindar definitely says that Zeus freed the Titans,
and Aeschylus, in the *Prometheus Unbound,* seems not only to have
introduced them, released, as witnesses of the freeing of Prometheus from his rock,[7] but also to have represented Zeus as coming
somehow to terms with Prometheus himself. Precisely what lies
behind the legend is a disputed point. According to some mythologists, it is a nature-myth, a contest between the wilder and the
more benignant powers of Nature ; others prefer to see in it
a vague reminiscence of the victory of the Olympian cult, brought
by the invading Greeks, over the older religion of the pre-Hellenic peoples. Personally, I think both sides in a measure right.
It seems very reasonable to suppose that invasion and conquest
should reflect themselves in a story of this kind, when we remember how regularly the gods of ancient peoples, in the classical
sphere and out of it, were supposed actually to take part in the

battles of their worshippers and to share their victory or defeat ; but on the other hand, the imagery of the battle is so reminiscent of earthquakes and volcanic eruptions that I do not believe the resemblance merely accidental.   The Greeks had at all periods good opportunities of observing such phenomena in their own part of the world.   To say nothing of Asia Minor, the island of Santorin (anciently called Thera) and the neighbouring islands are known to have been in a state of activity more or less intense from the second century B.C. to the year A.D. 1866, from which it can be deduced with some confidence that they were still more active at the time when this legend may be supposed to have formed.   Many other signs of volcanic activity have also been noted, in antiquity and by modern observers, in various parts of the Aegean.[8]

Later authors had not a little to say about the fate of Kronos after his defeat.   In conformity with the idea that he was king of the Golden Age, certain theologians began quite early to make him lord of the Islands of the Blessed.[9]   Plutarch has an exceedingly picturesque tale,[10] according to which there is a holy island near Britain (i.e., at the extremities of the known world) where Kronos sleeps with his followers around him, and Briareos on guard.   Finally, Euhemerizers and rationalizers represented Kronos as having been a great king of the West,[11] which story was improved, in Italy, by making him take refuge in Latium from the pursuit of Zeus, where he founded a city, Saturnia, on the future site of Rome, and gave the district its name from his hiding (*latere*) in it.[12]
It might perhaps be suggested that the revolt of Kronos against Uranos is merely a doublet of the struggle between Zeus and Kronos. Whether this prominence of the youngest son points to the former existence in Greece of the custom by which the youngest child is the heir (*Jüngstenrecht*, Borough English) is doubtful.[13]   It is noteworthy that to Homer Zeus is the eldest son, *Il.*, XV, 165, 187.

Kronos' consort and sister RHEA is a grandiose but somewhat vague figure, not very often worshipped under that particular name.   In a considerable number of places, however, we find one cult or another which might be called hers.   Apart from her common identification with the great Anatolian goddess Kybele, we constantly find her practically indistinguishable from Ge, and moreover, blended with a very old and widely worshipped power, the Mother, who, if she is not herself the Earth, at least has close relations with earth-goddesses.   From Cretan times onwards, in Greece and Asia Minor, we find this sympathetic and majestic figure under all manner of names, sometimes associated with a god, sometimes alone.   It must not be rashly assumed

that all the peoples of the Greek world and the neighbouring
regions had once a common cult, however ; rather is it the case
that they all developed a common conception, namely, that
there existed a divine power whose chief characteristic was
inexhaustible fertility, comparable, but on a far larger scale,
to that of a woman.   Such a concept might and did lead to at
least three results.   It might give rise to the beautiful idea, which
lasts to our own day, of a superhuman power tender and sympathetic as a mother ;   it might, from undue emphasis on the
idea of physical fertility, give rise to hideously immoral practices,
like those of Mylitta in Babylon, and here and there, even among
Greeks, to unseemly forms of worship addressed to Aphrodite ;
or finally, it might produce a sort of dogma, the fruit of reflection
and an attempt at systematization, that all or most of the gods
had a particular goddess for their mother.[14]   It is in this capacity
that Rhea, both in her proper form and in conjunction with
Kybele, is prominent.   She sides very decidedly with her children rather than with her husband, and it has been suggested[15]
that her position as consort of Kronos is due simply to the fact
that in Cretan legend she was the mother of that god whom the
Greeks identified with their Zeus.   Here again an error must
be avoided ;   we have no sort of right to say that Rhea, or the
Mountain Mother, or whatever name we may prefer to use for
this ancient goddess, was the only deity, or even the only goddess, worshipped in Minoan Crete.[16]   What we may say on good
grounds is, that she was very prominent there.   Of legend, apart
from the tales of Oriental goddesses with whom she was identified, she has but little, but that little probably very old.   Her
deceit of Kronos has already been mentioned ;   her children,
according to Hesiod, were Hestia, Demeter, Hera, Hades, Poseidon, and lastly Zeus.[17]   Concerning the birthplace of Zeus
two tales were current in antiquity ;   one, in all probability
much the older, according to which he was born in Crete ;   the
other, also quite ancient, which placed the great event in Arkadia,
that home of old traditions.[18]   In Rome, Rhea is identified with
Ops, the goddess of plenty.   In cult, however, Saturnus has for
his partner Lua, Ops being paired with Consus.

As regards the Cretan story, mention must be made of a very
curious tradition recorded by Boios in Antoninus Liberalis.[19]   The
cave which had been the scene of the birth every year sent forth
fire, ' when the blood of Zeus' birth boils '.   It seems likely, as Nilsson
supposes, that the divine child worshipped in Crete was born (and
probably died) every year.   This cave was no doubt an ancient sacred
place, and the same passage tells of how thieves tried to steal the

honey of the sacred bees who bred there, but were turned into birds for their impiety, their lives being spared by Zeus because no blood may be spilled there. The identification of Rhea with Anatolian goddesses leads occasionally to the birth of Zeus being located somewhere in Asia Minor.

Rhea was not the only mate of Kronos, although only she is represented as his wife. Philyra the Okeanid became by him the mother of the Centaur Cheiron, who is consequently called Philyrides in a number of passages.[20] He met her in Thessaly (while searching for Zeus, according to Hyginus), and the twy-form shape of her son was accounted for by the story that Kronos turned himself into a stallion, either by way of disguise, because Rhea surprised him, or because Philyra had turned into a mare to escape him.[21] Philyra was much shocked at the shape of her child and prayed to be changed into some other form : therefore Zeus turned her into a lime-tree (φιλύρα).[22]

To attempt anything more than the briefest of sketches of Zeus is obviously impossible. Many Wiro-speaking peoples have a divine figure (Iuppiter in Italy, Dyaus in India, Tiu among the Germanic peoples, and so forth) who more or less corresponds to him. The root meaning of his name is apparently ' bright ', and he is the god of the sky, or rather of the phenomena of the sky or, more accurately, of those of the atmosphere. His primary functions appear to be connected with rain and the return of fine weather, also, very characteristically, with thunder and lightning. Hence he is associated also with what depends so largely upon the weather, the fertility of the soil, although that is never a very prominent aspect of his cult or nature. To all this a long string of titles bears witness, such as Ombrios and Hyettios (Rainer), Urios (Sender of favourable winds), Astrapaios (Lightener), Bronton (Thunderer), Georgos (Farmer), and so forth. But he is so widely worshipped that there is scarcely a department of nature or of human activity with which he has not some connexion. He is closely associated with political life (in Homer, kings derive their authority from him, and Polieus, He of the City, is an ancient title of his), early represented as interested in moral concerns, and from Homer down, so firmly established as the supreme god that we feel no surprise at finding his name used by philosophers of a monotheistic tendency practically as equivalent to ' God ', while others, who do not go so far, still are very ready to extend his functions to include, for instance, those of Hades, who is ' another Zeus ' or ' Zeus of the lower world ' (Katachthonios) in many passages. Although his myths include many that are early and grotesque, or late and frivolous, he never quite loses his majesty, and is consistently represented in art as a stately figure, a vigorous man in the prime of life, standing or sitting in a dignified attitude, usually draped from the waist down, bearing sceptre or thunderbolt, or both, and attended by his familiar, the eagle. He also is often represented, in literature and art alike, as associated with the oak, a tree marked out as appropriate not only by its beauty and majesty and its long life, but by two conspicuous facts, namely, that in antiquity it grew very commonly, and not least so in those regions where Zeus was most fervently worshipped, such as Dodona and Arkadia, and that it is very commonly struck by lightning, as the ancients noticed and modern forestry has proved statistically.[23]

Two important attributes of Zeus are the thunderbolt and the aigis. Of the former it need only be said that the universal explanation, before modern researches made the true character of electrical phenomena known, of the destructive effect of lighting was that with the lightning-flash some kind of heavy and pointed missile was thrown. In Greek art, this is usually shown as a bi-conical object, often having conventional lightning-flashes attached, and sometimes wings also. The aigis is described, by various authors from Homer down, as a fringed garment or piece of armour (apparently, at times, a shield or corslet). In the hands of a god, or worn by him, it is not only a potent defence, but a magically powerful weapon, which when shaken at an enemy fills him with terror. Being worn by the god of thunder, it is not surprising that it has been again and again interpreted as a thunder-cloud. But the plain meaning of the name puts this out of court. αἰγίς means simply a goat-skin, as νεβρίς means a fawn-skin. In its origin this mysterious object is nothing more than a cloak made of a goat's hide with the hair on, forming a fringe. Just such a garment is worn to this day by Greek peasants, and it doubtless clothed many ancient wooden or stone cult-objects intended to represent Zeus, for the clothing of statues is quite common in 'Greece. As it was of tough hide, it would serve its wearer as a defence, not only against the weather, but against an enemy's blows. But being worn by a great god, the aigis, or goat-skin coat, of Zeus would be full of his divine force, or *mana*, and therefore could, especially when used by him or his favourite daughter Athena, itself work wonders.[24]

Of his birth something has already been said. Once born, he was taken to Crete (according to those who do not place his birth there) and hidden in a cave at Lyktos,—he was born, according to the Cretan story, in a cavern on Mt. Ide or Mt. Dikte, —where he was tended by the local divinities. Food was provided for him by the goat Amaltheia, also by bees who brought him their honey ; and his cries were drowned by the noisy war-dance of the Kuretes. So far we have evident interpretation of ritual, and Cretan ritual at that. The caves were holy, and modern excavations have found several shrines in caves the style of whose furniture shows very clearly that they are of Minoan date.[25] The Kuretes seem to be of Minoan origin[26]; and it has been already mentioned that a divine child was a prominent object of Cretan worship. Leaving this pre-Hellenic stratum we pass now to legends definitely Greek.

Zeus grew and reached maturity [27]; this is doubtfully Cretan, for it is not certain that Cretan child-gods grew up. Having overthrown Kronos, he had three important affairs to settle : to divide the conquered universe between himself and his brothers, to provide himself with a consort, and to settle his relations with mankind.

The first of these matters was briefly and amicably arranged : Zeus, Poseidon and Hades cast lots for the three main divisions of the ancestral estate, heaven, the sea, and the lower world, holding Olympos and the earth in common.[28] The absence here of any notion of primogeniture, the exclusion of the sisters from the division, and the retention of a sort of glorified equivalent of the paternal hearth and the land immediately around it, are all quite in accordance with early Greek law, and indeed with early European law generally.[29] Nor need we hesitate to press the comparison because Kronos was not supposed to be dead, being as immortal as his sons. His position, and indeed that of the elder gods generally, is exactly that of the aged father of a Homeric chieftain, Laertes for instance in the *Odyssey*, who has retired from active control of his kingdom or barony.[30] As might be expected from the age of the legend, the characters in it behave precisely like rather primitive Greeks. The result of the lot was, that Zeus had the sky for his share, Poseidon the sea, Hades the infernal regions.

The nuptials of Zeus, however, were a much more complicated matter. We have already seen how Father Sky married Mother Earth, and that not in Greek tradition only, but in the fancy of very many races. Now Zeus is emphatically a sky-god ; it is therefore natural that he should wed an earth-goddess, or at any rate, a goddess connected with fertility. Hence we find him the consort of Demeter, Persephone, Semele, and Hera. But once he was paired, in various local legends, with several such goddesses, the result of any attempt to correlate these legends (and such attempts were clearly made very early) must be either that he was represented as polygynous, or that he was thought of as grossly unfaithful to his legitimate queen. The former solution was impossible, for the Greeks themselves were always monogamous, and naturally represented their gods as having the same practice ; the latter was more in accordance with their own ideas, which tolerated such irregularities and gave children resulting from them a recognized, though subordinate, place in the family.[31]   Hence Zeus is always represented as having but one wife (generally Hera), but as the father of a number of illegitimate children, who, if they are the sons of goddesses, acquire divine rank themselves, while if their mothers are mortal women, their position, though exalted, is not divine.[32]   The numerous unions with mortals (to be treated later) are easily explained, in some cases by the probable supposition that the women in question are forgotten, or, as they are technically called, ' faded ' goddesses, in the majority as particularizations of the general claim of old royal houses to be ' scions of Zeus ',[33] and the desire of less illustrious families to provide themselves with a lofty ancestry, at the price of a bend sinister many generations back. The same explanations hold good for the many pedigrees which go back, not to Zeus himself, but to some other Olympian. Even so, a certain number of the unions of gods are marriages with relatives in the first degree, full sisters or daughters.   This was never allowed in Greek society, and we must explain such cases, as it seems to me, by supposing that the connexion between a god and a goddess was explained by some as that of brother and sister, or father and daughter, by others as that of husband and wife.   The ancients themselves noticed this anomaly, and were puzzled by it,[34] in later times.

In this chapter I propose to deal with the divine consorts only of Zeus, leaving the mortal recipients of his favours for a later section.

In Hesiod, Zeus' first consort was Metis (wisdom, good counsel).   But this was a dangerous union, for Metis was destined to bear, first Athena, and then a god who should rule the gods. Zeus therefore took the precaution of swallowing her before the birth of Athena, who in due time was born from the head of her father.[35]   Plainly, we have here a very odd combination, the ancient and savage myth of swallowing being blended with what seems to be a sort of allegory ; the chief god has Wisdom always within him.   The close connexion between Zeus and Athena is probably due to historical causes.   The chief god of the invaders must come to some sort of terms with the powerful and well-established Minoan-Mycenaean goddess ;[36] but he cannot be her husband, since she, like the rest of her kind, has either no consort or an insignificant one ; therefore he must be her father.   But she can have no mother, for that would subordinate her to some other goddess, such as Hera or Persephone, and she is far too important for that. Hence her miraculous birth, which represents, if we could but recover the details, an interesting chapter in early diplomacy and ecclesiastical polity.

His next wife was Themis, i.e. Sky married Earth.[37] The offspring was appropriate, the Seasons (Horai : see Chapter V, p. 124), and the Moirai, already discussed (Chapter II, p. 24, and note 32, which explains their diversity of parentage).

Next came Eurynome, who, like Metis, is represented by Hesiod as a daughter of Okeanos and Tethys.[38] Her children were the Charites, more familiar in English under the Latin translation of their name, Graces (Gratiae). They also will be treated in Chapter V, p. 124.

A more important union was that of Zeus and Demeter, which again gives us Sky wedding, not exactly Earth, but Corn. The offspring of this wedlock was Kore, otherwise known as Persephone.[39]

There is another tale which is of Orphic origin, perhaps originally from some lost Thracian or Phrygian myth. Zeus loved his own daughter, Persephone, and finally was united with her in the form of a serpent or dragon. She bore a wonderful child, Zagreus (identified, rightly or wrongly, with Dionysos), whom the jealous Hera stirred up the Titans to attack. Beguiling him with toys of various sorts, including a mirror, they succeeded in killing him, whereupon they tore him in pieces and devoured him. Athena, however, contrived to save his heart, which she brought to Zeus. He thereupon swallowed it, and destroyed the Titans with his thunderbolts. From their bodies sprang mankind, who therefore are partly divine, as the Titans had eaten Zagreus before they were destroyed, and partly wicked, owing to the wickedness of the Titans. Zeus, having swallowed the heart of his son, was able to beget him once more, this time on Semele. This very quaint tale seems to owe something to the legend of Zeus and Metis ; but its details contradict normal Greek tradition at every turn, notably in mating Persephone to Zeus and not to Hades, in the crude doctrine of original sin, in the story of the origin of man, and in the whole part played by the Titans.[40] It has been abundantly proved that it is to be connected with various deities of the so-called Orphic ritual, which grew up in Greece about the seventh and sixth centuries B.C., and thenceforth continued to exist until the downfall of paganism, as a more or less potent influence, but never fully absorbed into native belief or cult.

The next consort after Demeter was Mnemosyne (Memory) the Titaness.[41] Of her were born the nine Muses, for whom see Chapter VII. This seems to be nothing but allegory ; by divine help, Memory produces the arts and crafts.

Next comes Leto, mother of Apollo and Artemis. This
group is far too important to be discussed here, but will receive
full treatment in Chapters V and VI.

Finally, Zeus wedded Hera.[42] In Homer, Hera is not his
last, but his first choice, apparently, and their intimacy began
before the downfall of Kronos.[43] This is natural enough for a
poet whose chief heroes are the great kings of Argos and Mycenae
and their vassals. For Hera is from time immemorial the great
goddess of Argos, near which the ruins of her temple are still
visible. It is evident that when the invading Achaioi got so far,
they soon realized that the native cult was too strong to be
neglected, even if they wished to do so, and therefore gave it once
and for all a footing in their own worship, by recognizing the chief
Argive goddess as the divine partner of their own chief god. The
genealogy already given which makes Hera also the sister of Zeus
may very well represent another attempt to combine the two
worships. The nature, functions, and legends of Hera will be
treated in Chapter V.

According to Hesiod, the children of the divine pair were
three—Hebe, Ares and Eileithyia. The first and last of these
are very appropriate children for a goddess intimately connected
with the life of women, being respectively the deities of youthful
bloom and of childbirth. It is to be noted, however, that both
are relatively insignificant. Both goddesses appear in cult,
especially Eileithyia ; [44] neither has much mythology. Hebe
can hardly, indeed, be said to have any, except that she is represented as wedding Herakles after he was raised to divine rank
at his death.[45] Eileithyia has one curious legend of her own,
which runs as follows.[46] At Olympia, on a certain occasion, an
attack was feared from the Arkadians. As the Eleans drew up
in battle array against them, a woman suddenly appeared,
carrying a child which she announced as her own, which she had
been warned in a dream to give to the Eleans for their ally.
The Elean leaders thereupon laid the baby naked in the van of
their army, and when the Arkadians advanced, the child suddenly
turned into a serpent. At this the invaders retreated in a panic,
the Eleans pursuing them. The serpent disappeared into the
ground ; a temple was erected on the spot, and thereafter divine
honours were paid to the child, under the name of Sosipolis
(' Saviour of the State '), and to Eileithyia, for the unconvincing
reason that ' she brought him into the world '. There seems little
doubt that Eileithyia, with her non-Greek name and her supposed
Cretan origin, appears in this myth as the divine nurse of a
divine child, quite on the Cretan model. To the Romans,

Eileithyia was equivalent to Lucina, or Iuno Lucina, goddess of birth.

As a counter-miracle to the birth of Athena from the head of Zeus, Hera produced Hephaistos without father.[47]   He and Ares will be considered in Chapters VI and VII ; for the present it is to be noted that the offspring of Zeus and Hera amount in all to five, of whom none is originally connected with both parents, for Ares is possibly an intruder from Thrace, Hephaistos is certainly Oriental, Athena is a great independent goddess, originally unconnected with the Hellenic Zeus, and in all probability not subordinate in any way to Hera ; Hebe is little more than an offshoot of Hera, Eileithyia is pre-Hellenic and so, like Athena, can have nothing to do with Zeus.

There is one consort of Zeus, very probably the oldest of all, whom Hesiod omits from his list, namely Dione.   He knows her name indeed, but only as an Okeanid,[48] and nowhere says anything about her marriage with Zeus.   But Homer has heard of her as mother of Aphrodite, who is invariably daughter of Zeus in his poems ; therefore he must know of the union between Zeus and Dione.   Other authorities show us that Dione is somewhat more important than one would imagine from the little mention made of her in the best-known poets.[49]   Her name is simply the feminine of Zeus (genit. Dios).   At Dodona, but scarcely anywhere else, the divine couple were regularly worshipped.   Since we know that Zeus was worshipped along with Earth at Dodona,[50] it seems a not unlikely conjecture that she is an earth-goddess ; but against Strabo in ancient and Farnell in modern times, I am inclined to think that, whatever her nature, she was brought into Greece with Zeus himself, and owes her insignificance to the fact that, apart from this one very old cult in a retired corner of the Greek world, she is driven out of Greek religious consciousness by the commanding figure of Hera.   In any case, her relation to Aphrodite is nowhere reflected in cult, and she is so very vague that she is often confused with her better-known daughter.[51]

Not in Hesiod's catalogue of Zeus' brides, but elsewhere mentioned in the *Theogony* (938), in the famous Homeric Hymn to Hermes, the newly-discovered *Ichneutai* of Sophokles, etc., is Maia, daughter of Atlas.   She was one of the Pleiades (the rest were Taygete, Elektra, Alkyone, Asterope, Kelaino, and Merope) and Zeus visited her in secret, in the dead of night when Hera was sleeping, on Mt. Kyllene in Arkadia.   She bore Hermes, whose further adventures will be told in Chapter VI.

Having overthrown Kronos, Zeus was by no means without disputes and rivalries to trouble him.   These came chiefly, apart from the revolt of the Giants, from two sources, his own family and mankind. The former seem to have made a serious attempt to overpower and bind him, from which he was saved by Thetis, who brought to his aid Briareos.[52] The three conspirators were Hera, Athena and Poseidon ; it is noteworthy that the two former were constantly represented in the *Iliad* as not over-friendly critics of all that Zeus says or does, while Poseidon assists the Greeks against the will of his greater brother. It may be that this is ultimately due to the identification of Zeus with some Trojan god, but it seems quite as likely that the rivalry with the goddesses, at any rate, embodies a faint recollection that they are not of the same nation originally as Zeus. It is, however, very unsafe to found wide-reaching theories on episodes of this sort in poetry, especially as Athena is generally shown in the most friendly relations with her father, and nothing like a permanent hostility between him and Poseidon can be traced.

But Man found a champion, who according to some accounts was their creator, in the person of Prometheus (' the foreseeing ' [53]) the Titan, of whom mention has already been made in Chapter II, p. 25. It was the business of this demi-god to make man in the first place out of clay (the place where he got it, at Panopea, a couple of miles from Chaironeia in Boiotia, was shown to the curious in historical times, together with some stones, petrified remnants of the clay which had been left over), and when he had done so, Athena breathed life into the images.[54] Therefore, not unnaturally, he favoured and supported his own creation. Zeus had but little love for mankind at this time, and oppressed them, among other inflictions depriving them of fire. Prometheus came to the rescue ; he stole fire either from heaven, or from the forge of Hephaistos [55] (the former is much the commoner version, but the other as old as Aeschylus). This he carried to earth in a dry, pithy stalk of fennel (νάρθηξ: the plant *ferula communis* is meant). He also taught mankind all manner of arts and sciences, thus raising them from their brutish condition. So at least the matter is represented in the current classical story ; it is obvious that this is in conflict with the myth of the Golden Age, or can be brought into agreement with it only by supposing some kind of degradation to have taken place. It is in fact, in part at least, the product of early reflection. Prometheus appears as a sort of divine culture-hero, or inventor, a very well known figure of folklore, which always answers the question ' How did we get such-and-such a custom, or piece of knowledge ? ' by naming a person, human or divine, who discovered or originated it.

The theft brought down upon Prometheus the wrath of Zeus,

whose unfriendly designs towards mankind (in Aeschylus, he had intended to destroy them utterly [56]) were thus frustrated. He had already a decided reason for disliking the Titan, who possessed the fatal secret of the marriage of Thetis (see Chapter II, p. 26), and in addition, according to an old and obviously popular tale, had cheated him outrageously as follows. It being agreed that men should sacrifice to the gods and share the victim with them, the question arose which part should be for men and which for the gods. Prometheus was called upon to arbitrate. He killed an ox, cut it up, and separated the flesh and entrails from the bones. The latter he wrapped in fat and made, with the hide, into a bundle ; the rest he enclosed in the stomach. Zeus, on being given his choice, at once snatched the inviting-looking parcel of fat, and was furious to find that he had got little but bones. Hence it is that men sacrifice little or none of the best meat to the Olympians, but eat it themselves at the sacrificial banquet.[57]

Zeus plotted vengeance, and therefore caused to be created a woman to beguile Prometheus to his ruin. Hephaistos formed her out of wet clay ; Athena made her alive and dressed her ; the Charites and Peitho (the spirit of Persuasion) decked her with jewellery ; the Horai wreathed her with flowers, Aphrodite gave her beauty and charm, and finally Hermes taught her all manner of guile and treachery. This lovely plague was sent, not to Prometheus himself, but to his brother Epimetheus (Afterthought), who was more easily deceived and accepted her, despite his brother's urgent warnings to have nothing to do with any gifts from Zeus. She had, or somehow found, a jar containing all manner of evils and diseases ; this she opened, and they all flew out, leaving only Hope under the lid.[58] From this woman, who was called Pandora (All Gifts) from the part which the various gods had taken in her creation, comes the race of women, who have plagued men ever since.

Finally, Zeus took stern measures to make Prometheus submit. Hephaistos, accompanied by Kratos and Bia (Strength and Force, the children of Styx), carried the Titan to an isolated mountain peak,[59] and there chained him to a rock. Daily an eagle visited him, and tore his liver ; every night, the liver grew again, thus making the torture unending. Thus he remained in agony for long ages,[60] possibly, in the intention of the original narrators, for ever ; but in the usual story, he was released by Herakles,[61] who wandered into that region in seeking for the apples of the Hesperides.[62] There seems to be a double version of the legend here, for it is also said that he finally yielded and gave up the

3

secret of Thetis' fatal child in time to prevent Zeus from marrying her. The classical accounts generally harmonize the two ; Prometheus had yielded, and Herakles acted by Zeus' direction, or with his consent.[63]

As to who Prometheus originally was, it would appear that he is an ancient fire-god, native Greek to judge by his name, whose cult was early thrust into the background by the Oriental, but early and soon naturalized, worship of Hephaistos. This would harmonize very well with the fact that they are represented to some extent as rivals, Hephaistos being in one variant robbed by Prometheus, and also acting as his executioner. In historical times Prometheus was still worshipped here and there, sometimes with torch-races, while one or two places claimed to possess his grave, i.e., he was degenerating, as several minor deities did, into a hero.[64]

As the story was very popular, and is handled by a long series of writers, good, bad and indifferent, from Hesiod down, it is only to be expected that many variants should exist. Thus, the parents of Prometheus are normally Iapetos and Klymene or Ge-Themis, but various more or less obscure writers give as his father Eurymedon (a giant) or Uranos, while his mother is also given as Asia or Asopis.[65] His wife is variously named ; according to one account, supposed to be Hesiodic,[66] he did after all marry Pandora, and their son was Deukalion. Other names given in various authorities are Kelaino (presumably not the Harpy), Pyrrha, Klymene, Asia (here again the same name recurs in two different generations ; for some lost reason he is associated with a mythical personage who is called now his mother and now his wife), Pryneia, Hesione, and Axiothea ; this last seems due to a real connexion in cult with the Kabeiroi, several of whose names begin with the syllables axio-.[67] The locality of his punishment, not given by Hesiod, is different in different authors, but usually it is somewhere in the Caucasus. Finally, he appears in one late account [68] as in a sense creating men a second time, for after the Flood he came with a torch of celestial fire and gave life to the stones thrown by Deukalion and Pyrrha.

But now Earth began to bring forth monstrous and huge births, the Giants, to do battle with the new race of gods. Concerning the origin of these vague if formidable beings, it is unwise to be too dogmatic ; but this much may be noted, that they are continually represented as imprisoned, after their defeat, under one or another of the volcanic regions known to the Greeks. Thus, Typhoeus is in or under Arima, wherever exactly that may be ; later ages identified it with the volcanic island Inarime, not far from Naples ; [69] Enkelados is under Aitna, and so forth. It is further noteworthy that Typhoeus, at any rate, is not always a helpless prisoner there, for it is there that he begets his hideous offspring on Echidna.[70] We shall therefore probably not be far wrong if we consider them to be, not exactly personifications of volcanic forces and other formidable phenomena of nature, but anciently-conceived beings supposed to be responsible for such things. Their nature, in pure Greek tradition, is rather violent than positively wicked ; Greek theology knows no devil. It is further to be noted that of the Giants proper a great number have good Greek names, as Agrios (Wild), Phoitos (Goer ?), Thoon (Swift), Hippolytos (Looser of Steeds, *i.e.*, probably, Rider or Charioteer), Ephialtes (elsewhere the name of the nightmare-demon), and so on.

Despite all this, there are sound reasons for thinking the myth neither pure Greek nor early known to the Greeks. There are analogies between it and the various Oriental stories of conflict between the gods and formidable monsters of various shapes. There is no evidence, archaeological or literary, that it was familiar in Greece until about the early sixth century. See for particulars F. Vian, *La guerre des Géants*, Paris, 1952. It is further noteworthy that the earliest surviving representations in art of the battle show the Giants in fully human form (Vian, p. 20 ff.), and armed like Greek soldiers. The wild and monstrous Giants who fight with tree-trunks and rocks are later.

What may be called the orthodox account of them is, that they were born from Earth when the blood-drops from the mutilation of Uranos fell upon her. Hence they are often called Gegeneis, *i.e.*, earth-born.[71] We do indeed find stories, some of them very early, in which the Giants, either under that name or under that of Gegeneis, are wild and savage men, something like the Kyklopes, whom in some ways they resemble in their nature. This is true of the Giants in Homer, of the Gegeneis in Apollonios Rhodios,[72] who usually draws upon early and good sources for his tales. This seems to be a piece of early rationalizing, which need not prevent our holding to the above interpretation of the Giants as spirits of wild natural forces (not necessarily always volcanic, for the Greeks did not always distinguish very sharply between these and other striking phenomena), and not as, for example, representing an exaggerated account of some savage and backward people.

These Giants, then, were stirred up by their mother to attack the Gods, whether out of desire to avenge Uranos (an inconsistent motive, seeing that she herself prompted the revolt against him), or to avenge some insult or wrong done to herself later.[73] We have, in ordinary mythology, three distinct attempts. There is first the Gigantomachy proper ; second, the assault by Typhoeus ; and third, the attempt of the Aloadai.

Of the first we do not find any detailed account in any surviving author [74] older than Pindar, although there are allusions to it in Xenophanes and the *Batrachomyomachia*, a poem of uncertain but fairly early date, parodying Homer.[75] Herakles was a participant in it, fighting on the side of the gods and vanquishing the formidable giant Alkyoneus.[76] The scene of the contest was Phlegra ; on this point most versions of the story are agreed, but as might be expected, all are not so clear as to where Phlegra was.   Properly, it seems to be a district of the isthmus of Thrace, but the name of the Campi Phlegraei near Vesuvius still bears witness to the desire of early Greek settlers in Italy to take the famous myth with them.   Other localities are also named.[77] In the fullest account we have, that of Apollodoros, the sequence of events was as follows.[78] The Giants were of formidable and monstrous shape, part human, but of vast size, and with serpents for feet (a detail in which most accounts agree).   Furthermore, Earth had caused a certain plant to grow which should make them utterly invincible, and even without this, they could not be defeated by the gods alone, but only by a combination of the gods with a mortal.   Zeus however took measures to meet the danger, engaging his son Herakles as an ally and forbidding Sun, Moon and Dawn to show the where-abouts of the magic herb, which he himself gathered.   Even so, it was a most desperate fight, for the Giants advanced hurling vast rocks and torches made of whole oak-trees.   The gods on their side performed prodigies of valour, strength, and policy, which the fancy of sundry poets detailed at considerable length.[79] At last the Giants were defeated and crushed, some being buried under islands, Enkelados for example under Sicily, which Athena threw at him, while Polybotes was overwhelmed by Poseidon under a large fragment broken off from Kos, which formed the little volcanic islet of Nisyra.

Earth, however, found means to cause a new upheaval, for she brought forth one most prodigious monster, Typhon or Typhoeus.[80] On the description of this extraordinary creature poets from Hesiod onwards have lavished much ingenuity ; the groundwork is surely Oriental, and not Greek.   According to Hesiod, he was the child of Earth and Tartaros ; ' stout were his hands and full of labours ; untiring were the feet of the mighty god : also from his shoulders there sprang an hundred heads of a serpent, a terrible dragon, licking with dark tongues, and from the eyes in his monstrous heads fire sparkled beneath his brows ; and in all the dreadful heads was a voice that sent forth a sound unspeakable ; now he spake in the speech of the gods, now again like a bellowing bull, untameable of might, proud in voice ; and again like the cry of whelps, a wonder to hear, and again with whistlings; till the tall hills echoed.' Then follows an eloquent description of how Zeus arose in his might against him, hurling his thunder and lightning until the whole universe shook and was afraid, setting Typhoeus on fire and bringing him down helpless, after which he hurled him into Tartaros. He was still not dead, being indeed as immortal as his great conqueror, and lived to be the father of the Winds, except the South and West (Notos and Zephyros), which are kindly breezes and of divine origin (compare Chapter II, p. 36). But there was another story, yet more obviously ancient and containing stronger reminiscences of savagery, and consequently of the backward East, not the progressive West. According to this tale, the battle was not so simply decided. Typhon (as he is called in this variant especially[81]) was indeed put to flight by Zeus, but turned at bay when he got to Mt. Kasion, on the borders of Syria. Grappling with Zeus, he wrenched from him his sword (*harpe*, a kind of sickle or scimitar, the same weapon with which Kronos overcame Uranos and Perseus the Gorgon ; doubtless it has some ancient sacral connotation[82]), and with it cut out the sinews of his hands and feet. Thus disabled, Zeus was thrust by his opponent into the Korykian Cave (in Kilikia ; not the cavern of that name on Mt. Parnassos), and the sinews were hidden away under the ward of a monster called Delphyna, half serpent and half woman. Hermes and Aigipan, however, stole them back (according to Nonnos, Kadmos disguised himself as a herdsman and distracted Typhon's attention with his piping) ; Zeus flew up to heaven on a winged chariot, resumed his thunderbolts, and pursued Typhon to Mt. Nysa. There the Moirai beguiled him into eating the food of mortals, which of course was no fit diet for him, and weakened him. Still he resisted valiantly, and made so furious a stand in Thrace that Mt. Haimos (the Balkan massif) was named from the blood (αἷμα) which he shed there. Thence he was pursued into Sicily, and there buried under Mt. Aitna. We need not trouble ourselves with the last detail ; it is part of the natural attempt of the Western Greeks to get famous legends localized in their own territories ; the rest has every appearance of being ancient, and the geography indicates, what we might have guessed, that it is Anatolian. (See p. 77)

Another story of this great contest is falsely attributed to Pindar, but is clearly a late bit of aetiology. The gods so feared Typhon that they fled to Egypt, and there disguised themselves as various beasts, Zeus as a ram, Apollo as a raven, Dionysos as a goat, Hera as a cow, Artemis as a cat, Aphrodite as a fish, Hermes as an ibis. Clearly, this is nothing but the most foolish of all the attempts to explain why

Ammon, identified with Zeus, has a ram's horns, the raven is sacred
to Apollo, the goat to Dionysos (who sometimes has the form of a goat),
Hathor, identified with Hera, has the shape of a cow, and Hera herself
is traditionally called βοῶπις (cow-eyed), the Syrian Atargatis, who
was identified with, and probably is really related to, Aphrodite, has
sacred fish in her shrine, and Thoth, identified with Hermes, is ibis-
headed.   The identifications are in most cases old, as old at any rate
as the fifth century B.C.[83]   Typhon himself is the traditional Greek
equivalent of the Egyptian Set, the enemy of Osiris.

As to the origin of this monstrous figure, save that he is, as
has been already said, Oriental rather than Greek, we are quite in
the dark.   The etymology of this name is very uncertain ;   his
association with the winds suggests that he is a wind-daimon of
some sort himself, which would fit very well his monstrous and
violent strength, also the grotesque variety of noises which,
according to Hesiod, he was capable of producing.   It is to be
remembered that in such figures as his, which have no place in
classical cult, imagination has much freer play than in depicting
a god, whose supposed activities in response to prayer and sacrifice,
together with the form of cult thought to be pleasing to him, tend
to stabilize his myths, indeed in very great measure originate
them.   Typhon had no temples, no ritual, and no cult-statues,
and therefore the fancy of poet and artist was quite unfettered.
As in the case of the Giants and Titans, the imagery clearly
owes something to volcanic phenomena ;   it is worth noting that
an early and widely popular theory credited subterranean winds
with producing eruptions and earthquakes.[84]

Lastly we must mention the Aloadai, Otos and Ephialtes.
Their story is best told in the words of Homer's Odysseus : [85]
' And . . . I saw Iphimedeia the wife of Aloeus, who said that
Poseidon lay with her, and so she bare twin sons, that were but
short-lived.   Tallest they were of all that the fertile earth
nurtured, and goodliest by far, next to famous Orion ;   nine years
old were they, and nine cubits was their breadth, but in height
they were nine fathom.   And they twain threatened to arouse the
din of furious battle even against the gods in Olympos.   Ossa
they were minded to pile upon Olympos, and on Ossa, Pelion
with its waving forests, that the heavens might be climbed ;   and
this they had accomplished, if they had come to the measure of
their full growth ;   but the son of Zeus, whom Leto Fairlocks
brought forth, destroyed them both, before the down blossomed
beneath their temples and their cheeks were covered with the
bloom of a young beard '.   Another fragment of their legend is
given in the *Iliad* : [86] ' Ares suffered, when Otos and mighty

Ephialtes, sons of Aloeus, bound him with a fast bond, and he was prisoned in a bronze vessel thirteen months. And then had Ares, insatiable of battle, even perished, but that their stepmother, fairest Eeriboia, told Hermes thereof, and he stole Ares away, when now he was full weary, for the bitter bondage overcame him .' The accounts given in most later authorities are hardly more than explanations and expansions of these two passages ; what they owe to independent evidence and what to mere commentators' imagination is not easy to say.

First, as to their mother's meeting with Poseidon, two stories are told ; according to one, she was enamoured of the god and used daily to go to the sea-shore and pour water into her bosom, till at length he visited her ; [87] according to another, her love was the river-god Enipeus, and Poseidon deceived her by assuming his shape.[88] Yet another account makes them children of the Earth, not of Iphimedeia.[89] The reason for their quarrel with the gods was, that they desired to wed Hera and Artemis ; [90] their especial quarrel with Ares was that he had killed Adonis ; this is assuredly a late variant.[91] Their death was due to Artemis as well as Apollo,[92] or to Artemis only, in some variants ; a hind, or Artemis in the shape of one, ran between them ; both shot at her, and each hit the other. Hyginus has the curious story that they went to Tartaros and were there bound back to back against a column, serpents being used for the fastenings, while on the column an owl perches. This may go back to some forgotten picture.[93] These later authors calculate from Homer's description that the rate of growth of the monstrous brothers was nine inches (*digiti*) a month, or nearly nine feet, English measure, a year : or that their yearly growth was a fathom in height, a cubit in breadth.[94]

There is, however, a group of legends which is more interesting than these fanciful details, and serves to throw some light on the possible origin of the Aloadai. According to a tradition as old, at least in part, as Hesiod, they appear as beneficent beings, founders of cities and originators of the cult of the Muses.[95] The scene of their activity varies ; they are to be found in Thessaly and Boiotia, they go to Naxos to rescue their mother and sister, who had been kidnapped, and they are worshipped in the latter place as heroes. Otos also was reported to have been buried in Crete,[96] and Iphimedeia was worshipped in Mylasa [97] in Karia. Here we have no rebels against heaven nor upsetters of the established order of the universe, but rather some kind of culture-heroes or gods. It is perhaps worth remembering also that Iphimedeia and their sister Pankratis or Pankrato are represented as being nurses of Dionysos, which provides a link with the island of Naxos, where the cult of that deity flourished. As Naxos is also a seat of the worship of the Great Mother, in the form of Aphrodite Ariadne,[98] it may be that Iphimedeia ('Mighty Queen') is simply the Great Mother herself in one of her many forms;

this would certainly account for the version according to which the Aloadai were sons of Earth, and for the statement that their mother is worshipped in Karia, where one would expect an Anatolian goddess to be worshipped.

The Aloadai, like the Titans, may not unreasonably be supposed to be old gods ; and I would be inclined to see an indication of this in the identity of name between one of them and the demon of nightmare (Ephialtes, Epiales, Epheles ; other variants are also found; see Schultz in Roscher, article EPHIALTES). It is well known that the gods of an older religion are often the demons of a newer one, and this is occasionally true even among the tolerant Greeks. The name might well be interpreted as ' valiant warrior ', literally ' he who leaps upon ' his enemy ; [99] it might also be degraded into meaning an incubus or nightmare imp, who leaps or, as we say, ' sits ' upon the chest of the disturbed sleeper.

As a glance at the texts quoted in the notes will abundantly show, the Titans, the Giants, the Aloadai, and Typhon are frequently confused by our authorities, especially the later ones. Typhoeus and Ephialtes appear as names of Giants, for example, and the Giants are not infrequently said to have piled up mountains in order to reach the gods. Even the Hekatoncheires are sometimes added to the confusion, despite their usually friendly attitude towards Zeus.

The further mythology of Zeus is mostly concerned with his interventions in favour of or against particular gods or human beings. In literature, he is of course referred to by practically every writer, and no sketch of the subject is possible here. It may, however, be noted that apart from philosophers who treat of the nature of God, or of the gods, Zeus is especially prominent in the works of Aeschylus, the greatest theologian of all Greek poets. Usually, as in the passage chosen for the motto of this chapter, he embodies the tragedian's ideas of divine omnipotence and moral excellence ; a puzzling exception is the *Prometheus*, in which the god appears as a harsh and unjust tyrant. A solution of this difficulty plausible enough to find general acceptance has yet to be hit upon. That Aeschylus believed in the evolution of Deity and that his Zeus developed into the ideal ruler of the universe portrayed in his other works is contrary to all we know of Greek thought in general and his in particular.[100] In general, as already mentioned, Zeus is a dignified figure, always vastly superior to the other gods, and passing without great effort into the God of a monotheistic, or practically monotheistic, philosophy. This throws into even greater prominence the many passages in sundry writers which treat in a frivolous way the numerous

stories of his light loves and other undignified adventures. As
Ovid well says : [101]

> Non bene conueniunt nec in una sede morantur
> maiestas et amor,

particularly where the *amor* is treated in the spirit of a senti-
mental romancer, who neither reads into it any mystic meaning
nor perceives the primitive dignity of the ancient conception
underlying it, the wedding of the Sky-father with the Earth-
mother.

Passing now to Zeus' brother POSEIDON (*Ποσειδάων, Ποσειδῶν,*
Doric *Ποτειδάν*) we have a simpler figure, less popular, less universally worshipped, and much less capable of development
into a grandiose and enlightened theological concept. Perhaps
the most likely etymology of his name is Kretschmer's, ' husband
of Da ', Da being plausibly thought to be an old, probably pre-
Greek, name of the earth-goddess. This agrees with his common
title Gaiaochos, ' holder (embracer, husband) of Earth '.[102] If
he is Greek, his original realm cannot have been the sea, for the
Greek invaders came from somewhere inland ; when they took
to navigation, their god too became marine. It is not at all
certain that he was originally conceived as of human form ;
several legends (cf. pp. 66–7) and his standing title Hippios,
' He of the Horse(s) ', are consistent with his having horse-shape.
That he was always connected with water is, however, very
likely ; water fertilizes the earth, and earthquakes, which he
governs, may have been thought due to water undermining the
ground.[103]. However, his most prominent function is that of
sea-god, and it is in this capacity that we find him, in Homer,
wrecking Odysseus, who had earned his hatred, and again and
again rising from, plunging into, or journeying over the sea, which
was given him when the sons of Kronos cast lots for the universe.
The Romans, for want of a better equivalent (for they had originally no maritime gods whatsoever), equated him with a rather
obscure water-deity Neptunus, anglicized into Neptune. In art,
he is shown as a tall and stately figure, not unlike Zeus in general
appearance, but distinguished by his emblem, the trident,[104] and
by his wilder and more uncouth appearance, a feature exaggerated
in Hellenistic art especially.

His consort is the not very important AMPHITRITE. This
goddess is worshipped here and there, along with the Nereids,
of whom she is generally reckoned as one, although one lyric
passage of doubtful date calls her their mother,[105] apparently
through a blending of Poseidon with Nereus. She was an un-

willing bride, according to one story at least, for she was carried
off by Poseidon,[106] or at any rate ran away from his advances
and took refuge with Atlas, or with Okeanos, until at last the
dolphin found her ; in gratitude for which Poseidon turned him
into the constellation of that name.[107]　Once married, she was a
jealous wife, and not without cause.　Poseidon paid court to
Skylla, daughter of Phorkys and Hekate or Krataïs.　Amphitrite
heard of it, and put magic herbs into her rival's bathing-place.
The effect was to turn her from the loins down into a horrible
monster, encircled with a ring of dogs' heads, who thenceforth
became a terror to all mariners, seizing on and devouring them as
they sailed past her cave (traditionally located in the Straits of
Messina ; rationalizers of various dates are at pains to explain
away this picturesque sailors' yarn by assuming a whirlpool,
rock, or other natural danger).[108]

The children of Amphitrite were even more insignificant than
herself.　Hesiod names only Triton, the well-known Greek
merman, who, after the fashion of minor figures of mythology
and cult, is now one, now many.[109]　The etymology of his name
is quite uncertain, but it sounds as if it were connected with the
latter half of his mother's equally puzzling appellation.　It is
of course in no way certain that it is Greek, for the Greeks may
have taken Triton, name and all, from Minoan or Anatolian belief.
In shape, he is human from the waist up, fish-shaped from the
waist down, a type which probably is to be traced to twy-form
Oriental gods like the familiar Dagon of the Old Testament.
Hence he tends to be confused, in art and perhaps in belief also,
with other sea-creatures, such as Nereus, Proteus, and so forth.
A favourite subject with artists, especially for the decorative
details of sea-pieces, he is multiplied in a variety of shapes, sometimes male, sometimes female (here of course he trespasses on the
domain of the Nereids, a confusion very readily understood).
He can scarcely be said to have a mythology of his own, although
he enters commonly enough into tales of the greater sea-gods,
in literature as in art.　Doubtless many stories of him passed from
mouth to mouth among sailors and fishermen, but they are
practically all lost to us.　A few fragments from the wreck are
as follows.　When the Argonauts were making their way back
from Libya, Triton gave a clod of earth to one of their number,
Euphemos, in token that his descendants should bear rule in those
parts ; it fell, or was thrown, into the sea, and grew into the
island of Thera, colonized long afterwards by Euphemos'
descendant Theras,[110] and destined in still later times to send
out a colony to Kyrene.　This Triton (Pindar calls him Eurypylos)

seems to be a local Libyan god, worshipped at Lake Tritonis. A genuine native Greek Triton is the central figure of the legend told at Tanagra in Boiotia ; as certain women were bathing in the sea to purify themselves for the ritual of Dionysos, Triton appeared and offered them violence ; they cried on Dionysos for aid, and he appeared and overcame the would-be ravisher after a sharp fight ; another version was, that the Tanagraians set a large bowl of wine for him, and when he was helplessly drunk, one of them chopped off his head. In proof of this they showed his dried and headless body in the temple of Dionysos.[111] In general he, like most mermen, was regarded as an unchancy creature, apt to be jealous, and very dangerous if provoked ; hence Vergil's story [112] of how Misenos, having rashly challenged Triton to a contest in trumpeting, was drowned by him. As Triton is commonly represented as blowing a conch-shell, such a piece of presumption would of course be especially likely to offend him.

According to Apollodoros, Triton had two sisters, Benthesikyme (Wave of the Deep) and Rhode or Rhodos, the nymph of the island of Rhodes, who is elsewhere called daughter of Helios by Aphrodite or Amphitrite, or daughter of Aphrodite and Poseidon ; a good example of the artificial way in which gods of very varying origin are combined into genealogies.[113]

In considering Poseidon's mythical nature, we have to remember that he owes something on the one hand to foreign sea-deities, whose influence we can trace in later times (for example, the Mylasian Zenoposeidon, i.e., Zeus-Poseidon, who developed out of the Karian god Osogos [114]) and may reasonably guess at for earlier periods ; on the other, to gods not originally of the sea at all. The Greeks came by land to the country they occupied in historical times, and brought with them no sea-mythology, whatever they may have found there ; hence it is a tenable hypothesis, at all events, that some part of the god's violence and roughness is inherited from deities of the wind or the earthquake, or perhaps of mountain torrents. He is nearly always shown (unlike Nereus) as violent and ill-tempered, whether by sea or on land ; a sea-god pure and simple would surely be sometimes calm. Hence it should surprise no one that in mythology (with cult the case is different) no very sharp line can be drawn between Poseidon and such figures as Briareos, who indeed is sometimes represented as either the son or the son-in-law of Poseidon.[115]
The early stages of Poseidon's development are not easy to trace, for in Homer we already meet him as a fully-formed god, completely anthropomorphic, whose nature is assumed by the

poet to be known to everyone. He is a violent partisan, who from first to last does everything possible to help the Achaians and harm the Trojans.[116] For this he has an intelligible reason enough ; Laomedon, father of Priam, had employed him and Apollo to build the walls of Troy, and when they had finished their task, refused to pay them. It is curious that Apollo, who throughout the *Iliad* is the constant friend of Troy and in particular of Hektor, is associated with Poseidon in this matter ; in fact, Poseidon himself remarks upon it.[117] Poseidon, then, is consistent in his hatred and desire for revenge ; the reason for his servitude to a mortal was the rebellion against Zeus. There is an interesting variant of the tale in Pindar ; the task was shared by a mortal, the hero Aiakos, and as his work was less strong than that of the gods, it was his part of the wall through which the Greeks finally broke.[118] In the *Odyssey*, Poseidon's enmity to the hero is one of the chief motifs of the whole story. Odysseus had blinded the Kyklops Polyphemos, Poseidon's son by the nymph Thoosa, daughter of Phorkys.[119] In both poems he is a savagely majestic figure, represented as of enormous strength, even for a god, and prodigious speed ; when he descends to battle with the other gods, Hades fears that he will split the earth above his head,[120] and four strides take him across the sea from Samothrace to Aigai, where his palace is.[121] His standing epithet is Earth-shaker (ἐννοσίγαιος, ἐνοσίχθων), and a stroke of his trident is enough to shatter a rock and drown the man standing on it ;[122] a mere trifle to some of his recorded feats of destruction.

Violent in all things, Poseidon was a violent lover, although stories of this kind are less common in his case than in that of Zeus. This is very natural ; the standing epithet of his element is ' unharvested ' (ἀτρύγετος), i.e., barren, and his activities as god of fresh water are not very prominent. Hence there is no special reason for exhibiting him as lover or husband. His connexion with Medusa has already been mentioned (Chapter II, p. 30) ; he is also represented as either the father or the lover of the Harpies, or one of them.[123] More important, and illustrating another side of his activities, is his connexion with Demeter Erinys (' Raging '). The legend, as told at Thelpusa in Arkadia, was as follows. While Demeter was searching for her lost daughter, Poseidon saw and loved her. To avoid him, she took the form of a mare ; but he assumed the shape of a stallion, and so forced his attentions upon her. From this union was born the wonderful horse Areion or Arion (? ἀρι—Ϝίων, ' the very swift '), also a daughter, whose name only the initiated might know.

Practically the same legend was told at Phigaleia, where Demeter was represented as black and horse-headed, but here the child of the union was the goddess Despoina ('The Mistress'; one of the names for the queen of the under-world).[124] It seems not unlikely that we have here a very old tale indeed, in which a female and a male power of fertility (the horse is connected with corn-daimones in many parts of Europe [125]) unite and have offspring; and that later the female power was hellenized into Demeter, because she was corn-goddess, and the male into Poseidon, in his capacity of Lord of Steeds, already noted. But this is mere conjecture, and does not explain why the anger of the goddess should be so strongly insisted upon, not only in the legend, where it might be thought no more than a picturesque detail, but in her cult-title. That the offspring of the union should be the horse Arion in one case, Persephone or a goddess equated with her in another, need not be part of the original story; Arion is famous in epic as the horse of Adrastos, who will be discussed when we come to the Theban cycle; in another legend, preserved only in a scholiast on Homer,[126] he is the offspring of a Harpy and Poseidon.

A very considerable number of heroes are credited with being sons of Poseidon; his children in general were, like their father, of ungentle character. Indeed, his reputation as a begetter of strong but rough men lasted quite late; Sextus Pompeius, for example, gave out that he was the son of Neptunus, who of course had been fully identified with Poseidon long before that time.[127] To confine our attention to his divine consorts, the most noteworthy is Ge herself (cf. p. 63), and his association with 'Demeter' points the same way, for her name is plausibly explained as 'Mother Da'. Although he and Earth are sometimes enemies (he fights against her sons, the Giants), it is very understandable that a god whose domain includes fresh water should now and then be thought of as fertilizing the Earth; indeed, one of his cult-titles is Phytalmios, or nurturer of plants. The son of this union was the giant Antaios, with whom Herakles wrestled. This monster was unconquerable by any ordinary wrestler, or even by one of his own prodigious strength, for every time he was thrown he arose stronger than ever, from contact with his mother. Herakles, however, perceived this, and so heaved him in the air and managed to crush him to death with his hands.[128] At least, so the story is commonly told; but writers up to and including Diodoros of Sicily describe the contest as simply one of wrestling, with the loser's life for the stake, and those representations in art which show the hero lifting his antagonist in the air are not very early. The point of this, as of not a few Greek stories, may be the superiority of civilized skill, exemplified by Herakles, over savage brute force.

Poseidon is credited with some minor love affairs with beings known or plausibly supposed to be goddesses. They are as follows. By Alkyone or Halkyone, one of the Pleiads, he became the father of several persons of heroic rank, mostly connected with the sea in one way or another, namely Hyrieus or Urieus, founder of Hyria or Uria on the coast of Boiotia ; Aithusa, important only for having had by Apollo a son Eleuther, founder of the town Eleutherai ; Hyperenor, Hyperes and Anthas, of whom the last two also founded sea-coast towns.[129] By a sister of Alkyone, Kelaino, he had three more children, Nykteus, Lykos, and Eurypylos. There is nothing remarkable in the sea-god being represented as husband or lover of those stars whose rising and setting marked important dates in the Greek seaman's calendar. Another not inappropriate bride of the god was Chione, *i.e.*, Snow-girl, daughter of Boreas and Oreithyia, who threw her child Eumolpos into the sea when he was born, to hide her shame. Poseidon however rescued him.[130] She may conceivably be a deity of snow-storms.

The best-known tale concerning Poseidon is a local Attic legend, which perhaps reflects the contests between a Greek (Ionian ?) people, coming, it may be, by sea, and the natives of the place with their ancient cult of a Minoan goddess. Poseidon and Athena strove for the land of Attica, and the gods, or the king, or the people judged between them. Poseidon wrought a miracle : with a blow of his trident he produced a salt spring from the rock of the Akropolis ; the marks of his blow are to be seen to this day, underneath the porch of the Erechtheion, with an opening left in floor and roof above them, that they may always see the sky.[131] According to another account, he produced a horse, the first ever seen. But Athena planted, or magically evoked with a touch of her spear, an olive-tree, and the divine or human judges pronounced her victor. Poseidon in great wrath flooded the Thriasian Plain. At last the gods brought about a reconciliation, and henceforth Poseidon was much honoured in Athens, and especially was worshipped as Poseidon Erechtheus, a title behind which there certainly lies some early connexion between him and the mythical king Erechtheus, but the question is too complicated and obscure to be discussed in a book of this kind.[132] The salt spring was still shown to visitors in the days of Hadrian, together with the sacred olive, which had grown again, two cubits in a day, after the Persians burned it.[133]

This is the most familiar legend of its kind, but there are others. At Argos stood a temple of Poseidon Proklystios (the Flooder), con-

cerning which the local legend ran as follows ; Poseidon and Hera
strove for the Argolid, and Inachos and his fellow-judges decided in
favour of the great native goddess.   Poseidon then flooded the
country, but Hera appeased him, and when the waters retired his
temple was built.[134] At Trozen again, he strove with Athena for
possession of the land, until Zeus adjudged that both should hold it,
the god under the title of Basileus (King), the goddess as Sthenias
(the Mighty) and Polias (Queen of the City).   Whether for this cause
or some other, he flooded the land and made it unfruitful with his
salt waters, until he yielded to the sacrifices and prayers of the people,
who thenceforth worshipped him also as Phytalmios.[135]

Another series of legends tells how he created the first horse, or at
least first introduced the art of taming horses.   The tale of Areion
or Arion has already been told ; the other horses of the other local
legends were, like him, marvellous creatures, winged and gifted with
the power of speech.   One of these miracles was located at Petra in
Thessaly.   Poseidon, there worshipped as Petraios (He of the Rock),
was said, while asleep, to have fertilized the rocky ground, from which
sprang the horse.   Elsewhere, he is said to have struck the rock with
his trident to produce it.[136] Poseidon also sends or creates bulls, a
frequent embodiment of the powers of water, whereof the legends of
Pasiphae and of Hippolytos furnish examples.

Finally, Poseidon in his capacity as an earthquake-god is
credited with the authorship of some striking natural formations,
notably the pass of the Peneios, the natural drain which carries
off the waters of the plain of Thessaly.[137]

NOTES ON CHAPTER III

[1] The ancients commonly supposed the name to be a variant form
of χρόνος ; but the change from χ to κ at the beginning of a word is
impossible, and in any case, Time is too abstract and philosophical a deity
to be the object of an early and rather barbarous cult.   Another etymology connected it with κραίνω, and made it mean ' completer ', ' ripener,'
an appropriate meaning enough, but again philologically very doubtful,
if not impossible.   For Kronos in general, see Farnell, C.G.S., I, p. 23
foll.
[2] Op. et dies, 109 foll., and therefrom a host of later poets, as, for
instance, Ovid, Metam., I, 89 foll.; Verg., Georg., I, 125 foll.   It seems to
be rather a quasi-philosophic speculation than a tradition.
[3] Hesiod, Theog., 453 foll., followed more or less closely by later
writers, as Apollod., I, 4 foll. (ibid., 6, says that Metis, not Rhea, forced
Kronos to vomit up his children) ; but another version, given in Hyginus
139, 1, says that he did not swallow his children but threw Poseidon into
the sea and Hades into Tartaros ; the daughters apparently were not got
rid of.   Homer, as is clear from Iliad, XIV, 295, either knows nothing
of or ignores the swallowing.   There were local variants of the story, as,
for instance, that Poseidon escaped swallowing, Kronos devouring instead

a new-born foal (Pausanias, VIII, 8, 2). This clearly is the legend of
pious worshippers of Poseidon, who is among other things a horse-god, to
save their deity from such indignity. See further Preller-Robert, I, p. 55,
n. 2, and for interpretation of the myth in the light of savage and barbarian parallels, A. Lang, *Custom and Myth*, p. 45 foll.

⁴ Hesiod, *Theog.*, 501 foll.; Apollod., I, 6–7.

⁵ Hesiod, *ibid.*, 617 foll.

⁶ See preceding chapter, p. 36.

⁷ Pindar, *Pyth.*, IV, 291, who states that Atlas was not included in
the amnesty. Aesch., frag. 190, 193 N².

⁸ For examples of the two theories, see Preller-Jordan, I, p. 40;
Farnell, *C.G.S.*, I, p. 25. For the geological facts, see Lyell, Vol. II,
p. 65 foll. (the classical description); Bonney, pp. 161, 241; Geikie,
Vol. I, p. 1 foll. I owe these references to the courtesy of my friend
Prof. W. J. Pugh, of Aberystwyth.

⁹ So already Pindar, *Olymp.*, II, 77 foll. Hesiod, *op. et dies*, 169–169ᵉ,
if genuine, is of course older still; Rzach brackets it.

¹⁰ *De defect. orac.*, 420 A.

¹¹ As Diodoros Siculus, V, 66.

¹² See, for the best-known handling of this form of the story, Vergil,
Aen., VIII, 319 foll., 355–8; see also Dion. Hal., I, 34, 5; also 36, 1,
where he says the Golden Age was in Italy, under Kronos.

¹³ So Farnell, *op. cit.*, p. 25.

¹⁴ See the very judicious remarks of Farnell, *C.G.S.*, III, 291; for
Rhea in general, consult the chapter (VI) in which this passage occurs,
also Roscher, art. RHEA, Preller-Robert, I, 638 foll.

¹⁵ Preller-Robert, I, p. 54.

¹⁶ This has been well pointed out by Nilsson, *Hist. Gk. Rel.*, p. 18;
M.M.R.², p. 389.

¹⁷ Hesiod, *Theog.*, 453 foll., *cf.* Diod. Sic., V, 68, 1, Apollod., I, 4;
for other references, see Rapp in Roscher, IV, 89, 32 foll.

¹⁸ Crete, see the passages cited in n. 18, and add Diod. Sic., V, 65,
4, 70, 1 foll.; Aratos, 30 foll.; more refs. in Rapp, *op. cit.*, 89, 51 foll.
Arkadia, Kallim., *hymn.*, I, 4 foll., who also mentions, but rejects, the
Cretan tradition; *cf.* Hyg., *fab.*, 139; Lucian, *de sacrif.* 5. It is clear
from Paus., VIII, 47, 3 (at Tegea there was a very old altar with a representation of Rhea, the infant Zeus, and the local nymph Oinoe) that it
is a genuinely old story in Arkadia.

¹⁹ Anton. Liber, 19; see Nilsson, *Hist. Gr. Rel.*, p. 31; *M.M.R.*,
p. 471.

²⁰ As Hesiod, *Theog.*, 1002; Pindar, *Pyth*, III, 1, etc.

²¹ The story is common enough: see for full refs. Stoll in Roscher,
s.u. PHILYRA. The main passages are Apollonios Rhodios, II, 1231
foll., with the passage from Pherekydes quoted in the scholiast on that
passage; Verg., *Georg.*, III, 92 foll., and the ancient commentators there;
Hyginus 138. For one or two other children said to have been born of
this union, see Stoll, col. 2354, 36 foll. The first two passages cited place
the scene not in Thessaly but in the island called Philyreis, in the Euxine.

²² Suidas (the historian, not the Byzantine lexicographer) cited by
the schol. on Apoll. Rhod., II, 1231.

²³ For Zeus in general, see Farnell, *C.G.S.*, I, p. 35 foll.; Preller-
Robert, I, p. 115 foll.; Daremberg-Saglio, art. ZEUS; O. Waser in Roscher,
VI, 564, 23 foll.; Decharme, p. 15 foll. A huge amount of material,
relevant and otherwise, will be found in Cook. For the oak, see Warde

Fowler, 1920, p. 39. The following notes give only a few of the chief references to this often-told myth.

²⁴ Representations of the thunderbolt will be found, held in the hand of Zeus or lying beside him, in any work which reproduces statues or paintings of him (*e.g.*, Cook), or in any museum which possesses such works of ancient art. It also is not infrequently shown by itself, for instance on coins (examples in Cook, II, Plate XXXVI), either as an emblem of the god or because supposed thunderbolts were often venerated objects, in Greece as elsewhere (abundant examples in Blinkenberg, *The Thunderweapon*). The aigis is mentioned in Homer, *Iliad*, II, 446, where its tassels, like most things belonging to the gods, are of gold ; XVII, 593 (Zeus raises a storm with it) ; *Odyssey*, XXII, 297 (Athena uses it to spread panic among the Wooers), and many other passages, see any Homeric dictionary ; also commonly in later authors, as *e.g.*, Horace, *Carm.*, III, 4, 57, where it seems to be a piece of metallic armour (*sonantem Palladis aegida*).

²⁵ See Nilsson, *M.M.R.*, Ch. I.

²⁶ See Kallimachos, *Hymn.*, I, 46 foll., with the commentators there, especially the old, but learned, notes of Spanheim. For the Kuretes, see Chapter VII, p. 170.

²⁷ Hesiod, *Theog.*, 492 ; Kallim., *Hymn.*, I, 55 foll.

²⁸ Homer, *Iliad*, XV, 197 foll. ; a quaint criticism of the legend in Kallim., *Hymn.*, I, 60 foll.

²⁹ See Rose, *P.C.G.*, Chapter VIII and notes.

³⁰ Homer, *Odyssey*, I, 189 foll., and a score of other passages.

³¹ See, *e.g.*, Homer, *Iliad*, VIII, 281 foll. ; *Od.*, XIV, 199 foll. ; *cf.* Euripides, *Andromache*, 224–5.

³² *E.g.*, Apollo is divine, Sarpedon mortal. The apparent exceptions (Dionysos, Herakles) are easily explained, as will be seen in discussing their myths.

³³ διογενεῖς, the standing epithet of kings in Homer, see any Homeric dictionary.

³⁴ Hence endless attacks upon the morality of the gods in various critics, Christian and other, of the traditional religion ; *cf.* also Ovid, *Metam.*, IX, 500, *sunt superis sua iura*.

³⁵ Hesiod, *Theog.*, 886 foll.

³⁶ For this explanation, which I consider the most plausible, see Kern, 1926, p. 180 foll., Nilsson, *GgR*, I², p. 438.

³⁷ Hesiod, *op. cit.*, 901 foll. For Themis = Earth, cf. Chapter II, p. 21.

³⁸ Hesiod, *op. cit.*, 907, 358.

³⁹ Hesiod, *ibid.*, 912 foll. See further Chapter VI.

⁴⁰ ' Orpheus ', frags. 210 foll., Kern. For the age of the story of Zagreus, see Rose in *Greek Poetry and Life* (Oxford 1936), pp. 79–96 ; I. M. Linforth, *The Arts of Orpheus* (Berkeley and Los Angeles 1941), pp. 307–64, and refs. there.

⁴¹ Hesiod, *op. cit.*, 915 foll.

⁴² *Ibid.*, 921 foll.

⁴³ See *Iliad*, XIV, 295 foll.

⁴⁴ See Farnell, *C.G.S.*, II, pp. 608 foll., 623 foll., and the arts. EILEITHYIA and HEBE in Roscher. The name Eileithyia is sometimes pluralized.

⁴⁵ Homer, *Odyssey*, XI, 602–4 ; Hesiod, *Theog.*, 950–5, and numerous later passages.

⁴⁶ Pausanias, VI, 20, 4 foll.; see Farnell, *C.G.S.*, II, p. 611.

⁴⁷ Hesiod, *Theog.*, 927, is the earliest definite mention of this.

⁴⁸ *Theog.*, 353. It is, however, worth noticing that *ibid.*, 17, he mentions her in the middle of a list of great deities.

⁴⁹ See Roscher, art. DIONE; Farnell, *C.G.S.*, I, 39 foll.; Strabo, VII, 7, 9 foll., and fragments 1 foll.; best archaeological account of Dodona, Carapinos, *Dodone*.

⁵⁰ Pausanias, X, 12, 10; Farnell, *loc. cit.*

⁵¹ See, for example, *Theokr.*, VII, 116 (apparently the earliest instance); Ovid, *Fast.*, II, 459. It is much the same kind of telescoping of parent and child which we get in the case of Hyperion and Helios.

⁵² *Iliad*, I, 396 foll., which van Leeuwen justly calls *uestigia fabulae nostro carmine* (*i.e.*, than the *Iliad*) *antiquioris*. According to the scholiast, *ibid.*, 400, Apollo had a share in the revolt, and some ancient editors altered the text to bring in his name.

⁵³ This is the plain and obvious meaning of the word, clearly connected as it is with προμηθία, foresight, forethought. As he steals fire, it was long sought to equate his name with Skt. *pramantha*, a fire-stick, an etymology as unnecessary as it is unlikely.

⁵⁴ See Hesiod, frag. 268; Hyginus, *fab.*, 142; Pausanias, X, 4, 4; M 1, 1; M 2, 63.

⁵⁵ From heaven, Hesiod, *op. et dies*, 50 foll., and numerous later passages; from the sun, several late writers, as *S.B.*, VI, 42; from Hephaistos' workshop, Aesch., *Prom. Vinct.*, 7. The chief sources for the legend are Apollod., I, 45, II, 85, III, 169, in which we have the story connectedly but very briefly told; Hesiod, passages cited in notes 58 foll.; Aeschylus *Promētheus Vinctus* and the fragments of the lost companion play, the *Prometheus Solutus*. References and allusions are to be found in practically every ancient poet, and considerable parts of the story in Hyginus, *fabulae*, 31, 54, 142, 144; M1, 1; M2, 65, 66; M3, 10, 9. Full refs. are given by Bapp in Roscher, art. PROMETHEUS.

⁵⁶ Aesch., *P.V.*, 233 foll.

⁵⁷ Hes., *Theog.*, 535 foll. He, or some interpolator, out of regard for Zeus' omniscience, spoils the story by saying that the god was not really deceived.

⁵⁸ *Ibid.*, 570 foll.; *op. et dies*, 60 foll. See p. 77.

⁵⁹ More or less fully told in all the authorities cited above. See especially Hes., *Theog.*, 521 foll.; Aesch., *P.V.*, 1 foll. Sundry little variations are to be found; Hesiod does not specify the locality, and while some authors name the Caucasus, some, including Aeschylus, lay the scene elsewhere; in Aeschylus (frag. 193, 10, N²) the eagle came every other day, not every day; it was the offspring of Typhon and Echidna (Pherekydes *ap.* Schol. on Apollonios Rhodios, II, 1249) or was specially made by Hephaistos (Hygin., *Astron.*, II, 15, who also has a story that it was the offspring of Earth and Tartaros). It is to be noted that the whole tale shows signs of being comparatively recent. The punishment vaguely suggests that of sundry giants who were imprisoned *under* mountains; the part chosen for the eagle to tear is the liver, anciently supposed the seat of the passions, and this detail suggests the punishment of Tityos, whose crime was lust. Indeed, the historian Duris of Samos (schol. Ap. Rhod., *loc. cit.*) says that Prometheus' offence was a passion for Athena.

⁶⁰ Thirty thousand years, *i.e.*, three myriads (innumerable lengths) of years, according to a tradition claiming to go back to Aeschylus; see

Hyginus, *loc. cit.* (in *fabulae*, 144, 2, F. has *triginta*, clearly a mistake; the figure $\overline{XXX}$, for 30,000, has been misread XXX) and M2, 64.

[61] So first, Hesiod, *Theog.*, 526 foll.

[62] So Apollod., II, 120. From the fragments of the *Prometheus Solutus* it seems as if Aeschylus made Herakles' objective the cattle of Geryon.

[63] So, for instance, Hyginus, *fabulae*, 54.

[64] See Farnell, *C.G.S.*, V, p. 378 foll.; A. Mommsen, p. 324 foll.; Bapp, *op. cit.*, col. 3036, 41 foll. With the occasional tombs of Prometheus we may compare the fact that he was made immortal; according, *e.g.*, to Apollod , II, 85, he finally won immortality on his release only because Cheiron, incurably wounded, wished to die and gave up his own immortality to him.

[65] Iapetos, Hesiod in all passages and most other authors; Klymene, Hes., *Theog.*, 508, and many other authors; Ge-Themis, Aesch., *P.V.*, 18, 211. For the obscurer accounts, see Bapp, col. 3035, 58 foll.

[66] Hes., fr. 2 Rzach.

[67] See Bapp, col. 3036, 21 foll. The association of Prometheus and Axiothea rests on Tzetzes on Lykophron, 1283.

[68] M1, 189; postea uenit Prometheus et uiuificat homines illos, face caelesti adhibita.

[69] Homer (*Iliad*, II, 792–3). εἰν ’Αρίμοις, ὅθι φασὶ Τυφωέος ἔμμεναι εὐνάς. As, of course, neither he nor any other early writer of Greek divided the words, it was possible to take εἰν ’Αρίμοις (in Arima ? among the Arimoi ?) as one word, Εἰναρίμοις, ‘at Einarima’, and so Vergil did.

> Tum sonitu Prochyta alta tremit, durumque cubile
> Inarime, Iouis imperiis imposta Typhoeo (*Aen.*, IX, 715–6).

For the real position of Arima, or the ’Άριμα ὄρη, somewhere in Asia Minor, see the commentators on the above passages.

[70] Hesiod, *Theog.*, 304 foll.

[71] See Drexler in Roscher, art. GEGENEIS; Hesiod, *op. cit.*, 183 foll.

[72] See Homer, *Odyssey*, VII, 56 foll., 206; contrast, however, X, 120, where ‘men’ and ‘Giants’ are opposed. Apoll. Rhod., I, 943 foll. In both poets, they are a monstrous race, not exactly human.

[73] Earth bore the Giants because she ‘was wroth with Zeus,’ Apoll. Rhod., II, 40; the reason for her wrath was the sending of the Titans to Tartaros, schol. *ibid.*, *cf.* Apollod., I, 34; Claudian, XXXVII (*Gigantomachia*), 1–2; because Athena had killed her monstrous child Aigis, Diod. Sic., III, 70, 3 foll., 6; or because the gods laughed at her and Tartaros (*ob sui atque Tantali derisionem;* read, with Köpp, *Tartari*), M1, 11 (a very confused and fanciful account); or because the gods preferred to live in heaven rather than on earth; M2, 53, which confuses Titans, Giants and Hekatoncheires. For more particulars, see Drexler in Roscher, I, 1640, 48 foll.

[74] *Theog.*, 185, merely mentions their birth from the blood of Uranos.

[75] *Batrachom.*, 283; Xenoph., frag. 1, 21 Diehl.

[76] Pind., *Nem.*, I, 67 foll.; *Isthm.*, VI, 32 foll.

[77] In all manner of regions from Arkadia to Spain, see Drexler, *op. cit.*, 1649, 8 foll.

[78] Apollod., I, 34 foll.

[79] As, for instance, the unknown, probably Alexandrian, poet followed by Apollod., *loc. cit.*; Horace, *Carm.*, III, 4, 49 foll.; Claudian, *op. cit.*, and various other writers.

⁸⁰ See especially Hesiod, *Theog.*, 820 foll. ; fuller accounts, and complete references, will be found in Roscher, art. TYPHON, TYPHOEUS. In [Hom.] *hymn.*, III, 351, he is son of Hera without father.

⁸¹ Apollod., I, 40 foll. ; Nonnos, *Dionys.*, I, 154 foll., II.

⁸² See Cook, *Zeus*, II, 549, 550.

⁸³ See Apollod., I, 41 ; Ovid, *Metam.*, V, 321 foll. ; Anton. Lib., 28 ; Hyginus, *fab.*, 96. See Rose in *Class. Quart.*, XXIV, p. 107.

⁸⁴ See for an elaborate form of this theory, Aristotle, *Meteor.*, II, 365ᵇ21 foll. ; Anaxagoras had already, in the early days of philosophy, put forward a very simple form of practically the same theory, *ibid.*, 365ᵃ17 foll. So, if we may believe Ammianus Marcellinus, XVII, 7, 12, had Anaximandros.

⁸⁵ *Odyssey*, XI, 305 foll.

⁸⁶ *Iliad*, V, 385 foll.

⁸⁷ Apollod., I, 53 ; *cf.* Chapter X, p. 293.

⁸⁸ Ovid, *Metam.*, VI, 116.

⁸⁹ Erastosthenes, cited by schol. on Apollonios Rhodios, I, 482.

⁹⁰ Apollod., *loc. cit.*, 55.

⁹¹ Scholiast on *Iliad*, *loc. cit.*

⁹² Schol. on Pindar, *Pyth.*, IV, 88 ; Apollod., *loc. cit.* ; *cf.* Hyginus, *fab.*, 28.

⁹³ Hyginus, *ibid.*, *qui ad inferos dicuntur hanc poenam pati* : *ad columnam, auersi alter ab altero, serpentibus sunt deligati. est styx inter, columnam sedens, ad quam sunt deligati.* The passage is not corrupt, see my note. This might well be a misunderstanding of some old cult-monument, a sacred pillar with a bird on top of it, indicating the epiphany of a god, flanked in the heraldic fashion of Minoan art by two daimones. Vergil, *Aen.*, VI, 582, places them in Tartaros but gives no details.

⁹⁴ See Servius on Vergil, *loc. cit.* ; also the passages of Apollodoros and Hyginus already quoted.

⁹⁵ Hesiod cited by schol. Apoll. Rhod., *loc. cit.* (this fragment seems to have been overlooked by Rzach) ; Alos in Aitolia named after their reputed father. Stephanos of Byzantion says (*s.u.* 'Αλώϊον) that they themselves were the founders of Aloion. Pausanias, IX, 22, 6, their graves were shown at Anthedon in Boiotia ; *ibid.*, 29, 1–2, they founded Askra (Hesiod's native town) and originated a cult of the Muses on Helikon. Diod. Sic. V, 50, 6 foll., Parthenios 19 (kidnapping and rescue of their mother and sister, and death of the latter ; their worship in Naxos as heroes, which may point to their having been formerly gods) ; there is a little inscriptional evidence for this, see Schultz in Roscher, I, 254, 30.

⁹⁶ Pliny, *natural. hist.*, VII, 73 ; Sallust *ap. SA* III, 578.

⁹⁷ Paus., X, 28, 8. For fuller refs. to the whole legend, see the article of Schultz already quoted in note 87.

⁹⁸ Plutarch, *Theseus*, 20 ; Farnell, *Hero-Cults*, p. 48.

⁹⁹ See any Homeric dictionary *s.u.* ἐφάλλομαι.

¹⁰⁰ For discussion of this and other problems, see L. Séchan, *Le Mythe de Prométhée*, Paris 1951, especially p. 28 foll. Cf. E. Vandrik, *The Prometheus of Hesiod and Aeschylus*, Oslo 1943.

¹⁰¹ *Metam.*, II, 846–7.

¹⁰² A recent and full account of this and other matters is given by Fr. Schachermeyr, *Poseidon und die Entstehung des griechischen Götterglaubens* (Bern 1950). Interesting, but often hazardous speculations in Paula Philippson, *Thessalische Mythologie* (Zürich 1944). See also Nilsson, *GgR*, I², pp. 444–52.

¹⁰³ For the best account in English of Poseidon, see Farnell, *C.G.S.*,

IV, p. 1 foll. Add, for his mythology, Bulle in Roscher, s.u.; Preller-Robert, I, p. 566 foll.

104 Commonly interpreted as a fish-spear with three prongs, an explanation to which I can see no serious objection. As three-pronged thunderbolts are not uncommon in the art of various peoples, an attempt has been made to interpret the trident in this way, see for example Cook, Zeus, II, p. 789 foll., which gives plentiful further references. I do not accept it, owing to the paucity of real evidence for any sort of connexion between Poseidon and the sky; but it is not impossible.

105 For Amphitrite in general, see Stoll in Roscher, s.u. She is wife of Poseidon in Hes., Theog., 930, who also mentions her, ibid., 243, 254, as a Nereid. Homer speaks of her several times in the Odyssey as a sea-goddess (III, 91; V, 422; XII, 60, 97), but does not mention her connexion with any other deity. Pseudo-Arion, frag. 1, 10 Bergk, calls the Nereids her daughters.

106 Scholiast on Odyssey, III, 91, and some evidence from art, see Stoll, op. cit., 319, 18 foll.

107 Pseudo-Eratosthenes, catasterismi, 31; Hyginus, astron., 2, 17.

108 The story is told in this form only by scholiast on Lykophron, 45 and 650; Ovid, Metam., XIV, 1 foll., attributes her transformation to Kirke, who was jealous of Skylla because Glaukos loved her. It is to be remembered that in all such legends the monster is probably primary, the explanation of how he or she became a monster secondary, the rationalisation certainly latest of all. Unknown seas are great breeders of tales of wonder. Glaukos was originally a Boiotian fisherman, who found a marvellous herb that made him immortal. See, e.g., the fragments of Aeschylus, Glaukos Pontios, with Nauck's notes.

109 For an exhaustive study of the matter in all its aspects, see Dressler in Roscher, art. TRITON, TRITONEN. The passage of Hesiod is Theog., 930 foll.

110 Pindar, Pyth., IV, 20 foll.; Apoll. Rhod., IV, 1551 foll. More citations are given in Mooney's notes on the latter passage, and the scholiast.

111 Pausanias, IX, 20, 4–5; the next chapter describes this and another 'Triton' which he had seen; they appear to have large dried sea-beasts of some kind, probably improved by the addition of artificial parts. See, for more details on this curious topic, Aelian, histor. anim., XIII, 21.

112 Verg., Aen., VI, 162 foll.

113 Apollod., III, 201; I, 28; Pindar, Olymp., VII, 14, where see the scholiast. The text of Pindar runs, παῖδ' Ἀφροδίτας Ἀελίοιό τε νύμφαν 'Ρόδον, and the idea that Rhode is the daughter of Helios arises apparently from a misinterpretation of it as 'the nymph R., child of Aphrodite and Helios', whereas it probably means ' R., child of A., and bride of H.'

114 Theophrastos ap. Athenaios, II, 42 A; Pausanias, VIII, 10, 4, where see Frazer's note; Strabo, XIV, 2, 23; Preller-Robert, I, p. 580; Preller-Robert and Frazer give further references, including some to inscriptions recording the cult.

115 Son, Iliad, I, 404, see schol. on l. 400; son-in-law, Hesiod, Theog., 817 foll.; the daughter of Poseidon whom he marries, Kymopoleia, appears to be nowhere else mentioned.

116 Particularly in Iliad, XIV.

117 See Iliad, VII, 452–3; XXI, 441 foll., where Apollo serves Laomedon as a herdsman, not a mason.

118 See scholiasts on Iliad, I, 400 and Pindar, Olymp., VIII, 31 (41);

Pindar, *loc. cit.* Vergil, *Aen.*, II, 608 foll., avoids the difficulty of letting the divine work be overthrown by men, by making Poseidon himself destroy it at the taking of Troy. *Cf. supra*, p. 54 and n. 52.

[119] *Odyssey*, I, 68 foll., and many other passages.

[120] *Iliad*, XX, 57 foll.

[121] *Iliad*, XIII, 17 foll.

[122] *Odyssey*, IV, 505 foll.

[123] Father, *SA* III, 241, *alii dicunt eas Neptuni filias, qui fere prodigiorum omnium pater est;* lover, schol. Hom., *Iliad*, XXIII, 346, the Harpy bears the horse Arion, generally child of Demeter Erinys.

[124] Pausanias, VIII, 25, 4 foll. ; 42, 1 foll. In the former passage, Pausanias quotes Antimachos for the statement that Arion was born from the Earth. The two tales are not incompatible, for ' Demeter ' may well be some local earth-goddess. The scholiast on *Iliad*, XXIII, 346 (*cf.* Ovid, *Metam.*, VI, 119) says that Poseidon lay with an Erinys near the spring Tilphussa in Boiotia. For conjectures as to the priority of this story, see Stoll in Roscher, art. AREION, Bulle *ibid.*, III, col. 2803, 15 foll. According to the same scholiast, Poseidon gave Arion to Kopreus king of Haliartos (his name, ' Dunger ', suggests some local godlet like the Latin Stercutius, connected with the manuring of the fields ; an appropriate person to appear in this agricultural legend), who gave him to Herakles, from whom he passed to Adrastos. See further, Ovid, *Metam.*, VI, 118 ; Apollod., III, 77 ; *PG* III, 122 ; Tzetzes on Lykoph., 153, 766.

[125] Abundant examples in Frazer, *G.B.*³, see Index *s.uu.* Horse, Horses, and for this legend in particular, Vol. VIII, pp. 21, 338. *Cf.* Farnell, *C.G.S.*, III, p. 50 foll.

[126] See note 125.

[127] See A. S. Pease on Cicero, *de nat. deor.*, I, 63.

[128] Pindar, *Isthm.*, III, 70 (IV, 52) ; Plato, *Theaet.*, 169 B ; *Laws*, VII, 796 A ; Diod. Sic., IV, 17, 4. The common story is in Apollod., II, 115 ; Ovid, *Ibis*, 391 foll. (these two passages show that it is at any rate an Alexandrian story, whatever its ultimate source), and several passages of later authors in both languages. See Oertel in Roscher, art. ANTAIOS. E. Norman Gardiner, *Greek Athletic Sports*, p. 390, suggests that it may have arisen from representations in art of Herakles swinging Antaios off his feet, an ingenious but unlikely theory.

[129] Alkyone, Apollod., III, 111 ; Paus., II, 30, 8 ; IX, 22, 5 ; more refs. in Roscher, *s.u.* Kelaino, Apollod., *loc. cit.*, and Roscher, *s.u., cf.* art. CHIMAIREUS. This Alkyone is not the wife of Keyx, but probably is the same as the mother of Glaukos of the Sea, Mnaseas *ap.* Athenaios, VII, 296 B. For Eleuther, see also Stephanos of Byzantion, *s.u.* 'Ελευθεραί.

[130] Lykurgos, *cont. Leocratem*, 98 ; Apollod., III, 201 ; see, for more references and a number of other minor persons called Chione, von Sybel in Roscher, *s.u.*

[131] See any modern description of the Akropolis, as E. A. Gardner, *Ancient Athens*, p. 358. An attempt has been made to make this support the view mentioned in note 106, on the supposition that these marks were, or were thought to have been, made by lightning ; but a sacred object wholly unconnected with the sky may be uncovered, as for instance the stone of Terminus on the Capitol at Rome, which might not be covered in, Wissowa, *R.K.R.*, p. 137. *Cf. Folk-Lore*, XXXIII (1922), p. 43.

[132] See Preller-Robert, I, p. 202 foll. ; the chief classical references are Herodotos, VIII, 55 (*cf.* Eurip., *Ion*, 1433, *Troad.*, 801) ; Apollod., III, 177–179 (the gods judge the contest, and those who say it was Kekrops

and Kranaos, or Erechtheus, are wrong) ; Ovid, *Metam.*, VI, 75 foll. (Athena produces olive by striking rock with spear-point, Poseidon produces horse by blow of trident ; *cf. SG* I, 12) ; Varro *ap.* Augustine, *ciuit. Dei*, XVIII, 9 (people judge ; women all vote for Athena, and so outvote the men by one ; men, to appease Poseidon, punish them in various ways) ; more references in Preller-Robert, *ibid.*, p. 203, n. 1.

[133] Herod., *loc. cit.*
[134] Pausanias, II, 22, 4.
[135] *Ibid.*, 30, 6 ; 32, 8.
[136] Scholiast on Pindar, *Pyth.*, IV, 246 ; Philostratos, *imagines*, II, 14 ; PrG., I, 12. See further, Preller-Robert, I, p. 590.
[137] Herodotos, VII, 129, 4 ; Philostratos, *loc. cit.* ; see Frazer, *F.O.T.*, I, p. 171.

ADDITIONAL NOTES (see Note 58).

For discussion of the many difficulties in these passages, see Otto Lendle, *Die " Pandorasage " bei Hesiod*, Würzburg 1957.

Page 59.—Mr. Jaan Puhvel, of the University of California, obligingly furnishes the following Oriental parallel to the loss of Zeus' sinews and their recovery. The myth, which is Hittite, is in J. B. Pritchard, *Ancient Near Eastern Texts*, ed. 2 (Princeton 1955), p. 126. The Storm-god is defeated by the dragon Illuyankas, who robs him of his heart and eyes. The Storm-god then begets a son, who marries the dragon's daughter and recovers the heart and eyes. The Storm-god, thus restored, goes forth once more against the dragon.

CHAPTER IV

THE CHILDREN OF KRONOS—II

> qualis
> demissus curru laeuae post praemia sortis
> umbrarum custos mundique nouissimus heres
> palluit amisso ueniens in Tartara caelo.
>
> —STATIUS, *Thebais*, XI, 443-6.
>
> So steered his downward car
> He whom the fortune of a luckless lot
> Named ruler of the ghosts, the world's third heir,
> When, losing Heaven, he paled to look on Hell.

IN discussing the third of the brothers, Hades (Aïdes), Aïdoneus or Pluton, it is well to remember that in Greek mythology and in their thought generally there is no figure corresponding to the Devil of Persian and later Jewish belief and of traditional Christian theology. Hades is grim and mournful in character and in functions, severely just, and inexorable in the carrying out of his, or Fate's, decrees ; his realm includes a place of torment for the wicked ; but he is no enemy of mankind, does not tempt to wickedness nor delight in it, is not opposed in nature to his more fortunate brothers, and can reward the good as well as punishing sinners. He is a terrible, not an evil god.

Being feared, he is not named, indeed he has no name, properly speaking, nor has his kingdom, at any rate in the earlier documents. Ἀϝίδης means simply ' the Unseen ', and becomes Hades, Ἄιδης, by phonetic changes familiar enough in some dialects of Greek. The lower world is properly called ' The House of Hades '. Pluton is ' the Rich ', and may likely enough refer properly, not to any god of the dead, but rather (like Plutos) to the spirit of the fertility of the earth. Polydegmon (' Hospitable '), Eubuleus (' Wise in Counsel '), and several other complimentary (or hypokoristic) names are given him, for the Greeks as a rule did not like to speak of death in connexion with themselves or their friends, but preferred to say that some one had ' departed ' (βέβηκεν) or refer to him as ' the blessed one '

(ὁ μακαρίτης), even beginning such matter-of-fact documents as
wills with the formula ' All will go well ; but if anything happens,
I make the following dispositions '.[1]

The Romans either had no death-god, or had forgotten him, if
ever they did have one. Hence they took over the Greek name
Pluton, or translated it by Dis, the contracted form of *diues*.
The name of his consort was corrupted into Proserpina, and
nothing was added to the existing mythology. In cult they
remained unaffected for the most part, since indeed there was little
to affect them, Hades being worshipped almost nowhere in Greece,[2]
and represented comparatively seldom in art. When he is shown,
his form and features differ but little from those of Zeus, save in
expression ; Seneca describes the difference epigrammatically
when he says of him [3] *uultus est illi Iouis, sed fulminantis*, ' he
hath Jove's own look, But Jove's when he doth thunder '.

His kingdom is usually conceived of as being underground. In
such matters, however, consistency is not to be looked for in the
traditions of any people, and as already explained (above, p. 18),
there was a tendency to place the abode of the dead in the West,
while the two ideas were reconciled at an early date (we find the
process complete in the *Odyssey*) by supposing some locality in the
farthest known West to be the entrance, or at least the normal
entrance, to it. This naturally did not drive out the local traditions of places which claimed to possess a Hellmouth of their own,
such as Tainaron near Sparta. The topography of the place is
fairly consistent, and does not vary much from that described by
Homer. Somewhere beyond the stream of Ocean is the land of
the Kimmerians, who never see the sun. Here is a headland,
with groves of poplars and willows, sacred to Persephone :
apparently these stand outside the House of Hades. Near by
are the Gates of the (setting) Sun and the country of Dreams.
Somewhere in this region is a landmark, the White Rock (Leukas
Petra), where two great rivers meet, presumably two of the rivers
of the underworld, or one of them and Ocean. Passing this, one
comes to the Plain of Asphodel, where dwell the departed, great
and small, living a tasteless and colourless life, with a sort of
shadowy continuance of their former occupations in this world.
The ghosts are the merest shadows of the living men, εἴδωλα
καμόντων, ' phantoms of folk outworn ', lacking the essentials of
real vigorous life, the θυμός, probably the blood-soul, and also
the φρένες, literally ' midriff ', which a living man has. All that
is left is the ψυχή or breath-soul, which by itself is a poor thing,
being quite bodiless.[4]

Not all the dead, however, go to this dreary place. A very

few highly favoured mortals are taken away, body and soul together, to Elysion, which to judge from its name is a pre-Greek Paradise, ruled over by Rhadamanthys, alone or as assessor to Kronos, and identified by the Greeks with their own happy land, the Islands of the Blessed.[5] Here all is perfect happiness, materially but not grossly conceived, and no one ever dies. The beauty of this lovely fancy attracted even deeply religious writers whose own conception of a future life was much more developed, as for instance Pindar, who says of the final abode of the glorified righteous :

'There the breezes of Ocean breathe about the Islands of the Blessed, and flowers of gold blaze, some on land, upon fair trees, while others the water nurtures, with garlands whereof they entwine their hands and brows.' . . . 'Before their city lie meadows ruddy with roses, shaded with balsam-trees, heavy-laden with golden corn. And some take their pleasure in horses and in sports, some in draught-playing, some in the lyre, while all manner of wealth flowers fair among them. Also a sweet savour wafts over that lovely land, as they ever mingle every kind of incense in the far-shining fire upon the altars of the gods.'[6]

In other words, it was the life a Greek gentleman led when he could, active and joyous, even strenuous, but with no compulsion to labour, ' for with the might of their hands they trouble not the earth nor the waters of the sea, to gain them a bare living ', as he elsewhere puts it, in describing a somewhat less desirable place, a kind of half-way house to this Paradise.[7] The whereabouts of Elysion, or the Elysian Fields (or Plain), naturally remained vague, for it is sometimes spoken of as if quite distinct from the House of Hades, which is indeed the logical way to conceive it, since the latter is the abode of ghosts, not of living men made immortal ; oftener, however, and especially in the well-known descriptions in Aristophanes and Vergil, it is part of the underworld, separated from the world of the living, like the rest of Hades, by one of the infernal waters of which we shall speak presently. Entrance to it was originally gained purely by favour ; Menelaos is promised it explicitly because he is husband of Helen and therefore son-in-law of Zeus ;[8] but later belief placed therein the heroes and patriots of mythology and history, Achilles, Diomedes, the Athenian tyrannicides, and others. This is in keeping with the general growth of ethical feeling.

Opposed to Elysion or the Islands of the Blessed is Tartaros, as it is usually called, the place of punishment of the wicked. Here again the earliest ideas preserved to us are not ethical ; those who suffer there are not all sinners, or even all great sinners, but simply certain persons who have directly offended or insulted the gods. Odysseus sees there the following : [9] Firstly, Tityos the giant, who is bound fast and cannot keep off two vultures who tear, one on either side, at his liver. His offence was that he tried to rape Leto. Next is Tantalos, who is everlastingly hungry and thirsty. He stands in a pool of water which plashes against his chin, but always vanishes when he tries to drink it ; overhead hang all manner of fruit-trees, which are always tossed out of his reach by a wind when he tries to gather their fruit. His sin was, that he tested the omniscience of the gods by serving them at a banquet with the flesh of his own son Pelops, to see if they could tell it from that of some beast. Demeter, distraught with grief for the loss of Persephone, ate part of one shoulder, but the rest discovered the cheat, and Pelops was brought to life again and the missing part replaced by a shoulder of ivory. [10] Another variety of his story tells that he was plagued with eternal fear, with or without hunger ; a rock continually hangs over his head and seems just about to fall and crush him. [11] His sin also is variously reported, for in various forms of the story he did not tempt the gods, but (a) stole their nectar and ambrosia and gave them to his friends ; or (b) he blabbed their secrets ; or (c) he asked for a life like theirs (surely another version of the stealing of the food of immortality) ; or (d) when Pandareos stole a golden dog from the shrine of Zeus, Tantalos concealed the stolen goods and swore to Hermes that he knew nothing of the matter. Or finally, and these are clearly late versions, (e) it was he, not Zeus, who kidnapped Ganymedes, or (f) he anticipated the physicists of later times by denying that the Sun was a god, declaring that it was nothing but a mass of fiery matter of some kind. [12] Except this last bit of silly moralizing, all these stories agree on the essential point ; Tantalos was admitted to the friendship of the gods and somehow abused his privileges. His punishment became proverbial in antiquity, [13] although the verb ' to tantalize ', in the sense in which we use it, seems not to be ancient ; it is found indeed in one or two passages, but in a quite different meaning. He was equally proverbial for his wealth, a use of his legend which is no longer familiar, Kroisos having quite ousted him, as indeed he had begun to do in ancient times.

Third in Odysseus' list of those whom he saw ' suffering great anguish ' was Sisyphos. He was condemned eternally to roll a great stone up a hill ; every time he reached the top with his burden, it slipped from him and rolled down again. This, with insignificant variations, is the one form of his punishment, as given by authors of all dates. [14]

It is noteworthy that, save perhaps for Tityos (as intimated in the last chapter, the liver was anciently thought to be the seat of the desires, so that it is possible, even in so early an author as Homer, to think of him as suffering in that part wherewith he lusted against Leto), none of these sinners is tormented in a way reminiscent of his sin ; a sharp contrast to later visions of Hell, in which much ingenuity is spent in making the punishment fit the crime.[15]   Hence a good deal of rather useless effort has been made by modern writers to find why each of them meets his particular fate.   Thus, Sisyphos has been taken as representing all manner of things, from the futility of human endeavour to the ceaseless action of the waves against the rocks of his native region, the Isthmus of Corinth.   Perhaps the least wildly impossible sugges- tion is that the story arises from some very old representation in art of the hero rolling a huge block of stone to build the fortifica- tions of the Akrokorinthos, traditionally assigned to him.[16]   In like manner, various guesses have been made at the why and wherefore of Tantalos' misery, but without any convincing results. In my opinion, we must resign ourselves to ignorance on these matters, remarking only on the ingenuity of the Greek imagina- tion, which has in two cases out of the three hit upon the most miserable of all things, ceaseless and endlessly frustrated effort, instead of some crudely material torture.

Hardly less famous than the Homeric sinners is Ixion.   He also was a direct offender against the gods, having tried to seduce Hera.   For this violation of divine hospitality, he was bound to a wheel which eternally revolves.[17]

Frustrated endeavour is also the punishment of the Danaids. For slaying their husbands, they must eternally try to fill a large water-jar ; but it has no bottom, or their pitchers are broken, so that their efforts are always in vain, for the water flows away as fast as they pour it in.   It is a not improbable explanation that they are trying unavailingly to provide themselves with a bath, either the lustral bath of the bride, or one intended to form part of a ceremony of purification from the sin of blood-shedding.[18]   A sort of comic parallel to them is the figure of Oknos, who obviously comes straight from popular imagination.   He eternally plaits a straw rope, which his ass eternally eats.   One may doubt whether he was originally sup- posed to be a punished sinner in Hell at all ; the tale reads rather like a droll pure and simple, a part of the rich literature dealing with the doings of fools.[19]

Other sinners are mentioned often enough in one authority or another ; as might be expected, the inhabitants of Tartaros vary more or less according to the sympathies of the particular writer, although the ones just mentioned are, so to speak, part of the regular furniture of the place. In like manner, Dante takes occasion to place in his Inferno numerous people of whose conduct he disapproved, but no writer, however different from him in political sympathies or moral judgments, would have disagreed with him in putting Judas there. From quite early times,[20] Greek tradition was fairly consistent in setting among the damned a pair of famous heroes, Theseus and Peirithoos, who in punishment for their attempt to carry off Persephone, as will be told in a subsequent chapter, were bound (or rather, seated in chairs which magically held them fast) by Hades. The common story, however, doubtless influenced by the great vogue of Attic literary tradition, represents Theseus as having been released after a short detention, which one or two patriotic writers even made out to have been voluntary, inspired by a generous wish to save his friend or share his fate.

Vergil, apparently, is the first to place Salmoneus in Tartaros. Here for once we have a fairly clear idea of how the story arose. Numerous authorities, none of them very early,[21] say that this king, whose genealogy is given in Chapter IX, disguised himself as Zeus and appeared as Zeus' rival, driving about in a chariot of bronze, which rattled, to imitate the noise of thunder, and flinging firebrands to imitate thunderbolts. In the midst of this impious occupation, he was smitten by a real thunderbolt, and destroyed either alone or with all his people. The likeliest explanation is, that we have here a dim recollection of weather-magic, and that the real Salmoneus, whether king or commoner, was a powerful wizard, who by mimicking the noise of thunder and lightning could make real storms come, whether to smite his enemies or to bring rain to the thirsty land. Later times misunderstood this, and took the magic for blasphemous mockery. It is noteworthy that Homer knows nothing of any evil reputation of Salmoneus, of whom indeed he speaks respectfully.[22]

Other enemies of the gods, such as Prometheus, are occasionally said to have been punished in Hades, a natural result of the tendency towards uniformity in these quasi-theological stories, which, however, cannot quite overcome the variety of the Greek imagination.

Where there are tormented, there must be tormentors, and where there are persons condemned, there must be some one to condemn them. Hence we find, although not in the earliest authorities, infernal judges with their executioners, usually the Erinyes, although monsters such as the Chimaira are not infrequently represented in this capacity. In Homer there is simply a vague mention of ' you who beneath the earth take vengeance on men, even on all that swear falsely ',[23] names and number being left unspecified ; elsewhere he speaks of the Erinyes listening to a curse and bringing it to pass, but in this world.[24]   It is the later poets who are more definite on both points.   The judges of the dead are usually not Hades himself nor his consort, although the former does fulfil that function at times,[25] but the three just men of early days, Minos, Rhadamanthys, and Aiakos.   Of these the first is already a judge in Hades in the *Odyssey*, but in a different sense ; he is a king among the dead and settles their quarrels, as he did in life among living men ; their destiny is not in his hands. In both Homer and Pindar, as we have already seen, and in many other authors also, Rhadamanthys is lord of the Elysian fields. Various authors apportion the functions of the different judges more or less fancifully ; thus, Vergil makes Rhadamanthys alone judge the wicked, Horace apparently makes Minos judge all the dead, as do most authors, at least of the later times ; Plato ingeniously supposes that Rhadamanthys judges the Asiatic dead, Aiakos the Europeans, while Minos has the last word in case of their judgments needing revision.[26]

Here and there we find Aiakos degraded to a mere doorkeeper of the infernal regions, see Chapter II, note 74.   There is a tradition, wrong but fairly old, since the scholiast of the Codex Venetus of Aristophanes mentions it, which calls the doorkeeper of Hades in the *Frogs* Aiakos.[27]   This may well have had something to do with the occurrence, in Lucian, of the same idea, for he was well acquainted with Aristophanes and presumably with the then existing commentaries on him.

Of the birth of the Erinyes [28] something has been said in Chapter II.   It is less easy to say what their real origin was, *i.e.*, what gave rise to the belief in them.   They appear regularly in literature from Homer down as terrible, but just, avengers of crime and executors of curses invoked by one wronged on those who have wronged him, but most especially on those who have violated the ties of kinship.   Thus above all they hear the prayer of a father or mother wronged by a son.   The most famous example of their activity is their pursuit of Orestes after the killing of Klytaimestra, and on that basis Aeschylus has built one of his greatest plays, the *Eumenides*.   They know no pity, they understand no mitigating circumstances ; the deed, and the deed only, interests them.   They thus embody the earlier ideas of justice, before mankind, with growing enlightenment, began to see that *animus* was a necessary part of every crime, and that a deed which was done through mere accident or as the result of *force majeure* did not carry with it the full moral or legal responsibility of a deliberate act.   Yet even so, they are a long way from representing the beginnings of moral consciousness, for they punish, not families or clans, but individuals. They may, however, be said to represent the moral ideas of the clan, for they are regularly on the side of the elders, not only of father or mother but of elder brothers.[29] The sins which they avenge are those for which, originally, human law provided no redress, for if clansman has wronged clansman, the usual remedy of the blood-feud is obviously not applicable ; how can the clan avenge itself upon itself ?   The wrong-doer is polluted and dangerous, and so is eithei driven out or else made to die of himself (*e.g.*, by shutting him up to starve). In either case it is the Erinyes who punish him, in this world or the next ; man does not, for there is no man in a position to do so. Thus the Erinyes embody a just, although rude and undeveloped, idea of law and punishment. It is not surprising that we find them, as early as Homer, intervening to stop an unnatural prodigy,[30] and Herakleitos is less obscure than usual when he says [31] that if the sun went off his course the Erinyes would bring him back.

But this does not answer the question what the Erinyes originally were. An attractive theory, urged with no little force by Rohde and Miss Harrison, would make them the ghosts of those wrongfully put to death, who seek for vengeance on the slayer. This, however, does not satisfactorily explain the many cases in which they are invoked where there is no ghost in question, no one having been killed, and it seems better to take them, *pace* Farnell, as embodied curses. Etymology does not help, for the only word connected etymologically with 'Ερινύς is the verb ἐρινύειν, which is clearly derived from it, and simply means ' to rage like an Erinys '.

In art and in literature, they are regularly represented as formidable beings, stern of aspect, carrying torches and scourges, and generally wreathed with serpents, or having serpents in their hair or carried in their hands. Much of the most terrifying part of their shape is due to the vivid description of Aeschylus, in the *Eumenides*, but it is noteworthy, as an example of the Greek hatred for all that is monstrously hideous, that no artist makes the Erinyes ugly or misshapen ; they are rather beautiful, but fierce-looking women, known for what they are by their expression and the scourges or other implements which they carry, and in general as unlike Etruscan or medieval devils as possible. Latin has no equivalent for them, the name Furiae being a mere attempt at translation (from *furere*, to be raging mad), although once or twice confusion arises between these Furiae and the very obscure native goddess Furrina.[32]

The Erinyes appear in a number of legends, and also are a regular piece of epic machinery.[33] The most characteristic tale is perhaps that of Orestes. Agamemnon having been murdered by his wife Klytaimestra and her lover Aigisthos,[34] it naturally devolved upon his only son, Orestes, to take up the blood-feud. This, when he came to man's estate, he accordingly did, and, by force or fraud, killed Aigisthos. Being, moreover, the senior surviving male of the household, he naturally executed judgment upon his erring ward, who happened to be his mother also. His action was perfectly right and proper, although doubtless painful to him, and his reputation was much increased thereby. Such was the judgment of the non-introspective, patrilineal Achaians who told the story in later days, as interpreted for us by Homer, who, to put the matter beyond all doubt, makes gods and not only men sound the praise of the dutiful and pious son.[35] Such, also, is the verdict of Sophokles, who with an insight rare in Greek poets or any other admirably recaptures the tone of the Homeric story in his *Elektra*.[36] That the Erinyes should take up Klytaimestra's cause never enters Homer's head for a moment, although he is perfectly well acquainted with them and their functions. But in the non-Homeric tradition another view was taken of it, at first sight more humanitarian than that of Homer, but really simply less enlightened, for, like the Erinyes themselves, it takes no account of Orestes' motive. The rule is absolute ; a clansman must not shed the blood of a clansman, or of a clanswoman, and still less must any one slay a member of his own immediate family circle. Orestes had undoubtedly killed his mother, and the fact that he did so as a righteous executioner (for no one else was competent to act, seeing that a married woman normally passed into the guardianship of her husband's clan) and by the explicit orders of Apollo, counted for nothing. Therefore the Erinyes relentlessly pursued him. Aeschylus tells inimitably the tale of his subsequent adventures. He took refuge at the shrine of his divine monitor, at Delphoi. Thence he was bidden to go to Athens, to be tried by Athena's own court, the Areiopagos Apollo himself appeared as his advocate ; the Erinyes pled their own cause with terrible eloquence ; the court was equally divided, and Athena as president gave the casting-vote in favour of Orestes, thus forever establishing the precedent that if the votes were equal, a verdict of acquittal should be registered. The Erinyes themselves were appeased by Athena, and henceforth were worshipped in Athens, at the foot of the Akropolis, under the new name of Eumenides, ' the Kindly Goddesses '.

There, for Aeschylus, the story ends, but others had different versions, with the common idea that Orestes got rid of his persecutors, not by any form of trial or by divine defence, but by some kind of expiation. The most famous story is that told by Euripides, in the *Iphigeneia in Tauris*. Orestes was told to go to the country of the Tauroi (in the Crimea) to get an ancient image of Artemis, which the barbarous natives worshipped with unholy rites of human sacrifice. This he brought to Halai in Attica (one of half-a-dozen places which in after-times claimed to possess it) and henceforth it was worshipped as Artemis Tauropolos, and in the ritual there a pretence was made of cutting a man's throat, the supposed victim being really let go after one or two drops of blood had been drawn. In Euripides, this all happens after Orestes' acquittal, a very lame combination of the two stories.[37] Pausanias shows us a coarser variant. Orestes did not get rid of the Erinyes by an act of piety towards any deity, but gave them the blood they sought by biting off one of his own fingers ; when he did this, the goddesses, who had appeared black, suddenly turned to white, and he was free. So, at least, we may interpret the story,[38] complicated as it is by the rationalistic assumption, found also, where we might expect to find it, in Euripides, that Orestes was simply mad with remorse. Shrines near Megalopolis in Arkadia marked the spot where the expiation had taken place, and the Eumenides were there sacrificed to along with the Charites. Finally, there are numerous references [39] to Orestes having been purified by Apollo from his blood-guilt, in the usual manner, that is, by pouring over him the blood of a pig.

It is to be noted that the Erinyes frequently appear in company with other goddesses. We have already seen [40] that the Harpies carried off the daughters of Pandareos to be their attendants ; Aeschylus, and many others, identify them with the Eumenides and other powers of fertility ; and their dwelling is in Tartaros, where they punish the guilty, besides their pursuit of such offenders as Orestes in this world. If we are right in accepting the view that they are a sort of embodied curse, the last functions are the primary ones. But the connexion with the Eumenides, Charites and so forth is easily explained. Any underworld power is apt to be connected with fertility, because it is out of the ground that the crops grow. Conversely, any fertility power is apt to be assimilated to those grimmer spirits who live underground because they are ghosts, or because they belong to the world of ghosts, as rulers, guardians, executioners, or what-not. Finally, the ghostly associations of the Erinyes, and the close relations existing, in Greek as in other languages,

4

between the ideas of ghost, spirit, breath, wind and air are enough to connect them with beings such as the Harpies, whom we have seen reason to consider wind-daimones of some kind.

In dealing with the rewards and punishments of the future life, it is to be remembered that two ideas existed side by side in classical Greece. One was the ancient belief, already described, which is at least as old as Homer, according to which the other world is for the most part a miserable place of vague, undifferentiated existence; Achilles, in the *Odyssey*,[41] had rather be the meanest serf alive than king of all the dead. But another idea was also ancient, and had greater capabilities of moral development. According to this, the future life was a sphere of reward and punishment for the deeds done in this world. Here the influence of the Mysteries, those of Eleusis in particular, seems to have been considerable.[42] Another influence was that of Orphic, or Orphic-Pythagorean beliefs, which included a most elaborate scheme of Hell, Purgatory and Paradise. Thus in the second Olympian Ode of Pindar, already several times quoted, we have the following doctrine. The sins committed in this world are punished in the next, those committed there are atoned for here (presumably by a life of suffering in one form or another). In like manner, virtuous deeds performed in either of the worlds are rewarded in the other. Final bliss is reserved for those who have kept themselves free from unrighteousness three times on either side of the grave ; they go to ' the Tower of Kronos ', the Paradisal place of which the description has already been cited. Plato again [43] owes much to the Orphic doctrines for the imagery of those great myths which adorn his works ; while later, many other religious and quasi-religious beliefs, some of them derived in large part from Plato himself, added their contribution as we find, for instance, in Vergil. The general underlying principles of Orphism include a divine origin of man, a sort of dogma of original sin and a doctrine of reincarnation, which can be escaped, and a condition of entire and eternal happiness reached, by virtuous conduct coupled with the fulfilment of certain ceremonial obligations. Some at least of these ideas seem to have existed in other cults and beliefs also, and were certainly prominent in Pythagoreanism. The blend of these with the Homeric ideas gives us, in late writers, curiously mixed descriptions of the life after death, with a more and more elaborate and definite topography of Hades.

As a sort of general average of the various ideas known to have existed, the following description may be adequate. The world of the dead, however entered, is separated from that of the living by a body of water, one of the waters of the underworld, which are five in number, Styx, Acheron, Pyriphlegethon (or Phlegethon), Kokytos and Lethe. The names are in all cases significant ; they are respectively the Abhorrent, the Woeful (?), the Fiery, the Wailing and Forgetfulness. Pyriphlegethon has nothing to do originally with penal fires (although it is mentioned as a place of torment in occasional late passages), but simply refers to the flames of the funeral pyre. Lethe is closely connected with the idea that those about to be reincarnated are given a magical drink which makes them forget their former existence, although this need not be its original meaning in this context. At all events, we find it first in Aristophanes,[44] where it is a plain, perhaps with a river flowing through it ; then it seems to be alluded to, although not mentioned, in the famous Orphic gold tablet found at Petilia in Southern Italy,[45] which dates from about the fourth century B.C.   Here it is a spring, opposite which is another, the well or spring of Memory.   In Vergil it is a river.[46] Acheron is usually a river,[47] not infrequently a lake or mere ; in Homer, Kokytos and Pyriphlegethon, the former a branch of Styx, flow into it.   All these waters, save Pyriphlegethon and Kokytos, are in a sense real, for Styx is a famous stream in Arkadia, as already mentioned ; Lethe was the name given to one of two springs in the cavern of Trophonios at Lebadeia, the other being Mnemosyne (Memory), and consultants having to drink of both, that they might forget all other matters and remember what was revealed to them by the oracle ; it was also the Greek name of a river of Galicia in Spain.   Acheron is found as a river or a lake in more than one place.[48]   The boundary is usually Styx, not infrequently Acheron.[49]

To cross this boundary river, or lake, it is necessary to be ferried.   The ferryman is a quaint and probably very old figure, although he does not appear in Homer, namely Charon.   This of course involves a certain inconsistency in the tradition ; if the House of Hades is literally a house, as it seems to be in the older documents, the entrance is a door, guarded by a porter, Kerberos or another, as already described.   If it is a country, the river with its ferryman is a more appropriate boundary.   But Kerberos is never displaced by Charon, but only moved to the far side of the river, where living visitants at least have to quiet him by throwing him a honey cake, in other words giving him his share of the food of the dead, since such cakes were a very common form of offering.[50]   Charon must be paid for his services, and consequently the dead were buried with a small coin in their mouths, Charon's obol.[51]   He is consistently represented as an old man of formidable but squalid aspect.   Whether he was originally a ferryman may be doubted ; arguments have been adduced for considering him an ancient and popular death-god.   In modern Greek folklore he has become Charos, and is generally represented as riding a horse and carrying off young and old.   How much of this is original and how much due to conflation with Hades himself, who, as will presently be shown, is a charioteer, or with such figures, obviously of popular origin, as Death (Thanatos) in the *Alkestis* of Euripides, we cannot tell.   In Etruscan tradition Charun, as he is called in their language, is a grim enough demon, who carries a heavy hammer to dispatch his victims.[52]

Having crossed the water in Charon's boat, the dead are led to judgement before one of the infernal judges already described. They then are assigned to their appropriate place.   In the clearest and most consistent account in any great classical writer, that of Vergil, a path leads through the regions or zones in which dwell those who are neither in Elysion nor in Tartaros.   These include all who have died before their time (as we say ; and similar phrases exist in Greek),[53] such as children, suicides, and those slain in battle.   But even of those not all are to be found in this neutral region, for to enter the domains of Hades it is necessary to be buried.   This is one of the few beliefs which seem to have remained quite untouched and unmodified (save of course for those whose enlightenment placed them above all such superstitions) through- out antiquity.   It is natural enough ; as the House of Hades is regularly underground, and the very old belief that the dead continue to have a sort of life in their graves never died out, it is clear that the body or ashes must be put underground somehow, and that in a formal and orderly manner, as becomes so important a threshold-rite.   In practice, various methods of disposal of the dead were in use at various times and places ; but the minimum was that a little dust (three handfuls at least) should be thrown over the body.   This was hardly ever refused to friend or foe, and not to grant it was an act of the direst vengeance, shutting the ghost out, at least for a long while, from the place of his rest.

Passing, then, along this path, the traveller who, like Aeneas or his literary predecessors, upon the stories of whose adven- tures Vergil undoubtedly drew, dared to explore these regions, came to a cross-road, which led to Tartaros on one side and Elysion on the other.   Here, permanently or not, according to the particular beliefs of whoever might describe the place, were respectively the desperately wicked and the outstandingly right- eous.   Vergil succinctly describes the inhabitants of Tartaros as *ausi omnes immane nefas ausoque potiti,*—those who had dared a monstrous and unspeakable deed, and had accomplished that which they dared.   He specifies violation of the closest ties of blood-relationship and social obligation, treason against one's native land, gross abuse of power, and direct offences against the gods.   With this account few in antiquity would have

disagreed Of Elysion or the Islands of the Blessed we have
already spoken. Here Vergil places, among others, great and
successful patriots, renowned warriors, priests and poets of
more than common inspiration.

With the various theories of philosophers and theologians which
placed the abode of the good not in any underground world but off
the earth entirely and among the stars or even beyond them, we have
no concern here. They are indeed of vast importance for the history
of eschatology ; but theology is one thing, mythology another. To
those who believed in them, or at least adopted their imagery (Lucan,
for example), Hades-Pluton and all his realm were nearly, if not quite,
as much matters of the imagination as they are for us.[54]

To return to Hades himself, the chief and indeed almost the
only story connected with him is the tale of his marriage to
Persephone. This goddess, whatever her ultimate origin may
be,[55] is invariably, in classical literature as we have it, identified
with Kore, the daughter of Demeter. She thus has a two-fold
character, as goddess of the dead and as one of the principal goddesses of the fertility of the earth ; in the latter capacity, she is
the younger double of her mother, the two perhaps embodying
the ripe and the young corn,[56] although the details of their evolution are by no means certain. Consequently she corresponds to
the dual nature of Hades who as Pluton has become (whatever
he was originally) a god of terrestrial fertility as well as of death.
As the tale is told, with few important variants, in a number of
authors from the writer of the Homeric *Hymn to Demeter* down
to Claudian, Kore-Persephone was a virgin goddess of extraordinary beauty [whom her mother kept safe, as she supposed,
in Sicily, the island traditionally sacred to the two deities].[57]
But Hades desired a wife, and schemed to carry off Persephone.
In this he had his brother Zeus as his confederate ; according
to Greek, and indeed to most European ideas, his consent would
be necessary to a legal marriage, since he was the father and
natural guardian of the proposed bride. But Demeter's unwil-
lingness to have so grim a son-in-law had to be reckoned with,
and Hades made arrangements to seize his bride by a mixture
of force and fraud. As she was gathering flowers [at Henna,
a very old seat of the worship of the corn-goddesses], Hades
caused a flower of marvellous size and beauty to grow out of
the ground. When the goddess plucked it, the earth opened,
and Hades appeared in his chariot, for he, like Poseidon, is connected with horses. The reason for this is obscure, but it seems
certain that the horse, to the Greeks, was to some extent an

uncanny beast, connected with death, although they were from very early times quite well acquainted with its use and able to domesticate it. Seizing Persephone, he carried her off despite her struggles. Demeter grew anxious and came hurrying to look for her. Not finding her, she lit two torches [at the fires of Aitna] and sought for her all over the world. By reason of her mourning, the earth grew desolate and famine-stricken, for without her influence nothing could grow or reach maturity. After nine days the Sun, who had seen everything, told her who had carried off her daughter,[58] and she departed full of indignation against Zeus, Hades and the gods in general for thus wronging her. After further wanderings, she came to Eleusis, where she took the form of an old woman, and sat down to rest near the well Parthenion, where the daughters of the king of the place, Keleos, found her and spoke courteously to her. She returned home with them, and was employed by their mother, Metaneira, to nurse her young son Demophoon. By this time the goddess was somewhat past the first fury of her grief, having been persuaded to smile by the maiden Iambe's jests ; whence ever after jesting and raillery formed part of the Eleusinian Mysteries. She also, though she refused wine, drank *kykeon*, a mixture of water, meal and pennyroyal.[59] Now she proceeded to tend her nursling, whom she rubbed with ambrosia ; by night she laid him in the fire to burn away his mortality and make him divine. But one night Metaneira discovered her doing this, and screamed with terror. Demeter cast the child on the ground,[60] took her own form, sternly reproached Metaneira, and commanded that rites should be instituted in her honour at Eleusis, also foretelling that in future a sham-fight should be held yearly in honour of her nursling.[61] On her commands being obeyed, she promised to teach her secret rites, which ever afterwards were practised at Eleusis, the famous Eleusinian Mysteries.

Meanwhile, negotiations had been set on foot to bring about a reconciliation between Demeter and Hades. The goddess insisted on having her daughter back, but on inquiry found out[62] that Persephone had thoughtlessly eaten food (a seed [or seeds] of a pomegranate) in the lower world. This constituted a bond which there was no breaking, and a compromise had to be agreed to ; Persephone was to remain in the house of Hades for a third (or a half) of each year, spending the rest on earth with her mother.

Demeter now fulfilled her promise to the Eleusinians, and also restored the fertility of the ground [making Triptolemos, another son of Keleos and Metaneira, or the son of the hero Eleusis, after whom the town was named, her messenger to carry the art of corn-planting and the seed of corn to lands yet unacquainted with it].[63] Inconsistently with the ' Homeric ' story, which assumes that the use of grain was already known, but intelligibly enough in a legend of this sort, which clearly has grown out of the cult of the corn-goddess, Demeter is said by several of the later authors to have produced corn now for the first time. To have been the first recipients of this gift became a traditional Athenian boast.[64]

Triptolemos is an interesting figure, apparently a local god whose cult spread with the increase in importance of Athens and hence of the Mysteries which that city took under her protection after Eleusis was annexed, at a very early date. He appears very commonly in art ; in literature, references to him are frequent enough,[65] but his story consists of hardly more than the statement that he went through the world, in a magical car drawn by winged dragons, which Demeter had given him. Plato however names him as a judge of the dead.[66]

Ovid has one further tale to tell, namely that when he came to the land of the Scythians, their king Lynkos tried to murder him, in order to pass himself off as the giver of corn to mankind. Demeter intervened, and turned the would-be murderer into a lynx.[67]

The widespread cult of Demeter, of which Eleusis, although the best-known centre, was by no means the only one, cannot be dealt with here, nor need the bulk of the local legends be told, for most of them consist simply in the statement that Demeter had visited such-and-such a place in her wanderings, or had given them her gift of corn ; in fact, they are more or less the same as the Eleusinian legend, which, it is to be remembered, owes its prominence partly to the world-wide renown of the local mysteries, partly to the fact that all Attic legends came to have behind them the enormous literary prestige of Athens.

Three or four seem worthy of passing mention. At Lebadeia in Boiotia,[68] Kore once played with the local nymph Herkyna. The latter accidentally let a pet goose escape, and Kore found it hidden in a cave under a stone. When she raised the stone to get the goose, a river gushed forth, which was named Herkyna after her playfellow. At Argos there was an ancient cult of Demeter, and it was said in later times that as late as the third century B.C. she had wrought a notable miracle ; for when Pyrrhos king of Epeiros attacked the city after his unsuccessful expedition to Italy, the goddess smote him that he died. Such at least was the Argive story ; unbelievers would have it that it was a mortal woman who, seeing her son and Pyrrhos fighting each other, settled the matter with a well-directed tile from a house-top.[69]   At Pheneos in Arkadia, Demeter heard news of the kidnapping of her daughter (it is one of the very many places where Hades plunged into the earth with his prey), and gave them, not only her usual gift, but also the assurance that they should never lose as many as one hundred men in any war.[70]   At Enna or Henna in Sicily, the inhabitants would have it that both Demeter and her daughter had been born, and that she had also discovered corn there.[71]   It seems likely enough that in this very fertile region there had been a cult of a corn-goddess of some kind before any Greek had settled there.

A minor adventure of Demeter occurred on her search for Perse-phone.   Tired out, she was received by a woman called Misme who lived in Attica.   Misme gave her a drink of *kykeon*, which she swallowed eagerly, whereat her hostess' mannerless son, Askalabos by name, laughed at her greed.   In wrath, she threw the dregs of the drink in his face, and he was transformed into a kind of lizard, called *askalabos* in Greek, whose hide still bears the marks of the meal in the *kykeon*.[72]

There are, in addition, two legends concerning the goddess, one very old and very simple, the other appearing for the first time in a fragment of Hellanikos, and first fully told, so far as the surviving literature goes, in Kallimachos.   According to the former, which is already known to Homer,[73] Demeter loved Iasion, and lay with him ' in a field that had lain fallow and was thrice ploughed '.   The fruit of the union was the child Plutos, *i.e.*, Wealth, meaning of course the wealth of the ground, abundant harvests.   What the name Iasion (or, as later writers call him, Iasios) means is very doubtful ; nor do our authorities agree as to what became of him afterwards.   In Homer, Zeus smites him with lightning.   In Ovid, he lives to a good old age ; in several lateish authorities[74] he is a great sinner, who tried to violate the goddess, and was deservedly struck down by Zeus for it.   Nor is it certain what his native land was supposed to be, for while Hesiod places the scene in Crete, and therefore may be supposed to make Iasion a Cretan, several authorities, among whom is doubtfully reckoned Hellanikos,[75] say that he was a Samothracian, son of Zeus and the Atlantid Elektra, and brother of Dardanos.   As the story obviously points to some rite of a real or simulated marriage on the cornfield, like the Prussian custom which Frazer appositely compares, and as his name is doubtfully Greek and both his supposed fatherlands centres of pre-Hellenic cult, we may conjecture that he is a very old godling of agriculture, whom the Greeks found, perhaps already mated to a pre-Hellenic Demeter.   Certain it is that he is frequently mentioned along with her.

As to the other tale, it runs as follows.[76]   Erysichthon, son of Triopas, or of Myrmidon, a Thessalian, wanted wood to build a new hall or palace. In an evil hour, he chose to cut down for that purpose the trees of a grove sacred to Demeter, although the goddess herself took the form of her own priestess and warned him against such impiety. As he would not listen, she bade him go on with his work, for he should need a banqueting hall in future. From that moment, he was plagued with ravenous hunger, which nothing would satisfy, and grew thinner and thinner although he ate continually. So he was reduced to beggary, or, in a later form of the tale, lived on the profits of his daughter Mestra's powers of shape-changing.

The odd thing about the story is, that the cutting down of trees should so bitterly offend Demeter in particular. One would rather expect that a Nymph of some sort, probably a Hamadryad, would take offence at the felling of the tree in which she lived ; and indeed, such stories are to be found in connexion with the Hamadryads, as we shall see in a later chapter. This defect was perceived by Ovid, himself one of the best of story-tellers, who therefore altered the tale so as to make Demeter avenge the death of a Nymph killed by the felling of her tree.

Altogether, the tale has many obscurities, due probably to the fact that we have it only in comparatively late authors, and so cannot trace its growth. Various guesses, none very probable, have been made as to the original significance of Erysichthon ; a reference to note 76 will make it clear that the ancients were by no means agreed as to whose son he was, whether he or his father sinned against Demeter, and what the exact consequences were ; while the tale of Mestra is pretty certainly a later addition.

To make the matter still more obscure, there is another Erysichthon, an Attic hero, son of Kekrops, of whom Plato mentions that nothing is known. Phanodemos, however, who wrote an *Atthis*, or History of Attica, of which a few fragments survive, had heard that he went to Delos ; thence he brought back, according to Pausanias,[77] the most ancient known statue of Eileithyia, but he died on the way back and was buried in Prasiai.

Of considerable importance for cult, but of almost none for mythology, is the god Iakchos,[78] who, with Demeter and Kore, formed the triad of deities invoked in the Eleusinian ritual. Except that he was equated with Dionysos (apparently for no better reason than that his name sounds like Bakchos) it is evident that no one really knew anything about him, *i.e.*, such legends as there might have been were probably part of the content of the Mysteries, and not to be heard (or, more properly, seen, for the Mysteries appear to have included a sort of miracle-play) by the general public. Hence he is variously called son of Demeter, Baubo apparently being his nurse ; son of Persephone, whence he is often identified with Zagreus ; husband of Demeter, and finally, son of Dionysos, yet another instance of the confusion, in a mythical genealogy, of son and father. When identified with Dionysos he is sometimes distinguished by the epithet ' chthonian.'

He is connected with one notable miracle, recounted by Herodotos. Just before the Battle of Salamis, certain Greek allies of the invading Persians both heard and saw a supernatural cloud of dust (for there was no one left in Attica to make one) moving from Eleusis, and heard the Iakchos-hymn of the mysteries proceeding from it. This moved towards the Greek naval camp at Salamis, and the eye-witnesses knew that disaster was imminent for the Persian fleet.[79]

His cult is found at a few places outside Attica, and the Roman triad of Ceres Liber and Libera may be said to include him, for Ceres and Libera are Demeter and Persephone, and the third figure is probably Dionysos-Iakchos, Liber being usually identified with Dionysos.[80]

NOTES ON CHAPTER IV

[1] See, for instance, the testament of Theophrastos in Diogenes Laertios, V, 51.

[2] Pausanias, VI, 25, 2, says that Hades is nowhere worshipped, so far as he knows, save in Elis ; but cf., for example, ibid., I, 35, 9, where he mentions a shrine of Klymenos (' the Famous One ') whom he rightly conjectures to be the same as Hades. See further, Farnell, C.G.S., III, p. 280 foll. ; Preller-Robert, I, p. 798 foll. ; Scherer in Roscher, art. HADES.

[3] Herc. fur., 724-5.

[4] This is a composite picture, put together from Odyssey, X, 508 foll., XI, 13 foll. and XXIV, 11 foll. It is well noted by Preller-Robert, I, p. 809, that all the vegetation is of a useless and unfruitful character (asphodel, Asphodelus ramosus, is a weed which grows on barren land). For the different words for ' soul ' and their interpretation, see Rose, P.C.G., 89 ; Actes du congrès international d'histoire des religions (Paris, 1925), II, p. 139 foll.

[5] Elysion, first in Homer, Odyssey, IV, 563 ('Ηλύσιον πεδίον) ; Islands of the Blessed, first in Hesiod, op. et dies, 171. That ἠλύσιον is not a Greek word, despite attempts, ancient and modern, to derive it from the stem of ἐλεύσομαι and make it mean ' Gefild der Hinkunft ' (Preller-Robert), ' Land der Hingegangenen ' (Rohde) or the like, is now, I think, pretty generally recognized. See Nilsson, M.M.R.², p. 624, n. 18.

[6] Pindar, Olymp., II, 77 (70) foll., combined with frag. 114 Bowra.

[7] Olymp., II, 69 (63) foll.

[8] See the passage of the Odyssey cited in note 5, with which contrast Pindar, Ol., II, 86 (78), and the Harmodios-song (Kallistratos ? see Bergk, Scolia, frag. 10, in P.L.G.).

[9] Odyssey, XI, 576 foll. Tartaros, in Homer, is the place where defeated gods live, such as Kronos, see Iliad, VIII, 13, 478 foll., not a place of punishment for men, however wicked.

[10] See Pindar, *Ol.*, I, 49 foll. For full references, see W. Scheuer in Roscher, art. TANTALOS.

[11] Pindar, *ibid.*, 59, cf. *Isthm.*, VIII (VII), 10 ; Eurip., *Orest.*, 4 foll. ; probably Verg., *Aen.*, VI, 602 foll., where it is likely, but not certain, that a line mentioning T. has fallen out. See further, Schroeder in *A.R.W.*, 1922, p. 47 foll.

[12] (*a*) Pindar, *Ol.*, I, 63 foll. (*b*) Eurip., *loc. cit.* (*c*) *Nostoi*, frag. 10, Allen (= Athenaios, 281 B). (*d*) Schol. Pind., *Olymp.*, I, 62 (97) ; Anton. Lib., 36 (both say that T.'s punishment was to have Mt. Sipylon flung upon him, which seems to assimilate it to that of the Giants) ; Paus., X, 30, 2. (*e*) Mnaseas *ap.* schol. Venet. B on *Iliad*, XX, 234. (*f*) Schol. Pind., *loc. cit.* More refs. in Schroeder, col. 78, 52 foll.

[13] As Pindar, *Isthm.*, VIII, 10 (the stone) ; Plato, *Protag.*, 315 C (a ' tantalizing ' situation).

[14] See further, Wilisch in Roscher, IV, 964, 65 foll.

[15] See, for instance, Dieterich, *Nekyia*,[2] p. 4 foll. (frag. of Apocalypse of Peter).

[16] See S. Reinach, *Cultes, Mythes et Religions*, II, p. 176.

[17] Pindar, *Pyth.*, II, 21 foll., and many later passages, see Preller-Robert, I, p. 823, note 3. The first authority to locate his punishment in Hades ̄is Apollonios Rhodios, III, 62.

[18] See Harrison, *Proleg.*, p. 614 foll. ; S. Reinach, *op. cit.*, p. 193 foll., for various theories more or less plausible. *Cf.* Bernhard in Roscher, art. DANAIDEN. The literary mentions of this punishment are all late, as pseudo-Plato, *Axiochos*, 371 E, Ovid, *Metam.*, IV, 462, Horace, *Carm.*, III, 11, 25, etc. There are, however, representations in art of this or something like it which are much earlier.

[19] For Oknos, see Höfer in Roscher, *s.u.* He was represented in the famous picture of Hades painted by Polygnotos at Delphi, see Paus., X, 29, 1–2 ; Kratinos, frag. 348 Kock (Suidas, *s.u.* ὄνου πόκαι, clearly from a lost commentary on Aristophanes), is the earliest author to mention him ; several later mentions in Höfer, *op. cit.*

[20] See Paus., X, 29, 9, for the representation of them by Polygnotos ; conceivably he drew upon the lost epic *Minyas*, cited by Paus., *ibid.*, 28, 2. Rescue of Theseus by Herakles, Eurip., *Herc. fur.*, 1170, Apollod., II, 124 (Peirithoos left behind) ; Theseus eternally punished, Verg., *Aen.*, VI, 617, which Servius *ad loc.* says contradicts the (then) common story ; he seems to imagine that it is Vergil's own invention. The lost, doubtfully Euripidean play *Peirithus* (see N[2], p. 546), followed by Horace, *Carm.*, IV, 7, 27, made Theseus stay of his own free will. For more evidence, literary and artistic, see Weizsäcker in Roscher, III, 1767, 1786.

[21] See Vergil, *Aen.*, VI, 585 foll. ; Servius, *ad loc.* ; Apollod., I, 89 ; Hyginus, *fab.*, 61 ; Diod. Sic., IV, 68, 2, and VI, frag. 6, 4 ; Valer. Flacc., I, 662 foll. See further Ilberg in Roscher, IV, cols. 291–2. For Salmoneus as a weather-magician, see Frazer, *G.B.*[3], I, 310, II, 181 ; Reinach, *C.M.R.*, II, p. 159 foll. ; Rose, *P.C.G.*, p. 60.

[22] *Odyssey*, XI, 236.

[23] *Iliad*, III, 279, reading τίνυσθε. The variant τίνυσθον (' ye twain who punish '), although excellently supported by the MSS., is apparently a conjecture of Zenodotos, see commentators *ad loc.* It would refer to Pluto and Persephone.

[24] As *Iliad*, IX, 571.

[25] For instance, in Statius, *Theb.*, VIII, 21 foll.

[26] Vergil, *Aen.*, VI, 566 ; *ibid.*, 432, Minos judges those who have been

unjustly put to death on earth. Horace, *Carm.*, IV, 9, 21, *cf.* Lucian, *Dial. Mort.*, 30 ; Plato, *Gorg.*, 524 A.

[27] See Schol. Ven. on *Ranae*, 465.

[28] See Farnell, *C.G.S.*, V, p. 437 foll., and literature cited there : Rapp in Roscher, art. ERINYS ; Preller-Robert, I, p. 834 foll.

[29] *Iliad*, XV, 204.

[30] They silence the speaking horse Xanthos, *Iliad*, XIX, 418.

[31] Frag. 29 Bywater, 94 Diels-Kranz.

[32] See Wissowa, *R.K.R.*, p. 240.

[33] *Aen.*, VII, 310 foll.

[34] See Chapter VIII, 2, p. 247.

[35] See *Odyssey*, I, 35 foll., 298 foll. ; it appears from III, 310, that he killed Klytaimestra as well as her paramour.

[36] I unreservedly reject the too subtle interpretations of Sheppard, *Class. Rev.*, XLI (1927), p. 2 foll. ; see Owen, *ibid.*, 50 foll.

[37] See Eurip., *I.T.*, 940 foll., *cf.* 77 foll., 1435 foll.

[38] See Pausanias, VIII, 34, 1–2, with the parallels collected by Frazer (*Comm. on Paus.*, IV, p. 355).

[39] As Aesch., *Eumen.*, 282–3 ; for the many representations of this in art, see Höfer in Roscher, III, 983, 60 foll.

[40] Chapter II, p. 28.

[41] *Odyssey*, XI, 488 foll.

[42] See, *e.g.*, Aristophanes, *Ranae*, 145 foll.

[43] For the best discussion in English of this matter, see J. A. Stewart, *Myths of Plato* (Oxford, 1905), especially p. 66 foll.

[44] *Ranae*, 186. Two other fairly early mentions of Lethe, if certain, could be added, namely pseudo-Simonides, *Anth. Pal.*, VII, 25 (*Epigr.* 184 Bergk, 126 Diels) and *trag. frag. adesp.*, 372. N². But in both of these it is quite possible that the phrase λήθης δόμοι means simply ' home or place of forgetfulness ', not ' home of Lethe '. In Plato also (Rep. X, 621 A) Lethe is a plain, through which flows the river Ameles (Care-not), the water of which produces forgetfulness. A little lower, *ibid.* C, it is called ὁ τῆς Λήθης ποταμός. See Adam's commentary.

[45] Olivieri, *Lamellae Orphicae* (Kleine Texte, Lietzmann, No. 133), p. 12.

[46] *Aeneid*, VI, 714.

[47] River, for instance, in Verg., *Georg.*, II, 492, and perhaps in Homer, *Od.*, X, 513. Lake, for example, in Euripides, *Alcest.*, 443. The terrestrial Acheron was both, see note 48. We have already seen that Styx, presumably the nymph of the infernal river, is thought of on occasion as more or less anthropomorphic (Chapter II, p. 36), so once or twice Acheron is treated like an ordinary river-god. As such, in Ovid (*Metam.*, V, 539) he is by Orphne (or Gorgyra, Apollod., I, 33) the father of Askalaphos, the betrayer of Persephone. Natalis Comes, writing in the sixteenth century, calls him son of Ge or Demeter and adds that the Titans drank of his waters in their fight against Zeus, and that is why he was made an infernal river (*Mythologia*, III, 1 ; p. 190 of the Geneva edition of 1620). This may go back to a genuinely old source now lost.

[48] For Trophonios's cavern, see Pausanias, IX, 39, 8. For the Spanish Lethe, see Plut., *Q.R.*, 34, and my notes, *Rom. Quest.*, p. 184. For the best-known terrestrial Acheron (a river in Triphylia), see Strabo, VIII, 3, 15 ; hardly less famous was the Acherusian Mere in the neighbourhood of Cumae, *ibid.*, V, 4, 5. In general, see the articles ACHERON, LETHE, etc., in Roscher.

[49] Acheron in Euripides, *Alc.*, 443 ; Styx, in innumerable passages,

for example Vergil, *Aen.*, VI, 384 foll.   Note that *ibid.*, 369, it is spoken of as a swamp (*palus*).   The conception in all cases seems to be that of a marshy, sluggish stream.

⁵⁰ Charon first appears in the *Minyas*, as cited by Pausanias, X, 28, 2 ; but it is highly likely, judging by his obscure name and the popularity of his figure in later literature, that he is much older than this not very early work.   Besides the art. CHARON in Roscher, see Lawson, p. 114 foll., for interesting evidence of the modern belief concerning him ; *cf.* also Politis, I, 612 foll.

⁵¹ This, the classical explanation, I see no reason to doubt.   Mr. Lawson, it is true (*op. cit.*, p. 108 foll.), prefers to take it as originally a charm to prevent the body being possessed by evil spirits.   There is evidence for such an idea existing, as he points out ; but it is wholly non-classical, and the idea of providing the dead with journey-money is simply part of the almost universal custom of furnishing them with such things as a traveller would need.

⁵² The fullest account of Charun is in F. de Ruyt, *Charun démon étrusque de la mort*, Brussels, Lamertin, 1934, which gives abundant examples from Etruscan art.

⁵³ ὑπὲρ μοῖραν or μόρον.   See, for instance, Hom., *Il.*, XX, 336.   It was an article of faith, especially with necromancers in later times, that such persons (ἄωροι, βιαιοθάνατοι) became particularly spiteful and dangerous ghosts.

⁵⁴ Lucan, *Pharsalia*, IX, 1 foll.   The subject is fully discussed, for example, in Rohde, *Psyche*,⁴ II, p. 296 foll., who also sketches the older and genuinely classical beliefs, *ibid.*, I, 301 foll. ; Dieterich, *Nekyia*², p. 114 foll.   See p. 101.

⁵⁵ For Persephone, see Farnell, *C.G.S.*, p. 112 foll.   See also Leo Bloch in Roscher, art. KORA.

⁵⁶ That this cannot be accounted certain is clear from Farnell, *loc. cit.* ; but I think it rather likelier than not, seeing how common the names ' maiden ' and ' mother ' are in connection with corn-ceremonies, see Frazer, *G.B.*³, VII, p. 35 foll.   Since we find both Hades and Persephone fully developed in our earliest records, we can but conjecture what they were originally ; again I think the balance of probability (it is no more) is in favour of supposing that a death-god and death-goddess, whom we may call Hades and Persephone, coalesced at some early date with a god and goddess of the fertility of the earth, Pluton and Kore, who however, to judge by the name of the latter, cannot originally have been husband and wife.   The name of Persephone has a great variety of forms, Persephoneia (epic), Phersephone or Persephone, Phersephatta or Pherrephatta, with further variants, local, dialectic and so forth, of all these.   The Latin Proserpina is simply a corruption of Persephone, not the name of a native goddess, see Carter in Roscher, III, 3141, 58 foll.

⁵⁷ Beyond a bare mention in Hesiod, *Theog.*, 913, the earliest authority is the Homeric Hymn to Demeter, which dates perhaps from the seventh century B.C.   The other important authorities are Ovid, *Met.*, V, 359 foll. ; and *Fast.*, IV, 419 foll. ; Apollod., I, 29 foll. ; Hyginus, *fab.*, 146, 147 ; and the unfinished poem of Claudian, *de raptu Proserpinae* (Claudian XXXIII, XXXV, XXXVI).   References and allusions in all manner of authors are innumerable ; there is also an Orphic version, *Berliner Klassikertexte*, V, p. 7 foll. (frag. 49 Kern).   The account in the text follows ' Homer ', the passages in square brackets are taken from one of the later writers, generally Ovid.   See further Preller-Robert, I, p. 798 foll.

⁵⁸ So ' Homer ' ; the authority followed by Apollod. says it was the people of Hermione. See the note of Sikes and Allen on the hymn, line 17. According to Ovid Alpheios was the informant ; Claudian supposes a conspiracy of silence on the part of the gods, by order of Zeus.

⁵⁹ This is of course an aetiological detail ; the drink was a very old-fashioned preparation of wheat- or barley-meal, a kind of thin porridge or frumety, and was ceremonially used in the Mysteries. For Iambe the Orphic tradition substitutes Baubo, and attributes to her gestures, to our ideas highly obscene (see frag. 215 Abel, 52 Kern), which no doubt were of magical value. In Apollod., Iambe was an old woman.

⁶⁰ It was the child's father who interfered, Hyginus, *fab.*, **147**, where he is called Eleusios or Eleusinos, and is said to have perished. In Apollod., the child dies in the fire.

⁶¹ For this rite, see Sikes and Allen, note on lines 265–7, and for sham-fights in general, see Rose in *Folk-Lore*, XXXVI (1925), p. 322 foll.

⁶² From Persephone herself, in ' Homer '. In Apollod. and Ovid, Askalaphos, son of Acheron and Gorgyra or Orphne, saw her eating and betrayed her ; for which Demeter took vengeance on him, crushing him under a rock (Apollod.). Ovid (l. 543) says that Persephone threw the waters of Phlegethon on him and turned him into a screech-owl (the meaning, probably, of the word ἀσκάλαφος, see Liddell and Scott⁹, *s.u.*). Vergil (*Georg.*, I, 38–9) implies that Persephone remained willingly, to enjoy the delights of Elysion, *cf.* Claudian, XXXV, 282 foll. ; Lucan (VI, 739), that she had eaten something so horrible that she could not be purified from it and Demeter would not have her back.

⁶³ Ovid, *Metam.*, V, 645 foll. ; *Fast.*, IV, 507 foll. ; Hyginus, *fab.*, 147, and *astron.*, II, 14 ; Apollod., I, 32 ; *SdG* I, 19 ; M1, 8. Ovid. Servius and the Mythographer all tell the story with Triptolemos for Demophoon. For the cult of Triptolemos, see refs. in Farnell, *C.G.S.*, III, p. 360, ref. 228 ; in general, see Preller-Robert, I, p. 769 foll. ; Fehrle in Roscher, *s.u.*

⁶⁴ For example, in Isokrates, IV, 28.

⁶⁵ See note 65. His name is of doubtful signification, perhaps ' he who thrice (or ' greatly ') toils (at tilling the ground) '. See Fehrle, *op. cit.*, 1139, 58 foll., and the article of Kretschmer there quoted.

⁶⁶ Plato, *Apol.*, 41 A (which Cicero translates, *Tusc. Disp.*, I, 98), mentions him alongside of Aiakos, Minos, and Rhadamanthys ; a vase or two from Southern Italy put him in place of Minos, see Harrison, *Proleg.*, p. 610 foll., Rohde, *Psyche*⁴, I, 311, n. 1 ; clearly this is Attic, a by-product of the traditional Athenian hatred of Minos.

⁶⁷ Ovid, *Metam.*, V, 648 foll. *Cf.* Soph., frag. 604 P., with Pearson's notes.

⁶⁸ Pausanias, IX, 39, 2.

⁶⁹ Pausanias, I, 13, 8, *cf.* Plutarch, *Pyrrhus*, 34.

⁷⁰ Konon, *narrat.*, 15.

⁷¹ Cicero, *in Verrem*, II, iv, 106 ; see the whole passage for the Sicilian cult of the Two Goddesses, as Demeter and Kore were commonly called.

⁷² See Nikandros *ap.* Anton. Lib., 24 ; Ovid, *Met.*, V, 446 foll.

⁷³ Homer, *Odyssey*, V, 125 foll. *Cf.* Hes., *Theog.*, 969 foll. ; Theokritos, III, 50, and the scholiast (who says Demeter came upon him as he slept) ; Ovid, *Met.*, IX, 422 ; Hyginus, *fab.*, 270. For full references, besides the next note, see Seeliger in Roscher, *s.u.* ; add Frazer, *G.B.*⁹, VII, p. 208 foll.

⁷⁴ For instance, Apollod., III, 138 ; for the rest, see Seeliger.

⁷⁵ Evidence in Seeliger, *op. cit.*, 60, 43 foll. ; Apollod., *loc. cit.*, is one of those who tell the tale in this form.

⁷⁶ See in general, O. Crusius in Roscher, I, 1373 foll. The main authorities are Kallimachos, *Hymn.*, VI, 24 foll., where see Spanheim's notes (that the story is mentioned by Hesiod seems a mere blunder of the scholiast on Lykophron, see *fragm. fals.*, 5*b* ; but Hellanikos seems to have told it, for at least he mentioned that Erysichthon was son of Myrmidon and was called Aithon, or Blazing, because of his insatiable appetite, see Athen., X, 416 B) ; Ovid, *Metam.*, VIII, 738 foll. (note that in his version E. is old enough to have a marriageable daughter, whereas in Kallimachos he is a very young man) ; Lykophron 1393 (the first to introduce the magic tricks of Mestra, for which *cf.* Chapter X, p. 294), with the scholiast there ; Diod. Sic., V, 61, 2, who says that it was E.'s father Triopas that cut down the grove, and that he was forced to leave the country (Thessaly) and go to Knidia, where the promontory Triopion was named after him ; there is nothing here about the vengeance of the goddess.

⁷⁷ Plato, *Critias*, 110 A ; Phanodemos *ap.* Athenaios, IX, 392 D ; Pausanias, I, 2, 6,; 18, 5 ; 31, 2. For further references, see Seeliger, *op. cit.*

⁷⁸ Iakchos identified with Dionysos, *e.g.*, schol. on Aristeides, Vol. III, p. 648, Dindorf ; Diod. Sic., III, 64, 1. Son of Demeter or Persephone, see the above passages and *cf.* Suidas *s.u.* Ἴακχον, who calls him ' Dionysos at the breast '. *Cf.* note 61 for Baubo. Identified with Zagreus, schol. Pind., *Isth.*, VII, 3. From the passage in Diodoros it would appear that he was an agricultural deity or culture-hero, the inventor of ploughing. Husband of Demeter, schol. Aristoph., *Ranae*, 324, which repeats the statements about his parentage already given, and says that some denied his identity with Dionysos ; son of Dionysos, schol. Arist., *loc. cit., cf.* Nonnos, *Dion.*, XLVIII, 943 foll. See further, Höfer in Roscher, *s.u.*

⁷⁹ Herod., VIII, 65.

⁸⁰ Wissowa, *R.K.R.*, p. 297 foll.

ADDITIONAL NOTE (see p. 99, Note 54)

For later developments in popular thought and art, see F. Cumont, *Recherches sur le symbolisme funéraire des Romains* (Paris 1942), especially Chaps. I–III.

CHAPTER V

THE QUEENS OF HEAVEN

I am a goddess of the ambrosial courts.
—BROWNING, *Artemis prologizes.*

THE principal goddesses discussed in this chapter have several characteristics in common. All are deeply concerned in the life and functions of women ; and all have something in common with the great Minoan goddess or goddesses, although not all can be proved to have originated from that fertile source. It is not, therefore, to be wondered at if they show at times a certain resemblance in legends and function to Demeter and her daughter.

Of HERA something has been said in Chapter III. It may be stated without grave inaccuracy that her cult has little to do with her husband Zeus, but her legends are greatly concerned with him. The legend of Herakles seems to indicate that in very early times she, like the Italian Iuno, with whom she was identified, had ceased to be purely and simply a goddess of the life of women (if indeed she ever was confined to that sphere) and had become a great divinity, worshipped by nobles and kings. The story of Jason points the same way, but seems to be of later date.[1] Her union with Zeus, chief goddess to chief god, was perhaps an inevitable idea, but somewhat artificial, although it may be that she was always conceived as married to some male power ; the many tales of quarrels between the divine king and queen perhaps reflect actual breaches in friendly relations between the Greek and non-Greek sections of their worshippers. In art, she is shown as a tall and stately figure, usually fully draped, crowned with a sort of diadem (an ornament indicating high rank, but not definitely a badge of sovranty) or wearing a wreath, and carrying a sceptre.

The idea, championed for example by Roscher, that Hera was a moon-goddess, rests on no solid foundation, but contains a sort of reversed image of the truth. The moon is very commonly supposed to influence the physical life of women in important ways; she therefore tends to become a goddess of women. Therefore also any goddess who has similar functions will have certain points of resemblance to a moon-goddess. Similarly, the idea of Welcker, that she is an earth-goddess, has this much truth in it that, like the Earth, she is much concerned with fecundity. It is, however, that of women, not of plants, which she governs. In fact, she represents no natural phenomenon or object, but is chiefly the divine governor of the all-important human activity, marriage.[2]

Hera, then, is most typically a goddess of women, and it is for that reason that she is on occasion worshipped as Maid, Wife, and Widow,[3] the last title giving no little trouble to interpreters of her myths in classical times, seeing that her husband was immortal. It is around the second of these titles that we may group the bulk of the stories concerning her. She is normally thought of as the wife of Zeus, and Greek fancy was busy explaining how she came to marry him.

The ordinary story has already been told, and need not be repeated here. But all manner of local rites existed involving a marriage between two deities, a holy marriage (ἱερὸς γάμος) as it was technically called. Very often these were explained as the marriage of Zeus and Hera. Like the union of Demeter with Iasion, such weddings had for their object the production of fertility, especially perhaps that of the soil; and it is not without reason that a reminiscence of this is found in the famous passage of the *Iliad* in which all manner of flowers and also thick soft grass spring up to make a marriage-bed for Zeus and Hera on Mt. Ida.[4]

In Boiotia, there are two legends, neither consistent with normal mythology, and all the more interesting for that very reason. According to the one, Hera was brought up in the island of Euboia, from which Zeus ran away with her, and they took refuge on Mt. Kithairon, 'which', says Plutarch, 'provided them with a shady cave, forming a natural bride-chamber'. Makris, the nymph of Euboia and Hera's nurse, came to look for her, but was warned off by Kithairon (*i.e.*, the tutelary deity of that mountain), who assured her that Zeus was taking his pleasure with Leto; whence in later times Hera and Leto were worshipped together and even identified by some. This is of course in the sharpest possible contrast to the usual tale of Hera's enmity towards Leto.[5]

Another story from the same region can be traced clearly to a local rite. Hera had quarrelled with Zeus, and he planned to win her back. Therefore, with the connivance of a local hero, Alalkomeneus, he gave out that he was going to marry again. A log of wood was cut, decked with bridal ornaments, and given the name Daidale (the Cunningly Wrought). As this was carried along in a bridal procession, Hera saw it, and rushed from the place on Mt. Kithairon (or in Euboia) where she had hidden herself, with all the women of Plataiai at her heels. Interrupting the procession, she found out the trick, and the whole affair ended in laughter and good humour. In commemoration of this, the Plataians used at intervals to prepare wooden statues, from the oak-trees of a certain grove, choosing the particular tree by a process of divination from the action of the ravens who haunted the place. Every sixty years, by which time fourteen such images had been made, the whole of Boiotia joined in the festival of the Great Daidala, in which these figures were taken to the top of Mt. Kithairon, and there burned on a great pyre of wood, after preliminary sacrifices to Zeus and Hera. The legend has pretty certainly grown out of the rite, as usually happens ; the rite itself can be paralleled from the ritual of Artemis and of Herakles, besides some less exact resemblances in other cults. Its exact significance is obscure.[6]

As might be expected, Euboia also claimed to have been the scene of the divine union, and a cave on one of the islets near by was shown as the veritable place where the marriage had been consummated.[7] In Crete also a spot was pointed out in the territory of Knossos, near the river Theres, where, says Diodoros, a shrine stood in his day, at which the inhabitants yearly performed certain rites ' imitative of the marriage '.[8] Once more, doubtless, the ritual has produced the legend. As was only to be expected, Samos, one of the most famous seats of Hera's cult and her traditional birthplace, also localized the story, and indeed claimed to be the place where, before their marriage, in the days when Kronos still ruled, the lovers had secretly met, as Homer relates.[9] In Naxos apparently the same claim was made, for in later times, the local marriage rites included a curious custom by which a pretence was made of deflowering the bride before marriage, a young boy sharing her bed the night before.[10] This was explained as a commemoration of the loves of Zeus and Hera. In Samos the ritual of Hera included fetching her statue out of its temple, once a year, carrying it down to the shore, and there hiding it under withies and setting cakes before it. This was explained as a commemoration of the attempted stealing of the image by Tyrrhenian pirates, which had been frustrated by a miracle ; but when we remember that in many countries marriage rites include the real or simulated hiding of the bride, we shall perhaps not be far wrong in taking this as part of the 'annual ceremonies after the fashion of a marriage' which Varro says the Samians celebrated.

At Argos itself, Hera used every year to bathe in the spring Kanathos and so renew her virginity.[11] At Hermione, the statue of the goddess had a cuckoo on its sceptre ; this was supposed to commemorate the stratagem of Zeus, who disguised himself as a cuckoo and, when Hera sheltered him from a storm of rain which he had himself caused to spring up, took advantage of her.[12] Birds, in early Greek belief, had obviously not a little of divinity about them (they continued to be of great importance in divination), and we shall see that Zeus won the favours of Leda in a very similar manner. It has been suggested that the cuckoo, which by its cries announces the rain, was a particularly appropriate bird to be the agent of divine fertility in this case.

Lastly we may mention that at Stymphalos in Arkadia she was worshipped by all three of her titles of Maid, Wife, and Widow ($\pi a \tilde{\iota} \varsigma$, $\tau \varepsilon \lambda \varepsilon \tilde{\iota} a$, $\chi \acute{\eta} \varrho a$), and the explanation was given, as regards the first, that Temenos nurtured her there when she was young ; as to the second, that it commemorated her marriage with Zeus ; and for the third, that she quarrelled with Zeus and came back to Stymphalos for a while. It may be conjectured that more than one of these tales of a separation between the divine husband and wife have reference to the title of Widow (or Bereft, Deserted) ; the real explanation of such epithets is that, like other deities of Greek cult, she is often identified with her worshippers by giving her titles appropriate to them, and all women, whatever their condition, worshipped her.[13]

Apart from these actual legends, we may note that Hera was worshipped almost everywhere under one of several titles signifying 'bride' or 'wife' ; such stress indeed was laid on this function that we hear but little of her, in mythology or elsewhere, as mother ; as mentioned in the last chapter, her children are insignificant, as compared with the offspring of more than one lesser deity, and one of them (Hephaistos) is certainly a foreigner, although early naturalized. It may be mentioned that she is not infrequently identified with her own daughter Eileithyia ; this we may explain either by supposing that the greater goddess absorbed the cult of the lesser (an explanation which I think on the whole slightly the more probable) or that a title of Hera was, so to speak, detached and made into an independent figure. If the latter be what really occurred, it must have happened very early, for the two goddesses are distinct in Homer.[14]

The tales of the cat-and-dog life which was led by the divine pair clearly date from a time of not very refined manners, for the Homeric Zeus treats Hera as no Achaian chieftain would dream of treating his wife, beating her on occasion and once at least hanging her up with a heavy weight attached to her feet, a form of torture which we find inflicted on slaves in classical times.[15] Her jealousy of his numerous light loves is a regular motif in every story of that kind, and we shall come to it again and again, in speaking of Leto, Io, and other goddesses and heroines.

It need hardly be said that these tales of Hera's violent temper led, in ancient and also in modern times, to explanations of her as a personification of atmospheric disturbances.[16] For these there is little or no real foundation.

One very famous legend concerns not Hera only but two others of the great goddesses discussed in this chapter, Athena and Aphrodite. Once, as the gods were at the wedding-feast of Peleus and Thetis, Eris (Strife) flung among them an apple, inscribed : ' Let the fairest take it '. Straightway a discussion arose as to whom it was meant for, and Hera, Athena and Aphrodite each claimed it. Zeus decided that the quarrel should be adjudged by reference to the handsomest of all mortal men, Paris, son of Priam, who was then living on Mt. Ida. Therefore Hermes announced the contest to him, and led before him the three goddesses, upon whom he looked in all the divine glory of their beauty. Each of them offered him a bribe to decide in her favour ; Hera promised him royal greatness, Athena success in war, and Aphrodite the loveliest of all women for his wife. Paris decided in her favour, and by her help carried off Helen from Menelaos, thereby earning the undying hatred of the other two goddesses, and also the vengeance of all the other wooers of Helen, who had sworn to respect her choice and champion her husband. So began the War of Troy, and so also was achieved the plan of Zeus, who saw that mankind were growing too numerous and burdening Earth with their weight, and therefore wished to lessen their numbers by a destructive war.[17]

Such is the tale ; what originated it is less easy to say. It bears no signs of being a nature-myth ; it explains no ritual and connects with no religious belief ;[18] and the conduct of the goddesses is extremely human. Also, the tale seems unknown to Homer, and to every one else, before the Epic Cycle. None of these arguments would singly be of much avail; but taken all together they amount to a suspicion at least that the famous Judgment of Paris is part of the epic machinery of the *Kypria* (a poem which appears in language and in plot to have presupposed the existence of the *Iliad* and *Odyssey*); *i.e.*, that the author of that poem simply invented it, as Homer invented the machinations of Athena at Ithake in the *Odyssey*, to set his story going. Moreover, if we note that the goddesses are so to speak incorporated in their own gifts, Hera becoming royalty, Athena conquest, and Aphrodite love incarnate, we may I think recognize a literary handling of the old problem, so familiar to folklorists, ' Which good thing is the best ? ' the more so when we remember that all three of the bribes offered held a very high place in the popular Greek table of values. [19]

Homer, who as I have said knows nothing of the Judgement, does mention a tale [20] about Paris and the goddesses, but a different one; Paris ' railed against the goddesses (Hera and Athena) when they came unto his courtyard, but praised her who gave him woeful lust ' (Aphrodite). Here is no contest of beauty, and the ' lust ' in question is μαχλοσύνη, that is to say female passion, *i.e.*, the power to arouse it in any woman he desires. This passing reference to a lost legend in which Paris managed to behave insultingly to Hera and Athena may indeed have given the hint for the story of the Judgement; but to identify the two is quite uncalled for.

Such variants as exist in the legend appear to be the fruit of later writers' ingenuity. Thus, in Hyginus, Athena offers skill, not conquest (his text is not corrupt, merely bad Latin); in various post-Alexandrian writers the beauty of the goddesses is stressed by making them appear naked, [21] instead of elaborately and richly dressed, as in the earlier accounts.

Scarcely less important than Hera herself, and of greater importance in Athens, where she was worshipped as the city's patron goddess, was PALLAS ATHENA (Athene, Athenaia, Athenaie, Athana), whom Nilsson has shown pretty conclusively to be a pre-Hellenic goddess, probably in origin the protector of the citadel and person of some Mycenaean prince. [22] This fact accounts most plausibly for her martial character; the divinity, male or female, worshipped by a warlike baron would naturally tend to become warlike; similarly in Italy, Iuno, who generally is a peaceable goddess, presiding, like Hera, over the life of women, is occasionally shown armed in places where she has become the chief goddess of a community of warlike Italians.

such as Lavinium. It is equally natural that among such excellent craftsmen as the Greeks, she should also become a goddess
of handicrafts (Athena Ergane), from which, it would appear, she
develops more and more as a goddess of wisdom in general
(σοφία is both wisdom and technical skill), until late theologians
can consider her a personification of Wisdom in the abstract.[23]
Nor is it at all to be wondered at that being worshipped by the
people to whom we owe most of our notions of ethics, she should
be represented as a moral and righteous deity, one of whom
few, if any, unworthy tales are told. In Rome, Athena was
equated with the important Italian goddess Minerva, patroness
of the arts and crafts.[24]

Something has already been said of the legend of her birth.
Needless to say, the older school of mythologists were of opinion
that it was an imaginative account of a thunderstorm, but such
aberrations need not detain us. After Zeus had swallowed
Metis, there came the time when the immortal child was ready
to come forth into the light. She emerged therefore from her
father's head, which according to a tradition as old as Pindar,
one of the lesser gods (Prometheus, Hermes, or Hephaistos,
generally the last, as being the most appropriate for this piece
of exalted smith's work) clove with an axe. At this, all creation
shook with awe, and the very sun stood still; for she was in full
armour, shouting her war-cry and brandishing her spear, most
terrible to behold. When she laid aside her armour, the terror
passed; and the first of mankind to do her honour were the
children of the Sun, Ochimos and Kerkaphos, who made sacrifice, being forewarned by their father. In their haste, however,
they brought no fire, whence ever after the Rhodians, in whose
island this primeval rite took place, offered fireless sacrifice to
Athena. The goddess was well·pleased, it would appear, with
their good intentions, and granted them skill in all manner of
craftsmanship, so that the statues they made seemed alive.[25]

This is an ordinary story of the birth of Athena; but it is not the
only one. An ancient title of the goddess is Tritogeneia; whatever
that may mean—and Homer seems already to have forgotten—it
certainly does not mean 'daughter of Zeus'. The syllable *gen*, if it is
Greek, would most naturally mean 'born', and *trito-* suggests the
sea-gods Amphitrite and Triton. It is therefore by no means impossible that it refers to her birth or origin from water of some sort;
and as Preller justly remarks,[26] her cult is commonly found connected
with a stream or body of water of some kind, from the little river
Triton near Aliphera in Arkadia, which worshipped her and told the
ordinary story of her birth from the head of Zeus, to Lake Tritonis

in Africa, on which continent she was identified with native goddesses. If we knew to what language the names of Triton and his etymological kin belonged, and what they originally meant, it would doubtless throw some light on the origin of Athena and her mythology in prehellenic times; but unfortunately we do not.

As might be expected in the case of so important and popular a goddess, a clear idea of her personal appearance was early formed. She is represented in art and in literature as a stately virgin, with a beautiful but severe face, grey eyes,[27] and powerful yet graceful build. She normally wears a full suit of armour, with an elaborately crested helmet, and carries a long spear and a shield, on which, or on her cuirass, is the traditional Gorgon's head, already discussed in Chapter II, p. 29 foll. In representations of the battle with the Giants she is always prominent, and shown or described as striking down some of the most formidable of the enemy. Her titles continually bear witness to her warlike character; in various places she is called Promachos (Champion), Sthenias (Mighty), Areia (Warlike, or Companion of Ares), and so forth. The other side of her character, as the peaceful protectress of her worshippers and their leader in all manner of skilled occupations, is brought out likewise by a series of titles. She is Polias (Goddess of the City), Bulaia (She of the Council), Ergane (Worker), Kurotrophos (Nurturer of Children, a title shared by several other goddesses). From Macedonia to Sparta, her importance was second only to that of Zeus himself, whose favourite daughter she was (in Homer he has his special pet-name for her, ' dear grey-eyes '[28]), and whose aigis and thunderbolt she frequently carries.

Of her contest with Poseidon, at Athens and elsewhere, we have already spoken. Another very old legend, or rather pair of legends, deals with her relations to the shadowy ancient kings of the land, and not improbably reflects actual fact; for, as already mentioned, she was probably the goddess who guarded Mycenaean castles in old days. Even in Homer, when she returns to Athens after going far afield to help Odysseus, she enters the house or palace of Erechtheus, who is elsewhere spoken of as son of Earth, a tradition which we know from Herodotos to have been current in Athens.[29] To have been born of the earth ($a\dot{v}\tau o\chi\theta\acute{o}\nu\epsilon\varsigma$, *i.e.*, aboriginal) was the boast of more than one Greek people, and not least of the Athenians, although as a matter of fact they were a mixed population, comprising elements whose arrival in the country was of widely different dates. Hence it is not surprising that Athens, like other places, had tales of kings who had actually and literally sprung, not from the womb of any mortal mother, but from the land over which they ruled. In Athens these legends centre from the most part about Erichthonios, who is sometimes identified with, but more usually distinguished from, Erechtheus. The tale runs as follows; Hephaistos desired to wed Athena, who preferred to remain virgin, and hid from him. Finally he caught her and struggled with her, she defending herself with her spear. In the struggle, Hephaistos' seed fell on the earth, which was thus fertilized. In due time Erichthonios was born, and Ge handed him over to Athena to be cared for. She put him in a covered chest, and gave it into the care of the three daughters of Kekrops, Aglauros, Herse and Pandrosos, bidding them not open it. But two of the three could not restrain their curiosity, and so were driven mad and leaped from the Akropolis. Athena then herself took charge again of the child, who henceforth lived in her temple. What exactly the over-curious daughters of Kekrops saw is a matter on which our authorities differ; the earlier ones say the child was guarded by one or two serpents; the later, that he was himself snake-footed (like Kekrops).[30] Also, the earliest tradition now surviving does not make Hephaistos his father, but rather his brother, both being sons of Ge.[31]

This raises a curious question, namely whether Athena was always considered a virgin. There is nothing astonishing in the suggestion that she was not, for we have seen that she was pre-Hellenic, and pre-Hellenic goddesses were often mothers (we have no right to say they were always such), and therefore Athena may have been. Indeed, at Elis she was worshipped as Mother ($\mu\acute{\eta}\tau\eta\rho$); this, however, proves little or nothing, for we may very naturally explain it as meaning that the mothers of Elis worshipped her (see notes 3 and 13).[32] That she was rather a maternal than a virginal goddess at Athens has been held by so excellent a scholar as Fehrle, and more recently by E. Kalinka.[33] We shall see that such a change has in all probability taken place in the case of Artemis. But the evidence for Athena is not convincing. As already mentioned, the tale of Hephaistos' attempt to marry the goddess is not in the earliest version of the story of Erichthonios; the other arguments are, that she is connected with certain fertility-rites, i.e., such rites are not infrequently carried out at festivals of hers, and that she is connected in mythology with several personages who are not virginal in character. Thus, in one or two lateish accounts, the union of Poseidon and Medusa is said to have taken place in her temple;[34] at Athens she is connected with, and may not improbably be supposed largely to have absorbed the cult of, the three daughters of Kekrops, whose names (Bright, Dew, and All-Dewy) seem to mark them clearly as spirits of the dew which refreshes and fertilizes the land, and the union of Herse and Hermes suggests maternal characteristics in the triad. But all this is quite as reasonably explained by saying that so great a goddess would tend to absorb the cult of smaller ones, whether their functions exactly fitted hers or not.

The story of Hermes and Herse, mentioned above, runs as follows. The god saw and loved Herse, thereby provoking the jealousy of her sister Aglauros. The latter, when Hermes visited Herse, barred his way and declared she would not move. ' Agreed ! ' said Hermes, and turned her into stone with a touch of his wand.[35]

It is but natural that a war-goddess should be interested in warlike implements, and therefore we find Athena credited with having invented the taming of horses, or the use of chariots. In this connexion there is a very interesting myth concerning her assistance of the hero Bellerophon. His endeavours to catch and tame the immortal and winged horse Pegasos which sprung from the body of Medusa were of none avail for a while, since no earthly bridle could control him. But one night as he slept, Athena stood before him and placed in his hand a celestial bridle, bidding him use it to tame his divine mount. When he awoke, the bridle was veritably in his hand, and he used it successfully.[36] Warships were also interesting to Athena (this may well be the reason why the sports at her great festival, the Panathenaia, included a regatta, which is somewhat unusual in ancient games), and we shall see that she taught Argos to build the Argo. Then, on the borderline between her peaceful and her warlike occupations, we may put her connexion with music. She was actually worshipped as Salpinx (Trumpet) in Argos,[37] and the flute (*aulos*, Latin *tibia* ; really more like the oboe than the flute of to-day) was her invention. According to Pindar, she took a hint from the wild lamentations, mingled with the hissing of their snaky hair, raised by the surviving Gorgons at the death of Medusa.[38] Later accounts add that she disliked her own invention, because it distorted her face unbecomingly when she played, and that therefore she threw her flutes (they were generally played in pairs) away. Marsyas the satyr picked them up, to her great annoyance, and to his own perdition, as it turned out. For, undeterred by the thrashing which Athena gave him for not leaving the flutes alone, he became so proficient in playing on them as to venture to challenge Apollo himself to a contest. The god agreed, on condition that the victor might do as he chose to the vanquished, and having won by his divine skill, he flayed Marsyas alive. From his blood, or the tears which the satyrs and other minor deities shed for him, sprang the river which bore his name. The origin of this legend is quite obscure.[39]

Patroness of all peaceful arts, Athena is especially the mistress of the characteristically feminine accomplishments of spinning and weaving, which in a Greek household were regularly done by the housewife and her daughters and serving-maids. In this connexion she is extensively worshipped, and representations of her unarmed and with a spindle are less common, indeed, than those which show her in armour, but not unknown.[40]

In this capacity also she came into conflict with a mortal artist Arachne, and if Ovid is to be believed, behaved in a most unfair way towards her. Arachne was the most skilful weaver in Lydia, and boasted that she could outdo Athena herself. The goddess appeared to her in the form of an old woman, and warned her against presumption ; as Arachne would not hear reason, she took her own shape and accepted her challenge to a contest. Athena wove into her web the stories of sundry persons who had aroused the wrath of the gods and been signally punished ; Arachne's subject was a collection of scandalous tales of the loves of the gods.

This was too much for Athena's temper, never of the mildest, and she tore the insulting web to pieces and beat Arachne with her batten. In rage at this treatment, Arachne hanged herself ; Athena saved her life, but turned her into a spider, in which shape she still weaves, and has incidentally provided modern zoologists with a name for the spider-kind.[41]

One obscure story even connects Athena's best known title with her hot temper ; while Athena was young and living with Triton, she used to practise warlike exercises with the latter's daughter, Pallas. One day they quarrelled, and as Pallas was about to strike Athena with the weapon she held, Zeus intervened on behalf of his daughter and stretched forth his aigis. Pallas' attention being thus averted, Athena killed her, but was afterwards sorry for her playfellow's death, and so made an image of her, which she clad in the aigis. This was the famous Palladion, which fell from heaven into the land of Troy and was the 'luck' of the city until Odysseus and Diomedes stole it during the Trojan War.[42] The real meaning of the name Pallas, and how it came to be attached to Athena, are quite obscure ; it is seldom if ever a cult-title, but a poetical appellation of the goddess, from Homer down.

We now pass to another virgin goddess, of whom we can say with some certainty that originally she was a mother-deity, and that she is not Greek, ARTEMIS.[43] All accounts agree in

making her interested in wild life (hence her title Agrotera,
She of the Wild), and especially in the young of all living things,
particularly but not exclusively of man. Hence she is a goddess
of birth, appealed to by women on that occasion, and is called
Locheia, She of the Child-bed, and Kurotrophos, Nurse of Youths.
By men she is chiefly worshipped as a patroness of hunting.[44]
Kindly on occasion, she is also a formidable goddess, and in particular, any sudden but not violent death among women is
attributed to a shot from her bow.[45] It is almost needless to
say that her connexion with the life of women led to her identification with the moon, precisely as in the case of Hera ; a
further confusion is produced by confounding her with the
infernal goddess Hekate. Once more, any real arguments for
these identifications are wanting, and in particular, neither the
oldest mentions of Artemis in literature nor the earliest forms of
her cult with which we are acquainted in any way hint at her lunar
character. Of her confusion with Phoibe the Titaness, her
mother's mother, I have already spoken (Chapter II, p. 21).

The first point to notice is the evidence for Artemis' non-
Hellenic character, which is manifold. In the first place, she
has not a Greek name ; in the second, although mythology represents her as Apollo's sister, she is found worshipped in places
with which he has little or no concern, not only Ephesos, where
she is adored in a most un-Hellenic form and has a temple-legend
connecting her with non-Greek peoples, but at scores of places
in Greece proper. Thirdly, her association with wild animals
connects her, not with any Greek deity, but with the Minoan
goddess whom we commonly call the πότνια θηρῶν or Lady of
Wild Things, her Cretan name being unknown to us. We may
add that one of the most famous of her attendant nymphs,
Britomartis, is a Cretan goddess, clearly of great local importance.
Finally, Homer has but little respect for her, as appears from the
undignified and grotesque part she plays in the battle of the
gods.[46] There, she ventures to oppose Hera, who whips her
soundly with her own bow, and sends her off the field weeping
bitterly. This contrasts so sharply with the respectful treatment accorded to her mother Leto [47] as to suggest that there is
more than a trace of *odium theologicum* behind it ; Artemis is
a goddess of the conquered race, not yet fully naturalized a
Greek, as Hera is.

Her original maternal character is very clear in the cult of
Ephesos [48] ; but it might be objected that Artemis of Ephesos
and Artemis of Greece proper have nothing in common save
the name. For the mainland of Greece we have as evidence a

series of tales in which the nymphs who attend Artemis are represented as becoming mothers. These will be told later ; at present it should be noted that one of the most important of these figures is the Arkadian Kallisto, whose name so strongly suggests Artemis' own title Kalliste (Fairest) as to make it highly likely that she was originally Artemis herself. Moreover, although too much weight ought not to be attached to her title of Kuro-trophos, since a nurse is not necessarily other than a virgin, her functions as a goddess of childbirth remind one rather distinctly of the matronly figure of Hera, and suggest that Artemis' virginity is not original.

If we ask how the lovely classical conception of the virgin huntress came about, one answer is, that the original pre-Hellenic goddess may well have had no prominent male partner, and quite possibly was represented as being vaguely associated with a lover or lovers whose names varied from one locality to another. The husbandless goddess may have become the virgin goddess. The parallel case of Kybele and the various accounts of the male companion of Demeter make this plausible enough. But also, fertile deities are often attended by the unfertile, whatever exactly the reason may be,[49] and so it is quite likely that the goddess owes her title of $Παρθένος$, if it really means Virgin, which it does not always, to the virginal character of her worshippers. Whatever produced the idea, we have no reason to quarrel with it, since it gave us one of the most gracious of the many divine figures of classical antiquity, the Artemis of Euripides' *Hippolytos* and of developed Greek art.

The ordinary legend of the birth of Artemis and her brother Apollo is as follows. Leto the Titaness was loved by Zeus, and conceived twin children. But no land of all the many which Leto visited when she felt her time draw near would receive her, until at last she came to Ortygia, wherever that may be ;[50] it was identified fairly early with the rocky and inhospitable island of Delos, a form of the story which is very likely due to the fact that the Ionian cities of Asia Minor chose this central but politically unimportant spot as the site of their great common festival, the Panionia. For the fear of the other lands to receive her, two motives are assigned. The earlier, as we have it, is sheer terror of the formidable son, Apollo, of whom she was destined to become the mother. This is found in the ' Homeric ' Hymn to that god,[51] but for that very reason is somewhat suspicious, since the poem is written for his festival and is couched in a strain of most enthusiastic praise of him. The other motive, although later, seems more natural and a better story ; the whole earth feared Hera, who either had set her son Ares and her servant Iris to warn all and sundry not to receive her rival, or had decreed that Leto should not bring forth her children in any place where the sun shone. In addition, she allowed Python, the dragon of Delphi, to pursue Leto.[52] At all events, Delos received her, and there the divine twins were safely born ; Poseidon, in one version, evaded Hera's decree by keeping the island, which at that time was afloat and not bound fast in one place, covered with his waves, so that the sun should not shine on it. As to who attended their mother, the tradition again varies ; the quaintest version is perhaps that in Apollodoros, that Artemis was born first and at once gave Leto that help for which in later times mortal women often looked to her, thus insuring the safe arrival of her brother. In the Homeric hymn, all the goddesses were there save Hera and Eileithyia, but the latter was finally bribed into coming. In the island there grew an ancient palm-tree, which was believed to have been clasped by Leto in her pains.

Artemis' adventures began as soon as she was born, as might be expected in a babe of such divine parentage. So far as they are not common to her and her brother Apollo, they may be said to begin with the killing of Orion. His story may be told in the words of Apollodoros.[53] ' They say that he was a child of Earth, and of enormous stature ; Pherekydes, however, states that his parents were Poseidon and Euryale. Poseidon gave him power to walk across the sea. His first wife was Side, whom he (? whom Zeus) cast into the House of Hades, because she strove to rival the beauty of Hera. He then wooed Merope, daughter of Oinopion. But Oinopion made him drunk and when he was asleep put out his eyes and cast him down by the sea-shore. So he went to a forge (? text uncertain) and snatching up a boy, put him on his shoulders and bade him guide him eastwards. Arriving there he regained his sight from a ray of the sun, and hastened back after Oinopion. Poseidon however had provided him with an underground house wrought by Hephaistos (follows the story of Orion and Eos, told in Chapter II, p. 35). Now Orion, according to some, was killed because he challenged Artemis to throw the discus against him, while others say he tried to violate Opis, one of the maidens from the Hyperboreans, and so was shot by Artemis.'

The legends we have concerning Orion are for the most part rather obscure and late ; most of them seem to cluster about either Boiotia or Chios. There is first the strange story of his birth.[54] Hyrieus, the Boiotian hero after whom the town of Hyriai was supposed to be named, had no children. Consequently, when he was visited by three gods (generally stated to be Zeus, Poseidon and Hermes), and in return for his hospitable reception of them was asked to name a wish, he begged for a son. The gods fulfilled his request in a curious fashion ; taking the hide of an ox, they made water upon it, and ordered it to be buried in the ground for ten (lunar) months ; at the end of that time a child was born from the ground, and named Urion in commemoration of the act (οὐρεῖν) of the gods. Later his name was altered to Orion. Of his adventures one may be named, viz., his persistent pursuit of the Pleiades, the daughters of Atlas. This is one of the few stories in all mythology which we may definitely trace to an astronomical source ; for the constellation Orion, which maintains a somewhat erratic connexion with the hero, is in the neighbourhood of the Pleiades. According to one version,[55] he met them with their mother Pleione in Boiotia and straightway pursued Pleione with amorous intent. She and her daughters fled, and the flight was stopped, or immortalized, by pursuer and pursued alike being turned into constellations. In another Boiotian tale he appears as the father of two daughters, the Koronides (Metioche and Menippe), who were minor local heroines or goddesses. In keeping with the sidereal affinities of their father, these were turned into comets.[56] Apart from these stories, Orion appears to have been a mighty hunter in Boiotian tradition, and on the whole a benevolent being, if rather too amorous. He was here and there worshipped. The name of his wife Side is noteworthy ; it is the Boiotian word for a pomegranate ; the town of Sidai (i.e., City of Pomegranates) was said to be named after her, and the story that she went down untimely to Hades may be connected with the fact that the pomegranate has, as we saw in discussing Persephone, under-world connexions.

The tale of Oinopion connects itself with Chios ; it is very natural that the 'son of Wine-face', a sort of Greek equivalent of old Sir Simon the King, should be lord of one of the most famous wine-growing districts in all the Greek world. Besides Apollodoros', or rather Pherekydes' account of what happened, already given, there are two others ; one,[57] that Orion paid a friendly visit to Oinopion, set about clearing the island of wild beasts, and while so employed met Artemis, whom he tried to violate. The goddess thereupon caused a great scorpion to grow out of the ground, which stung Orion to death ; both of them may still be seen in the heavens. Another tale [58] is that Orion desired to marry Oinopion's daughter Hairo, and so proceeded to work for her father, ridding the country of wild beasts, and also reived cattle from neighbouring regions and brought them as bride-price. But Oinopion delayed the marriage until at last Orion, in a fit of drunkenness, anticipated his marital rights, whereat the injured father blinded him. Several minor variants are known ; very likely, if we had all that is now lost of Greek literature, we should not consider some of them insignificant. It is by no means clear what relation he originally bore to the constellation Orion. Homer knows of Orion

the hunter and also of Orion the constellation, but never so much as
hints that they are one and the same ; but several later writers apparently found their stories on the relative position of that constellation,
Scorpius, and the Pleiades. One reason for this state of affairs seems
to be that no one great poet or group of poets ever put forth a version
which imposed itself on the world at large. Hence the popular local
legends often told no doubt by country folk, or by worshippers of the
Koronides or other local godlings, remain to us more or less in their
original shape.

Artemis of course took part in the battle of the gods and
giants, according to every artist who represents it. This is an
event of conveniently vague date, due no doubt to its comparatively recent introduction (see above, p. 57), and it was not
good art (and also, perhaps, neither pious nor safe) to omit from
representations and descriptions of it such picturesque figures as
Artemis with her bow, Herakles with his club, Dionysos in one of
his bestial shapes, and so on. Hence it is brought down late
enough in mythical chronology, never very rigid, to include these
younger figures.

Some of the nymphs in the train of Artemis (who was commonly worshipped in company with the nymphs) are so plainly
goddesses themselves that it will be convenient to give their
myths here. It will be seen that they are invariably closely
connected with their divine mistress and protectress, and that
in a way which suggests that they are one and the same, or at
any rate that they are old deities very like her in nature.

BRITOMARTIS is one of the oldest. We have Solinus' word
for it that her name is Cretan and means ' sweet maid ', while
both he and Hesychios say that she is simply Artemis called
by her Cretan title.[59] Moreover, she and Artemis share the
title Diktynna. Her cult was Cretan, and her principal temple
near Kydonia in Crete.[60] She was the daughter of Karme, an
obscure figure whose parentage is variously given, and of Zeus.
Minos loved her, but she would have none of him, and avoided
him by flight or hiding for nine months.[61] At last, in running
away from him, she leaped over a cliff into the sea, but was
caught, unhurt, in the nets (δίκτυα) of fishers, hence her title
Diktynna. Thence Artemis rescued her ; according to the most
detailed account we have,[62] Britomartis had simply hidden under
the nets, and sailed across to Aigina, as soon as Minos had gone
away, in a fishing-smack belonging to one Andromedes. In
Aigina Minos tried again to take her, but she vanished away
in a grove sacred to Artemis and was thenceforth worshipped
by the Aiginetans as Aphaia. The story is, in a way, likely enough

to be true.   Several mythological persons are found jumping
over cliffs (this seems to be connected with a rite of purification
by air[63]), and that the ancient cult of Aphaia goes back to Minoan
days or even came from Crete is in no sense unlikely.   Probably
if we knew more of her ritual we should see that the story of
the flight and search was invented to explain details of it.   If
Britomartis was a power of fertility, as is highly likely, considering the company she keeps, there is nothing absurd in supposing that her worshippers used annually to go and look for her,
probably in spring, when fertility is coming back again after
the barrenness of winter, just as to this day in some places the
Maypole, which is a sort of embodiment of spring, is sought and
found in the woods.[64]

KALLISTO is likewise an ancient figure, whose myth, as told by
Ovid, runs as follows.   Zeus loved Kallisto, and deceived her
by taking the form of Artemis.   Later, as they bathed together,
the real Artemis perceived that her votary was pregnant, and
in great wrath drove her away.   After her son, Arkas, the ancestor
of the Arkadians, was born, Hera changed her into a she-bear,
and in that shape she wandered for fifteen years.   At the end
of that time her son met her while out hunting, and would have
hurled his spear at her when Zeus in pity snatched them both
up into heaven, where they became the constellations Vrsa Maior
and Arctophylax.[65]

This is Ovid's skilful patching together of several different
versions, and it is a tribute to his ability as a story-teller that it
is by far the best known.   The oldest known version is simpler ;
Hera plays no part, Artemis changes Kallisto into a bear by way
of punishment, and the reason for Arkas' pursuit of her was that
she had ventured into the sacred enclosure of Zeus Lykaios, into
which any creature that entered must be put to death.[66]
Another variant,[67] which seems to be native Arkadian, for it is
represented on their coins and they had a tomb of Kallisto to
show, is that Artemis shot her.   A more ingenious form of this is
apparently due to Kallimachos ; Hera changed her into a bear
and persuaded Artemis to shoot her in that shape, as a wild beast.[68]
In either case, the child was saved and given to Hermes, who
entrusted it to his own mother Maia.

A curious variant is that of 'some authorities' in Apollodoros,
according to which Zeus disguised himself as Apollo, not Artemis.
Another oddity, if not a totally different legend, makes Arkas the son
of Zeus and Themisto, daughter of Inachos the river-god.[69]
Another Peloponnesian legend represents Zeus as becoming, by
Taÿgete (the nymph of the mountain Taÿgetos), father of Lakedaimon,

the legendary ancestor of the Lakedaimonians. A variant makes her mother of Eurotas, the river of Sparta, which comes to much the same. The legend seems to have been of considerable local importance, since Pausanias saw, on the great throne of Apollo at Amyklai, one of the most notable monuments of Lakedaimonian cult, a representation of Taÿgete and her sister Alkyone being carried off respectively by Zeus and Poseidon. We have to patch it together from a few scattered references, mostly in very obscure authors ; according to one of them, a late scholiast on Pindar, Artemis turned Taÿgete into a hind to help her to escape from Zeus. A mountain-goddess (incidentally she is a star, one of the Pleiades), who can on occasion take bestial form, and who becomes the mother of a famous race, may very well be a local form of Artemis herself or of some goddess hardly to be distinguished from her.[70]

IPHIGENEIA is not a goddess, but a princess of epic story, although not in Homer. Yet a princess who is constantly in association with a goddess, as victim, protégée, or priestess ; whose name is a title of that goddess, as Hesychios and Pausanias assure us ; [71] and who is variously stated to have had substituted for her a hind, a bear, or a bull, all creatures associated with Artemis, can hardly complain if she is suspected of being herself no other than the deity in question. Her well-known legend runs, with little variation, as follows.[72] She was a daughter of Agamemnon and Klytaimestra. Her father, or her uncle Menelaos, generally the former, had offended Artemis, by boasting that he was a better hunter than she, or by killing a deer sacred to her.[73] Hence, when the great expedition against Troy assembled at Aulis, Artemis caused contrary winds or none at all to blow, and prevented it sailing. Kalchas the seer was consulted, and announced that Artemis must be appeased by the sacrifice of Agamemnon's daughter. Iphigeneia was therefore fetched from home under pretence of being married to Achilles, and the sacrifice was about to be made when the goddess relented, snatched Iphigeneia away, and put a hind in her place.

There was another version, presumably Attic, according to which the sacrifice took place, not at Aulis, but at Brauron in Attica, and the substitute was a bear.[74] This legend clearly is due to the very curious and ancient cult of Artemis at that place, where a dance was performed in her honour by girls who were called bears and wore saffron robes, possibly a substitute for the tawny hide of the beast. Other variants are that a bull or a calf was substituted, or that Iphigeneia was turned into an old woman.

Thus rescued, she was carried off by Artemis to the land of the Tauroi, in the Scythian Chersonese, *i.e.*, the Crimea. Here

5

she became priestess of the goddess, who was worshipped there in savage fashion, all strangers being sacrificed to her. Iphigeneia held this hateful office for some years, until at last her brother Orestes, as already stated (Chapter IV, p. 87), came there to expiate his blood-guilt by carrying off the image of Artemis to more civilized surroundings. He was taken prisoner by the natives, and handed over to Iphigeneia to sacrifice, along with his constant friend Pylades. But by some accident Iphigeneia recognized her brother, and so by stratagem or by divine inter- vention she and the two friends escaped from the Tauroi and made their way back to Greece.[75]

Nemesis, of whom something has already been said in a former chapter,[76] is a deity who to some extent overlaps with Artemis ; another such is OPIS or (in Ionic) UPIS. That this was a name or title of Artemis we are assured by several respectable, although not very early authors, from which we are justified in concluding that if not actually a by-form of the goddess herself, she was at least a being of similar character ; nor is it surprising that she sometimes appears as a companion of the greater deity.[77] But the most famous Opis is one of the Hyperborean virgins. Of the Hyperboreans we shall have more to say in the next chapter, when dealing with Apollo ; at present it is to be noted that accord- ing to an old tradition, doubtless the orthodox doctrine of the ancient sanctuary of Delos,[78] Artemis and her mother and brother were accompanied to that place by two Hyperborean maidens, Opis and Arge ; it is also said that they died there, and were buried in a tomb behind the temple of Artemis,—this despite the fact that the extreme holiness of Delos made it no place for a grave of any sort.[79] Finally, we may note that one of the stories of Orion says that Artemis shot him because he tried to assault, not herself, but Opis.[80] The tradition, however, was not consistent with regard to these dim figures ; Herodotos himself names two more, Hyperoche and Laodike, and Kallimachos[81] yet another two, Loxo and Hekaerge, which names are too like Apollo's title Loxias and the epithet Hekaerge (worker from afar, or Averter) of Artemis herself (Apollo is commonly Hekaergos), for the resemblance to be accidental.

Not unlike Artemis in many respects was the Italian goddess Diana,[82] who was a deity connected with fertility and childbirth, worshipped, in the most ancient cult of which we know anything, in a grove near Nemi, the famous seat of the *rex nemorensis* or King of the Grove familiar to every one from *The Golden Bough*. Hence it is not surprising that the Romans identified the two. The Italian goddess had of course no native statues, so in art the

familiar figure of the huntress Artemis (' Diane chasseresse ') is
used for both alike.   The goddess is shown as a young and beautiful woman, wearing buskins, with her chiton girt up to the knee,
generally armed with bow and quiver and regularly accompanied
by a stag or other beast.   On her head are frequently little
crescent-shaped horns, which in later times no doubt stood for the
moon with which she was identified, but are no part of her earlier
type.   Her emblems, besides attendant beasts and her weapons,
include the torch which is a common attribute of goddesses of
fertility, from the very common association of light with life or
birth.

   This is one of her many points of resemblance with another
goddess of fertility, HEKATE.   One is almost tempted to speak of
two goddesses here, so much do the earlier and later conceptions
of her differ.   She is quite unknown to Homer, but in Hesiod we
find her a great deity, in Boiotia at any rate, already so far
developed as to be credited with all manner of good gifts, wealth,
success in sports, skill in horsemanship, victory in war, good
council ; she is said to be mighty alike in heaven, on earth, and at
sea.[83]   Here we have a great goddess, probably Karian in origin,
though Greek in name (perhaps ' Worker from afar '), who in the
belief of her worshippers has expanded her functions until they
begin to rival those of Zeus himself.   Her near relation to Artemis
in functions is mirrored in her mythological kinship to her, for her
mother is Asterie, Leto's sister ; she and Artemis are therefore
cousins.   Or her father is Zeus, and her mother Demeter, who is
occasionally Artemis' mother also, or Pheraia daughter of Aiolos,
who has been identified with Artemis herself.   Hence, apart from
those regions (notably in Asia Minor) where she was worshipped
as a principal goddess, she preserves a respectable position as an
attendant or companion of Artemis.[84]   In this, or in the old
Boiotian and Asianic cult, she is the subject of few or no surviving
legends of any account ; but she is obviously connected with the
earth in some way or another, for she can make it bring forth
abundantly.   Now, as we saw in the case of Kore-Persephone,
such goddesses tend to become connected with the world of the
dead underground, if they are not so to begin with.   Hence we
find a grim and fantastic Hekate who is queen of the ghosts, and
therefore of all manner of magic, the blacker the better.   In this
capacity, she is also goddess of the cross-roads and of roads generally (Enhodios, Trihoditis), for cross-roads are great centres of
ghostly and magical activity in wellnigh all countries.   It is
apparently for this reason that her statues are often triple, so that
she may look down all three at once of the roads which meet at the

point where she stands. At this uncanny spot, then, offerings of food for Hekate were commonly placed, which were popularly called ' Hekate's suppers ',[85] and here the goddess was believed on occasion to appear, especially by night, in terrible aspect, reminiscent of the Erinyes (a scourge is indeed one of her attributes, besides the familiar torch), attended by hell-hounds. In such a form also she was invoked by witches like Medeia, and it is this Hekate who appears constantly in all manner of magical formulae.[86]

A goddess originally connected with fertility and believed to appear at night could hardly help being connected, sooner or later, with the moon, and so Hekate duly was. Indeed the three faces on her statue are not infrequently taken to stand for her three personalities,[87] Selene in heaven, Artemis on earth, Hekate in hell. But, since our earliest authority says nothing about either the moon or the infernal regions, and does not hint that she and Artemis were the same, nay definitely distinguishes them, we have no right to suppose that Hekate was originally either Artemis or a moon-goddess ; it remains merely a not impossible suggestion, favoured by some modern mythologists.

We pass now to a deity the popular conception of whom is as unlike the virgin Artemis or the infernal Hekate as could well be imagined, yet who is in origin near akin to them, APHRODITE. Her mythical birth from the sea has already been described ; [88] of her real origin it may safely be said that she owes a great deal, probably all, to Oriental influences. She is called Kypris, ' Lady of Cyprus ', where her cult was certainly very old and as certainly not Greek ; her name sounds vaguely Greek, and was by the Greeks themselves connected with ἀφρός (foam), but this at best explains only the first two syllables, has no connexion with her most important functions, and is probably a mere accidental resemblance. At Thebes, she is connected with the foreigner Kadmos, and nowhere do we find clear evidence of a cult certainly primeval and certainly Hellenic. At best, we may suppose, what is in itself not unlikely, that here and there, in the early days when she was adopted into the Greek pantheon, she found and absorbed some local goddess of similar functions. It is therefore reasonable to take her as an adaptation of one of the great goddesses of the type of Ishtar, who were worshipped throughout a great part of Asia.

Wherever she came from, she was certainly worshipped practically in every place where Greek was spoken. Generally she was the goddess of love, beauty and marriage, not infrequently a protectress of sailors, but also, in Sparta especially, a war-goddess, a conception of her which seems to have come originally from

Cyprus itself (warlike goddesses are not uncommon in Asiatic cult), by way of the ancient worship of her just off the Lakonian coast, at Kythera (hence her very common title, Kythereia). This is no doubt the real reason why she is so commonly united with Ares, who is her cult-partner here and there, and in mythology her lover and sometimes the father of Eros. Of her connexions,—clearly secondary and the result of a natural desire to prove this important foreigner of good Greek stock,—with Zeus and Dione, something has already been said. To the same desire we may attribute her mythical position as mother of EROS. This was a respectably old god, worshipped at Thespiai in Boiotia, and at Parion in Mysia. Despite the constant association of the pair ' Venus and Cupid ' in literature, Eros has nothing whatever to do with her in any but late cult, and little in any literature before the Alexandrian period ; although in Hesiod he attends Aphrodite, he is not her son, but an ancient cosmogonic power, which indeed he continued to be in theological and philosophic speculation. In the places where his worship is of importance, he is quite markedly the deity of the loveliness of young men and boys, to which, as is well known, the Greeks were exceedingly susceptible. In Alexandrian times, however, the idea of romantic love (not mere desire) between the sexes took possession of literature, which is why most of the famous love-stories date from that time. Eros therefore became more and more important, at the same time losing his dignity ; for whereas he was previously shown for the most part as a handsome young athlete,—his famous bow dates only from the fourth century B.C.,—he is now generally shown as a pretty child, a little winged archer, capricious and mischievous, delighting in working magic (by shooting an invisible arrow at them) on gods and men alike.[89] In literature, therefore, he appears for the most part late and in a subordinate part, as part of the divine machinery for making some one fall in love with some one else.

When we do get a story told of the god, it is one rather of lovers than of Love ; for instance, the altar of Anteros near the Akropolis at Athens had the following tale attached to it. One Meles, a beautiful Athenian boy, looked with scorn on the offer of friendship of a metic, or resident alien, called Timagoras, and bade him jump off the Akropolis if he really wanted to prove his devotion. Timagoras took him at his word, and Meles in remorse took the leap likewise. In commemoration, the metics set up the altar of Anteros. The latter deity is simply ' counter-love ', ' love returned,' and provides a deified equivalent of the lover as Eros does of the loved. Another tale is preserved by Ovid and Antoninus Liberalis. A man named Phylios

or Phyllios was infatuated with a lovely boy called Kyknos (Swan),
who imposed upon him all manner of extraordinary tasks, such as
taking savage beasts bare-handed. At last Kyknos bade him capture
a bull, which he managed to do by the help and advice of Herakles,
but refused to give it to Kyknos. The latter, in a pet, jumped over a
cliff, or into a lake, and was turned into a swan. It is rather a libel
to call such rubbish mythology.[90]

Aphrodite is not uncommonly associated with the CHARITES,
already mentioned in passing.[91] Although these goddesses
(vague in number, but generally represented as a triad, on the
authority of Hesiod), whose parentage is variously given, are
commonly conceived as simply grace or loveliness embodied, there
is little doubt that they are old goddesses of vegetation (*i.e.*, they
make the ground ' delightfully ' productive) ; hence, for example,
their Athenian cult under the names of Auxo (Increaser) and
Hegemone (She who leads, *sc.* brings the plants forth from the
earth). They are common enough in art, where their three
comely and maidenly figures, draped or undraped, are a favourite
subject, and also in legends where an attendant for one of the
greater goddesses, a beautiful wife for a god, or celestial dancers
or singers at any great festival, are required.[92] But they can
hardly be said to have any legends of their own.

Equally vague and likewise connected with the fruits of the
earth are the HORAI. As the word in classical Greek does not
mean ' hour ', in the Latin and English sense, but simply ' time,
season ', they are the seasons of the year. Hence their varying
number, for the ancients recognized anything from two seasons
(summer and winter) up to four, as we do. They are oftenest
three (spring, summer, winter), and tend slightly to become deities
of ethical character ; as early as Hesiod they are named Eunomia,
Dike and Eirene, *i.e.*, Law and Order, Justice, and Peace. But
this is not their most important side in what little cult they have,
and generally they, like the Charites, remain picturesque but
subordinate deities, attendants on the greater ones, including
Aphrodite. They have no real mythology.[93]

In considering the myths relating to Aphrodite herself we shall
do well to begin with the most easternly stories, of which the best
known is her love for Adonis ; for here we have, without doubt,
the familiar Oriental tale of the Great Mother and her divine lover.
The name Adonis is probably the Semitic *'adon*, ' lord ', and he is
often identified with Tammuz, for instance in the Vulgate of
Ezekiel.[94] To begin his story at the beginning, Myrrha or
Smyrna, daughter of Theias king of Assyria or of Kinyras king
of Cyprus, was smitten by Aphrodite, whom she refused to honour,

with an incestuous love for her own father. With the connivance of her nurse and under cover of darkness she contrived to satisfy her desires ; but at last he found her out and would have killed her had not the gods listened to her prayer for deliverance and turned her into the tree (myrrh or balsam) which still bears her name. At full time a lovely boy was born from the tree, concerning whom two stories are told ; according to one, Aphrodite put him into a chest and gave him to Persephone to take care of ; Persephone refused to give him back, because of his beauty. They appealed to Zeus, who decided that Adonis should spend a third of the year where he would and a third with each of the two goddesses. Adonis henceforth spent two-thirds of each year with Aphrodite (the resemblance of this to the story of Kore is obvious, and in all probability the Greek legend has influenced the foreign one), but later was killed by a boar when out hunting. This suddenly and unskilfully drags in the other form of the story, according to which Aphrodite met Adonis as he hunted, and was enamoured of him because of his beauty : she had apparently not seen him before, and he had been brought up by the nymphs. She warned him to be careful, but he persisted in going hunting, and so was killed by the boar,—either an ordinary one, or one specially sent by Artemis, who for some reason was angry with him, or by Ares, who was jealous, or even by Ares himself disguised as a boar. From his blood sprang the rose, or the anemone, or else the latter sprang from the tears Aphrodite shed for her dead love ; roses, which once were all white, were reddened by the blood of Aphrodite, who had pricked herself on a thorn as she ran to help the dying Adonis.[95] Under the prettiness of this story we can see the outlines of an Oriental myth of the Great Mother and of her lover who dies as the vegetation dies, but comes to life again,—a detail which is lacking from the second version, but is clearly visible in the first. The rites of Adonis were popular in Greece from the fifth century B.C. ; besides the ceremonial wailing and singing of dirges, which went on sometimes over an effigy of the dead boy, they included the preparation of the famous ' gardens of Adonis ', seeds planted in shallow soil, which sprang up quickly and withered quickly.[96]

Very much the same story, although at first glance a different one, is told of Anchises and Aphrodite. The goddess, either by the machinations of Zeus, who wanted to be revenged on her for all the trouble she had caused him and the other gods, or out of sheer wantonness of desire, fell desperately in love with Anchises, then a young and handsome man, and granted him her favours on Mt. Ida, near Troy. The fruit of this union was Aineias. As Ida is in the country of the Asianic mother-goddesses, and as Anchises, although he may be to start with a more or less historical person, has here and there a little cult, we may safely recognize the Great Mother and her lover once more. In the ' Homeric ' hymn which is our best authority for the story, Anchises is much afraid, after he discovers who his mistress is, that he will become 'strength-less' in consequence,—not that he will die. I interpret this in much the same fashion as Mr. A. B. Cook, viz., that the business of fertilizing the Great Mother was so exacting as utterly to exhaust the strength of her inferior male partner, who consequently, if he did not die, became a eunuch. That Anchises was afterwards smitten by the thunderbolt for revealing the goddess' secret may well be a misunderstanding ; to be thunder-smitten is a quite well-known way of becoming immortal.[97]

So far, we have been dealing with legends which represent the goddess, not as married, but as forming more or less temporary unions with some one much inferior to herself,—a proceeding quite characteristic of Oriental goddesses, who are essentially mothers, not wives, and beside whom their husbands or lovers sink into comparative insignificance, although some of them are not unimportant gods. This aspect of Aphrodite is reflected only here and there in Greece ; under the title Urania (Celestial ; Astarte is Queen of Heaven) she is occasionally, as at Corinth, worshipped with definitely immoral rites, including temple-harlots. But the Greeks were in general a people of clean life, and rapidly modified, in most places, the less reputable features of the cult. Hence it is that in Athens, for example, Aphrodite Pandemos (' of all the folk ') is a quiet and staid marriage-goddess, in whose worship nothing objectionable seems to have taken place. The statement so often found that Aphrodite Urania is celestial and Aphrodite Pandemos vulgar or mercenary love is merely a pretty conceit of Plato.[98] Not dissimilar is the compromise which takes place in mythology ; Aphrodite is a wife, but far from a model one. Her husband is another noteworthy Oriental, the fire-god Hephaistos. But as she is not infrequently connected in cult with Ares, we get as early as Homer (if indeed the passage is not interpolated by a later hand) the story of her love for the war-god.[99] Hephaistos soon learned of the intrigue, for Helios, who sees everything, warned him. Not daring to meet Ares on equal terms, he contrived a subtle net of invisible but very strong meshes, which fell upon the guilty couple and caught them ; whereupon Hephaistos called in all the other gods to see the sight. At first he was very angry, and talked of a divorce and of reclaim-ing the bride-price he had paid Zeus for his erring daughter ; but

Poseidon managed to get him pacified and went surety for Ares' payment of the damages due to Hephaistos. So all was smoothed over, and Aphrodite continued to live more or less peaceably with her injured husband. The tale is very obviously not meant to be taken seriously ; indeed, Hephaistos is not a very serious figure in mythology, as will be seen later.

As in mythology, so in art, Aphrodite wavers between several types. Her Oriental figures, as the archaic idols found in Cyprus, are naked and hideous things, with their sex emphasized in a way which would be obscene if it were not so innocently frank ; the early Greek statues show a draped figure, having a certain stiff dignity, such as would be not inappropriate to Aphrodite Pandemos ; the later ones are for the most part nude or nearly so, and vary with the skill of the artist from meritorious studies of the body of a healthy and well-proportioned woman to monuments of that divine beauty which no one has ever again seen quite so clearly as the best of the Greeks.

The Romans, who had no love-goddess of any sort, identified Aphrodite with an Italian deity, Venus (the name means practically the same as Charis) who seems to have been the power who made tilled ground and especially gardens look trim and neat (*uenus'os*), as they do when flourishing. The Greek deity, coming in from Sicily, where her cult on Mt. Eryx was famous, thrust this puny native wholly into the background, and stamped her own cult, in its more respectable form, on Rome. The Julian *gens* were active in introducing the new worship, whence ultimately their claim to be descended from her through Aineias.[100] See p. 340B.

NOTES ON CHAPTER V

[1] See in general for Hera, Farnell, *C.G.S.*, I, p. 179 foll. ; Preller-Robert, I, p. 160 foll. ; H. Graillot, art. Hieros Gamos and J. A. Hild, art. Junon, in Daremberg-Saglio ; Roscher, *Iuno und Hera*, also his art. Hera in the *Lexikon* ; and Eitrem, *s.u.* Hera, in Pauly-Wissowa.

[2] For further criticism, see Farnell, *loc. cit.*

[3] See below, p. 105. *Cf.* Farnell, *Class. Quart.*, IV (1910), p. 186 ; *Higher Aspects of Greek Religion*, p. 44 ; Rose, *P.C.G.*, 82.

[4] *Iliad*, XIV, 346 foll.

[5] Plutarch, *de Daedalis Plataeensibus* (*ap.* Eusebios, *praep. euang.*, III, 1 foll.), 3 (Plut., Vol. VII, p. 44, Bernardakis).

[6] Plut., *ibid.*, 6 ; Paus., IX, 3, 1 foll. For the latest discussion of these rites, see Nilsson in *Journ. Hellen. Stud.*, XLIII (1923), p. 144 foll., where some of the earlier literature is referred to.

[7] See Soph., frag. 437 Pearson (schol. Aristoph., *Pax* 1126) ; Steph. Byzant., *s.u.*

[8] Diod. Sic., V, 72, 4.

⁹ *Iliad*, XIV, 294–6, with the scholiast there ; Varro, *ap.* Lactantius, *instit. diuin.*, I, 17 ; August., *C.D.*, VI, 7 (Vol. VII, p. 154 E, Benedictine ed.) ; Menodotos of Samos *ap.* Athen., XV, 672 A foll. That the rite (known as the Tonaia) described in the last passage had to do with a marriage ceremony is asserted by Fehrle, *Kultische Keuschheit*, pp. 142, 173, and denied by Eitrem, *op. cit.*, 393, 53, who however gives abundant instances of other rites of Hera which certainly did have this meaning.

¹⁰ Kallimachos, frag. 75, 1 foll. Pfeiffer ; see the editor's notes for parallels and comments, and cf. Argenti-Rose, *Folklore of Chios* (Cambridge 1949), p. 331.

¹¹ Pausanias, II, 38, 2, which also mentions certain secret rites of Hera at Argos, a somewhat exceptional thing in her cult. Argos, of course, also claimed to be the goddess' birthplace, Strabo, IX, 2, 36.

¹² Paus., II, 36, 2 (Zeus worshipped there under the title of Kokkygios, He of the Cuckoo) ; Aristotle *ap.* schol. Theokr., XV, 64 (the story as told in the text). See further, Hild, *op. cit.*, p. 671 *a*.

¹³ *Cf.* note 3. In Homer (*Iliad*, XIV, 303) it is Okeanos and Tethys who brought up Hera.

¹⁴ Hera called Eileithyia, see Farnell, *C.G.S.*, I, pp. 247 and 250 (notes 28c and 39) ; the Eileithyiai daughters of Hera, *Iliad*, XI, 270 ; Eileithyia mentioned without reference to Hera, *Iliad*, XVI, 187 ; *Odyssey*, XIX, 188.

¹⁵ *Iliad*, I, 567, 587 ; XV, 18 foll. *Cf.* Plautus, *Asinaria*, 303–4.

¹⁶ See Preller-Robert, I, p. 166 foll., and references there.

¹⁷ *Kypria*, frags. 1, 3, 4, 5 Allen ; Proculus, *Chrestomathia*, I, epitome of *Kypria* (*Homeri Opera*, T.V., p. 102 Allen). These remains are supplemented by the following, which probably draw upon the *Kypria*, directly or otherwise : Euripides, *Androm.*, 274 foll. ; *Troad.*, 919 foll. ; *cf. Helen*, 23 foll., *Hec.*, 644 foll., *Iph. in Aul.*, 180 foll. ; Isokrates, X, 41. Further particulars are given by Türk in Roscher, III, 1587. The episode of Eris and the apple is found only in late authors, Hyginus, *fab.*, 92 (which mentions that Eris was not asked to the banquet, and threw in her apple from the door) ; Lucian, *dial. marin.*, 5 ; Sallustius, *de dis et mundo*, 4, p. 6, 11 foll. Nock ; and some others. But I do not think (with von Sybel in Roscher, I, 1338, 58) that it is Alexandrian or later ; rather does this good folktale theme (see Chapter X, p. 293) appear likely to be really old.

¹⁸ I am quite unconvinced by the ingenuities of Miss Harrison, *Prolegomena*, p. 292, but thank her for pointing out, *ibid.*, p. 298, the quasi-identity of the goddesses and their gifts.

¹⁹ There were plenty of Greek sayings on this theme, for instance the famous skolion (*scolia anonyma*, 8 Diehl) gives health, beauty, wealth honestly won, and good company as the four best, in that order ; Theognis, I, 255, gives justice, health, attainment of desire as respectively the noblest, best and pleasantest of things. For the particular ' bests ' from which Paris had to choose, *cf.* Solon, frag. 23, 5 Diehl (absolute power) ; Euripides, *Bacch.*, 877, 897 (victory) ; Mimnermos, frag. 1, 1 Diehl, and indeed the erotic poets generally (love or beauty).

²⁰ *Iliad*, XXIV, 28–30. See Rose in *Humanitas*, III (Coimbra 1950–1) pp. 281–5.

²¹ For instance, in Propertius, II, 2, 13, and cf. Chapter IV, note 36.

²² See Nilsson, *Hist. Gr. Rel.*, p. 26 ; *M.M.R.²*, p. 487 foll. ; *GgR*, I², p. 346 foll. In general, see Farnell, *C.G.S.*, I, p. 258 foll. ; Preller-Robert, I, p. 184 foll. ; also the article ATHENA in the various classical dictionaries.

[23] *E.g.* the pagans cited by S. Augustine, *contra Faustum*, XX, 9 (338 A, *edit. Bened.*). (*Cf.* M3, 10, 7, *Minerua id est sapientia.*) Varro (*ap.* Aug., C.D., VII, 28) identified her with the Platonic Forms or Ideas.

[24] For Minerva, see Wissowa, *R.K.R.*, p. 252 foll.

[25] To the reference given in Chapter IV, note 35, which is the earliest mention of this tale, add especially ' Homer ', *hymn.* 28 ; Pindar, *Olymp.*, VII, 35 foll., with the scholiast, who gives, as other claimants for the honour of having split Zeus' head, Palamaon (an insignificant daimon connected with Hephaistos, see Roscher *s.u.*), Hermes, and Prometheus. Later references are numerous ; Pindar is the first surviving author to mention the splitting of the head ; whether the famous Parthenon pediment representing the Birth shows Hephaistos or Prometheus present is doubtful, see L. Malten in Pauly-Wissowa, VIII, 313, 43. The account in the text is put together out of ' Homer ' and Pindar. Cf. also Apollod., I, 20.

[26] Preller-Robert, I, p. 186 foll.

[27] γλαυκῶπις is her epithet in Homer, and is most naturally taken as meaning ' grey-eyed ', as the ancients interpreted it, or else ' bright-eyed '. It is true that it can also mean ' owl-faced ', for a kind of owl, sacred to Athena and now called *Athene noctua*, is termed γλαῦξ. But anything like definite evidence is wanting that the goddess was ever conceived as having owl-shape, although the assertion is often and confidently made. See below, p. 177. It seems more natural to suppose, if the word really means ' grey ', that the goddess' eyes and the bird were both so called from their colour ; if, on the other hand, it means ' bright ' (see Liddell and Scott⁹, *s.u.*), that this common characteristic led to the name and the epithet ; certainly ' bright-eyed ' would be a very natural adjective to use of so vigorous a deity, and of any owl.

[28] φίλην γλαυκώπιδα, *Iliad*, VIII, 373.

[29] Hdt., VIII, 55 ; for Erechtheus, cf. also Chapter IV, note 134.

[30] See for the story of Erichthonios, pseudo-Eratosthenes, *cataster.*, 13 ; Hyginus, *astron.*, II, 13 ; schol. on German. *Arat.*, p. 73, 6, all drawing upon Euripides, frag. 925 N² ; Eurip., *Ion*, 20 foll., 268 foll., 1427–9 ; Amelesagoras cited by Antigonos of Karystos, *histor. mirab.*, 12 ; Ovid, *Metam.*, II, 755 foll. ; Apollod., III, 188 foll. The later authorities are schol. Plat., *Tim.*, 23 D ; *S.G.*, III, 113 ; Hygin., *fab.*, 166. Apollod. mentions that according to some, the guardian serpent killed the daughters of Kekrops. For modern discussions, see, besides the authorities cited in note 22, Harrison, *Proleg.*, p. 287, and Sittig in Pauly-Wissowa, art. HERSE. The name Erichthonios means probably ' good earth ', or the like ; he is clearly an old power of the fertility of the soil, hence his parentage and his association with serpents.

[31] Harpokration *s.u.* αὐτόχθονες, citing Pindar (frag. 268 Bowra) and the author of the *Danais*, an obscure Cyclic epic.

[32] Paus., V, 3, 2. I neglect, as obviously the product of late theological speculation, based on the legend of Erichthonios in part, the story given by Cicero, *de nat. deor.*, III, 55, cf. Iohann. Lydus, *de mens.*, IV, p. 135, 7 Wuensch, that Hephaistos became by Athena the father of Apollo (*sic*) ; it is necessary only to read the context to see how utterly divorced this rubbish is from any real mythology.

[33] E. Fehrle, *Die kultische Keuschheit*, p. 176 foll. ; E. Kalinka, in ἐπιτύμβιον *Heinrich Swoboda dargebracht* (Reichenberg, 1927), p. 116.

[34] Ovid, *Metam.*, IV, 798. Fehrle (*op. cit.*, p. 192) observes also that in some forms of the story of Auge, who is pretty certainly a goddess of childbirth, she is more or less closely connected with Athena.

[35] See Ovid., *Metam.*, II, 708 foll. ; Apollod., III, 181.

[36] Her protégé Erichthonios was a great charioteer, pseudo-Eratos., 13 ; in Arkadia she was supposed to have invented the four-horse chariot, Cic., *de nat. deor.*, III, 59. For the Bellerophon episode, see Pind., *Olymp.*, XIII, 64 foll. (cf. Rose, *P.C.G.*, p. 152). To this event was traced her title Hippeia (or Chalinitis, Pausan., II, 4, 5) at Corinth.

[37] Paus., II, 21, 3.

[38] Pind., *Pyth.*, XII, 6 foll.

[39] See Arist., *Pol.* 1341b3 ff. ; Apollod., I, 24 ; Paus, I, 24, 1 ; Ovid, *Metam.*, VI, 382 foll. ; *Fast.*, VI, 691 foll. ; Hygin., *fab.*, 165 ; MI, 90, 125 ; M2, 115, 116 ; M3, 10, 7. *Cf.* Jessen in Roscher, art. MARSYAS.

[40] Pausanias saw one such at Erythrai, VII, 5, 9 ; see further Furt-wängler in Roscher, I, 688. Another seated statue existed on the Akropolis at Athens, see Paus., I, 26, 4.

[41] See Ovid, *Metam.*, VI, 1 foll. More references (mostly very obscure) in Schirmer in Roscher, art. ARACHNE. Vergil knew the story in some form, see *Georg.*, IV, 246 ; Servius, *ad loc.*, seems to draw upon Ovid.

[42] See Apollod., III, 144–5 (an interpolation) ; Tzetzes on Lykophron, 355, which also gives a number of other explanations of the name, and looks as if it might be the source of the interpolation in Apollodoros. Cf. Roscher, *Lexikon*, art. PALLAS, -ADIS.

[43] See, besides the dictionaries, Preller-Robert, I, p. 296 foll. ; Farnell, *C.G.S.*, II, p. 425 foll. ; Nilsson, *GgR*, I², pp. 481–500. For the Ephesian Artemis, see C. Picard, *Ephèse et Claros*, Paris, 1922.

[44] See, for example, the *Kynegetika* of Xenophon, Arrian, and Grattius.

[45] For example, *Odyssey*, XI, 172.

[46] *Iliad*, XXI, 479 foll.

[47] *Ibid.*, 497 foll.

[48] Notably by the many-breasted form of the cult-statue. I can see no plausibility in the view of Sir Wm. Ramsay that this is meant to represent a queen-bee (see *Asianic Elements in Greek Civilization*, London, 1927, p. 82, for the latest assertion of the theory), for (*a*) I find no resemblance in the shape of the idol, as shown by the copies of it surviving in museums, to any insect ; (*b*) it seems most unlikely that the true sex of the queen-bee should have been known to the half-barbarous Ephesians of early times, seeing that Greek biologists consistently imagined it to be a male.

[49] I have briefly studied some aspects of this curious fact in *Class. Quart.*, XVIII (1924), p. 14 ; *Class. Philology*, XX (1925), p. 240.

[50] The name seems connected with ὄρτυξ, a quail, and is one of the titles of Artemis herself ; see Farnell, *op. cit.*, p. 433, for the suggestion that the goddess was anciently worshipped under that form, or at least in some way intimately connected with quails. Asteria, Leto's sister, took the form of a quail, Apollod., I, 21, and in that shape plunged into the sea to escape from Zeus' amorous pursuit ; she then became the floating island of Delos, Kallim., *hymn.*, IV, 36–8. For the various identifications of the place in ancient times, see Preller-Robeit, I, p. 297 ; Ephesos in particular claimed to be the original Ortygia. In *hymn. Homer.*, III, 16, Artemis is born in Ortygia, but Apollo in Delos.

[51] *Hymn. Homer.*, III, 47 foll. ; Delos itself is much afraid that Apollo will consider it too insignificant for his birthplace, *ibid.*, 66 foll. This poem is our earliest detailed account of the birth-legend.

[52] See especially Kallim., *hymn.*, IV (*ad Delum*) ; Apollod., I, 21 foll. ; Hygin., *fab.*, 53, 140 ; *cf.* Pindar, frags. 78–79 Bowra.

53 Apollod., I, 25–27. See further the arts. ORION, OINOPION, and SIDE in Roscher. As will be seen, the text of Apollodoros is none too certain at this point ; in speaking of the forge, some would introduce a mention of Hephaistos, as one important variant (' Eratosthenes ', *cataster.*, 32, who cites Hesiod as his authority) says that Orion visited Lemnos after being blinded, and that Hephaistos gave him a servant of his own, called Kedalion, to guide him. Sophokles seems to have written a play on this subject, frags. 305–310 N², 328–333 P., unless indeed this dealt with some other legend concerning K., now lost. Cf. Pindar, frag. 68 Bowra.

54 The chief authorities for this odd story are Ovid, *Fast.*, V, 495 foll. Nonnos, *Dionys.*, XIII, 96 foll. ; *SA* I, 535, and several other scholiasts, see for full references Küentzle in Roscher, III, 1036, 18 foll.

55 Pindar, frag. 239 Bowra, and scholiast on *Nem.*, II, 16 ; *Etym. Magnum*, p. 675, 36 ; schol. Apoll. Rhod., III, 225. More references in Küentzle, *op. cit.*, 1031, 41 foll.

56 They killed themselves as willing victims to appease the underworld powers in a time of plague or drought, and were in consequence worshipped after their death by the people of Orchomenos, Anton. Liber. 25, who draws upon Korinna and Nikandros. Ovid, *Met.*, XIII, 685 foll., says they lived in Thebes and that the gods caused two young men, the Korones, to spring from their ashes.

57 See Aratos, 634 foll., with the scholia of Konon. Usually the scorpion kills him in Crete, while he is hunting with Artemis, not molesting her, and is sent by Ge because Orion boasted that he would destroy every wild beast, see, *e.g.* [Erat.], *catast.*, 32.

58 Parthenios, 20. It does not appear whence Parthenios got this story, nor what, according to it, happened to Orion afterwards.

59 Solinus, II, 8 (p. 81, 16 Mommsen) ; cf. Hesychios *s.uu. Βριτόμαρτις, βριτύ*. See in general Rapp in Roscher, art. BRITOMARTIS.

60 Strabo, X, 4, 13.

61 Kallim., *hymn.*, III, 189 foll. ; Pausan., II, 30, 3 ; Anton. Lib., 40 ; pseudo-Verg., *Ciris*, 286 foll.

62 Ant. Lib., *loc. cit.*

63 Cf. Eitrem in *Λαογραφία*, Z' (1922), p. 127 foll.

64 Examples of this kind of thing in Frazer, *G.B.³*, II, p. 66 foll. With the same author's treatment of the legend of B., *op. cit.*, IV, p. 73, I am not in agreement.

65 Ovid, *Metam.*, II, 405 foll. ; *Fast.*, II, 155 foll.

66 Pseudo-Eratosthenes, *catast.*, 1, 2, 8, citing Hesiod. Cf. Eurip., *Hel.*, 375 foll.

67 This and several other variants are gathered by Apollod., III, 100–101.

68 Schol. on *Iliad*, XVIII, 487, who cites Kallimachos as his authority. Yet another tale (Apollod., *loc. cit.*) makes Zeus change K. into a bear ; a detail suggested, perhaps, by the stories of Philyra and of Io.

69 Istros, frag. 57 ; pseudo-Clement, *Recognitiones*, X, 21. For fuller refs. and analysis, see Franz in Roscher, art. KALLISTO.

70 Hellanikos, frag. 19a Jacoby ; Apollod., III, 116 ; pseudo-Eratosth., *catast.*, 23 ; Hygin., *fab.*, 155 ; pseudo-Clement, *Recog.*, X, 21 ; Paus., III, 18, 10. The episode of Taygete being changed into a hind is in *schol. recent.* Pind., *Ol.*, III, 53, where the text of Pindar and the older scholia say only that the golden-horned hind which Herakles had to catch was dedicated to Artemis by Taygete. There are some variants of the tale, late and not very interesting, in pseudo-Plut., *de fluuiis*, 17, 1 and 3. For more refs. see Höfer in Roscher, art. TAYGETE.

[71] 'Ιφιγένεια · ἡ "Αρτεμις, Hesych., cf. Paus., II, 35, 1. As the literal meaning of the name is ' mightily born ', *i.e.*, princely or royal, it clearly is a possible title for a great goddess and equally a very understandable name for a princess. See Farnell, *C.G.S.*, II, p. 452 foll., *Hero-Cults*, p. 55 foll.

[72] The leading ancient authorities are the *Kypria*, in Proklos' *Chrestomathia* (*Homeri Opera*, V, p. 104, Allen); Pind., *Pyth.*, XI, 23; Aesch., *Agam.*, 184 foll. (cf. Lucret., I, 84 foll.) ; Soph., *Elect.*, 563 foll. (here the cause of the delay is a calm, see Jebb's excellent note) ; and Euripides' two tragedies, *Iphig. in Aulide* and *Iphig. Taurica*. For full refs. see Stoll in Roscher, art. IPHIGENEIA.

[73] So most of the above-named authorities, together with Hyginus, *fab.*, 98. Euripides, however, gives (*Iph. Taur.*, 20 foll.) a variant which has all the ear-marks of a popular tale. Agamemnon had vowed to sacrifice to Artemis the fairest of the yield of a certain year ; in that year Iphigeneia was born, and the goddess claimed her. This is allied to *Home-Comer's Vow*, see Chapter X, p. 291.

[74] For these variants, see Anton. Liber., 27, and Tzetzes on Lykophron, 183, who cites sundry authorities for them.

[75] See the authorities in the above notes, especially Eurip., *Iph. Taur.*, and Hygin., *fab.*, 120.

[76] Chapter II, p. 23.

[77] Title or name of Artemis, Alexandros Aitolos fr. 4, 5 Powell ; Kallimachos, *hymn.*, III, 204, who certify the name for Ephesos and Crete respectively ; also some later authors. Companion, *e.g.*, Verg., *Aen.*, XI, 532, 836. See in general, Farnell, *C.G.S.*, II, p. 486 foll. ; Höfer in Roscher, *s.u.*

[78] Hdt., IV, 33, 3–35. He cites as his authority the very ancient hymns of Olen, which were sung at Delos. According to him, Hyperoche and Laodike came after the birth of the divine twins, to make a thankoffering to Eileithyia for Leto's delivery. For more variants, see the commentators *ad loc.*

[79] See Thucydides, I, 8, 1 ; III, 104, 1–2. Cf. Nilsson, *M.M.R.*[2], p. 611 foll.

[80] Apollod., I, 27.

[81] Kallim., *hymn.*, IV, 292. Opis and Hekaerge have in some late sources masculine parallels, Opis (the word may be of either gender) and Hekaergos, see Höfer, *op. cit.*, 928, 50 foll.

[82] See Wissowa, *R.K.R.*, p. 247 foll.

[83] Hesiod, *Theog.*, 411 foll., generally considered spurious, defended by Kern, 1926, p. 245. See further, besides the dictionaries, Farnell, *C.G.S.*, II, 501 foll. ; Preller-Robert, I, 321 foll. ; Nilsson, *GgR*, I[2], pp. 722–5.

[84] See Preller-Robert, pp. 322–3.

[85] See, for instance, Aristophanes, *Plut.*, 595, and schol. on 594.

[86] For an apparition of Hekate see the burlesque description in Lucian, *Philopseudes*, 22–24 (Hekate is 300 feet high and attended by dogs bigger than elephants), or the serious one in Apoll. Rhod., III, 1211 foll. For her invocation by magicians, see, *e.g.*, Theokritos, *Id.*, II, 12.

[87] See Vergil, *Aen.*, IV, 511, with the note of Servius. Sophron, *ap.* Schol. on Theokritos, II, 12, has a curious story which seems to be meant as an explanation of Hekate's various functions. Zeus and Hera had a daughter called Angelos (' Messenger ' ; this is, among other things, a title of Artemis ; of course the meaning ' angel ' is much later), who stole her mother's perfume. Hera pursued her to punish her, and she took

refuge in two impure places, one defiled by a birth, the other by a death. This secured her from further pursuit by any celestial deity, and so Hera gave up the chase and told the Kabeiroi to purify Angelos. For this purpose they took her to Acheron, and so she became an infernal goddess.

⁸⁸ Chapter II, p. 22. In general, besides the classical dictionaries, see Farnell, *C.G.S.*, II, p. 618 foll. ; Preller-Robert, I, 345 foll. Need it be said that some of these (not Farnell) try to identify her with the moon ? The latest attempt to make her name purely Greek is to be found in Kern, 1926, p. 206 (' die auf dem Schaume wandelnde ').

⁸⁹ For Eros, see especially the good and learned article of Friedländer in Roscher, *s.u.* For the story of Eros and Psyche, see Chapter X, p. 286. Add A. D. Nock in *Class. Rev.*, XXXVIII (1924), p. 152 ; C. T. Seltman in *Ann. Brit. School at Ath.*, XXVI, p. 88.

⁹⁰ Pausanias, I, 30, 1 ; a yet sillier version (not taken from Pausanias, as Seltman, *op. cit.*, p. 102, implies) in Suidas, *s.u. Μέλητος (a)*. Ovid, *Met.*, VII, 371 foll., who adds that Kyknos' mother Hyrie cried for his loss until she turned into a lake ; Ant. Lib., 12, who says that Thyrie, as he calls her, jumped into the lake, which was named after her.

⁹¹ Chapter II, p. 51.

⁹² See Stoll-Furtwängler in Roscher, art. CHARITEN. Charites as attendants, e.g., Hom., *Odyssey*, VIII, 364 (wash and anoint Aphrodite) ; as wives, besides the statement in the *Iliad* (XVIII, 362) that 'Charis' was wife of Hephaistos (probably no more than an allegory, Charm allied to Craftsmanship), and in Hesiod (*Theog.*, 949) that he was married to Aglaie, the youngest of the Charites, see *Il.*, XIV, 267, where Hera promises that Sleep shall marry Pasithea, one of the younger Charites ; as entertainers, Theognis 15 (they and the Muses sing at the wedding of Peleus and Thetis).

⁹³ See Rapp in Roscher, *s.u.* The reference to Hesiod is *Theog.*, 902.

⁹⁴ Ezekiel, 8, 14, *et ecce ibi mulieres sedebant plangentes Adonidem ;* the LXX (γυναῖκες . . . θρηνοῦσαι τὸν Θαμμούζ) and the A.V. keep the name as in the Hebrew text.

⁹⁵ The chief accounts of Adonis in ancient literature are Apollod., III, 182–185 ; Ovid, *Met.*, X, 298 foll. (this was no doubt the account Shakespeare used for *Venus and Adonis*, for he was a tolerable Latinist and knew his Ovid) ; Hyginus, *fab.*, 58 ; Bion, *epitaphium Adonidis*, and the anonymous εἰς νεκρὸν ῎Αδωνιν (Appendix, Nos. X and XI, in Wilamowitz-Moellendorf's *Bucolici Graeci*, Bib. Class. Oxon.) ; SdB X, 18 (which also gives an utterly different variant) ; SdA V, 72 ; Anton. Lib., 24. For modern discussion, see, besides the mythological dictionaries, Frazer, *Adonis Attis Osiris* (GB³, Vols. V and VI).

⁹⁶ Rites of Adonis, see, for instance, Plut., *Nikias*, 13 (date of event, 415 B.C.), Aristoph., *Lysistr.*, 388 foll. (refers to same event). Gardens of Adonis ('Αδώνιδος κῆποι) ; besides the paroimiographoi, see Hesychios and Suidas *s.u.*; Plato, *Phaedrus*, 276 B ; Theophrastos, *hist. plant.*, VI, 7, 3 ; *de causis plant.*, I, 12, 2.

⁹⁷ See *hymn. Homer.*, V (to Aphrodite) ; Apollod., III, 141 ; Verg., *Aen.*, II. 647, with the notes of Servius. *Cf.*, besides the articles in Roscher and Pauly-Wissowa, Rose in *Class. Quart.*, XVIII (1924), p. 11 foll. ; Cook, *Zeus*, I, pp. 394–5. See, on the other side, A. D. Nock in *Arch. f. Religionswissenschaft*, XXIII, p. 25 foll.

⁹⁸ For these rites, see Farnell, *loc. cit.* The reference to Plato is *Sympos.*, 180 D.

⁹⁹ *Odyssey*, VIII, 267 foll. ¹⁰⁰ Wissowa, *R.K.R.*, p. 288 foll.

CHAPTER VI

THE YOUNGER GODS

ἰὼ θεοὶ νεώτεροι, παλαιοὺς νόμους
καθιππάσασθε.
—AESCHYLUS, *Eumenides*, 778, 808.

Ah, ye younger gods, that have ridden rough-shod over ancient use !

THE deities of whom this chapter has to treat have all one feature in common, that mythology represents them as young, the sons of Zeus or of some other of the great gods already discussed. As a matter of fact, most if not all are demonstrably quite old, but they are generally imagined under the forms of young, or at least not old men, and some of them are, as it were, an embodiment of the new and progressive character of Greek civilization and thought.

APOLLO, whatever his origin, is in his developed form the most characteristically Greek of all the gods. He is also, from the picturesque beauty with which Hellenic art and literature surrounded him, perhaps the best known to-day, and it is a commonplace with those writers, such as Swinburne, who love to contrast Hellenism with Christianity, to draw a sharp anti-thesis between him and Christ. He has no Roman equivalent or parallel, although here and there in Italy, as elsewhere, he is identified with a local deity, such as the god worshipped on Mt. Soracte, and the somewhat obscure figures of Semo Sancus Dius Fidius and of Veiouis seem to have been influenced by him. He also, as already mentioned, is identified with the sun by many theorists; this was a popular doctrine among ancient theologians from the fifth century B.C. onwards, but has really nothing to recommend it, save the fact that they both are archers.[1] His developed type in art is well known ; his is the ideal male figure, which has reached its full growth, but still has all the suppleness and vigour of youth. He generally holds either a lyre or a bow. While all Greece worshipped him, and references to him are almost as numerous as those to Zeus himself, his most famous shrines in Greece proper were Delphoi on the mainland and the holy island of Delos ; in Asia Minor he had many shrines, the best known being Klaros, Branchidai and Patara.

In discussing his attributes and functions, it is well to start from his title Lykios, or Lykeios, which is admitted on all hands to be very ancient. The question is, whether it means ' Lykian ' or ' Wolf-god.' The former alternative is vigorously supported especially by Wilamowitz-Möllendorff, who points out that he is the son of Leto, who is identical with the Lykian goddess Lada ; that he is much worshipped in Asia Minor, including Lykia ; that he is commonly called Letoides, ' son of Leto,' suggesting the Lykian custom of mother-kin, or counting descent through the female side ; that in Homer he sides with the Trojans and against the Greeks.[2] These and other arguments have convinced several scholars, such as M. P. Nilsson ; but I cannot think them in the least cogent. The identity of Leto and Lada is not certain, and in any case, mythical parentage does not prove much ; the children of the Hellenic Zeus include the non-Hellenic Athena and Dionysos, and Hera of Argos is the mother of the Asianic Hephaistos. Worship in Asia Minor need mean no more than that the Ionian Greeks brought Apollo there, as they did Poseidon, and the occasional Oriental features in Apollo's cult, such as his connexion with the number seven, which Nilsson stresses (his birthday was the seventh of the month, for instance), cannot be proved to be very early. If he sides with the Trojans, that is no more than Ares does, who is certainly not from Asia Minor, and he is invoked on several occasions by Greeks, in a formula which bears every sign of being ancient, along with Athena and Zeus. The epithet Letoides proves nothing, for many of the sons of Zeus have such epithets ; Hermes, for example, and Dionysos are often spoken of as ' son of Maia ' and ' son of Semele '. On the other hand, we have positive facts of Apolline cult to indicate strongly that he came, not from the east, but from the north, notably the ancient route of the Hyperborean offerings, and the fact that the great procession of the Stepteria at Delphoi went northwards, not improbably following the route by which the first worshippers of the god came to that shrine, although in reverse direction.

The Hyperboreans, of whom all manner of fables are told, are nevertheless real enough to send actual and visible offerings to Delos, by a route passing through real country, in historical times, as described by Herodotos (IV, 33, where see the commentators). The name looks as if it meant ' beyond or north of the North Wind ', and so the ancients took it, and described how, far north, there dwelt a highly virtuous people who worshipped Apollo ; but the probability is, that they were a race or clan of some kind living on an ancient route (the amber trade-route ?) which led north from Western Greece, who reverenced, presumably, Apollo in one of his earlier forms. Their name has been ingeniously explained as meaning ' those who carry around or over ' in Macedonian or some allied tongue ; it is thus equivalent to the name Περφερέες by which certain traditional guardians of the offerings and their bearers were called.

We must therefore fall back on the meaning ' wolf-god ', which the ancients themselves gave to the epithet, although we need not suppose some of them right in taking it to mean simply ' slayer of wolves '. Rather may we suppose that, to begin with, Apollo (' destroyer and healer ' then as in later times) was a deity worshipped by herdsmen, as being very potent either to bring down the dreaded wolves upon their flocks or to keep them away ; in this respect he was not unlike that picturesque figure of Slavonic folklore, the Shepherd of Wolves.[3] This accords well enough with the epithet Nomios (He of the pastures), and with the attribute of the bow, a very likely weapon to use against wolves and other wild beasts ; nor does it clash with his repute as a god of healing, for the shepherd is also the physician of his flock. Nor need it surprise us that he is a musician ; shepherds who play and sing are no creation of the fancy of pastoral poets, but plain fact, in antiquity and to-day, all over the classical area.

As to Apollo's prophetic gifts, it is noteworthy that his methods are not unlike those of the spirits who inspire a Siberian shaman ; he possesses his prophets and speaks through their mouths.

Altogether, since his name apparently is not Greek, or at least, no reasonably certain Greek etymology has yet been found for it, we may suppose that the invaders, on their way into Greece, found and adopted him, no one can say where or when, but certainly before they reached Greece proper ; and we may also not improbably suppose that, once in Greece, they identified the god they had made their own with local deities of somewhat similar character.

Be Apollo's development in early times what it may, when we find him in Greek authors, from Homer down, he is a very definite and glorious figure. He is the patron of medicine, of music, particularly that of the lyre, and of archery ; he never quite loses his connexion with flocks and herds ; and he is the true and unerring prophet, who knows the will of his father Zeus and reveals it to mankind. His prophecies are, almost without exception, on the side of that advanced morality which he championed in defending Orestes against the Erinyes. Of his birth we have already heard, in dealing with Artemis. Like the wonder-child he was, he began his adventures immediately, and his first act, or nearly so, was to take vengeance upon Python. According to sundry versions of this tale, Apollo himself, on going to Pytho (Delphoi), his future abode, found his way barred by a formidable dragon (a female and nameless in the earliest account), which he slew with his arrows. Another version of the story names this creature Python, and yet another says that it persecuted Leto before the birth of her children, which it tried to prevent. As the constant and perfectly credible tradition of Delphoi represents the place as having formerly been an oracle of Earth, and as the serpent is a chthonian animal, we may connect this slaying with the taking over of the shrine.[4]   Certainly Python is closely interwoven with the traditions and ritual of the place in historical times.   For example, the ritual of the great festival held every eight years and known as Stepteria included a curious pantomime in which a lightly constructed house was burned down.   This was called the ' palace of Python '.   Then a handsome and well-born young Delphian, obviously personating the god, if not originally incarnating him, made a show of going into exile, and did actually go, with attendants and much ceremony, a long journey by the sacred Pythian Way through Thessaly to the Vale of Tempe, where he was purified and whence he returned crowned with laurel, Apollo's own plant and a great purger of magical ills. Whatever all this curious ritual may really mean, there is no doubt that the ancients connected it with the slaying of Python, who according to some had fled northwards sore wounded and pursued by the young god, whereas the greater part were of opinion that Apollo, like any other slayer, was obliged to go into at least temporary exile and be purified.[5]   At the great Pythian games, one of the leading ' events ' was a contest in flute-playing.   The subject was a descriptive piece, intended to represent the combat between the god and the monster.[6]

The other great features of Delphoi, besides scores of less note, were the omphalos and the tripod.   The former means here ' central point ', and it was thought for a while that the holy thing itself had been recovered by the French excavators, or at all events an ancient model or representation of it.[7]   More thorough examination of the object (a block of wrought stone with an iron knife-blade sticking in it) has, however, put it quite beyond doubt that it is nothing of the kind, and especially that the blade is that of a modern knife and certain letters on the stone spell the name of a modern Greek.   But that it did exist and was supposed to mark the middle point of the earth's surface is abundantly attested.   And this accords well enough with the tradition that the shrine originally belonged to Earth, for where would she give oracles more appropriately than at her own centre ?   See for further details Bousquet in *Bulletin de Correspondence hellénique*, Vol. LXXV (1951), pp. 210–23.   For anything we know to the contrary, the shrine may once have belonged to a Minoan-Mycenaean goddess, later identified by the Greeks with their own Ge.   The ancient belief concerning this most venerable monument we have in the words of one of the most famous of Apollo's priests, Plutarch, who says that two eagles were sent, one from each extremity of the earth, and met at that very spot. Some said, however, that they were not eagles (the birds of Zeus) but swans or ravens (Apollo's birds). In art, we have numerous representations of the omphalos, often with the eagles on it, and it is referred to again and again as the seat of Apollo. Occasionally we find Python coiled around it.

The tripod was still more the seat of prophecy, if possible. On it sat the Pythia, or prophetess who gave the oracles.[8] Apparently the idea was that, her body being thus lifted clear of the ground, the holy influence of the god could come beneath and enter her; a semi-rationalizing tale stated that a certain vapour came out of a cleft in the ground and passed into her. The Pythia was originally, it is said, a young virgin; but an impious wretch having violated her, it was decided that in future only old women should be employed.

Not infrequently since classical times the Pythia has been confused with another figure, the Sibyl, with whom she has in reality nothing whatever to do.[9] The oldest form of the tale seems to be simply, that there was a woman named Sibylla, a native of the village of Marpessos in the territory of Troy, although the more important town of Erythrai tried to claim her as its own, and there was much controversy on the subject in antiquity. This Sibylla won the favour of Apollo, to whose service she was much devoted, and he inspired her to give marvellous and infallible, if rather riddling, prophecies. The meaning of her name, which is probably Oriental, is quite obscure. These oracles, of which an ever-increasing number was in circulation, were very popular. They were extant in many places, and consequently many towns claimed to be the birthplace of their author; in the end, as Sibylla was taken to be a common noun, a whole series of Sibyls sprang up, some with personal names, such as Herophile or Phyto; there were, besides the original Marpessian, Phrygian, Erythraian or Hellespontine Sibyl, the Delphic (a sister of Ápollo, by some accounts) and the Sibyl of Sardes, according to one of the briefest lists, while finally we get what may be described as the orthodox list of Varro, which gives ten—the Persian, the Libyan, the Delphian, the Kimmerian (who, being located in Italy, seems to be the same as the Cumaean), the Erythraian (Herophile), the Samian (Phemonoe), the Cumaean (Amalthaia, the authoress of the celebrated Sibylline oracles of Rome), the Hellespontine (i.e., the Erythraian or Marpessian over again), the Phrygian (again the Marpessian), and finally the Tiburtine (the result of an attempt to find a Greek equivalent for the local goddess

Albunea ; hence the name 'Sibyl's Temple' quite unjustifiably
given to one of the most famous ruins in Tivoli).   To this must
be added the Jewish or Babylonian Sibyl, usually identified
with the Marpessian-Erythraian, who is in some ways the most
famous of all, since the collection of Sibylline oracles which we
have,—obviously late forgeries, containing Jewish and Christian
propaganda disguised as ancient revelations,—are in her name.
Behind all these shadowy figures lurk, in all probability, a certain
number of real women.   The centuries intervening between the
Dorian invasion and the rise of the full classical civilization were
a time of great religious upheavals.   From them survive several
names, not only of prophetesses like Sibylla, but also of prophets,
such as Bakis, whose oracles were very popular during the
Peloponnesian War, and Epimenides of Crete.   No doubt many
of these persons never existed ; but we may reasonably suppose
that many of them did, and had in some cases a more than local
reputation.

There is no reason why we should suppose either the Sibyl or the
Delphic prophetess to have been frauds.   The modern interest in
spiritism has made everyone familiar with the fact that certain persons
can, voluntarily or otherwise, pass into an abnormal condition in
which they speak, or even write, more or less intelligibly, without
being conscious of it at the time, or remembering it afterwards.
Apollo, like many African deities who speak through prophets or
'mediums', no doubt found many of these abnormal persons to serve
him in all sincerity.   What the inquirer at Delphoi or one of the other
shrines took away with him was not the actual words of the seer,
but an edited official record, generally in indifferent hexameters,
couched for the most part in very riddling and obscure language, so
that if the apparent sense of the prophecy proved false, the god could
always take refuge behind another interpretation.[10]

Another early adventure of Apollo was the slaying of Tityos,
who tried to violate Leto.   Tityos' punishment in Hades has
already been described.[11]

A healer himself, Apollo was the father of the god of medicine,
ASKLEPIOS (the name was corrupted into Aesculapius on Latin
lips when, in 293 B.C., Rome imported the god to heal a stubborn
pestilence).   On the subject of this deity's original nature a
controversy rages.   No one doubts that he was worshipped in
historical times as a god ; the question is whether he was originally god or hero.   Fortunately this delicate point need not be
decided in order to tell his legend.   Apollo loved Koronis,
daughter of Phlegyas ; but she played him false with a mortal
lover, one Ischys of Arkadia.   Apollo was warned of her perfidy

by his faithful messenger the crow (Pindar characteristically omits this and makes him know by his own divine omniscience). He therefore sent Artemis to take vengeance on her, or (in Ovid's version) himself shot down the culprit. But his love for Koronis overcame him when it was too late ; he turned the crow, which had hitherto had white plumage, into the black bird it still is, and, seeing that he could not bring Koronis to life again, tried at least to save her unborn child. In this he was successful, and the infant was handed over to the care of Cheiron the good Centaur. Under his able tuition he learned medicine, and soon brought the art to the very highest state of perfection. By his wife (variously named Epione, Xanthe, etc., in various authors [12]) he had a curiously mixed family, corresponding to his own mixed nature as a deified hero, or heroized god. Homer knows of two sons, Podaleirios and Machaon, sturdy epic heroes with nothing hieratic about them, who took part in the campaign against Troy, and, having inherited their father's skill in some measure, were invaluable as surgeons. Alongside these come several pale and shadowy figures, with no legends, or none of any account. Such are Hygieia (Health), Iaso (Healing), Panakeia (Cure-all), Asklepios' daughters, and a child-deity, Telesphoros (Accomplisher) who was worshipped along with him.

But Asklepios' zeal for healing all manner of ailments carried him too far. When Hippolytos died, Artemis besought him to restore her favourite to life. [13] When to her persuasions was added the cogent argument of a huge fee, he exerted his skill to the utmost, and succeeded brilliantly. This interference with the established order of nature was too much, however, for Zeus, who promptly dispatched Asklepios to the lower world with a thunderbolt.

Apollo was furious at the death of his son, but did not dare attempt vengeance on his mighty father. He therefore consoled himself by killing the Kyklopes who had made the thunderbolt. Having thus become guilty of bloodshed within his own divine clan, he suffered the usual penalty, according to Greek law, namely banishment for a year to be the serf of a mortal man. His sentence was made as easy as might be by putting him under the rule of a man eminently just and kindly, Admetos king of Pherai. His cattle throve and increased prodigiously, and he did not omit to show his gratitude and respect towards his mysterious thrall. Apollo was grateful, and sought to do Admetos further service. On inquiry of the Moirai, he discovered that his temporary master had but a short time to live ; but he so far softened their hearts with wine that they consented to allow Admetos a longer life if he could induce anyone to die in his stead. On hearing how matters stood, Admetos sought a substitute. All, even his father and mother, refused, save his wife Alkestis. The fatal day arrived, and Alkestis died. Admetos, however cowardly his conduct may appear to us, and indeed to the best-known teller of the tale in antiquity, Euripides, was probably quite justified, in the opinion of those among whom the legend first took form, by the immensely greater value of a man as compared to a woman ; the idea of the equality of the sexes (which, like most modern ideas, is classical Greek) had not yet been developed. He now went on to add to his blameless conduct a deed of outstanding devotion to a sacred duty. In the very beginning of his mourning for Alkestis, he received a visit from Herakles, on his way to win the mares of the Thracian Diomedes. The claims of hospitality could not be ignored ; pretending that no member of his family was dead, but only a sojourner under his roof, he welcomed the hero and bade the servants see to his comfort. Herakles, however, found out the real state of affairs, and took measures to put matters to rights. According to popular belief, Thanatos, the death-daimon, literally carried off the dead, much as Charos is represented as doing in modern Greek folklore. Going to the tomb, Herakles awaited the coming of this messenger from the lower world, and when once he came, set upon him and compelled him to let go his prey. Alkestis was thus revived, and brought back safely to her home. The story shows in every detail, with its somewhat primitive morals, its Moirai who can be made drunk, and its Death who is so solid and material that a valiant man can overcome him by sheer force of muscle, that it is the offspring of popular fancy, in fact a folktale.[14]

Apollo was generally more or less unhappy in his loves. According to a pretty, if not very early tale, his sacred plant, the laurel ($\delta\alpha\varphi\nu\dot{\eta}$), was once a girl whom he wooed. She was daughter of a river, Ladon in Arkadia or Peneios in Thessaly, or of Amyklas, the son of Lake-daimon and Sparte, two very unsubstantial worthies after whom the district and the city were said to be named. A true follower of Artemis, she wanted no lovers, but soon found one in Leukippos, son of Oinomaos king of Pisa, who disguised himself as a girl to be near her. Apollo, who was jealous, put it into Daphne's mind to bathe with her companions ; Leukippos was thus found out and killed by the virgin huntresses. But his own addresses were equally unwelcome ; Daphne fled from him, and finding that he was over-taking her, prayed Zeus, or Earth (her mother, in some accounts), or Peneios to rescue her ; she thereupon was changed into a laurel.[15]

A very old tale of the rivalry of Apollo and a mortal has in

later accounts a rather pretty and romantic development.
Euenos, son of Ares by a mortal woman, had a daughter Marpessa,
of whom Homer knows that she married Idas and Apollo carried
her off, and that Idas, ' the mightiest of men that in those days
were ', bent his bow against the god himself. How much more of
the legend Homer knew, we cannot say ; but later authors tell
it more or less as follows. Marpessa was carried off by Idas,
hotly pursued by Euenos. Poseidon, however, had given Idas a
winged team, and although Euenos drove after them until he
reached the river Lykormas, he then, in despair, killed his horses
and drowned himself ; the river was ever afterwards called
Euenos in memory of him. Idas went to Messene, and Apollo,
who all the while had been a suitor for Marpessa's hand, now
carried her off in his turn. God and mortal fought for their
bride, but Zeus intervened and bade her choose between them.
She preferred Idas, because Apollo was immortal and might leave
her when she grew old.[16]

Apollo would not have been a Greek if his affections had not
turned towards beautiful boys ; the most celebrated of these was
Hyakinthos of Amyklai near Sparta, who was also loved by
Zephyros (the West Wind). Hyakinthos preferred Apollo, and
Zephyros took his revenge by blowing suddenly just as Apollo,
at play with his favourite, hurled a diskos. This, caught in the
gust, struck Hyakinthos on the head and killed him. This at
least is the fullest account ; the earliest narratives say nothing
about the jealousy of Zephyros, and lay the blame of the death on
mere accident, wind or the rebound of the diskos from a rock.
Apollo was bitterly grieved, and according to what appears to
have been the local saga contrived that the boy should be deified.
According to some versions, a flower marked with the letters
AI AI (alas, alas) sprang from Hyakinthos' blood and bore his
name.[17]

It so happens that we know something of the real facts from
the descriptions of the festival supposed to commemorate this
event, the Hyakinthia, and from the name of Hyakinthos himself.
The latter is certainly pre-Hellenic, having the characteristic
suffix,—*nth*—, of the language, whatever it was, which the earliest
inhabitants of the peninsula spoke. Moreover, we know that the
cult-statue of Hyakinthos was not that of a handsome boy but of a
bearded man,[18] and that the festival itself was very obviously a
ceremonial in honour of a vegetation-deity. Apollo, who is to
some extent connected with agriculture, clearly had absorbed this
older god on his arrival at Amyklai with the first Greek settlers ;
the rest of the story is aetiology and pretty fancy.

Yet another ill-fated passion of Apollo was for Kassandra (or Alexandra), daughter of Priam of Troy.[19] On her he showered his favours, including the gift of prophecy; but in the end she would not yield to him. Now no god can recall his gifts; but Apollo took measures to render her powers a curse rather than a blessing, for while she always foretold truly, this doom was on her and her people, that she should never be believed. Hence her warnings against the dangers threatening Troy fell on deaf ears. What, if anything, lies behind this sombre figure, one of the most impressive in all Greek legend, it is impossible to say; quite conceivably Kassandra was a real woman, a Trojan lady of high rank, who was, as the modern jargon has it, ' mediumistic ', and of whose strange powers a tradition remained to later ages. Besides her prophecies, the following events make up her career. At the time of the fall of Troy she was unmarried. Taking refuge in the temple of Athena in Ilion, she was dragged from the image of the goddess and violated by Aias the Lokrian. For this sacrilege his people, the Lokrians of Opus, were obliged yearly to send certain virgins of their noblest families (the Hundred Houses) as temple-servants to Athena. If they were caught on the way to the temple by the people of Ilion, they were put to death; if they reached it, they performed the duties of the meanest slaves, apparently for life. This is no piece of mythology but historical fact, for we have both literary and inscriptional evidence of the sending of these unfortunate girls to Ilion, and the term of the penance, a thousand years, expired somewhere near the beginning of the Christian era.[20] Noble families do not behave in this manner for a mere phantom of the imagination, and the only reasonable conclusion is that Aias' crime is a fact, whence it is not improbable that the name and rank of his victim have been correctly remembered. The story goes on to say that Kassandra was assigned to Agamemnon as his share of the booty, and was murdered with him by Klytaimestra.

The rather late story of Apollo and the Cumaean Sibyl appears to be partly modelled on the legend of Kassandra. According to Ovid, he would have made her immortal if she would have yielded to him. As it was, he bade her choose whatever she liked, and she asked to live as many years as she held grains of dust in her hand. Too late, she realized that she had not asked to continue young, and, as she still would not grant the god her favours, she gradually shrivelled up till, towards the end of her life of a thousand years (the number of the grains of dust), she was, according to the popular account, reduced to a tiny thing which was hung up in a bottle and could only answer the children who asked ' Sibyl, what do you want ? ' with the words ' I want to die '.[21]

More fortunate was Apollo's love for Kyrene, daughter of Hypseus, the son of the river Peneios, and a Naiad, Kreusa daughter of Earth. Kyrene was a huntress, a sort of local Artemis, and when Apollo first saw her she was wrestling, single-handed and unarmed, with a lion. His admiration for her courage turned to passionate love, and snatching her up, he carried her in a golden chariot from Mt. Pelion to that district in Africa which still bears her name.[22] There she became the mother of ARISTAIOS, a rustic deity, the inventor of various country labours and pastimes, such as bee-keeping, olive-growing, and hunting or some kinds of hunting. He is best known from a single episode ; he had a violent passion for Eurydike, wife of Orpheus, and pursued her ; in trying to escape from him she trod on a venomous serpent, from the bite of which she died. Her sister Dryads took revenge upon Aristaios by making all his bees die ; he then had recourse to his mother for advice. According to Vergil, she in turn referred him to Proteus, who, when Aristaios managed to catch him, explained the cause of the trouble. The Nymphs were consequently appeased, and a new swarm got from the decaying carcass of a bullock. This belief was apparently common, and not confined to the Greeks ; the fact lying behind it is the existence of a fly, *Eristalis tenax*, which lays its eggs in carrion, where they hatch out, and closely resembles a bee in outward appearance.[23]

A fervent lover, Apollo was not less vigorous in his hate, although it was by no means always on his own account that he exercised his terrible powers. His defence of his mother's honour against Tityos has already been described ; the case of Niobe was less to the credit of the divine trio concerned, but shows, by what is to our ideas (and those of the Greeks of the classical epoch) its injustice, a survival of the old principle of collective responsibility, the same which, in the case of the early Hebrews, for instance, caused the execution not only of Achan but of all his household. Niobe, daughter of Tantalos, had seven sons and seven daughters (or six of either sex, or ten). In an evil moment, she boasted that she was far superior to Leto, who had but two children. Thereupon Apollo and Artemis drew their bows, the former slaying the boys and the latter the girls. Niobe, thus bereft, wept over her dead children until she turned into a pillar of stone, from which the tears continued to flow, and in this shape she was shown to the curious in later times on Mt. Sipylos.[24]

Two famous musical contests are said to have taken place, one between Apollo and Pan, the other against Marsyas. The latter story has been briefly told in Chapter V (p. 111) ; the former runs as follows. Pan challenged Apollo to a contest. Tmolos, the deity of the mountain of that name, acted as judge, and the divine performers played in turn (the story is told prettily by Ovid,[25] grandly by Shelley). Tmolos decided in favour of Apollo ; Midas king of Phrygia dissented, whereat Apollo transformed his ears into those of an ass, as an appropriate punishment. The king was exceedingly ashamed, and contrived to wear his turban so as to cover the deformity. His barber, however, was perforce privy to the secret, and having the professional vice of garrulity, was ready to burst for lack of some one to confide it to. At last he dug a hole in the ground and whispered it into that. Unfortunately, reeds grew up from the spot, which every time the wind blew through them whispered audibly ' King Midas has asses' ears.' There is a variant according to which Midas was judge between Apollo and Marsyas and voted for the latter ; the sequel is the same.

Apollo is in art the ideal type of young manhood ; a similar figure in appearance, but younger and less muscular, is his half-brother HERMES. There the resemblance stops, for Apollo has perhaps a higher moral development than any other Greek god save Zeus himself, whereas Hermes remains largely non-moral. Yet their beginnings were not very dissimilar. Hermes seems to be native to Arkadia, where his birth took place and where he always was much worshipped ; his connexion with fertility and with all manner of beasts, and the fact that he is god of luck and can give wealth, honest or dishonest in its origin (he is god of traders and also of thieves), all suggest that he is, like Apollo Nomios, a deity whose influence extended over the traditional ancient form of wealth, flocks and herds and their increase. He likewise is connected with human fertility, and one of his oldest cult-monuments is simply the phallos, which remained a prominent feature of his cult. Occasionally he governs the fertility of the earth also. While not a fire-god, he is credited with having invented fire-making ; and as he is the servant and messenger of the greater gods, he even appears as a cook. But his principal character is that of the divine herald, in which capacity he is regularly represented as wearing the broad hat (*petasos*) with which Greek wayfarers kept the sun out of their eyes, and carrying a herald's staff (*kerykeion, caduceus*). All this is explicable enough if we suppose that he was and long continued to be the deity of a rather simple and backward folk, as we know the Arkadians were, but developed to the extent of having many functions, including the protection of travellers in wild and ill-policed country. He certainly was god of roads, and a very plausible etymology of his name Hermeias or Hermes is that which connects it with ἔρμα (rock, stone, ballast) ; for in ancient Greece, as in many other countries, piles of stone were common objects on a roadside, not to supply road-metal, but to mark holy spots, where a kindly or dangerous power dwelt. Hermes then is perhaps simply the Power in the Stone-heap ; but we must not forget the possibility that the Arkadians found him in Arkadia when they arrived there, and that his name is not Greek at all. Certain it is that he was very often worshipped under the form of a mere stone, and that his most characteristic monuments, the *hermai* or herms which bear his name, are not statues but square pillars, tapering a little towards the bottom, crowned with a human head, and having a phallos part-way up the front. If then he remained a somewhat backward god, we can understand why he holds no very high place among the Olympians, but is the younger son of the family, running errands for the rest and especially for his father Zeus.

But, perhaps for that very reason, he is no less dear to man than many of the greater deities. A friendly and rather an amorous god, he delights in the assemblies of men for all manner of purposes, and not least in their deliberations, for he is among his other functions god of eloquence, whether in prose or in verse. He also is a musician and patron of music. Also, he is the especial god of young men, and every gymnasium contained a herm. In those statues which show him in fully human shape, his body is that of a slim and graceful but nowise effeminate Greek *ephebos*, a youth of about seventeen or eighteen. It is thus that he appears in the marvellous statue by Praxiteles which forms the chief glory of the museum at Olympia.

Nor does his connexion with mankind cease at their death, for he is also Guide of Souls (Psychopompos). I need hardly repeat that a deity of fertility is apt to form connexions with the underworld ; in Hermes' case, the fact that he is a messenger perhaps had something to do with the idea ; he is the go-between who carries tidings from one of the divine brethren to another. It is apparently on account of his chthonian functions that he is identified with Kasmilos or Kadmilos, one of the Kabeiroi.[26] Even so, he never is a grim or formidable god, but rather courteous, popular and kindly, as befits a herald, whose person is everywhere sacred.

The legend of his birth is preserved in one of the ' Homeric ' Hymns (the fourth), which handles the subject with just that good-natured humour which befits it ; for few Greek gods mind a harmless joke or so, and certainly Hermes does not. ' At dawn he was born ', says this merry author, ' by noon he was playing on the lyre, and that evening he stole the cattle of Apollo Fardarter, on the fourth day from the beginning of the month, when lady Maia bare him.'[27] The details are here and there a little obscure, but the outlines are clear. Hermes, soon after he was born, left his cradle and walked out of the cave where his mother lived. At the entrance he met a tortoise, which he promptly seized and took inside the cave, where he killed it and converted its shell into the sounding-board of the first lyre that ever was made. After an extempore song, he turned to a new amusement. Making his way to Pieria,—a very tolerable walk for a baby,—he stole fifty cows from a herd belonging to Apollo, and drove them off, making them walk backwards and following them, also walking backwards, with a sort of improvised snowshoes of plaited twigs on his feet, to confuse the tracks still more. In passing, he gave a broad hint to an old vine-dresser not to inform against him, and so made his way to the Triphylian Pylos, where he slaughtered two of the cattle. Having cut them up in proper ritual fashion for a sacrifice, he finally returned to Kyllene, just before dawn, and tucked himself up in his cradle, the picture of baby innocence. Maia, with a proper regard for her maternal duties, did her best to scold him, but was assured that he was quite capable of taking care of himself. Next day Apollo, who had been put on the track by the old man, arrived in a great rage. Distrusting Hermes' bland assurance that he was too young even to know what the word ' cow ' meant, he haled him off to appear before Zeus. The latter listened to a speech of consummate impudence made by Hermes in his own defence, and ordered him to restore the cattle. Hermes, who at some point in the proceedings [28] had stolen Apollo's bow and quiver, thought it best to comply, and soon mollified his elder brother by producing the lyre. Apollo in return gave Hermes, or got for him from Zeus, the various powers which have already been mentioned, save eloquence and ingenuity in theft, which he had already, and also taught him a little elementary divination, a gift of which he made some use, for he here and there gives oracles in a small way, not trespassing on the Apolline monopoly. He likewise gave him his marvellous staff, which tends in literature (art distinguishes it better) to be, not simply a herald's badge of office, but a magician's wand.[29]

If we could imagine a miracle-play written by Congreve, it would surely have the tone of this hymn, with its witty handling of a non-moral popular legend. It is most typically Greek, for a Greek was apt to be very indulgent to a rogue, provided that he was a clever one. Greek, again, is the light and playful handling, not simply of Hermes himself, but of Apollo. No race, save perhaps the Hebrews, has ever thought more becomingly of the divine majesty and power than the Hellenes ; but no race has ever been less prone to grovel before any power, human or divine. There is no reason to suppose that the author of the Hymn did not believe in Hermes or was not willing to worship him most devoutly. In like manner, he probably treated the temporal powers of his day with proper respect on occasion. But he also saw both in clear sunshine, and required of both that they should not take umbrage at being chaffed. It is no wonder that Shelley, one of the most Greek of English poets, was so attracted by the Hymn as to make an excellent translation of it.

Other poets add a few details to the story, mostly concerning the old man who saw Hermes go by and afterwards gave information to Apollo, and the reason for Apollo leaving his cattle untended. Magnes, after whom Magnesia was named, the son of Argos (son of Phrixos) and Perimele daughter of Admetos, had a very handsome son, Hymenaios, whom Apollo so admired that he was never long away from Magnes' house. Hermes profited by the elder god's abstraction, and drugged the dogs who watched the herds. As he drove them away,—the story here differs from that of the Hymn in some few unimportant details,—he met near home with an old man known as Battos (Chatterbox), who agreed, in consideration of the gift of a cow, to hold his tongue. Mistrusting him, Hermes disguised himself and visited Battos again, with the offer of a reward for information. On this being accepted, he punished the old man's perfidy by turning him into a rock.[30]

An obscure tale represents Hermes as befooling Hera into becoming his foster-mother, and therefore obliged to treat him as her own son. This he accomplished by disguising himself as her own infant, Ares.[31]

Hermes' love affairs mostly concern mortal women ; but one which is rather famous is with Aphrodite herself. The two deities are not seldom associated in cult ; according to a story preserved to us in Ovid, they are the parents of a bi-sexual godling, a Greek adaptation probably of Oriental gods, who frequently combine the two sexes. Hermaphroditos, as he was called after his parents, was exceedingly handsome, and a fountain-nymph, Salmakis, fell violently in love with him. He would have none of her, but gave her an opportunity at last by bathing in her spring. She prayed that she might always be united to him, and her prayer was answered by the combination of lover and loved into a single person, a hermaphrodite, as we and the ancients call such monstrosities. But from the fourth century B.C. onwards, when the taste of Greek sculptors was beginning to degenerate, this ambiguous figure was in high favour, and numerous representations, many having a morbid beauty, survive. The spring Salmakis, which was at Halikarnassos, was supposed to enervate any man who bathed in it.[32]

According to some genealogies, Priapos also was a child of Hermes and Aphrodite ; see next chapter.

Another tale represents him as uniting with Artemis, Hekate, or Brimo, the last being an obscure goddess worshipped, or at least mentioned, at the Eleusinian Mysteries. As the authors from whom we hear this story are all liable to identify deities of related function with one another (syncretism, to use the technical term) it is hard to say whether this is a very old tale in which Artemis is not yet a virgin, an obscure local legend (Thessalian ? the scene of the amour is Lake Boibeïs) of some community worshipping Brimo, or one of the many tales of the union of two powers of fertility, which in this case has become attached to Hekate.[33]

The Italians identified Hermes with Mercurius, whose functions, since he was god of traders and their wares, *merces*, did really correspond to those of Hermes to some extent, if indeed he is not simply a Latin offshoot of the Greek god.[34]

In discussing DIONYSOS, we are dealing with a god indubitably foreign to Greece, although it is likely enough that on his arrival he found similar deities here and there waiting to be absorbed. He is still quite obscure in Homer, who however has heard something of his wild rites and of his conflict with Lykurgos of Thrace.[35] That he is himself a Thracian deity we are abundantly assured ; but we know that the Thracians and Phrygians were closely allied races, and by good luck we know the Phrygian form of the god's name, Diounsis. Concerning the meaning of the name, since Thrako-Phrygian was a Wiro speech and fairly near akin to Greek, we can say with reasonable confidence that the first member contains the name of the sky-god, who was called in Phrygian Dios. As to the rest we are not so sure. A connexion with the legendary Nysa has been suggested ; another and very ingenious theory is that there existed a word *nyso-*, akin to Latin *nurus*, Greek *νυός*, and that it meant ' child ' or ' son '. But this raises the difficulty of accounting for the Phrygian form, which seems to give rise to the Homeric *Διώνυσος*.[36] In any case, there is no doubt that his mother's name is good Phrygian, for Semele is nothing but a Greek modification of Zemelo, the Phrygian earth-goddess. However, in mythology Semele is one of the mortal daughters of a mortal father, Kadmos son of Agenor. Zeus loved her, and thereby excited the jealousy of Hera, who plotted her rival's destruction. Appearing to her in the form of an old woman, she congratulated her on the exalted rank of her lover, but advised him to put his love to a further test ; let him appear to her in all the splendour of his divinity, as if she were his lawful divine consort. Semele won Zeus to promise her any favour she liked, and asked for this one, which the god reluctantly granted. But her human frailty could not endure the terror of his Olympian glory, nor the blaze of his thunderbolts, and she was consumed by the lightning, to be rescued afterwards from the under-world by her son and made a goddess.[37] Her unborn child, deified already in some accounts by contact with the divine fire, was caught up from the ashes of his mother's body by Zeus, who thrust him into his own thigh, whence at the fulfilment of the time of gestation he was born. Clearly we have here a barbarian myth ; Greek legend does not lend itself to such grotesques, but a parallel can be found in North America, at the other end of that series of Asiatic peoples, Mongolian and other, of whom the Thracians of antiquity form the Western extremity.[38]

A title of Dionysos and the name of a hymn commonly sung in his honour was Dithyrambos. This by dint of bad etymology was pressed into alluding to the story just told ; it was explained as meaning ' he of the double door,' alluding to the child's two entrances into life. This is of course absurd, and most of the modern etymologies are not much better. The likeliest seems to be that from *dithrera*, a Phrygian name for a tomb, for we know that in Phrygia Diounsis is one of the deities who guard tombs against violators.[39]

Being thus born, Dionysos must needs be provided with a nurse. Indeed, the nurses of Dionysos are his constant companions in mythology, occurring in the very earliest mention, that in Homer, already referred to. Here certainly it is not at all unlikely that we are dealing, if not exactly with a Greek belief, at least with a Cretan survival ; for the infant ' Zeus ' of Crete was constantly associated with a nurse of some kind, human or bestial, and we have seen [40] that the infant Erichthonios was tended by the daughters of Kekrops. One of the best-known stories names but a single nurse, Ino sister of Semele, whose misfortunes are told by several writers. Unfortunately, no account has survived which is at once complete and early, and the versions which we have are apt to contradict each other. However, putting them together, with the continuous narratives of Ovid and Apollodoros [41] as framework, we arrive at the following story. Ino, at the time when she undertook the care of Dionysos, was married to Athamas. She had borne him two sons, Learchos and Melikertes. Hera sought for vengeance against her, as against all who had helped her latest rival ; she therefore drove both Ino and Athamas mad. The result is variously stated. In one version, apparently that followed by Euripides,[42] Ino rushed out of the house in a frenzy like that of the votaries of Dionysos, and remained away so long that Athamas thought her dead, and married Themisto, daughter of Hypseus, in her place. After some time, when he had had two children by his new wife, he discovered that Ino was not dead, but restored to sanity, and she was secretly or openly brought back. Themisto tried to kill her stepchildren, but their nurse (in one account, Ino herself in disguise) foiled her. Themisto's directions were that her own children were to be dressed in white, Ino's in black, so that they could be easily told apart (presumably, the murder was to take place at night). Ino reversed this, and thus Themisto killed her own children, and in horror at her deed committed suicide But this episode breaks the continuity of the story and can hardly be originally part of it. Ino, then, and also her husband Athamas were driven mad by Hera. Athamas killed his son Learchos, either mistaking him for a deer or lion and shooting him, or seizing him and dashing his brains out. Ino rushed away with the other child in her arms. Hotly pursued by her husband, she jumped over a cliff into the sea. But Dionysos, or in Ovid's account, Aphrodite, took pity on her and brought about her transformation into a goddess of the sea, Leokothea (either ' White Goddess ' or ' Runner on the White ', *i.e.*, on the foam), whom we shall find later helping Odysseus. Melikertes also was deified, and henceforth was known as Palaimon.

Here again there is a variant, and an odd one, clumsily incorporated in the main story. Athamas or Ino threw Melikertes (or Learchos) into a boiling cauldron before Ino carried him off. This is pretty obviously another version of the manner in which he became a god ; the mortality was boiled or burned off him. Other variants are, that Ino killed both children, and that Athamas followed her, not in a fit of homicidal mania, but in just anger at her attempt to kill Phrixos and Helle.[43]

As to who Ino and Melikertes originally were, opinions differ. Why the latter should be called Palaimon (' Wrestler '), when he was only a baby, whether his name is Greek ('Honey-cutter,' *i.e.*, bee-keeper) or Phoenician (' King,' probably ; in this case his brother Learchos—' Ruler of the people '—may be simply his Hellenic double) ; whether Ino was always another name for Leukothea ; how it is that Ino is known to have been worshipped in a way which suggests a goddess of vegetation, including mourning for her death, although, if she was a sea-goddess, she did not die ; and finally, why the famous Isthmian games were partly at least in honour of Melikertes—all these are easy questions to ask and hard ones to answer. At present I merely indicate their existence, leaving their attempted solution to works on the religion, not the mythology, of the Greeks.[44]

A corrupt and puzzling passage of Plautus states that Palaimon was said to be a comrade of Herakles. No very successful attempt has yet been made to connect this with any known myth or rite.[45] It is to be remembered that all the mythology of this group was originally a Boiotian legend or cycle of legends, later overlaid with the popular myth of Dionysos, who had, to begin with, nothing to do with either Athamas or Ino-Leukothea.

To return, however, to Dionysos, he was rescued from all this complex of madness and murder, and handed over to divine nurses, the nymphs of Nysa. Of this mountain Hesychios says :

'Nysa, the Nyseian Mount. Not confined to any one place ; we find it in Arabia, Ethiopia, Egypt, Babylon, Erythra (? the Red Sea, ἐρυθρὰ θάλαττα), Thrace, Thessaly, Kilikia, India, Libya, Lydia, Macedonia, Naxos, the neighbourhood of Mt. Pangaion, and as a place in Syria.'

Wherever or whoever they were, they nursed him faithfully, and became his companions and followers. According to Ovid, he repaid their kindness by renewing their youth when they grew old.[46]

Once come to maturity, Dionysos' adventures fall into two great categories, namely his persecutions by unbelievers in his divinity, and his conquests, peaceful and warlike. Lykurgos has already been mentioned ; he attacked Dionysos and his nurses ' on holy Nyseïon ', and smote the nurses with an ox-goad ; Dionysos jumped into the sea, and there was kindly received by Thetis. Zeus smote Lykurgos with blindness, ' and he lived not long thereafter, for he was become hateful to all the deathless gods '.[47]

A more violent struggle was that with Pentheus, which is immortally handled in Euripides' *Bacchae*. Pentheus, son of Kadmos' daughter Agaue and successor of Kadmos himself on the throne of Thebes, declared that Dionysos was an impostor and his votaries deceivers or deceived. Hence, when most of the women in the city flocked out to Mt. Kithairon to take part in the revels of the god, he did his best to stop them. As their frenzy, and the power of the god which wrought miracles through them, made them formidable even to a strong armed force, he was ready, if prompted, to use gentler means, and these were soon suggested. A mysterious stranger, probably a priest of Dionysos, was made prisoner and brought before him Pentheus thrust him into the dungeons of his palace, only to find him miraculously delivered. Impressed, yet still hostile, he listened to the stranger's advice that he should disguise himself as a woman and go to see for himself what Dionysos' votaries were doing.

Spying on them from a tree, he was seen, flung from his post, and torn to pieces, his own mother taking a leading part in his death. Not till later, when her frenzy subsided, did she realize what she had done.[48]

Even more terrible was the manifestation of Dionysos' power in Argos. There, because they would not recognize his deity, madness fell upon the daughters of Proitos, or on the Argive women generally, and they rushed forth into the wilds, where they wandered about 'with all manner of unseemliness', says Apollodoros, and in particular, they destroyed their own children. At last the seer Melampus, after long haggling over terms, healed them, either by certain magical dances, for he was an expert on the Dionysiac mysteries, or by herbs. Another version, however, attributes their madness to an insult to their native goddess Hera, and states that they fancied themselves cows, Hera's beast.

Still there were unbelievers in Boiotia; the daughters of Minyas, Alkithoe, Leukippe, and Arsippe (or Aristippe, or Arsinoe) held out against the new cult, and when all their city, Orchomenos, had gone forth to worship, they sat at home and wove, although, by one account, Dionysos himself came to them in the form of a girl and advised them to take part. As his advice was spurned, he showed his power; phantoms of wild beasts filled the room, the web began to turn into vines, and invisible devotees of the god made wild music and raised their revel-shout. The daughters of Minyas were maddened, and in their madness cast lots to see who should offer sacrifice to the god. The lot fell upon Leukippe, whose son, Hippasos, they accordingly tore in pieces. Then they ran out, to revel or to hide (the authorities differ), and were turned into bats or other nocturnal flying things.[49]

Another opponent of Dionysos was Akrisios, king of Argos and father of Danae, of whom more will be said in a later chapter. His enmity to the god is but an obscure episode in his career.[50]

Yet a further form of the story of Dionysos' struggle for recognition concerns his earliest childhood. Kadmos—so the legend ran in Prasiai or Brasiai, a little town on the coast of Lakonia,—when he heard of Semele's frailty, put her and her newborn child into a chest and cast it into the sea. It floated ashore at Prasiai, and when it was opened, Semele was found dead, but Dionysos alive. Ino, conveniently coming upon the scene at that moment, was entrusted with the care of her nephew; Semele received a splendid funeral. A curious parallel to this is another tale, likewise preserved in Pausanias; at Patrai a chest came into the possession of Eurypylos, one of the warriors who fought against Troy; it had formerly belonged to Aineias or Kassandra. On being opened, it proved to contain an image of Dionysos, the work of Hephaistos, at sight of which Eurypylos went mad.[51] We shall find more floating chests later. That some kind of ritual lies behind all these tales seems highly likely; what it is, I am not prepared to guess.

So far we have had, pretty consistently, tales of the coming of Dionysos in which some one goes mad and some one else is torn in pieces. The god himself is always represented as followed by a revel-rout of beings, some divine and some human, Satyrs, Seilenoi, Nymphs and finally Mainades or Lenai (literally, 'mad-women'), human votaries, also known as Bassarides, probably 'wearers of fox-skins' from one form of their ritual costume; another was the skin of a fawn. They regularly perform curious miracles, making fountains of milk or wine spring up from the ground; they are madly strong, able to tear goats, bulls, and human beings in pieces with their bare hands; fire will not burn them, nor weapons harm them; and despite their violence to various animals, they have a deep sympathy with them, often suckling kids, fawns and so forth. All this, wild as it sounds, is but an idealization of the enthusiastic ritual of the god. His worshippers sought, by ecstatic dancing and perhaps also by the use of wine, to become possessed by their god; they were then called after one of his numerous [52] names, Bakchoi, from Bakchos. The tearing in pieces and devouring of an animal or even human victim is also fact; these wild sacrifices were due to a desire to assimilate the god himself, who was conceived some-times as human in form, sometimes as bestial, his most common avatars being the bull and the goat, although he often appears as a serpent. He was in fact a god of the fertility of nature; if in Greece he tends to become a wine-god merely (and even in Greece he is never wholly restricted to that one sphere) it is because there were already deities whose activities were directed to fertility, Demeter for example, and Dionysos occupied that part of the field in which there was least old-established opposition. That the stories of quarrels and forceful propagation of his rites are wholly due to the details of his cult is not, however, by any means certain; it is likely enough that real opposition to the new god was shown at least here and there.

Of stories in which Dionysos appears peacefully spreading his cult, the most famous is the Attic legend of Ikarios. He lived in Attica in the days of King Pandion, and received Dionysos with joy. The god gave him his gift of wine, from which he gave the country people to drink. They, feeling the effects, imagined that they were poisoned, and killed him. His daughter Erigone, whom according to one obscure story Dionysos loved, sought him everywhere, accompanied by her faithful dog Maira. Finding him at last, she hanged herself for grief. Then ensued a plague of some kind, either a suicidal epidemic among the young women, or dog-star heat and ruinous drought. Somebody, in one version Aristaios, asked Apollo's advice, and was told to honour Ikarios and Erigone. A festival was instituted, at which among other rustic rites little images were swung from trees, in commemoration of Erigone's death. Also, Aristaios prayed to Zeus, who sent forty days of cooling wind just in the heat of summer.[53] As a matter of fact the swinging was a fairly common rite, whose exact meaning is in dispute, but which probably was a kind of purificatory ceremony. Ikarios and Erigone (' Born in spring '; also called Aletis or Wanderer) were probably, to begin with, some kind of local deities.

One of the most charming of Dionysos' adventures is that related in the ' Homeric ' hymn (the seventh) which bears his name. ' I will make mention ', says the poet, ' how he appeared by the shore of the unharvested sea, on a jutting headland, in the likeness of a young man, one in his first manhood; beautiful were the locks that waved about him, all black, and the cloak he wore about his sturdy shoulders was purple '. Certain Tyrrhenian pirates, seeing him, promptly seized him and bound him, as an obviously desirable slave, ' for they said he was a son of Zeus-nurtured princes '; but the bonds fell off him, and the pilot warned them that this was a god they had on board. As they paid no attention, but went on their voyage, the ship began to run wine, a vine grew about the mast, and the god himself turned into a lion, in terror of which they all jumped overboard and were turned into dolphins, save the pilot, whom Dionysos spared. This is why dolphins are friendly to man.[54]

The god's triumphs were not limited to a handful of pirates. According to a fairly early saga (Euripides knows of it),[55] he penetrated as a conqueror far into the interior of Asia; after Alexander's real conquests, Dionysos' fabled ones were extended, and he was represented as having reached India. Here, however, the mythologist need not follow him; for we are leaving the realm of genuine myth and saga for a strange world in which pseudo-history and politics are blended together. On the one hand, it was obviously desirable, from the point of view of Alexander and his successors, that they should be treading in the footsteps of a god, especially one readily identified with all manner of Oriental deities, since he was at least partly Oriental himself. On the other, Dionysos was equated with Osiris, and Osiris in turn Euhemerized into an early king of Egypt who went about spreading culture, by force if necessary. So this Indian

Dionysos, as we find him in the long and very dull poem of
Nonnos, for example, is no Greek god, but a hodge-podge of the
mythology of several nations, stirred together by Hellenistic
princes and Hellenistic theories. The result does not lack
interest, but is outside our present scope.[56]

The loves of Dionysos and Ariadne will be dealt with in connexion with the saga of Theseus ; his other love-affairs are of
little interest, being restricted for the most part to an affection
for such obvious personifications as the satyr Ampelos (Vine),
or one or two episodes in late writers such as his unrequited love
for the Amazon Nikaia.[57]

The Satyrs of Dionysos' train are spirits of the wild life of woods
and hills, and particularly of their unrestrained and unguided
fertility. In shape they are regularly represented as quasi-
human, but more or less grotesque in build and features, always
male, always sexually excited, and with some part of them
definitely bestial ; usually, as in the earlier Attic art, they have
horses' tails, a feature reminiscent of the Centaurs whom we shall
discuss later. Others have something of the goat about them,
being shown with little horns, prick-ears, often goats' legs. This,
the type familiar from the famous Satyr of Praxiteles and other
well-known monuments of art, clearly resembles Pan. Of tales
concerning Satyrs there are plenty, but all of much the same
kind ; they are intensely lustful, fond of dancing and revelry,
usually cowardly, save in so far as the Dionysiac frenzy makes
them formidable. They are rather part of the *entourage* of
Dionysos, or,—since they are an independent creation of Greek
fancy and not merely an offshoot of his cult,—a sort of
mythological feature of the uncultivated lands, as the Tritons
are of the sea. In Italy, they are identified with the native wood-
spirits, the Fauni ; we still often speak of Praxiteles' statue as
' the dancing Faun '.[58]

Not dissimilar, but rather more substantial, are the Seilenoi,
or Seilenos (once again, we find a minor deity now one, now
many). Speaking generally, Seilenoi are older Satyrs,—we
sometimes hear of Papposeilenoi, *i.e.*, daddy Seilenoi,—and,
whereas the Satyrs are often merry with wine, the Seilenoi are apt
to be heavily drunk ; a not uncommon subject in art is a Satyr
supporting a Seilenos whose potations have been too deep. On
the other hand, such wisdom and sobriety as is to be found among
these wild creatures dwells with the Seilenoi. They are often the
nurses and tutors of Dionysos in his youth ;[59] they are skilled
musicians ;[60] and sometimes at least they are full of homely
wisdom. Thus, a fragment of Pindar[61] represents one of them

as preaching to Olympos,—the tutelary spirit, it would seem, of one of the mountains so called, but in this context a mortal,—on the vanity of worldly wealth ; and a famous story, probably a folktale, informs us that King Midas caught one at a spring variously located, but, it would seem, originally in or near Macedonia.[62] This was done by mixing wine in the waters of the spring, and thus making the Seilenos drunk ; on being brought in bonds before Midas, he reluctantly spoke, and told the king that the best fate for man was not to be born at all, the next best, to die as speedily as possible after birth. One Seilenos actually emerges into independent cult ; Pausanias found a temple in Elis which was dedicated to him, and him alone. Less impressive was his memorial in Athens ; on the Akropolis was ' a stone of no great size, big enough for a small man to sit on ', which had served Seilenos for a seat when he came to Attica in the train of Dionysos.[63]

Dionysos certainly is a foreigner ; ARES may be, for he is never very popular, from Homer down ; he is constantly associated with Thrace ; and he is not really needed, since other deities, as Zeus and Athena, to say nothing of some of the great heroes, have warlike functions in plenty. Be that as it may, he is already a recognized member of the Olympic circle by the time of Homer, and is the son of Zeus and Hera. He never develops into a god of social, moral or theological importance, in this respect contrasting sharply, not only with Apollo, but even with the Italian Mars, with whom he is identified in Graeco-Roman cult and legend ; for Mars has agricultural as well as warlike functions, however he came by them, and, at least in the Augustan cult of Mars Vltor, he was capable of embodying the idea of righteous vengeance, while Ares is little more than a divine swashbuckler.[64] As already told in the last chapter, he is from early times associated with Aphrodite, as lover or cult-partner. Apart from this, and from his constant appearance as stirrer up of strife, he really has but little mythology. War was not a subject on which Greek fancy dwelt with much complacency, although the Greeks of the classical epoch were brave and skilful fighters. It is perhaps as a result of this that Ares not infrequently gets the worst of it in his encounters, as when Otos and Ephialtes overcome and bind him.[65]

The scholia on Homer give a reason for this misfortune. The Aloadai were entrusted by Aphrodite with the care of Adonis ; when therefore Ares killed him, they were justifiably annoyed and imprisoned the god.

Ares was the father of a number of children. By Aphrodite, if we combine various accounts, he had Eros and Anteros, Deimos and Phobos (Fear and Rout, his attendants in Homer) and finally Harmonia.[66] But his affections were not concentrated on Aphrodite, for Eos is said to have been his mistress, and consequently to have been caused by Aphrodite to be perpetually in love with some one.[67] Several other children of Ares, notably Diomedes of Thrace and Kyknos, Herakles' opponents, will be mentioned later. One noteworthy union was that with the Attic heroine, or goddess, Aglauros, who bore him a daughter, Alkippe. Halirrhothios, a son of Poseidon, violated Alkippe, and was consequently killed by Ares. He was tried before the Areiopagos, which then met for the first time, and in connexion with this homicide he, like Apollo, underwent the penalty of a period of serfdom.[68]

Associated with Ares are two minor deities of war, Enyalios and Enyo. Neither has any myth to speak of, and the former is really, to judge by Homer's use of the word,[69] simply a name or epithet of Ares himself. He was often identified with the Roman Quirinus, she commonly with Bellona.

NOTES ON CHAPTER VI

[1] See Chapter II, notes 83 foll. For Semo Sancus and Veiouis, see Wissowa, Ges. Abh., pp. 290–2.

[2] See Wilamowitz-Möllendorff in Hermes, XXXVIII (1903), p. 575 ff. ; Greek Historical Writing and Apollo (Oxford, 1908), p. 30 foll. ; Wide-Nilsson, p. 277, and references there; Nilsson in Chantepie de la Saussave[4], II, p. 326; Hist. Gk. Rel., p. 132, and references; on the other hand, the short but excellent article of J. A. Scott, in Classical Journal, XVII (1922), p. 463. For Apollo in general, besides the classical dictionaries and Preller-Robert, I, 230 foll., see Farnell, C.G.S., IV, p. 98 foll., especially 119, for criticism of the theory just mentioned. The Homeric line referred to is αἱ γάρ, Ζεῦ τε πάτερ καὶ 'Αθηναίη καὶ "Απολλον, (Iliad, II, 371, and numerous other passages, never in the mouth of any but a Greek, as Scott points out). See p. 164.

[3] For the Hyperboreans, see Farnell, C.G.S., IV, p. 99 foll. ; for Apollo as wolf-god, see, e.g., Aesch., Septem, 145 ; interpreted as ' wolf-slayer ', Soph., El., 6–7. For the Slavonic belief, see F. S. Krauss, Slavische Volkforschungen, Leipzig, 1908, p. 141 foll. ; M. Vulpesco, Les Coûtumes périodiques roumaines (Paris, 1927), p. 7 ; the Croatian Shepherd of Wolves (vučji pastir) is a human being, who assigns the wolves their prey and exercises power over them. He also takes care of shepherds to some extent. St. George seems to have usurped some of his functions, Krauss, p. 138 ; in Roumania, S. Peter or S. Andrew. He may well have been a god in pagan times. Connected with Apollo Lykeios is a curious tale (Arist., hist. animal., VI, 580ª 17, copied by Aelian, hist. anim., IV, 4, with

a grotesque misunderstanding, and by Antigonos of Karystos, *hist. mirabil.*, lxvi [61]) : Leto came from the land of the Hyperboreans to Delos in wolf-shape, being thus disguised to escape Hera ; hence there are but twelve days in the year in which she-wolves drop their young, that being the time she took over her journey.

⁴ See *Hymn. Homer.*, III, 300 foll. ; Apollod., I, 22 ; Hygin., *fab.*, 140 ; further references in Preller-Robert, I, 239, and the classical dictionaries ; cf. also Farnell, *op. cit.*, III, p. 9, and IV, p. 180. For early history of the shrine see the Homeric hymn and also in Aesch., *Eumen.*, 1–8. In later belief (see *Acts*, 16, 16 ; Plutarch, *de defect. orac.*, 441 E ; Hesychios *s.u. πύθων*) a python was a spirit which possessed persons and caused them to give oracles.

⁵ For the Stepteria, see Plut., *quaest. Graec.*, 293 C ; *de defect orac.*, 418 A foll. ; Tertullian, *de corona*, 7 ; Aelian, *uar. hist.*, III, 1 ; Farnell, *op. cit.*, IV, p. 293 foll.

⁶ See Strabo, IX, 3, 10 ; Pollux, IV, 84. Their accounts differ slightly in detail, but agree in general.

⁷ For illustrations, see Cook, *Zeus*, II, p. 169 ff., with plate ix. Of the literature on the subject, much of which is cited by Cook in his notes, perhaps the most important work is Roscher, *Omphalos* (Leipzig, 1913), especially p. 54 foll., where the literary evidence is collected. For the E, see Plutarch, *de E apud Delphos* (the chief ancient treatise) and cf. Cook, *loc. cit.*, p. 176, n. 2, for a number of modern conjectures, to which a'ld W. N. Bates in *Amer. Journ. Arch.*, XXIX (1926), p. 239.

⁸ Material on the tripod conveniently collected by Cook, *loc. cit.*, p. 193 foll. Often in art and literature it is Apollo himself, or even Dionysos, who sits on the tripod. Cook's idea that the Pythia was thought of as the bride of Apollo is in no way proved by the evidence : her virginity would fit her admirably to be his ' medium '. For the alleged vapour, see, for instance, Strabo, IX, 3, 5 ; Pliny, *nat. hist.*, II, 208, which shows clearly that the whole story is a piece of rationalizing. Violation of the Pythia and her replacement by an old woman, Diod. Sic., XVI, 26, 6 ; the old woman, of course, need not have lived virgin, for any woman past child-bearing is likely to be magically potent in the beliefs of many countries. Diod., *ibid.*, 1–3, tells a quaint tale of the origin of the oracle ; some goats and then their goatherd came within range of the vapour and experienced its divinely maddening effects, whereat the matter was noised abroad and it was agreed that it must be an oracle of Ge.

⁹ For the Sibyl, see especially Bouché-Leclercq, II, p. 133 foll. ; Buchholtz in Roscher, *s.u.* The two lists of Sibyls I have quoted are from schol. Aristoph., *Birds*, 962 ; Varro ap. Lactantius, *diuin. inst.*, I, 6. Bouché-Leclercq, *loc. cit.*, p. 137, n. 1, gives many more ; Herakleides Pontikos is the first to recognize more than one Sibyl.

¹⁰ See H. W. Parke and D. E. W. Wormell, *The Delphic Oracle*, Vol. II, *The Oracular Responses* (Oxford, 1956).

¹¹ Chapter IV, p. 81.

¹² The controversy is well dealt with in Farnell, *Hero-Cults*, Chapter X. See also the classical dictionaries and Preller-Robert, I, 514. Besides passing references in Homer (*Iliad*, IV, 194 ; XI, 518), the principal authorities are Hesiod, frags. 122 foll. ; Pindar, *Pyth.*, III, with scholiast ; and of the later writers, Ovid, *Metam.*, II, 542 foll. The official legend of Asklepios' shrine near Epidauros apparently knew nothing of Koronis' lapse from virtue ; see Isyllos' paian (Powell, *Collectanea Alexandrina*, pp. 133–4). Pindar, like Homer, speaks of Asklepios simply as a hero.

The home of Asklepios is consistently placed in the Thessalian town of Trikke. For his wife, see Thraemer in Roscher, I, 621, 24 foll. The names of his parents also vary more than a little. See p. 164.

¹³ This is the commonest story. Pindar merely says (*loc. cit.*, 54) that through greed of gain he brought a dead man to life. The scholiast gives us our choice of Hippolytos, Tyndareos, Kapaneus, Glaukos (he presumably means the son of Minos, see p. 297), Hymenaios (this, he adds, is the Orphic account), Kapaneus and Lykurgos (Stesichoros' version), and those who died at Delphoi (Pherekydes), presumably all and sundry. Others, he adds, say it was because he healed the daughters of Proitos, or did something to Orion (raising him from the dead or curing his blindness ?), or cured the children of Phineus (Phylarchos). Clearly there was no consistent tradition. Those who told the tale of Hippolytos added, in later times, that Artemis brought him to Aricia, where he henceforth was worshipped as Virbius, a minor deity connected with Diana. This feeble tale was eked out by an etymology bad even for antiquity, Virbius = *uir bis*, since Hippolytos was restored to life and therefore became a man a second time (!), also by the fact that horses were not allowed in the grove, which was taken to be due to Hippolytos having had quite enough of them in his former existence. See Vergil, *Aen.*, VII, 761 foll.

¹⁴ The chief ancient account now surviving is the *Alkestis* of Euripides; the earliest, Hesiod frag. 127. Apollod., I, 104–6, gives more details. Pelias, the father of Alkestis, offered her hand to whoever would yoke a lion and a boar to a chariot, and Apollo did this for Admetos. At the bridal, Admetos forgot to sacrifice to Artemis, and consequently the bridal chamber was found full of serpents, obviously meant as a sign of early death. He also gives two variants of the return of Alkestis, one that Kore sent her back, the other that Herakles fought Hades himself for her, going down to the underworld to do so. This is of course different only in wording from the tale of the wrestling with Death. That Apollo made the Moirai drunk is stated by Aeschylus, *Eumen.*, 728. A great deal of dreary rubbish has been written on this delightful legend, in order to prove Admetos a sun-god, a by-form of Hades, or what not. All such trash is refuted, if it needed refutation, by A. Lesky's excellent and learned monograph, *Alkestis, der Mythus und das Drama (Sitzungsberichte der . . . Akademie der Wissenschaften in Wien*, 1925). For the minor variants, which are many, see the articles ADMETOS and ALKESTIS in Roscher and the other classical dictionaries. In some of them, Apollo loved Admetos, not for his virtues but for his beauty.

¹⁵ See Ovid, *Metam.*, I, 452 foll. ; Parthenios, 15 ; Pausan., VIII, 20, who mentions (cf. Philostratos, *Vit. Apollonii*, I, 16) that the story was also located at Antioch on the Orontes, where there was a famous shrine of Apollo in the suburb Daphne. Minor authorities in the classical dictionaries, *s.u.*

¹⁶ Homer, *Iliad*, IX, 557 ; Paus., V, 18, 2 (Idas shown on the archaic Chest of Kypselos taking Marpessa back ; hence this part of the story at least is old) ; Apollod., I, 60–61 (complete story).

¹⁷ Earliest mention of the legend, Eurip., *Helen.*, 1470 foll. ; then Nikandros, *Theriaka*, 902 foll. See also Apollod., I, 16–17, III, 116. Nikandros, his scholiast and Ovid, *Metam.*, X, 162 foll., mention the flower : it is not our hyacinth, which does not answer to the description of its colour (red) or of the markings, but perhaps a kind of fritillary, see Constance Garlick in *Class. Rev.*, XXXV (1921), p. 146. That Hyakinthos

was made a god is implied by Pausanias, III, 19, 4. Nonnos, *Dionys.*, XIX, 104, mentions an Amyklaian song in which H. is stated to have been brought to life again by Apollo. Ovid says that Apollo would have made him immortal if he had not died so soon. Zephyros is mentioned by Palaiphatos, 46 (47), and some other authors; Servius (on Verg. *Ecl.*, III, 63) names Boreas instead. See further Greve in Roscher *s.u.* Apollodoros also names Thamyris the bard as a former lover of Hyakinthos. See p. 164.

[18] Pausanias, *loc. cit.*; cf. Farnell, *C.G.S.*, IV, pp. 125, 264 foll.

[19] For Kassandra, see Engelmann in Roscher, *s.u.* Homer barely mentions her and says nothing of her prophetic gifts. The *Iliu Persis* of Arktinos (?), one of the Cyclic poets, mentions Aias' violence, Proclus, *chrestomathia (Homeri Opera*, v. V, p. 108, Allen), and Homer has probably heard of it, since he says (*Od.*, IV, 502) that Athena hated him. Pindar (*Pyth.*, XI, 33) is the first to speak of her as a seer; she had this from Apollo, to whom she played false, Aesch., *Agam.*, 1202 foll., *cf.* Apollod., III, 151; another story (Schol., *Il.*, VII, 44, Eustathios on the *Iliad*, p. 663, 40) is given below, Chapter X, p. 297.

[20] For the Lokrian maidens, see the inscription in *Jahreshefte des österr. arch. Inst.*, XIV (1911), 168–9; the clan of Aias undertakes in future to furnish the girls, and in return is relieved of certain disabilities; also Lykrophron, 1141 foll., with the scholion of Tzetzes; Plut., *de sera numinis uindicta*, 557 D, which dates the penance; it had ' not long ceased ' in about A.D. 100, the date of the work, therefore it began in the tenth century B.C., which fits very well with the foundation of the Lokrian city on the site of Troy, Hissarlik VII. See Farnell, *Hero-Cults*, p. 294 foll., for the best discussion of the whole matter, and Leaf, *Troy*, appendix, for more authorities.

[21] Ovid, *Metam.*, XIV, 130 foll.; Petronius, *Sat.*, 48, 8.

[22] Pindar, *Pyth.*, IX, 5 foll.; according to the scholiast, Pindar's source is the *Ehoiai* (Hesiod, frag. 128).

[23] See Vergil, *Georg.*, IV, 281 foll. For the variants of the legend of Kyrene and the fairly numerous mentions of Aristaios in literature, see the arts. ARISTAIOS, KYRENE in Roscher. For the superstition, see E. S. McCartney in *Trans. Am. Phil. Assoc.*, li. (1920), p. 106.

[24] The earliest account of Niobe is in Homer, *Il.*, XXIV, 599 foll., where, however, the lines (614–17) which mention her metamorphosis into a rock, though doubtless early, have been condemned as an interpolation by many scholars from the times of the Alexandrian critics down. According to Homer, all the people were turned into stone. Aeschylus wrote a tragedy on the subject, now lost. The best-known account is perhaps that in Ovid, *Metam.*, VI, 146 foll. Pausanias (I, 21, 3) says he had seen the Niobe on Mt. Sipylos, and it was a natural rock-formation ; for the opinions of modern investigators, see Frazer's note there. For more details and variants (they are not important, chiefly affecting the number of the children), see Sauer in Roscher, art. NIOBE UND NIOBIDEN.

[25] Ovid, *Metam.*, XI, 146 foll. Hyginus (*fab.* 191) and some later authorities (see M1, 90; M2, 116; M3, 10, 7) give the variant The story of the barber became famous, see Persius, *Sat.*, I, 119.

[26] For Hermes in general, see Farnell, *C.G.S.*, V, p. 1 foll.; Stein in Pauly-Wissowa, *s.u.*; Preller-Robert, I, 385 foll. The various attempts to make him a personification of some natural phenomenon, such as morning–twilight, wind, etc., appear to me merely foolish. For the Kabeiroi, see Chapter VII, p. 171.

²⁷ *Hymn. Homer.*, IV, 17–19. Good explanatory notes on the text of this difficult work will be found in the edition of Sikes and Allen. See for Zeus and Maia, Chapter III, p. 53.

²⁸ The stealing of the bow is mentioned by Horace certainly (*Carm.*, I, 10, 12), perhaps therefore by Alkaios, whose hymn to Hermes, unfortunately lost save for a few fragments, was imitated by Horace in this ode (see the commentators, ancient and modern, on Horace, and Bergk's notes on Alkaios, fr. 5 foll.). It is also mentioned by the scholiast on Homer, *Il.*, XV, 256, and possibly occurred in the hymn, the text of which is full of gaps, perhaps in the lacuna after 415. See p. 164.

²⁹ The two are distinguished, and the whole subject well discussed, by de Waele, p. 29 foll.

³⁰ Anton. Liber., 23, quoting Hesiod (frag. 153) and several Alexandrian poets ; Ovid, *Metam.*, II, 676 foll., who differs in a few minor details, very likely the result of his own fancy, at least in part. See further Roscher, *s.u.* HYMENAIOS. The name seems to have grown out of the cry ὦ ῾Υμὴν ῾Υμέναιε, raised at marriages; various late stories make him a handsome young Athenian, whose marriage was romantic and happy.

³¹ Nonnos, *Dionys*, IX, 232–4.

³² Ovid, *Metam.*, IV, 285 foll.

³³ Propertius, II, 2, 11–12, with the almost certain correction of Turnebus, *Brimo* for *primo* in 12. Hekate, schol. on Lykoph., 1176 ; she got the name Brimo because she ἐνεβριμήσατο, made angry noises at Hermes to make him stop molesting her. Artemis, Cicero, *de nat. deor.*, III, 60 ; the offspring of the union was Eros.

³⁴ Wissowa, *R.K.R.*, p. 304 foll.

³⁵ *Iliad*, VI, 130 foll. The mention of Dionysos in XIV, 323–5, is probably interpolated.

³⁶ See W. M. Calder, *Class. Rev.*, XLI (1927), p. 161 foll.

³⁷ Pindar, *Olymp.*, II, 27 (25) ; Pausan., II, 37, 5, and many other passages. The statement sometimes made that she was called Thyone after her reception into Olympos is a grammarian's fancy, see Schmidt in Roscher, V, 927, 48. The fact is that she has inherited the name Semele from her Thrako-Phrygian antecedents, while Thyone is her Greek appellation. For the whole story, see especially Eurip., *Bacch.*, *passim* ; Ovid, *Metam.*, III, 236 foll. ; Nonnos, *Dionys.*, VII, 190 foll. ; Apollod., III, 26 foll. ; Hyginus, *fab.*, 167, 170, 251. Of modern authors, besides the arts. DIONYSOS, SEMELE, THYONE in the classical dictionaries, Preller-Robert, I, 659 foll. ; Farnell, *C.G.S.*, V, 85 foll., will be found particularly useful.

³⁸ Rose in *Aberystwyth Studies*, IV (1922), p. 19 foll.

³⁹ Calder in *Class. Rev.*, XXXVI (1922), p. 11 foll.

⁴⁰ *Supra*, Chapter V, p. 110.

⁴¹ Ovid, *Metam.*, IV, 416 foll. ; Apollod., III, 28–9.

⁴² Hygin., *fab.*, 1, 4 ; cf. Nonnos, *Dion.*, IX, 243 foll.

⁴³ Ino kills both children, Eurip., *Med.*, 1283 foll., unless indeed τέκνων there is a rhetorical plural ; Athamas follows her to revenge her treachery, Philostephanos *ap.* schol., *Iliad*, VII, 86. The cauldron is in most of the authorities above quoted.

⁴⁴ The latest and best discussion is in Farnell, *Hero-Cults*, p. 35 foll.

⁴⁵ Plautus, *Rudens*, 160–2. See, for an attempt to make sense, J. D. Craig in *Class. Rev.*, XL (1926), p. 152, who points out that Portunus, who was identified with Palaimon, is in Imperial times associated with Hercules on one monument at least.

⁴⁶ Ovid, *Metam.*, VII, 294 ; Apollod., *loc. cit.*, who says that he was to be brought up as a girl by Ino (cf. Seneca, *Oedip.*, 418 foll.), and that after Ino's departure Zeus turned him into a kid, in which form Hermes took him to Nysa.

⁴⁷ Homer, *Iliad*, VI, 130 foll.

⁴⁸ See, besides Euripides' play, the fragments of the *Pentheus* of Aeschylus. There was also a *Pentheus* by Pacuvius, who closely followed Euripides, see *Class. Quart.*, XX (1926), p. 204 foll. Ovid tells the story in *Met.*, III, 511 foll., and Nonnos, *Dion.*, XLIV–XLVI.

⁴⁹ The Proitides : Hesiod, frag. 27 ; Herodotos, IX, 34, see commentators there ; Apollodoros, II, 26–29 ; see further, Rapp in Roscher, *s.u.* The Minyades ; Ovid, *Met.*, IV, 1 foll. ; Ant. Lib., 10. Both stories are connected with an obscure festival, the Agrania, for which see Nilsson, *Gr. Feste*, p. 271 foll.

⁵⁰ Ovid, *Metam.*, III, 559 ; IV, 607.

⁵¹ Paus., III, 24, 3–4 ; VII, 19, 6.

⁵² He is πολυώνυμος, Sophokles, *Antig.*, 1115 ; some samples of his many names are given by Ovid, *Metam.*, IV, 11 foll.

⁵³ The chief authorities are Eratosthenes *ap.* schol., *Il.*, XXII, 29 ; Hyginus, *fab.*, 130 ; *poet. astr.*, II, 4 ; Apollod., III, 191–2 ; for the love of Dionysos for Erigone see Ovid, *Metam.*, VI, 125. According to Hyginus and some other authorities (see Schultz in Roscher, *s.u.* IKARIOS, an article to be used with caution owing to its inaccuracies in quotation), Ikarios became a constellation, Bootes or Arcturus, Erigone Virgo, and Maira the Dogstar. See Additional Note A, p. 164.

⁵⁴ Besides the Homeric hymn, the story is told by Ovid (*Met.*, III, 597 foll.), Apollodoros (III, 37-38), Hyginus (*poet. astron.*, II, 17), and of course Nonnos (XLV, 105 foll.), with small variations of detail.

⁵⁵ *Bacch.*, 13 foll.

⁵⁶ The story is told by Nonnos in Books XIII foll. For the Euhemerized doings of Osiris, see Diod. Sic., I, 11 foll. ; in 11, 3 he is identified with Dionysos. There was a certain real resemblance. Dionysos was also supposed to have extended his influence West ; in Italy he was identified with Liber pater, for whom see Wissowa, *R.K.R.*, 298 foll.

⁵⁷ Ampelos, Nonnos, X and XI ; Nikaia, *ibid.*, XVI.

⁵⁸ See the elaborate article of E. Kuhnert in Roscher, *s.u.* SATYROS und SILENOS. He rightly points out that the evidence from literature is comparatively scanty, that from art abundant. The question of the Satyr-drama, and of drama in relation to Dionysos generally, is one for the historian of Greek religion or literature, not for the mythologist.

⁵⁹ For instance, in Euripides' *Cyclops*, 1 foll.

⁶⁰ For instance, in Vergil, *Ecl.*, VI.

⁶¹ Pindar, frag. 143 Bowra, from schol. Arist., *Nub.*, 223.

⁶² So our oldest authorities, Bion of Prokonnesos, frag. 3 Jacoby, and Herodotos, VIII, 138, 3. The story is told more fully by Xenophon, *Anab.*, I, 2, 13 ; Theopompos *ap.* Athenaios, II, 45 C, and at much greater length in Aelian, *Var. Hist.*, III, 18 (Seilenos reads Midas a long lecture on geography, chiefly that of fairyland) ; Aristotle as quoted by pseudo-Plut., *consol. ad Apollonium*, 115 D–E (frag. 40, Rose). What Midas, king of Phrygia, is doing in the north of Greece (the other authorities place the scene in Asia Minor, if they name the locality at all) is not apparent until we consider that the Thracians and Phrygians are the two halves of the same race. See Additional Note B.

⁶³ Pausan, VI, 24, 8 ; I, 23, 5.

[64] For Ares in general, see Preller-Robert, I, 335 foll.; Farnell, *C.G.S.*, V, 396 foll.; Kern, 1926, p. 118 foll., who is strongly of opinion that the name is pure Greek (= ' Schädiger ') and that he is chthonian, originally a god of fruitfulness, not merely of death; Stoll in Roscher, *s.u.*, cf. also the other dictionaries; for Mars, Wissowa, *R.K.R.*, p. 141 foll.

[65] See Chapter III, p. 61, and note there.

[66] Eros, Simonides, frag. 24 Diels (*ap.* schol. Apoll. Rhod., III, 26); Anteros, Cicero, *de nat. deor.*, III, 60. Deimos and Phobos (cf. *Iliad*, XV, 119), Hes., *Theog.*, 934; Harmonia, *ibid.*, 937; Hellanikos, frag. 41 Jacoby; and elsewhere.

[67] Apollod., I, 27.

[68] Euripid., *Electr.*, 1258 foll.; Apollod., III, 180, who says the Twelve Gods judged the case and Ares was acquitted; Panyasis *ap.* Clem. Alex., *Proptrept.*, 2, 35, says that he was a serf to a mortal man for a year.

[69] *Iliad*, XX, 69, Athena is opposed by Enyalios; but XXI, 385 foll., when the battle of the gods breaks out again, her opponent is Ares. For Quirinus and Bellona, see Wissowa, *R.K.R.*, 153 foll., 151.

ADDITIONAL NOTE A (see Note 53)

There is also an Erigone, a daughter of Aigisthos, who tried to secure the condemnation of Orestes for her father's death. See the fragments of Sophokles' *Erigone* with Pearson's notes.

ADDITIONAL NOTE B (see Note 62)

In another and rather famous story, Midas hospitably entertained Seilenos, whom his people had found wandering, and returned him to Dionysos. In return, he was given a wish, and wished that all he touched might become gold. But this made his food and drink do so, and, nearly starved, he begged to be deprived of the gift again. He was told to wash in the river Paktolos; he was freed from his golden touch, but the sands of the river have contained gold ever since. See Ovid, *Met.*, XI, 90 foll.

ADDITIONAL NOTE C (see Note 2)

See also Nilsson, *GgR*, I², pp. 536–8. Interesting review of existing theories, W. K. C. Guthrie, *The Greeks and their Gods* (London, 1950), pp. 73–87, cf. E. R. Dodds, *The Greeks and the Irrational* (Berkeley and Los Angeles, 1951), p. 69 foll.

ADDITIONAL NOTE D (see Note 12)

See further E. J. and L. Edelstein, *Asclepius* (2 vols., Baltimore, 1945).

ADDITIONAL NOTE E (see Note 17)

See further Machteld J. Mellink, *Hyakinthos* (Utrecht, 1943).

ADDITIONAL NOTE F (see Note 28)

Against this, see D. L. Page, *Sappho and Alcaeus* (Clarendon Press, 1955), p. 253 foll.

CHAPTER VII

LESSER AND FOREIGN DEITIES

πλὴν ἀλλὰ ἐμπέπληκάς γε τὸν οὐρανὸν τῶν ἡμιθέων τούτων . . . ἀλλ᾽ ὁ
Ἄττις γε, ὦ Ζεῦ, καὶ ὁ Κορύβας καὶ ὁ Σαβάζιος πόθεν ἡμῖν ἐπεισεκυκλήθησαν
οὗτοι, ἢ ὁ Μίθρης ἐκεῖνος ὁ Μῆδος ὁ τὸν κάνδυν καὶ τὴν τιάραν, οὐδὲ ἑλληνίζων
τῇ φωνῇ, ὥστε οὐδ᾽ ἢν προπίῃ τις ξυνίῃσι.

But you really have filled the sky with these half-gods . . . Attis
now, Zeus, and Korybas, and Sabazios—where did these tumble in on us
from ? Or Mithras yonder, the Median, with his caftan and his fez,
who can't even speak Greek, no, not enough to understand if one says
' To your health ! '

—LUCIAN, *Deorum concilium*, 7, 9.

HITHERTO, all the gods discussed have been worshipped
all over Greece, or at least have been associated with
deities so worshipped. It remains to discuss a few who,
either because of their insignificance or because they are foreign
and adopted late, never attained to such distinction. Several
of them are by no means uninteresting to the mythologist.

HEPHAISTOS has been pretty conclusively shown to be an
Oriental.[1] The distribution of his worship is intelligible only if
we assume that he was, to begin with, a fire-god adored by the
natives of the region of the Lykian Olympos, which was and is
remarkable for the presence of a considerable quantity of natural
gas. From this centre, his cult appears to have spread among
the Karians, not only on the mainland, but to adjacent islands,
notably Lemnos, whose mountain, Moschylos, geologists recognize
as obviously volcanic, and in which some traces of volcanic activity
seem to have lingered long enough for a memory at least of them
to survive in classical tradition. Here also, it would seem, those
Greeks who had settled on or near the coast of Asia Minor learned
to know of this god, and his cult spread to the volcanic regions
of the West, where the Liparaean Islands near Sicily became
connected with him, also to some extent Sicily itself, and Cam-
pania. By this time he was no longer, if he ever had been, simply
a deity who made fire come from the ground, and was become

165

a divine smith, whose forges were under the earth at sundry places and made their presence known by fire and smoke escaping therefrom. The population of Attica, which was largely industrial, worshipped Hephaistos with considerable zeal, and here and there in other parts of Greece proper he was honoured ; Crete, always backward in classical times, apparently never reverenced him at all.

In Homer, he is a fully accredited Olympian, a son of Hera. His father is apparently Zeus ; but in Hesiod he is already the child of Hera only, a counter-miracle to the miraculous birth of Athena. Even in Homer, he is rather a figure of fun, at whose clumsy activity the gods laugh ' unquenchably ' when he waits at table. He is lame from birth, and Hera was so ashamed of his deformity that she cast him out of heaven, when Thetis and Eurynome daughter of Okeanos caught him, and he lived with them nine years. Or,—the two accounts are three-quarters the length of the *Iliad* apart,—Zeus cast him out when he interfered in a quarrel between his parents. On that occasion he alighted on Lemnos, after falling all day, and was kindly received by the Sinties, as Homer calls the natives. But his usual workshop was neither with the sea-goddesses nor in Lemnos, but in heaven, and the poems are full of descriptions of the marvellous things he wrought, such as statues which would move of themselves, tripods which had the same wonderful power, immortal and impenetrable armour, all very natural things to be ascribed to him, seeing that he is foreign, and the Greeks of that day were but poor metallurgists compared to the Mediterranean peoples they lived among, and whose skill plainly had, to their eyes, not a little magic about it. [2] Other authors, Kallimachos, for example, and Vergil, love to portray him in an underground forge, with his soot-blackened workmen, the Kyklopes, about him, endlessly busy with divine tasks,—thunderbolts for Zeus, arrows for Artemis, arms for some favoured hero. [3]

Apart from this, and from the stories already told of him in connexion with the birth of Athena, the affair of Erichthonios, and the scandalous behaviour of Aphrodite, there is little to be said. [4] In Rome, he was very inappropriately identified witn Volkanus (Vulcan) ; for, as we have seen, Hephaistos became a smith-god, and is hardly remembered in any other capacity, whereas Vulcan was and remained, in native cult, the god of destroying fire, and had nothing to do with its industrial uses. [5]

That the smith is a magician is an idea expressed also in the curious tradition of the IDAIAN DAKTYLOI (' Fingers ') Their legends are extraordinarily complicated and fluctuating, but a few elements remain constant. They are generally smiths, and somehow connected with Rhea ; but as she is identified with Kybele, the Daktyloi are located now in Crete, now in Phrygia, since a Mt. Ida is to be found in both places. They were six gigantic smiths, helped by their five sisters ; or there were thirty-two of them who were magicians, while twenty more worked counter-magic, freeing from spells. Or, at the cave where Zeus was born, the nymph Anchiale threw dust, which turned into Daktyloi. Or, they somehow got to Olympia, and the Herakles who founded the games there was one of them, not the son of Alkmene. These scraps are just enough to tantalize the researcher, and give an idea of what a world of folklore was contained in the lost works of Greek literature.[6]

Not dissimilar are the TELCHINES, of whom Suidas is not certain whether they were daimones, or envious men who had the evil eye. A modern, acquainted with Northern European beliefs, would naturally say, as P. Friedländer does, that they are a sort of gnomes or kobolds. They lived on an island, generally Rhodes, until they were driven out or killed. They were skilful doctors and smiths, and at the same time excessively wicked and malicious. For the rest, their story, preserved to us in scraps in a score of authors, ramifies endlessly, for they are confused with all manner of other figures, such as the Kyklopes, and there is no agreement as to their names, number, or details of their history.[7]

A very different kind of fire-deity from Hephaistos is HESTIA ;[8] here, for once, we have a fully correct identification of a Greek with a Roman deity, for she really is the same as Vesta, etymologically and otherwise. She is simply the Holy Hearth, worshipped by numerous peoples, because it is a sort of natural centre of family cult, because fire and life are commonly identified, and, as regards public cult, because the king's or chief's hearth is of great importance in a primitive community, where fire is hard to make, and a public fire is often kept up by the chief, both for practical purposes, to supply a light to those who need it, and for ritual. But to the mythologist pure and simple there is not much that is interesting about Hestia, for she has practically no myth ; she is the child of Kronos and Rhea, and she chose to remain virgin,—a not unnatural corollary to the fact that the daughters of the house tend the hearth,— although Apollo and Poseidon wooed her.

Concerning PAN there are far more stories. His name is intelligible ; it comes from the same root as Lat. *pa-sco,* and means ' the Feeder ', *i.e.,* the pasturer of flocks. Like his father Hermes, he is an Arkadian deity, but unlike him, never fully human in form, being regularly shown with the horns, ears, and legs of a goat. Goatish also is his character, for he is lustful and playful, a vigorous and fertile deity, on occasion short of temper, especially if disturbed in his noontide rest. A characteristic power which is still mentioned in modern speech is that of causing ' panic ',—wild, groundless fear, affecting large bodies of men and causing them to behave like frightened and stampeded beasts. He is regularly god of shepherds, and in particular,—for he is a hill-god,—he haunts their summer pastures in the mountains. Like them, he is a musician, a player on the pipe which is nowadays named after him. It is therefore no wonder that he is above all prominent in pastoral poetry, and that, although his cult spread far beyond his native Arkadia, he remains chiefly Arkadian. Of higher moral and social developments he knows nothing, apart from the fancy of theologians, that his name meant ' All '.

I have called him son of Hermes, but, as so rustic a god has really no very close relation to any of the great Olympians, his parentage varies. Apart from sheer fancies (as, that his mother was Hybris, *i.e.*, Wantonness, or that he was the son of *all* the Wooers and Penelope), we have our choice, as regards his father, between Zeus, Hermes, Apollo, Kronos (the mother being Rhea), Uranos (the mother being Ge), Odysseus, Antinoos, and Amphinomos (the mother in these cases being Penelope), and Arkas, besides a quaint and obscure legend which makes him son of a shepherd called Krathis and a she-goat.[9] The mother is generally a nymph, sometimes a well-known one, such as Kallisto. The appearance of Penelope is very curious ; Pan lies utterly outside the epic tradition, and I see no reason to suppose that this Penelope is Odysseus' wife at all ; the ancients of course identified the two, hence the stories, all late, which make the father some person named in the *Odyssey*.

His love affairs were fairly numerous. Of his amour with Selene I have already spoken.[10] He and his music are closely connected with the pretty tale of Syrinx (' Pan-pipe '), which much resembles that of Apollo and Daphne. Syrinx was a lovely, but coy nymph, one of the Hamadryads. Pan loved her and, as she would have none of him, pursued her. Calling on her fellow-nymphs, or on the earth, for rescue, she either sank into the earth or was transformed into a bed of reeds. Pan, finding the reeds that now were, or grew over, her body, cut them and therewith made the first pan-pipes.[11]

A deity of the high hills, Pan was associated with pines, and is not unnaturally said to have loved Pitys, the nymph of the pine-tree ; as with Syrinx, his love was not reciprocated,[12] and in fleeing from him, she was turned into the tree that bears her name. A third unfortunate love was for Echo ; this time the issue was more tragic, for not being able either to persuade or to overtake her, he sent madness upon the shepherds, who tore her in pieces, only her voice surviving.[13]

There is another, quite different story concerning Echo. She used to be a nymph, but offended Hera by keeping her talking when she was trying to spy on an intrigue of Zeus with certain other nymphs. Hera therefore deprived her of the power of speech except for repeating the last words of whoever spoke to her. Thus handicapped, she did her best to make love to Narkissos, the loveliest of young men, son of the Boiotan river Kephissos and the nymph Leiriope. Being repulsed by him, for he was cold to all love, she hid herself and wasted away to a voice.

But Narkissos was punished for his cruelty. Happening to lean over a clear spring in order to drink from it, he saw his own reflection and at once fell in love with it. Unable to tear himself away, he remained by the spring until he died of exhaustion and unsatisfied longing, and was turned into the flower which bears his name.[14]

Pan was the friend and teacher of his unfortunate half-brother Daphnis, a son of Hermes and a nymph. A Sicilian herdsman, Daphnis was beloved by one of the nymphs of his native country : but either because he was unfaithful to her, or because he rejected her, she blinded him. He spent the short remainder of his life making sorrowful ditties on his own unhappy fate, the legendary origin of all shepherds' songs. Hermes took him up to heaven and made a river to spring up in the place where he died.[15] Thus far the common story ; Theokritos, however, in the first Idyll, has a quite different one, in which apparently he, like Narkissos, would not love, until at last Aphrodite punished him by smiting him with insatiable longing for some one unattainable, whereof he died.

Perhaps the most famous exploit of Pan was the help he gave the Athenians at Marathon. On the eve of that great struggle, they sent the runner Philippides (not Pheidippides) to ask help from Sparta. ' Now, as Philippides himself said and officially informed the Athenians, when he was near Mt. Parthenion above Tegea, Pan fell in with him ; and Pan called Philippides by name and bade him take a message to the Athenians, asking why they did not pay him any respect, seeing that he was their friend, had often helped them before, and would do so again.'[16] So, after the victory, they instituted a cult of him, with a shrine under the brow of the Akropolis.

Even more famous, perhaps, is the tale of Pan's death ; it is certainly more weird. In the days of Tiberius, a ship was making for

Italy from Greece, when she was becalmed near the islands of Paxos and Propaxos. Suddenly a voice from the shore cried 'Thamuz!' This was the name of their pilot, an Egyptian, who at first did not reply, but finally answered, when he was thus summoned for the third time. Then a voice called, 'When you come to Palodes, tell them that great Pan is dead.' After some discussion, Thamuz decided that if the calm continued, he would obey the voice; it did continue, and when they drifted near Palodes, he shouted from the ship, ' Pan the great is dead,' and was answered by a confused sound of wonderment and great lamentation. On arriving in Italy, the pilot was summoned by Tiberius, who loved quaint lore of all sorts, and after much argument, the scholars whom he kept always at his call decided that it must be the son of Hermes and Penelope, and, according to the then current theology, not the god Pan but a daimon of the same name.[17]

Just on the frontiers of classical belief and cult was the great Asiatic goddess KYBELE or KYBEBE, with her cult-partner ATTIS. Neglecting a rationalistic version in Diodoros, their tale runs thus. Agdistis, or Kybele, sprang originally from the ground, and was bi-sexual, until the gods reduced her by surgical methods to a female. (Here, at the very beginning, we find the Asiatic fondness for beings who were both god and goddess struggling with the normal Greek preference for one or the other.) From the severed part of her sprang up an almond-tree of marvellous beauty, and Nana, daughter of the river Sangarios, plucked a blossom and put it in her bosom. It disappeared, and she found herself with child. The baby, when born, was exposed, but a he-goat somehow contrived to attend him, and for some reason he was named Attis or Attes. Agdistis-Kybele loved him, and was frantically jealous. On his preparing to marry, or on his having an intrigue with a nymph of the Sangarios (clearly the various narrators are not certain what his relations to this river and its mythological offspring were), she drove him mad, and he castrated himself, whereof he died. The goddess repented of her harshness, and Zeus granted her prayer, that the body of Attis should never decay, the little finger should continue to move and the hair to grow. This is the extraordinary tale which, among other things, purports to explain why Kybele's priests are eunuchs.[18]

Both in cult and in legend, Kybele is frequently identified with Rhea. Hence it is that her attendants, the KORYBANTES, are frequently confused with the KURETES, who, as already mentioned,[19] attended the infant Zeus. So intimate is the confusion, indeed, that Immisch, in Roscher's *Lexikon*, combines them in one article. They were certainly alike in many ways, but it is worth while to distinguish them.

Beginning with the Kuretes, we must first of all set aside two peoples or tribes of that name, one mentioned in Homer[20] and other authors as fighting with the Aitolians of Kalydon (the quarrel arose over the division of spoils as a result of the Kalydonian boar-hunt) and a second, mentioned by Strabo[21] as inhabiting Chalkis. Nor need we take very seriously the assertion that there once was a people of that name in Crete, who were very old-fashioned in their ways, offering human sacrifice to Kronos;[22] a statement of this sort, not found in any early author, sounds too much like a rationalization of the daimonic Kuretes, to whom we now come. Hesiod, in a lost poem, stated that one Hekateros had by the daughter of Phoroneus five daughters, who became the parents of ' the divine mountain-nymphs, the race of rascal Satyrs, workers of naughtiness, and the divine Kuretes, dancers and lovers of play '.[23] For him, then, they are superhuman beings of a lower order than the gods ; and as such they seem to be mentioned in the celebrated hymn of Palaikastro in Crete, where Zeus Kouros, the Cretan child-Zeus, or boy-Zeus, appears at the head of his *daimones*, who apparently are the Kuretes themselves. Yet it is no way impossible that behind this belief lurks a very old reality, a worship of Zeus Kouros (or of the older deity out of whom he sprung) by veritable *kuretes*, or bands of young men from the Cretan cities.[24]

The Korybantes (' Whirlers ', possibly), so far as the jumbled condition of our evidence (mostly from late authorities) enables us to distinguish them from the Kuretes at all, are Asianic, not Cretan, attendants on Kybele, not Zeus. No two authorities agree as to their parentage (of course, occasionally they are provided with a single ancestor, Korybas, child without father of Kore), but they are constantly associated with ritual dancing, with mysteries and magical cures ; the latter it seems were taught only to women. Here again it seems not impossible that behind all lie the figures of very old medicine-men, dancers, like the Roman Salii, of sacred dances and performers of magic, and deified in process of time.[25]

The KABEIROI were more important, although the Greek world was hardly acquainted with them till the time of Athenian greatness. They are often confused with the Great Gods of Samothrace, whose mysteries were important ; they were also worshipped over a considerable part of Asia Minor, including Phrygia, which may be their original home ; also in Macedonia, in various parts of North and Central Greece, but particularly in Boiotia. The meaning of their name is doubtful; many explain it as a Phoenician word, *qabirim* or mighty, which agrees very well with their Greek titles of 'great' or 'mighty gods' (θεοὶ μεγάλοι, or δυνατοί), and with their appearance in Boiotia, the country of the 'Phoenician' Kadmos ; but there is nothing provably Semitic about their ritual or the history of their cult, though it is of course possible that in early times their worshippers included Phoenician sailors, and in no wise inconceivable that a Semitic name given them by these gained currency in Greece. Be that as it may, certain it is that they were deities of fertility, with famous mysteries connected with their cult, and also that they were supposed to afford protection against all manner of dangers, especially those of the sea. Apart, however, from identification of them with Greek gods, they have but little mythology that is known to us. There were two male powers, Axiokersos and his attendant son Kadmilos or Kasmilos ; also two females, of whom we hear rather less, Axieros and Axiokersa. The most popular identification was that of Kasmilos with Hermes ; the legend which a few ecclesiastical writers preserve for us is a quaint one. There were three brothers, whereof two killed the third, somewhere near Mt. Olympos (the Kabeiroi were worshipped in Thessaly, and so this is presumably the Thessalian version). From his blood sprang parsley, which therefore the initiates must not eat, lest the pollution of the death be upon them. The slayers cut off his head, wrapped it in a purple cloth, garlanded it, and, carrying it on a bronze shield, buried it at the foot of the mountain. Obviously this is a hieratic legend, intended to explain something which was done during the mysteries ; but, save that it has nothing Greek about it, we cannot understand it.[26]

Returning to a Greek belief, we may mention the NYMPHS.[27] The name means 'young marriageable women, brides'; and they are the beings inhabiting Nature in many of her aspects. As we saw in discussing Artemis, some of them are offshoots of her ; the Nereids are of their kind, and two or three of them rise to the rank of not unimportant goddesses ; but the majority, although popular figures of rustic cult, alone or with Pan or some such deity, rather appear incidentally in stories of greater deities, or of mortals, than possess any very definite mythology of their own. Nymphs are of several kinds, according to the province of nature which they inhabit or animate. There are the nymphs of trees, Dryads or Hamadryads : properly, δρῦς is an oak, and these should be oak-spirits, as the Meliai are the spirits of ash-trees ; but, either because the oak is one of the most important trees, or because its name is sometimes used to mean simply ' tree ', the Dryads are generally tree-nymphs in general. Nymphs are long-lived beings, but not always considered immortal ; tree-nymphs die when their trees decay or are cut down, or they live a very long term of years (so far beyond the life of even a long-lived tree that perhaps they are thought of as migrating from one to another), but die eventually.[28] A similar belief was held by some of mountain-nymphs or Oreads ; the author of the Homeric Hymn to Aphrodite says of them that ' they belong neither to mortals nor to immortals ; long do they live and they eat immortal food . . . together with them either firs or oaks of lofty crown grow on the nurturing earth . . . but when the doom of death stands near them, first the fair trees wither upon the earth, and the bark perisheth about them, and the limbs fall, and the soul of the nymphs therewith leaves the light of the sun '.[29] Aristotle is recorded to have held that neither Nymphs nor Satyrs were immortal.[30]

A late theory was that a Hamadryad animated a tree and perished with it, while a Dryad was simply a nymph who lived among trees. It is much to be doubted whether any such fine distinction existed in popular belief.[31]

The Naiads were the Nymphs of water, constantly associated with springs, rivers and lakes of all kinds. Here again we find sundry distinctions ; a few authors speak, for example, of Potamiads, nymphs of rivers ; the fact is that all these names are simply feminine adjectives, agreeing with the substantive *nympha*, and there was no orthodox and exhaustive classification of these shadowy beings. One and all, they are represented as beautiful, young, fond of dancing and music, and usually amorous, for they appear again and again as the brides, willing or otherwise, not only of satyrs, but of the greater gods and also of mortals. They have prophetic powers, and can inspire mortals, who thus become νυμφόληπτοι or filled with a divine madness. Like fairies, whom indeed they greatly resemble, they are on occasion formidable beings, as we saw in the legend of Daphnis.

Not unlike the Nymphs are the Muses, whose birth has already been described. They may have been in origin water-spirits. Water, as any one may hear, talks as it flows ; hence it is a widespread idea that water, or the spirits of water, can prophesy ; a drink from the fountain of Kassotis was part of the preparation of the Pythia, and similar rites were observed at many Greek oracles. But a prophet is also a poet. hence the idea that the

Muses could inspire whom they pleased to write, not only metrical oracles, but anything metrical. Moreover, as they were very wise, they knew all stories and could inspire any one to tell them. Hence they easily became the patronesses of every form of literature as it developed, and by a natural extension of other arts also. The ancient seats of their worship were the district of Pieria near Mt. Olympos in Thessaly, and Mt. Helikon in Boiotia ; hence they are very often alluded to as Pierian, Helikonian, and so forth. It is evident that a hilly region is a natural one for a cult of water-deities, for a mountain-torrent is a very audible body of water. On the other hand, the evidence for such an origin of the Muses is anything but cogent, amounting to no more than their association here and there with water, and does not explain their name ($Mo\~υσαι$ i.e.,* $Μόνσαι$, the Reminders). Whatever they were to begin with, their cult is of fairly wide distribution, although not of great importance anywhere. The Romans identified with them their very obscure native deities, the Camenae.[32]

Like other deities, they are jealous of their honour. On two occasions they were challenged by mortals ; the first so to presume was the Thracian bard Thamyris, who boasted that he could outsing even them. They met him at Dorion in the Western Peloponnesos, and there, says Homer, ' they stopped his minstrelsy . . . in wrath they maimed him (the word here probably means ' blinded ') and took away his marvellous song and made him forget his harping '.[33]

More obscure were certain mortal singers, called, like the Muses themselves, Pierides, as being daughters of Pieros of Pella in Macedonia by his wife Euhippe of Paionia. There were nine of them, and they challenged the Muses formally to a contest of song. This being accepted, the jury of nymphs who had been sworn in for the occasion voted unanimously for the Muses ; the Pierides, as a penalty for their presumption and their rudeness to the Muses during the contest, were turned into daws, which still have the power to imitate human speech.[34]

It is only in late authors that we find the Muses assigned each to one special department of the arts and sciences. According to them, Kalliope is the Muse of epic poetry, Kleio of history or of lyre-playing, Euterpe of tragedy or of flute-playing, Melpomene of the lyre or of tragedy, Terpsichore of flute-playing or of dancing, Erato of hymns to the gods, or of the lyre, Polyhymnia of dancing, Urania of astronomy, Thaleia of comedy,—there are yet more variants, but the reader will have had enough of this silliness of late pedants, which a very small knowledge of classical literature is sufficient to refute.[35]

The Muses are often spoken of as virgins, but against this must be set the legends of Rhesos and Orpheus, told in Chapter IX, both of whom were sons of Muses.

PRIAPOS, in Greece, where he arrives rather late, is an obscene little deity, a daimon of fertility, represented as a more or less grotesquely misshapen man, with a huge and erect phallos. He is the guardian of gardens, part scarecrow, part warning to human thieves, part luck-bringer ; and in his capacity of luck-bringer he is often found at the door of houses. He can hardly be said to have any mythology ; a number of obscure authors say he was the son of Aphrodite (the father is variously given), and that it was through Hera's ill-will that he came into the world so misshapen. Also, the stars known as the Asses, in the constellation Cancer, are sometimes connected with him. Dionysos had a favourite ass, which had carried him well once, when Hera had maddened him and he was journeying to Dodona to ask advice about his cure ; Priapos and it fell into an argument (the ass had been granted human speech by Dionysos), and Priapos, getting the better of the discussion, killed the poor beast ; Dionysos then made it into a constellation.[36] But in his native Lampsakos, and in many towns of Asia Minor, Priapos was an important god of fertility.

I pass over, as not germane to a book of this kind, some legends of foreign deities and peoples which had no very wide currency among Greeks, as that of Isis, which in its later form, as known to Plutarch,[37] had patently been influenced by the story of Demeter, or the weird version of the Exodus, made up of a few garbled scraps of the Pentateuch and a great deal of free imagination, which imposed upon writers who should have known better, such as Strabo and Tacitus.[38] Deserving of passing mention, however, are two figures, one an abstraction and one most certainly a false reading. The constellation Virgo is by many writers called Astraia (the Starry Maid), and identified with Dike or Justice, who, according to Aratos, for example, used to live among men in the Golden Age, retired to the mountains in the Silver Age, and finally, during the wickedness of the Bronze Age, fled to heaven, whence she may even yet be seen on starry nights.[39] The other is Demogorgon, whose name appealed to the imagination of Spenser, Milton, and above all, Shelley. It is rather quaint that such excellent poets should have built upon one scrap of a not over-reliable commentator. Statius makes his Teiresias[40] mention with awe ' the Most High One of the triple universe, whom it is not lawful to know '. The scholiast, generally known as Lactantius, says, as we have his note, that he

means Demogorgon ; but as no such name is ever heard of elsewhere, every scholar now agrees that it is a copyist's blunder for
Demiurgus, *i.e.*, the Creator.

Having now given an account of the gods, great and small,
it remains briefly to characterize them and to discuss one point
regarding their shape.

They are, generally, human in form, and human in character.
In philosophy indeed indignant protests are raised against any
unworthy conduct or motives being imputed to them, and most
lofty views of the purity and righteousness of Deity put forward; but the common man, to whose imagination we ultimately
owe mythology, was not a philosopher, and, then as now, he
did not insist on the highest standard of ethics from those he
respected. The gods are usually just and merciful, but on occasion, anger at some slight or injury, desire for the satisfaction
of their natural passions, or other strong motive, will force them
away from the paths of perfect uprightness ; and some, such as
Hermes, lay no claims to high morality. As to their ordinary
life, they do much as men do, living in houses in heaven or on
Mt. Olympos, or in the temples and shrines men prepare for
them ; like human beings, they eat, but theirs is magical food,
nektar and ambrosia, wherefore they have in their veins something other than the blood that flows in ours, and are sustained
so that they do not die. They can, however, be wounded or
made insensible. They are not bodiless, nor omnipresent, nor
omniscient ; but they can go immense distances in very little
time, see things from very far off, hear in heaven prayers made
on earth, and even help or harm without being actually present.
Their powers, then, are corporeal and finite, but very much less
limited than ours ; ' the gods can do all things ' generally speaking, but here and there a limit even to their power and knowledge
is mentioned or implied ; thus, none but Zeus and his favourite
Apollo has certain foreknowledge of the future, although any
god may know something, even a great deal, of what is to take
place.[41]

A notable point is that practically every god is somehow
connected with at least one animal. The eagle is Zeus' attendant . Hera is associated with the peacock, and also with the
cow ; her epithet, from Homer down, is βοῶπις, which Homer
probably took to mean ' having large round eyes, like a cow's ',
but which etymologically could be equally well rendered ' cow-
faced ', and we shall see that her priestess Io was turned into a
heifer. Their son Ares on one occasion at least is said to have
turned into a boar, that which killed Adonis.[42] Apollo is associ-

ated with the raven and the swan ; Artemis with deer and bears ;
Aphrodite's birds are the sparrow and the dove ; the bestial
shapes of Dionysos have already been mentioned[43] ; Hermes
is often accompanied by a cock ; Demeter and Persephone,
besides the horse-shape of the former,[44] are associated with
swine.   Poseidon and Hades are associated with horses, the
former also with bulls.   Pan and the Satyrs are half-bestial in
form.   Athena's bird is the owl ; the Muses are human in shape,
but the Pierides, their rivals, like them in number and musical
abilities, are turned into daws.   Generally, any god may on
occasion take the form of some animal.

The answer is that the evidence does not justify such a con-
Now, speaking generally and with reservations, people who
worship divine beasts are in a lower state of culture than those
whose deities have invariably or generally human form.   Are
we then to conclude that the Greeks, at an earlier stage of their
history than any we know, adored holy bulls, cows, horses and
so forth, and that they later developed the concept of human-
shaped or anthropomorphic gods ?

The answer is that the evidence does not justify such a conclusion.   The earliest mentions we have of many deities, indeed
of all, represent them as more or less completely human in shape.
We must judge each case on its merits, and if we do so, we
find no hint in any early author that Zeus was conceived as
being anything other than a glorified man in appearance ; Dionysos may have been a bull or a serpent before he took human form,
but he is no native Greek and cannot therefore serve as a cri-
terion.   Hermes' cock is certainly younger than himself, for it
was introduced into Greece in historical times,—long after
Homer,—and Hermes is a very old god.   He holds a fighting-
cock because the young men whose god he became liked them.
Hera may have been a cow-shaped goddess once, but if so, it
has left no trace on her cult or imagery, save the one enigmatic
epithet and perhaps the story of Io.   Artemis probably was
adored in bestial shape here and there, for her worshippers at
Brauron danced before her in yellow dresses and were called
she-bears[45] ; but Apollo shows no trace of having a non-human
shape, save for a tale or two in which he takes bestial form as a
temporary disguise.   As a general proposition, then, the statement that all or most Greek gods were once theriomorphic will
not stand ; it remains merely a more or less likely suggestion for
some of them.   What we can be perfectly sure of is, that none
of them was ever an animal totem.[46]

NOTES ON CHAPTER VII

¹ See especially the art. HEPHAISTOS, by L. Malten, in Pauly-Wissowa. Cf., for H. in general, Preller-Robert, I, 174 foll. ; Farnell, *C.G.S.*, V, p. 374 foll., and Roscher's *Lexikon, s.u.*

² Hesiod, *Theog.*, 927, cf. Chapter III, p. **53** ; Homer, *Il.*, I, 571 foll., 590 foll. ; XVIII, 369 foll.

³ Kallim., *Hymn.*, III, 46 foll. ; Verg., *Aen.*, VIII, 424 foll.

⁴ See Chapter V, pp. 110.

⁵ See Wissowa, *R.K.R.*, p. 229 foll.

⁶ For the Daktyloi in general, see v. Sybel in Roscher, *s.u.* The references in the text are to schol. Apoll. Rhod., I, 1129 (numbers, size, occupations) ; Apoll. Rhod., I, 1129–31 ; the language is ambiguous (οὕς ποτε νύμφη | 'Αγχιάλη Δικταῖον ἀνὰ σπέος ἀμφοτέρῃσιν | δραξαμένη γαίης Οἰαξίδος ἐβλάστησεν) and the schol. takes it that she was their mother, and clutched at the dust in her birth-pains ; Diod. Sic., V, 64, 6, and Paus., V, 7, 6–7 (Idaian Herakles).

⁷ See, for their very complicated mythology, P. Friedländer in Roscher, *s.u.* They were wizards, skilled in metallurgy, and cunning smiths, Diod. Sic., V, 55. Driven from Rhodes by the children of Helios, Nonnos, XIV, 36 foll. ; sunk in the sea by Zeus because they had the evil eye, Ovid, *Met.*, VII, 365 ; killed by Apollo in his wolf-shape, *SdA*, IV, 377 ; ? confused with Kyklopes, Kallim., *hymn.*, IV, 31 (they make Poseidon's trident, usually ascribed to the Kyklopes).

⁸ See Farnell, *C.G.S.*, V, Chapter VIII ; Preuner in Roscher, *s.u.*, see also his *Hestia-Vesta* ; her virginity, *hymn. Homer.*, IV, 21–8, *cf.* schol. Aristoph., *Vesp.*, 846.

⁹ For Pan in general, see Roscher-Wernicke in Roscher, *s.u.* ; Preller-Robert, I, 738 foll. ; Farnell, *C.G.S.*, V, 431 foll. Pan at noontide, Theokr. I, 15 foll. (shepherds dare not pipe then for fear of disturbing him and making him angry). In this connexion he often sends dreams, or even waking visions, in the mid-day siesta, see especially Kaibel, *epigr. Graec.*, 802 = *Anth. Graec.*, Vol. III (Didot ed.), 1, 214 ; one Hygeinos was cured by Pan who appeared 'visibly, not in a dream, at midday '. Son of Hermes, see especially *hymn. Homer.*, XIX, 28 foll. ; the other genealogies are in Roscher, III, 1379–80.

¹⁰ Chapter II, p. 34.

¹¹ Ovid, *Met.*, I, 689 foll. ; Achilles Tatius, VIII, 6, 7 foll. ; Longus, *Daphnis and Chloe*, II, 34. This, like the next two stories, is in all probability an invention of some witty Alexandrian.

¹² Nonnos, II, 108, 118 ; XLII, 258 foll. Theokr., *Syrinx*, **4**, however, says that Pitys loved Pan.

¹³ Theokr., *ibid.*, 5 ; Longus, III, 23 ; schol. on Lykophron, 310, however, says Echo became by Pan the mother of Iynx (a sort of bird, the wry-neck, used in love-charms ; he says she was originally a girl, turned into bird-form by Hera). Or their child was Iambe (Etymolog. Magnum, 463, 3 ; surely this means no more than that the musical god is allegorically said to have begotten the metrical foot called an iambus).

¹⁴ Ovid, *Met.*, III, 341 foll. ; the connexion with Echo may be his own invention. Without Echo, Konon, *narrat.*, 24 (Jacoby, Vol. I, p. 197), who makes his offence to have been that he caused the death of his admirer Ameinias ; Paus., IX, 31, 7–8, who has an explanation : N. had a twin sister whom he loved, and when she died he used to console

himself by looking at his own reflection in the spring, as a sort of picture of her. For other authorities, see Greve in Roscher, *s.u.* Attempts to explain the story (none perfectly convincing, but several ingenious), in Greve, col. 15-16 ; add Frazer, *GB*³, III, p. 94 (perhaps likeliest to be right ; he connects it with the belief, which existed in Greece, see Iamblichos, *Protrept.*, 21 ; Boehm, *de symbolis Pythagoreis*, p. 51 ; Artemidoros, *onirocr.*, II, 7, p. 91, Hercher, that it is unlucky to see one's own reflection).

¹⁵ The legend is known chiefly from Diod. Sic., IV, 84 ; Aelian, *uar. hist.*, X, 18 ; and the ancient commentators on Vergil, *Ecl.*, V, 20. There is also something to be gleaned from the scholiast on Theokritos I. From Aelian, who as usual is confused and silly, it dimly appears that Stesichoros handled the story. See further, Stoll in Roscher, *s.u.*

¹⁶ Herodotos, VI, 105.

¹⁷ Plutarch, *de defect. orac.*, 17 (419 B foll.). Despite the contrary opinion of some, I hold with S. Reinach (*Bull. Corresp. Hell.*, 1907, p. 1 foll. ; *C.M.R.*, III, 1 foll.) that the story is quite true ; but what they really heard from shore was Θαμοῦς, Θαμοῦς, Θαμοῦς παμμέγας τέθνηκε, ' Thamuz, Thamuz, Thamuz the all-great is dead '. The people were lamenting ceremonially for Thamuz, or Adonis ; Πὰν μέγας and παμμέγας are indistinguishable in pronunciation, or nearly so. Palodes (τὸ Παλῶδες) is puzzling ; if it is the harbour of Buthroton, Πηλώδης Λιμήν (so Reinach), that is some forty miles from Paxos, an impossible drift in a night of flat calm.

¹⁸ Principal ancient authorities, Pausanias, VII, 17, 10–12 ; Arnobius, *aduers. nat.*, V, 5 foll. ; Ovid, *Fast.*, IV, 223 foll. ; Catullus, 63 (Attis) ; Sallustius *de dis et mundo*, 4, pp. 4–10, Nock ; Julian, *orat.*, 5, 165 B foll. For more authorities and modern interpretations, see Frazer, *GB*³, V, p. 263 foll. ; H. Hepding, *Attis, seine Mythen und sein Kult*, Giessen, 1903 ; H. Graillot, *Le culte de Cybèle dans l'empire romain*, Paris, 1912 ; Roscher, arts. AGDISTIS, ATTIS, KYBELE. The ancient versions vary in detail, but not very importantly.

¹⁹ Chapter III, p. 49. Cf. in general, Roscher, art. KURETEN UND KORYBANTEN.

²⁰ *Iliad*, IX, 529, cf. Strabo, X, 3, 6.

²¹ Strabo, *ibid.*, 8.

²² Porphyry, *de abstinentia*, II, 56, citing Istros ; cf. Hesychios, *s.uu.* Κουρῆτες, Κουρήτεσσι, Κουρήτων.

²³ Hesiod, frag. 198.

²⁴ Hymn : text, Powell, p. 160 ; comment, Harrison, *Themis*², p. 1 foll ; Nilsson, *M.M.R.*, p. 475 foll.

²⁵ See the art. in Roscher cited in note 19 ; mysteries, Plato, *Euthyd.*, 277 D, *Laws*, VII, 790 D. Korybas ; *SdA*, III, 111.

²⁶ For the Kabeiroi, see the important article KABEIROS UND KABEIROI, by O. Kern in Pauly-Wissowa. The legend is preserved in Clement of Alexandria, *Protrept.*, II, 19 (who runs on into an odd tale in which Kabeiroi, Kuretes, Korybantes and Dionysos are hopelessly jumbled) ; Arnobius, *adu. nat.*, V, 19, who calls them Korybantes ; Firmicus Maternus, *de errore*, 11. Kern (col. 1416, 50) rightly says : *diese Zeugnisse sind spät und von tendenziöser Entstellung nicht frei.* Cf. p. 181.

²⁷ For the nymphs in general, see Bloch in Roscher, *s.u.* It is clear that no very sharp line can be drawn between them and the Horai and Charites on the one hand, the various local personifications and abstractions on the other. Of the little importance of the classification of nymphs

into Dryads, Hamadryads, Naiads, etc., let the following example suffice ; Propertius, describing Hylas carried off by the Naiads, says, *a dolor, ibat Hylas, ibat Hamadryasin* (I, 20, 32). This is no late and puzzle-headed scribbler, but one of the most learned of Augustan poets.

²³ So, in the famous passage of Hesiod, frag. 171 :

ἐννέα τοι ζώει γενεὰς λακέρυζα κορώνη
ἀνδρῶν γηράντων, ἔλαφος δέ τε τετρακόρωνος,
τρεῖς δ᾽ ἐλάφους ὁ κόραξ γηράσκεται, αὐτὰρ ὁ φοῖνιξ
ἐννέα μὲν κόρακας· δέκα φοίνικας δέ τοι ἡμεῖς
Νύμφαι ἐυπλόκαμοι, κοῦραι Διὸς αἰγιόχοιο.

i.e., ' Nine generations of men the chattering crow sees grow old ; a stag lives four crow-lives ; the raven grows old in the lifetime of three stags ; but the phoenix outlasts nine ravens, and we, the Nymphs of lovely locks, daughters of Zeus Aigis-bearer, ten phoenixes.' The many citations and allusions will be found in Rzach's notes. For a hamadryad perishing with her tree, see Ovid, *Metam.*, VIII, 771 foll. ; but Ausonius, in his imitation of the above passage of Hesiod (*Ecl.*, 5), calls the long-lived nymphs Hamadryads (*quam nos perpetuo decies praeuertimus aeuo | Nymphae Hamadryades, quarum longissima uita est*). Plutarch, however, says that the speaker is a Naiad (*de def. orac.*, 415 C).

²⁹ *Hymn. Homer.*, V, 256 foll.

³⁰ Arist. *ap* Lactant. on Stat., *Theb.*, IX, 376.

³¹ *SB* X, 62.

³² For the Muses, see, besides Roscher *s.u.*, Preller-Robert, I, p. 484 foll. ; Farnell, *C.G.S.*, V, p. 434 foll. Camenae, Wissowa, *R.K.R.*, p. 219.

³³ Homer, *Iliad*, II, 594 foll., where see the scholia.

³⁴ Ovid, *Metam.*, V, 300 foll. ; Anton. Liberal., 9, citing Nikandros. The latter informs us that Mt. Helikon grew up to the sky with sheer delight at the song of the Muses, until by order of Poseidon Pegasos stamped on it to stop it. This may be cited as an example of the rubbish which an Alexandrian sometimes produced when he tried to improve on a myth.

³⁵ *Anthol. Palat.*, IX, 504 and 505, will serve as examples of this attempt to refine on the Muses ; they disagree with each other on nearly every Muse. For really classical treatment, see, *e.g.*, Apollonios Rhodios, III, 1 (Erato invoked to inspire an epic), Horace, *Carm.*, III, 30, 16, and IV, 3, 1 (Melpomene as Muse of lyric poetry ; Horace elsewhere invokes Kleio, Kalliope, Euterpe and Polyhymnia, all in connexion with lyric).

³⁶ Birth-story, schol. Apoll. Rhod., I, 932–3 ; schol. on Lykophr., 831. Story of the ass in Hygin., *poet. astron.*, II, 23. Another tale of the same constellation is that Dionysos, attended by his train, together with Hephaistos, rode on asses to fight the Giants, who ran away at the braying of their mounts ; *ibid.*, and pseudo-Erat., 11. For full references concerning Priapos, see Roscher, *s.u.*

³⁷ *De Iside et Osiride*, 15, 16 (357 A foll.) ; Isis hears that the coffined body of Osiris is at Byblos, and goes there in search of it ; she becomes the nurse of the queen's child—the queen is variously styled Astarte, Saosis, or Nemanous, ' which in Greek might be called Athenais '—lets the child suck from her finger instead of her breast, and lays it in the fire every night ; the story goes on much like the legend of Demeter and Metaneira's baby.

³⁸ Strabo, XVI, 2, 35 foll. ; Tacitus, *Hist.*, V, 3–5 ; Josephus protests vehemently against fictions of this sort in the *contra Apionem*.

³⁹ Aratos, 100 foll. ; cf., *e.g.*, the famous passage of Ovid, *Met.*, I, 149.

⁴⁰ *Theb.*, IV, 514–15, *ni te, Thymbraee, uererer,* | *et triplicis mundi summum, quem scire nefastum.*

⁴¹ All these points can be illustrated from Homer. *Il.*, I, 606–8, the gods have houses which Hephaistos has made for them ; *Od.*, V, 196 foll., Kalypso gives Odysseus mortals' food, but takes nektar and ambrosia herself (generally the former is a drink, the latter a food) ; *Il.*, V, 340, the gods have *ichor* (fluid) of a peculiar kind in their veins, and not blood ; same passage, Aphrodite is wounded ; XXI, 406, Ares is knocked senseless by a heavy stone. The above passages show that the gods are not bodiless. The plot of the *Odyssey* turns largely on Poseidon not knowing what is done in heaven, or in the Mediterranean, while he is away with the Ethiopians ; *Il.* XIII, 17 foll., Poseidon walks from Samothrace to Aigai in four strides ; XIV, 153, Hera sees from Olympos what is happening at Troy ; I, 474, Apollo in heaven hears his worshippers singing hymns to him on earth. *Od.*, III, 231, ῥεῖα θεός γ' ἐθέλων καὶ τηλόθεν ἄνδρα σαώσαι, ' lightly can a god, if he will, save a man though from far away ', unless this be taken to mean ' bring him back safe from a great distance ' ; *ibid.*, 228, Telemachos is of opinion that some things are too hard even for a god. In the *Odyssey*, Proteus is able to foretell much to Menelaos, but Kirke, although a goddess, has to send Odysseus to get information from the ghost of Teiresias.

⁴² See Chapter V, p. 125.

⁴³ See Chapter VI, p. 154.

⁴⁴ See Chapter III, p. 66.

⁴⁵ See Farnell, *C.G.S.*, II, p. 436.

⁴⁶ See Rose, *P.C.G.*, p. 47 foll.

ADDITIONAL NOTE A

A few more very minor gods and spirits occur. Of these perhaps the best known is Morpheus (Ovid, *Met.*, XI, 633 foll.), a spirit, not of sleep in general, but of forms (μορφαί) seen in dreams, or so Ovid supposed. See Roscher, *s.u.*

The group of the Twelve Gods (Zeus, Poseidon, Apollo, Ares, Hephaistos, Hermes, Hera, Athena, Artemis, Aphrodite, Demeter, Hestia) is a matter of cult, not of mythology.

ADDITIONAL NOTE B (see Note 26)

For a full account of the Kabeiroi, the Samothracian gods and some other like groups of minor deities, see Bengt Hemberg, *Die Kabiren* (Uppsala 1950).

CHAPTER VIII—PART I

THE CYCLES OF SAGA

Non ergo ipsas res gestas finxerunt poetae . . . sed rebus gestis addiderunt quendam colorem.

The poets, then, did not invent the subject-matter of their sagas, but merely coloured the existing facts.

—LACTANTIUS, *diuinae institutiones*, I, ii, 23.

THE first thing to notice in connexion with those of the great heroic legends which form cycles is one which seems very obvious now that M. P. Nilsson [1] has had the sagacity to point it out. All of them, with the exception of the tale of Odysseus, which is not true saga, but *märchen* with saga-elements introduced, are closely connected with Minoan-Mycenaean sites. The original Argonauts are Minyai from Mycenaean Orchomenos ; the Theban saga concerns two attempts to take a Mycenaean city ; the tale of Troy has one end of its action at Argos and Sparta, the other at Hissarlik, and two out of three of those are classical sites of Mycenaean discovery. Herakles is lord of Tiryns, one of the oldest Mycenaean cities ; Minos has given his name to the ancient civilization of Crete ; Theseus plays his heroic part in Mycenaean Athens. The Kalydonian boar was hunted in a region not yet completely investigated, but it is known that Mycenaean remains exist there, and it would surprise nobody if the abode of King Oineus were one day to come to light and reveal the typical Mycenaean *megaron*, like those at Mycenae and Tiryns.

Who Minos really was we probably shall never know, nor even whether the word is a proper name or a title. To the Greeks, he was a great king of Crete in old days, who according to the general account was as just as he was powerful, while the Athenian story made him a cruel tyrant. Since the Athenian story said that he defeated the Athenians and imposed a tribute on them, we may discount this. But good or bad, just or unjust, the story of his origins was as follows.

Agenor king of Tyre had a fair daughter, Europê, whom Zeus loved. To attract her, he took the form of a magnificent white bull, which played about Europê so gently that she finally climbed, in sport, on his back, whereat he ran down to the sea-coast and swam away with her to Crete. There she bore her divine consort goodly offspring, Minos and Rhadamanthys ; some add Sarpedon. Minos became king of Crete (his brothers or brother are disposed of by a tale of a feud between them in which he was victorious) and wedded Pasiphaë, daughter of the Sun, by whom he had, among other children, two daughters, Ariadne and Phaidra, and two sons, Androgeos and Glaukos.[2]

I omit a crowd of relatives of Agenor and Minos, such as Europê's brothers Kilix and Phoinix, who are nothing but the eponymous ancestors of Kilikia and Phoenicia, and thus empty names ; the third son Kadmos is a much more substantial figure. Europê, herself probably no more than the eponym of the continent of Europe, is provided with a husband Asterios, who brings up her children and conveniently dies with- none of his own. Phoinix, in Homer,—*Il.*, XIV, 321, an interpolated passage,—and some later authorities, is Europê's father.

In answer to a prayer of Minos, Poseidon sent him up a most beautiful bull from the sea, which so delighted him that he would not sacrifice it, as he had promised to do, but substituted an inferior victim. The god, in revenge, made Pasiphaë conceive an unnatural lust for the bull. Now it chanced that Daidalos, the most cunning of all craftsmen, was an exile in Crete from his native Athens at the time. He had had for apprentice his nephew Talos or Perdix, who bade fair to out-do his master, for he invented the saw. The jealous Daidalos,—it is the well-known folktale of the Prentice Pillar in its Greek form,—flung him into the sea, whereat he was changed into the bird (the partridge) which bears his name ; Daidalos, either being actually condemned by the Areiopagos for his deed or fearing the unpopularity that would result from his unnatural conduct, escaped to Crete,[3] and there wrought many works for the king and queen. The latter confided her hideous passion to him, and by disguising her as a cow he contrived that it should be satisfied. She bore a horrible monster, half bull and half man, known as the Minotaur, or Minos' bull. To dispose of this creature, Daidalos made a maze, the Labyrinth, in the centre of which it was placed.

The story of Glaukos and the seer Polyidos is told in Chapter X ; it remains to add that Minos, before he finally let the prophet go, made him teach his craft to the child. Polyidos agreed, but on leaving his pupil, bade him spit into his mouth ; whereat, by a very natural piece of magic, Glaukos forgot all that he had learned.[4] The rest of the legend of Minos will be found in Chapter IX.

Without going into minute detail, it is apparent that we are dealing with divine and semi-divine beings in this story. Minos himself is said by Homer [5] to have reigned for nine (eight ?) years and to have been the gossip of Zeus ; behind this there may very well lie the faint recollection of days when divine kings, or at least kings who were also high priests, reigned in Crete, and perhaps were thought to incarnate, not the Greek Zeus, but the Cretan child-god identified with him ; it may be also that they were deposed or slain after a period of years, or at least went through some ceremony of re-commencing their reign then. Pasiphaë (' All-Shining ') is the name of a goddess, possibly lunar, adored in Lakonia.[6] Of Ariadne, apart from her adventures with Theseus, we know that she was worshipped at Amathus in Cyprus under the title of Aphrodite Ariadne, with most singular rites.[7] Even the Minotaur has some claim to be more than a mere bit of wild fancy, for we find one or two monsters, half-bull and half-man, in works of art of the Minoan period in Crete, and as for the Labyrinth, it is pretty certainly to be connected with the word *labrys*, which signifies a double-edged axe, a common sacred symbol among the ancient Cretans and their neighbours in Asia Minor, while the idea that it was a maze is not improbably to be connected with a very real maze, the intricate ground-plan of the great Minoan palace at Knossos,[8] some remains of which were probably above ground long enough to bewilder and puzzle the early Greeks, themselves accustomed to much simpler dwellings.

Returning to the rape of Europê, we trace the fortunes of the rest of her family.[9] Agenor sent forth his sons in search of their sister, with orders not to return without her. Neglecting the spectral Phoinix and Kilix, who duly stayed away and founded the peoples bearing their names, we must concentrate our attention upon Kadmos. Accompanied by his mother Telephassa, he got as far as Thrace, where she died. After burying her, he went on to Delphoi to ask for guidance ; Apollo bade him seek no more for Europê, but follow a cow which he should find and build a city where she lay down to rest. He did so, and the cow went as far as the present site of Thebes before lying down. Kadmos therefore founded a city, called after himself Kadmeia, which became the fortress of Thebes in historical times, and proceeded to sacrifice the cow to Athena. He needed water for the sacrifice, and the only spring available was guarded by a ferocious dragon, the son of Ares. Enraged at the killing by this monster of several of his men, Kadmos joined in the fray, and slew the dragon. Athena now advised him to extract its teeth and sow them, which he did. From them sprang up a host of armed warriors ; these he pelted with stones, and they, supposing each that one of the others was stoning him, attacked one another until only five were left. These were called Echion, Udaios, Chthonios, Hyperenor, and Peloros, *i.e.*, Snake-man, Ground-man, Earth-man, Overweening, and Monster, and from them sprang the nobility of future Thebes, the families known as the Spartoi, or Sown Men. The land itself was called Boiotia (which, with a little good will, can be taken as meaning Cow-land) after the guiding cow.

But Kadmos was guilty of the death of the sacred dragon, and to appease the wrath of Ares he, like Apollo, had to go into servitude for a year.[10] At the end of this time the god was mollified, and granted the hero marriage with his and Aphrodite's daughter Harmonia. The wedding was attended by all the gods, and Kadmos gave his bride, besides a festal robe, the notorious necklace (a thing of marvellous beauty, made by Hephaistos himself, and given to Kadmos by him or by Europê), which was afterwards to play a fatal part in the lamentable history of Thebes. For a while he and his queen lived together peaceably, he civilizing the rude natives and in particular teaching them to write. Here the legend touches fact, for the Greek alphabet is for the most part a modification of North Semitic script.[11] They had four daughters, Ino, Semele, Autonoe, and Agaue The first two have been dealt with in Chapter VI.[12] Agaue married Echion, and became the mother of the unfortunate Pentheus ; Autonoe's husband was Aristaios. Their son was Aktaion, whose fate has become proverbial. Three comparatively obscure forms of his story are, that he paid court to his aunt Semele, thus arousing the jealousy of Zeus, who killed him ; [13] that he boasted that he was a better hunter than Artemis,[14] or that, after making offerings at her temple, he proposed to marry her.[15] But the usual story, made famous by Ovid and by numerous artists ancient and modern, is that he came upon her bathing and therefore naked. She flung water in his face, and by her power converted him into a stag, in which form he was run down and killed by his own hounds.[16]

It does not appear that Kadmos in the earliest traditions had any sons. Various authorities give him one, Polydoros, a mere genealogical link, who is also called Pinakos, *i.e.*, Writing-tablet-boy ! [17]

Kadmos and Harmonia finally went away to Western Greece, and so to Illyria. Here they found a war in progress between the Illyrians and Encheleis ; the latter, in accordance with an oracle, begged them to become their leaders, and thus conquered their enemies. Kadmos became king of the Illyrians, who, one may suppose, were named after his child Illyrios, the son of his old age,—another shadowy figure. Finally he and his wife were turned into great harmless serpents. When Apollodoros adds that both were taken away to Elysion, he is telling the same tale twice ; they became venerable and worshipped ancestors, such as often appear in serpent-form, in Greece and elsewhere.[18]

We need not search the map for the ' Eel-people ' (Encheleis), although Lake Kopais with its famous eels has been suggested as a likely neighbourhood. The heroized or even deified pair went far away, which, as we have seen in discussing Hades and his realm, is just what would be expected.

The next dynasty was that of the Labdakidai. Its founder Labdakos left a son, Laïos, who was but one year old ; in the minority of the young king, a nobleman of the Spartoi, Lykos (' Wolf ') brother of Nykteus son of Chthonios, was made war-leader and soon made himself king, reigning for twenty years. Now Nykteus had a daughter Antiope, who won the favour of Zeus, and escaped from the wrath of her father by running away to Sikyon in the Peloponnesos, where she married Epopeus. Nykteus in despair killed himself, leaving to Lykos the charge of punishing Antiope. He captured Sikyon and carried her off, treating her with the utmost harshness and cruelty, which in some accounts was aggravated by the jealousy which his wife Dirke felt for her. But either on the way to or from Sikyon or during a period of escape from her prison, she bore twin sons, Amphion and Zethos ; these she was forced to leave at the place of their birth, somewhere on Mt. Kithairon, but they were found and brought up by shepherds. Zethos became a stout warrior ; Amphion, to his brother's disgust, a musician. Meanwhile their mother, unknown to them as they to her, languished in her dungeon. At last, when her sons were some twenty years old, she escaped,—by a miracle, according to one account at least, her chains falling off of themselves. She made her way to her sons, soon to be followed by Dirke, who was a votary of Dionysos, and wandered there during one of the orgiastic dances of his cult. Seeing the escaped prisoner, she gave orders to bind her to the horns of a wild bull and let her be dragged to death. But at this moment, mother and sons were made known to each other ; Dirke was put to death by the means she had intended for Antiope, Lykos was killed or dethroned, Laïos banished, and the two heroes became masters of Thebes, which they provided with walls, the stones following Amphion's lyre of their own accord.[19]

This is clearly another account of how Thebes was founded, for it is ridiculous to suppose it had all this while been an open town. Dirke is connected with the local fountain of that name, which sprang up from her blood.

Laïos in banishment found a good friend in Pelops, but proved himself ungrateful, for he kidnapped the latter's son Chrysippos, whose beauty fascinated him. This sin was at the root of the curse which brought his line to an end in two more generations. Zethos married Thebê, the local nymph, and thus Kadmeia was re-named Thebes ; Amphion became the husband of Niobe, and in some accounts shared her fate.[20]

A rather obscure legend gives the further adventures of Antiope ; Dionysos was wroth at the death of his votary, Dirke, and so, as he had already intervened to turn her into a fountain, he now avenged her by driving Antiope mad. In this state she wandered, until at last Phokos, son of Ornytion and grandson of Sisyphos, healed and married her. In later ages her grave was shown at Tithorea in Phokis, and if the inhabitants could contrive to steal some earth from the tomb of Amphion and Zethos and add it to her monument, their crops were good but those of the Thebans bad.[21]

Amphion and Zethos being dead,—their whole story is a sort of parenthesis in the saga,—Laïos regained his kingdom, and brought with him the burden of his sin against Pelops.[22] He married Iokaste (Homer calls her Epikaste) daughter of Menoikeus and sister of Kreon, but was warned by Apollo that if she bore him a son, that son should slay him. So when a son was born, he thrust a spike through his feet and gave him to a shepherd to expose. The place of exposure, Kithairon, was the hill-pasture or summer grazing grounds alike of Thebes and of Corinth, and a shepherd of Polybos, king of the latter state, who was child-less, found the baby and took it to the queen, Polyboia or Merope. The infant was named Oidipus (Swell-foot) from his swollen feet [23] and the royal couple reared him as their own son. On reaching manhood, Oidipus was taunted with being a suppositious child, and went to Delphoi to find who his real parents were. The oracle told him that he was destined to kill his father and wed his mother. Knowing no other parents than Polybos and Merope, he left the shrine resolved never to return to Corinth. Journeying on to the place called the Schiste Hodos (the Divided Way) on the road from Phokis to Boiotia, he met Laïos, whose attendants bade him clear the road. A fierce quarrel ensued, in which he killed Laïos, whom of course he did not recognize. He then arrived at Thebes, which he found in turmoil and distress. The king was missing, and the city was tormented with a monster, the

Sphinx (Hesiod calls her Phix ; the former name at least is intelligible, meaning the Strangler), which asked all and sundry a riddle, and killed those who could not answer, quite in the style of tyrants and monsters of folklore. She is described as a winged creature, with a woman's face and a lion's body, a familiar type enough in Oriental art. Kreon, acting as regent, offered the kingdom and the hand of his sister, the widowed queen, to anyone who would rid them of the pest. Oidipus undertook to do so ; he solved the riddle, the Sphinx killed herself in disgust, and he married Iokaste.

Naturally, the question was asked and answered what the Sphinx' riddle was. The traditional one is this : ' There is on earth a two-footed creature and a four-footed one with the same name, and also a three-footed, for it changes its form alone of all that move on the ground or through the air or in the sea. But when it walks supported on the most feet, then is the swiftness of its limbs the weakest.' Oidipus answered, ' Thou hast spoken of man, who when he goeth on ground is at first four-footed from his mother's womb ; but in eld he leaneth on a staff as a third foot.' [24]

If we could trust the evidence of two gems alleged to be Mycenaean from Thisbe in Boiotia, [25] we could date the death of Laios and the overcoming of the Sphinx from Minoan-Mycenaean times. One shows a young man attacking a sphinx, the other the same or a like figure aiming an arrow at a man in a chariot ; but their genuineness is highly doubtful, therefore nothing can be concluded from them. Homer now takes up the tale. ' I saw ', says Odysseus, describing his adventures in Hades, [26] ' the mother of Oidipodes, fair Epikaste, who wrought a dread deed in the ignorance of her heart, marrying her own dear son, that wedded her after he had slain his father ; and the gods speedily made it known to men. But he, by the cruel counsel of the gods, reigned on in woe over the Kadmeians at lovely Thebê, but she went unto the house of Hades, strong keeper of the gate, fastening a swift noose to the roof of the lofty hall, in the gripe of her grief ; but unto him she left sorrows very many, even all that the Erinyes of a mother accomplish.' Elsewhere he speaks of Oidipus as having ' fallen ' (this by all analogy should mean that he died by violence, perhaps in battle) and being buried with the usual funeral games. Here is a much simpler story than that in the later authors. ' I hold ', says Pausanias very reasonably, quoting the first of the above passages, ' that Oidipus had no children by her . . . for how did they " speedily make it known," if Epikaste really bore Oidipus four children ? The mother of his children was Euryganeia daughter of Hyperphas, as is clear from the poet of the epic known as the *Oidipodia*.' [27]

In the ordinary tale, then, Oidipus and Iokaste lived together for many years, and had two sons, Eteokles and Polyneikes, and two daughters, Antigone and Ismene. But at last the truth became known. According to Sophokles, Polybos died and the Corinthians sent a messenger to invite Oidipus to be their king. He refused, saying that he dared not go near his mother. The messenger, who was none other than the shepherd who had found him when exposed, told him that he was no child of Merope. Determining to find out his real parentage, and also to discover the murderer of Laïos,—for a plague had fallen on the city and Apollo had revealed that it could not be stayed until the slayer was driven out,—he found the thrall who had exposed him, and who had also been in attendance on Laïos at the Schiste Hodos. From him he forced the truth, and in utter despair put out his own eyes. Iokaste hanged herself, and in accordance with the oracle, Kreon banished Oidipus, becoming regent in the minority of his sons. Years afterwards, on the eve of the outbreak of war between Eteokles and Polyneikes, Oidipus wandered to Kolonos in Attica, attended by Antigone, and there died, or rather was transported to the next world, leaving his grave (whose exact place no one knew save Theseus) as a protection for the country.

But this is apparently the Attic story, the fruits of a very natural desire to claim as their own the bones of this great, if unfortunate hero. The normal tale says nothing of banishment ; Oidipus shut himself up in an inner room of the palace at Thebes, and lived there while his sons came to manhood, presumably under the regency of Kreon. One day, however, when serving him at table, they set before him certain ancestral vessels which Laïos had used, and which he had forbidden them to serve him in. On discovering what they had done, he invoked a curse of dis-union upon them. To make matters worse, on another occasion, by accident or design, they set the loin of the meat before him, instead of the more honourable shoulder-piece ; whereat he prayed that they might die by each other's hands.[28]

The curse was fulfilled. On the death of Oidipus, or in his helpless old age, or on their coming to years of discretion,—the accounts vary,—the two brothers could not agree which should be king ; it is to be remembered that primogeniture is not a Greek institution. At length they decided to rule in alternate years, and the first year fell to Eteokles. Polyneikes, by the terms of the contract, went into banishment, until his turn to rule should come.

He arrived at Argos, and there fell in with Tydeus of Kalydon, who was also in banishment, for homicide. The two quarrelled, and soon came to blows, when Adrastos, son of Talaos and king of Argos, came to stop them. He had been given a mysterious oracle that he was not to allow his daughters to marry any save a lion and a boar ; now Polyneikes had a lion's skin over his shoulders, Tydeus a boar's, or they had these beasts for their shield-devices. In them, therefore, Adrastos recognized the destined bridegrooms. Accordingly, Tydeus married Deïpyle, daughter of Adrastos, Polyneikes her sister Argeia, to whom he gave the fatal necklace of Harmonia, which he had somehow brought with him. Adrastos undertook to restore both his sons-in-law to their countries.

Pausanias preserves a tale according to which Polyneikes left Thebes before the quarrel began, in an attempt to avoid the curse of his father, and that on that occasion he met and married Argeia ; when Eteokles began to reign, he invited his brother back ; the quarrel and (second) exile followed. [29]

Eteokles had already given unequivocal signs that he was not going to yield the kingdom to Polyneikes, or to anyone else ; or it was assumed that he would not do so. In any case, no time was lost by Adrastos in getting together a large army. For leaders, besides himself and his two sons-in-law, he had Kapaneus son of Hipponoos, Hippomedon son of Aristomachos,—these two were both Argives,—Parthenopaios son of Meilanion and of Atalante the Arkadian huntress, of whom more will be said in discussing the Kalydonian saga, and finally Amphiaraos son of Oikles, the seer. These are the Seven against Thebes.

The list is not quite agreed upon ; Aeschylus includes in it Eteoklos son of Iphis, omitting Adrastos ; others, according to Apollodoros, included Mekisteus and Eteoklos, omitting both Tydeus and Polyneikes, presumably as not being leaders of independent contingents.

Amphiaraos, being a seer, foreknew that the expedition would be a failure and that he, if he went on it, would never come back, indeed that no leader save Adrastos would ever return. Knowing that Polyneikes would try to enlist the persuasions of his wife, Eriphyle, he forbade her to accept any gift from that quarter. She, however, disobeyed him, was bribed with the necklace of Harmonia, and at last won her husband to join the ill-fated enterprise. Departing reluctantly, he laid on his children the charge that they should avenge his death on their mother, and also that they should themselves make an expedition against Thebes when their time came. [30]

Tydeus was sent to Thebes to urge the claims of Polyneikes. According to a legend as old as Homer, his mission was a stormy one, for he was waylaid on his return ; Homer says it was because he had excelled all the Thebans in athletic prowess and they were jealous of him, while the later version is that it was sheer unmotived treachery on the part of Eteokles, but in any case his single valour was too much for the fifty who attacked him from an ambush, and he killed them all, save one, whom he spared to carry home the news.[31]

The expedition now set out, and marched uneventfully as far as Nemea. Here befell the incident which led to the founding of the Nemean Games. Hypsipyle, for reasons which will be given in discussing the Argonautic saga, had been driven from Lemnos, captured by pirates, and sold as a slave to Lykurgos, king of Nemea, who had a young son, Opheltes, whose nurse she became. Adrastos' army was short of water, or wanted running water for a sacrifice,[32] and Hypsipyle agreed to show them a spring. She left her nursling on the ground meanwhile, and it was killed by a dragon who infested the place. Returning, the Seven found the dead child, killed the dragon, gave little Opheltes a magnificent funeral, and celebrated the games for the first time ; for a considerable period, according to tradition, they were open only to ' soldiers' sons ', meaning apparently the descendants of those who served in the expedition.[33] Hypsipyle herself was protected from the vengeance of Lykurgos and his wife Eurydike by the army, and afterwards carried away by Thoas and Euneos, her children by Jason, who after a series of adventures of no great interest had arrived at Nemea, and recognized her, with the help of Amphiaraos, according to Euripides.[34] Amphiaraos named the dead child Archemoros (' Beginner of Death '), since his was the first of the many lives to be lost in the expedition.

The great stress laid upon the funeral rites of this baby, the association with the serpent, and the fact that it is his nurse, not his mother, who is prominent in the story, all suggest that he is originally a child-god of Cretan type, no human infant at all.[35]

The army now marched against the city, where after some indecisive fighting, or immediately on their arrival, they apportioned each of the seven gates of Thebes to one of their champions.

According to Aeschylus, the arrangement of attack and defence was as follows :

Gate	Assailant	Defender
Proitides	Tydeus	Melanippos
Elektrai	Kapaneus	Polyphontes
Neïstai	Eteoklos	Megareus
Onkaiai	Hippomedon	Hyperbios
Borrhaiai	Parthenopaios	Aktor
Homoloides	Amphiaraos	Lasthenes
Hypsistai	Polyneikes	Eteokles

However, the names in all three columns vary more or less in various authorities, for example, Euripides and Apollodoros.[36]

The result was the utter rout of the Argives. Kapaneus, as he mounted the wall, swore that not even Zeus should keep him out of the city now, for which impiety he was struck down by a thunderbolt. Tydeus, after fighting with desperate valour, got a mortal wound. Athena, who throughout had favoured him, was minded to bring him the gift of immortality. But his ungovernable rage had got the better of him, and as she came up, she found him gnawing the head of Melanippos, who had also fallen. In disgust, she withheld her gift, and Tydeus died. Amphiaraos fled in his chariot, but was swallowed up alive in the earth; in later times the spot was much renowned for the true oracles which the seer continued to give after death, as in life. Adrastos escaped, thanks to the speed of his horse, Arion, offspring of Poseidon and Demeter Erinys.[37] There remained now, for the other three (or four) assailants of the gates had fallen, only the two brothers; their combat ended in either killing the other.

Kreon was now master of the situation, and gave orders that the Theban dead, especially Eteokles, should be buried with all honour, but the bodies of the enemy left to rot. This was against all Greek ideas of piety, since the ghost of one unburied could not find entrance to the House of Hades; burial indeed is but the formal making over of the dead person to the powers of the nether world, and hence not to bury one dead, or to entomb one living, was to put him in a most dangerous magical state, namely, on a borderline.[38] Hence Kreon had offended, not only the common feelings of humanity, but the gods above and below, for the latter were defrauded of their due, the former polluted by the corpses left in their realm. Therefore vengeance descended upon him.

One well-known version of the legend [39] so redounds to the glory of the Athenians that it is probably their own. Adrastos, with the mothers of the dead chieftains, went to Attica and sat a suppliant at an altar. Aithra, mother of Theseus, associated herself with them, and Theseus was easily persuaded to espouse their cause. Collecting his army, he attacked Thebes, defeated

Kreon, and gave honourable burial to the slain.   Euadne, wife of Kapaneus, hurled herself into her husband's funeral pyre, an act very reminiscent of Hindu *sati*, but without parallel in Greek tradition.

It is a happy thought of sundry lateish authors [40] to make the suppliants take refuge at the famous altar of Mercy (Eleos) in Athens. But if this were more than a pretty invention, we should expect Euripides to have heard of it, which he has not, but places the whole scene at Eleusis.

More complicated is the version followed by Sophokles in his *Antigone*, which apparently represents more or less the common form of the saga.   Antigone, he and the other tragedians agree, refused to let her brother go unburied, and secretly contrived to throw a little dust over him, thus giving him the formal interment which was strictly necessary.   She was caught at this pious duty, and Kreon had her put alive into a sepulchre.   Now this was doubly impious.   In the first place, Antigone was not his to dispose of in this manner, for although he was her natural guardian, she was betrothed to his son Haimon, who should have been consulted in the matter.   In the second, an ordeal of this kind, in which a living person is put into the world of the dead, is against Greek custom, although the entombment of guilty Vestals is an obvious Roman parallel.   It was not an execution, for it was left to Hades to say what should become of Antigone.   She, however, settled the matter by hanging herself in the tomb.   Haimon, who had come to rescue her, killed himself over her dead body ; Hades thus reunited husband and wife.   Kreon's queen, Eurydike, killed herself on hearing of her son's death.   Kreon lived for many years longer, but was at last dethroned and slain by Lykos, whom we shall meet again in the story of Herakles.

There is another and very romantic tale of Antigone, brought into literature if not actually invented by Euripides.[41]   Kreon bade Haimon put Antigone to death, which command, however cruel, was at least correct, since he if anyone had the right to do so.   But he saved her alive, telling his father that she was dead.   Sheltered by some shepherds, she bore Haimon a son, whom years afterwards she brought into Thebes to a festival.   There Kreon recognized him as one of the Spartoi by the birth-mark, shaped like a spear-head, which all that stock had.   According to Hyginus, he ordered her execution, and, the intervention of Herakles proving vain, she and her husband killed themselves.   But what little is left of Euripides' play suggests that a happy ending came about somehow, possibly through the influence of Dionysos, whom some one addresses in terms of zealous adoration in a fragment supposed to come from that drama.

The war of the Seven had two important sequels. The sons of the fallen chieftains, together with Aigialeus son of Adrastos, set forth once again to attack Thebes, and this time were successful. This is the war of the Epigonoi, or Younger Generation. The Thebans evacuated the city, and the aged Adrastos, who had led the army, died on the way home at Megara, from grief for his son, who alone had fallen in the campaign. The date of this is supposed to be shortly before the war of Troy.[42] Setting aside the obviously fabulous elements of the whole story, we seem to touch on real events; it is noteworthy that the Catalogue of the Ships, in the *Iliad*, which is practically a survey of the geography of pre-Dorian Greece and a historical document of the highest importance, does not mention Thebes, but only Hypothebai, *i.e.*, Lower Thebes, doubtless a settlement which had grown up at the foot of the ruined and abandoned citadel.

The other event was the revenge of Alkmeon (or Alkmaion) son of Amphiaraos.[43] In accordance with his father's commands he, like Orestes, killed his mother. The result was similar; pursued from place to place by the Erinyes, although Apollo had formally approved his action and favoured him, after a time he came to Psophis in Arkadia, where Phegeus, king of that place, purified him and gave him his daughter Arsinoe in marriage. But famine fell on the country, and Alkmeon was bidden to seek a land on which the sun had not shone when he killed his mother. This he found at the mouth of the Acheloos, which had recently brought down some new land; there he settled, and married Kallirhoe, daughter of the god of the river. As his new wife longed for the necklace and robe of Harmonia (the latter, according to Apollodoros, had also been given to Eriphyle, to induce her son to go with the Epigonoi; a feeble doublet of the story concerning the necklace), he got them from Phegeus by a trick; this being found out, he was set upon and killed by the latter's sons, at the command of their father. Arsinoe, who protested, was put into a chest (again this curious motif of a chest, which as already stated I cannot explain[44]), taken to Tegea, and given as a slave to Agapenor, king of Arkadia. But Kallirhoe begged Zeus, who was her lover, to cause her sons by Alkmeon, Akarnan and Amphoteros, to grow immediately to manhood. This was granted her, and the young men killed the sons of Phegeus, then Phegeus himself and his wife; after which they reported their doings to their mother, dedicated the robe and necklace to Apollo at Delphoi (where, according to later legends, the latter was stolen during the Phokian or Sacred War and brought nothing but ill-luck to the thief), and then, gathering a band of followers, founded the land known in later ages as Akarnania.

Another figure intimately connected with the Theban saga is Teiresias the seer.[45] With him we step into pure fairy-tale. His fame is as old as Homer, who knows that he alone of mankind was given grace to keep his wits in the House of Hades, where the rest flit as shadows. He was a Theban, one of the Spartoi by descent, son of Eueres and grandson of Udaios ; his mother was the nymph Chariklo. He lived a prodigious while, seven generations according to Hesiod. The same authority, as also many later writers, assures us that once, on Mt. Kyllene (or more usually, Kithairon ; Kyllene, being both the older and the less natural site, is obviously the original one), he saw two snakes coupling, and killed the female. Promptly, he was turned into a woman, and so remained until at length, once more seeing a pair of coupling snakes, he killed the male, and regained his former sex. Now it chanced that Zeus and Hera had a quarrel as to which sex got the more pleasure of love ; on submitting their dispute to Teiresias, they learned that the woman has nine times as much delight therefrom as the man. Hera was furious, and blinded the umpire, but Zeus, to console him, gave him seercraft and long life.

Here we have most obvious folktale, plainly older than the other story, found first in Pherekydes and modelled on that of Aktaion. He came upon Athena as she was bathing, and although the goddess' mercy preserved his life, his eyes paid the forfeit. A third story makes him a prophet from birth, as indeed the son of a nymph might well be, and blinded as a punishment for revealing the secrets of the gods. In itself, it is a normal tale enough, the crime being like that of Tantalos in one version.[46] In any case, the blind prophet or poet is a familiar figure of Greek legend, for the very good reason that it is true to life. In a barbarous or semi-barbarous community, such as those of the earliest Greeks must have been, the blind man is enforcedly idle, left much to the company of his own thoughts, and therefore likelier than a sighted man to see visions and dream dreams, which take the form of poems or prophecies,—the two are not sharply distinguished. It is to be remembered that Homer was traditionally blind, and describes the bard Demodokos as being sightless, while an early Homeric poet, author of the Hymn to Apollo, states that he himself was blind.[47]

Teiresias, then, remained in great honour at Thebes throughout the troubled period we have just described. In the great siege by the Seven, he discovered that there was only one salvation for the city ; the blood-guilt for the sacred dragon still lay heavy upon them, and could be atoned for only by the sacrifice of one of the Spartoi. Menoikeus, son of Kreon, cheerfully undertook to provide the victim, and stabbing himself on the walls, fell dying into the very lair of the dragon, thus giving the Earth, as Teiresias explains in Euripides,[48] *a harvest of man's life for the harvest she had borne, and blood for her blood*. In the last extremity of the city, after the then king, Laodamas, had killed Aigialeus and himself been killed by Alkmeon, it was Teiresias who advised the Thebans to keep the Argives amused with a pretended negotiation for peace, while they themselves put their wives and children on waggons and slipped away from the city in the dead of night. This was the last act of his life. On the way he drank of the spring Tilphussa, and died, apparently of the chill of the water. His daughter, generally called Manto (Divineress), was captured by the victorious Epigonoi, and sent to Delphoi as part of Apollo's share in the spoil.

It need hardly be added that Manto and the Delphian Sibyl (Chapter VI, p. 138) are confused.

About contemporary with the reign of Oidipus, in the traditional chronology, but quite unconnected with Thebes, is the great exploit of the Argonautic expedition.[49] As the Argonauts are persistently called Minyai, and a very lame explanation given,[50] we must suppose that originally it was a tale of the inhabitants of Orchomenos, or perhaps of some other settlement of the mysterious Minyan people. But as we have it, the ' Argo which is all men's concern ', as Homer calls her,[51] has sailed far away from her original builders and owners ; the geography of the story, centering as it does about the Black Sea, leads us to suppose that the outline at least of the saga grew up at Miletos, which had relations with that part of the world early in the history of Greek colonization, and whose great family, the Neleidai, claimed Minyan descent. On the other hand, Thessaly has had no small share in it, for the great voyage was begun at Pagasai, and Thessalian heroes, notably Jason (Iason or Ieson) himself, figure largely in it. The claims of other cities (some of them no doubt justified) will be found discussed in the authorities cited in Note 49.

Something of the matrimonial adventures of Athamas, son of Aiolos the son of Hellen, has been told in Chapter VI (p. 150). His first wife was Nephele, *i.e.*, Cloud ; a cloud-fairy, in other words. She bore him two children, Phrixos and Helle. Ino, the second wife in the ordinary form of the story, hated and plotted against her stepchildren. She therefore, pretending, one may suppose, that it was a helpful charm, persuaded the women to roast the seed-corn for the next year ; as there was then naturally no harvest, Delphoi was consulted concerning the famine, and the messengers bribed by Ino to bring back a false answer, that Phrixos, or Phrixos and Helle, should be sacrificed.[52] They were, however, rescued by their mother, who brought them a golden-fleeced ram which carried them away. They went across the sea towards Kolchis ; Helle fell off at the point afterwards called in memory of her the Hellespont (Dardanelles), but Phrixos arrived safely. Here the king of Kolchis, Aietes, son of Helios and Perse or Perseis, received him kindly, and gave him his daughter Chalkiope in marriage. The ram Phrixos sacrificed to Zeus Phyxios (God of Flight), and hung its fleece up in a safe place, generally a grove where a dragon guarded it. Chalkiope bore him sons, Argos, Melas, Phrontis and Kytisoros. At length he died and was buried in Kolchis.

It is clear that this is a fairly complete story, and does not necessarily lead up to what follows. The original goal of the Argo is called Aia in Homer and many other authors, i.e., simply ' the Land ', and Aietes is ' the man of the Land '. It is a fairy place, ' east of the sun and west of the moon ', suitable for the hiding-place of a magical treasure, a pot of rainbow-gold.

All manner of variants exist. Phrixos was saved by the intervention of a servant who revealed Ino's treachery ; Athamas handed Ino and her son Melikertes to him for punishment, but Dionysos rescued them, and drove Phrixos and Helle mad ; in their crazed wanderings they met their mother, who gave them the ram, which was the offspring of Poseidon and Theophane.[53] Aietes killed Phrixos, and meant to kill all his children as well, because an oracle had warned him, or soothsayers had told him, that the son of the stranger would slay him.[54] These are merely samples, and do not include various silly attempts to rationalize the ram into a man called Krios, or a ship with a ram for figure-head.

The adventure of Phrixos, whatever the details, provided the future adventurers with a wonderful something to look for. The occasion of the voyage was as follows. Kretheus, Athamas' brother, king of Iolkos in Thessaly (a Minyan settlement), died, leaving a son Aison and a stepson Pelias, child of Poseidon and of Kretheus' wife and niece Tyro, and brother of Neleus the founder of the Pylian dynasty. Aison was of course the lawful heir, but Pelias somehow got possession of the throne, either deposing Aison,[55] or simply being left, on Aison dying a natural death, as guardian of the kingdom and of his young nephew Jason.[56] But the latter's mother did not trust Pelias, and her son was got safely out of the way, in charge of Cheiron the centaur, who, in contrast to the general wildness of his race, was just and wise, skilled especially in music and medicine. In his cave and under the care of him and his mother Philyra Jason lived for many years, enjoying the companionship of many other princes, who were sent from all parts to learn of Cheiron. Meanwhile Pelias was not comfortable, for an oracle had warned him to beware of the one-sandalled man. Also, whether he knew it or not, Hera, to whom he had neglected to sacrifice, hated him. One day a handsome young man with but one foot shod walked into Iolkos. It was Jason, who had one foot bare either because it was the Magnesian custom to dress so,— a bare foot gives a better grip on muddy ground,[57]—or for a reason savouring more of fairy-tale. There had been heavy rain, and as he came down from Cheiron's cave [58] he noticed, on the banks of a swollen river, a poor old woman, evidently afraid to cross. He carried her over on his shoulders, but not without difficulty, for the torrent was strong, and in so doing he lost one sandal in the mud. On the other side of the stream the woman revealed herself as Hera, who thenceforth favoured him in return for his courtesy.[59] Pelias recognized the man of destiny, and was by no means reassured on finding that it was his nephew, for his doom was to die by the force or cunning of one of the Aiolidai, his own line on the mother's side,[60] and Jason's on both. So he spoke the new-comer fair, and with a plausible story of being haunted by the ghost of Phrixos, who demanded the recovery of the fleece, he easily induced him to set out in search of it.[61]

Straightway, by Jason's own efforts and those of Hera, aided by Athena, who also favoured Jason, an expedition was got ready. Argos, son of Arestor, built them a ship, the first, or the first long-ship at least, that ever was made, and Athena helped him with advice and also fixed in the bows a piece of wood from the oak of Dodona, which had the power of speech. Some fifty of the noblest heroes in Greece came to join, from sheer love of adventure, or induced by Hera. As might be expected, no two lists agree as to their names, for an Argonautic ancestor was an addition to even the proudest pedigrees. We may, however, name a few,[62] who are regularly present and fall into three main classes. First there are the ' specialized ' heroes, such as Tiphys the pilot and Lynkeus the super-lookout, who are discussed in Chapter X, p. 294. Next comes an important class, the fathers of the heroes of the Trojan War, as Peleus father of Achilles, Telamon father of the greater Aias, and so on. Another category consists of those who took part in the Kalydōnian boar-hunt, to be described later. These include Meleagros himself, Laokoon his father's brother, Iphiklos his maternal uncle, and other members of the same family. To these must be added representatives of various

Greek states, put there no doubt by the local patriotism of later days, while two of the most prominent of the whole list are the obvious intruders Orpheus and Herakles. The former, who is not heard of till much later than Homer, obviously has no place in a saga already well known in Homer's own day ; the latter was too important to be left out of an adventure supposed to have happened in his days, but is simply a nuisance to the tellers of the story, since a subordinate rôle is absurd for him, and Jason, Argos, Tiphys and a few more have all the leading parts ; hence he is got rid of as early as possible.

Sailing up the coast from Pagasai, the port of Iolkos, the heroes made their first long halt at Lemnos. Here they found everything in the hands of the women, for there were no men left. Some time before, the Lemnian women had neglected the cult of Aphrodite, who in revenge caused them to have a foul odour which disgusted their husbands. The latter filled their places with Thracian women, captured in a raid on the mainland. The women of Lemnos plotted to avenge themselves, and in a single night killed every male in the island. Only Hypsipyle showed any natural feelings, getting her aged father Thoas, son of Dionysos and king of the island, safely down to the coast, where Dionysos helped him to get away. The women, after a feeble show of resistance, were glad to come to terms with the Argonauts, who lived with them for a year, during which time they begat many children, Jason in particular wedding Hypsipyle, who bore him two sons, Euneos and Thoas, as already stated.[63] Finally Herakles urged them to continue their adventure.

The next halt was, in some accounts, Samothrace, where they all were initiated into the famous local mysteries, by advice of Orpheus. This is of course a comparatively late episode. Next they came to Kyzikos, where they were hospitably received by the natives, the Doliones, and Kyzikos their king. They did good service in return for their welcome, for Herakles shot with his arrows the Gegeneis who infested the uplands.[64] Unfortunately, when they departed, a storm drove them back in the night ; the Doliones mistook them for enemies, and in the ensuing scuffle Kyzikos was killed. Having mourned for him, the Argonauts went on to Kios, where they landed because Herakles had broken his oar. He went to get material for a new one, and the rest prepared supper meanwhile ; Hylas, son of Theiodamas, Herakles' favourite, who acted as his page, went for water, and soon found a good spring. But the water-nymphs, attracted by his beauty, pulled him in, and Polyphemos and Herakles, coming in answer to his cry for help, could not find him. They roved the woods all

night, and at last the Argonauts, after a hot debate, went on
without them.   Later, Herakles met the two sons of Boreas,
Zetes and Kalais, who had advised leaving him, and killed them
both in the island of Tenos.   He set up grave-stones over them,
which always moved when the North Wind (Boreas) blew.
Glaukos, after the Boreadai had given their advice to the Argonauts, appeared from the sea and told them that Herakles was
destined to other exploits than this.[65]

As to Hylas, Apollonios says that in his own day the people of Kios
continued yearly to search and call for him, in obedience to orders
given by Herakles.   This is pretty clear indication that he is in origin
a godling, probably connected with vegetation, who annually disappears
and presumably comes back again after a search, no doubt in spring-
time.   Osiris is the stock example of this type of deity ; another is
the obscure Bormos, who was ' the brother of Iollas and Mariandynos,
child of king Upios, who died young when out hunting, in the summer-
time, and is honoured in a mournful rustic song '.[66]   Another is
Linos, who was the son of Apollo and of Psamathe (Sand-girl) daughter
of Krotopos king of Argos, but was exposed by his mother at birth,
and, then or later, torn in pieces by dogs ; or son of Amphimaros and
the Muse Urania, who was killed by Apollo for daring to rival him in
music ; or he was Herakles' teacher, and his unruly pupil, when Linos
tried to punish him, beat the teacher's brains out with his own lyre ;
and in any case, he seems to have grown out of the words, or word,
αἴλινον or αἲ Λίνον, in a very old traditional song of harvesters and
vintagers.[67]   Similar again is Lityerses, the Phrygian, whose name
may mean ' rain-dew '.   He was a son of Midas, used to challenge all
comers to contest with him in reaping, and would kill or beat those
whom he could out-do, till at last a more violent opponent (some say
Herakles) struck him dead.   An Egyptian figure of the same kind was
Maneros (? *maa-ne-hra*, ' come back ! '), son of the first king of Egypt,
who died young and was lamented.[68]   All these songs were mournful,
perhaps, because the dead vegetation-spirit was mourned for.   Hylas'
name may be no more than a scrap of his song ; Kretschmer would
connect it with Lat. *ululare*, and indeed there is nothing strange in the
idea that the dirge contained the words ' Howl, howl ', *ut litus Hyla,
Hyla, omne sonaret.*[69]

The Argonauts pushed on, and came to the land of the
Bebrykes, whose king, Amykos, was the son of Poseidon by a
Melia (ash-tree nymph) of Bithynia, in which region they had now
arrived.   He insisted on boxing with all strangers.   The crew of
the Argo included the Dioskuroi, Kastor and Polydeukes ; the
former was a mighty horseman, the latter a boxer.   He promptly
accepted Amykos' challenge and knocked him out after a brisk
set-to.   The Bebrykians, who had no sporting instincts, broke

into the ring with clubs and other barbarous weapons, but were soon routed by the Argonauts.[70] The next stop was Salmydessos and here they met with the aged king Phineus, who was blind and in great misery. The reason for this is variously given, as is the genealogy of this interesting character. Hesiod (the name is of course applied to the composers of many poems, no doubt by sundry authors) gave two accounts—one, that he was blinded by Helios, because he preferred a long life to eyesight ; another, that he was punished with blindness for having shown Phrixos the way to Aia,—a fragment of a version of Phrixos' story that has not survived. Another story, originating so far as we know in Attic authors, is that he had had two children by his first wife, Kleopatra daughter of the North Wind ; after her death he married another wife, who so wrought upon him that he either blinded his children himself, or let her do so. In one continuation of the story, Zeus gave him his choice between death and blindness ; he chose the latter, which offended Helios mightily, and induced him to send the Harpies as a further punishment. Or, and here again we meet a persistent theme, he had the gift of prophecy and misused it to betray the secrets of the gods to all and sundry, wherefore the double penalty of blindness and the Harpies fell upon him. The Harpies carry him away in one version, but generally they carry off or befoul his food, so that he nearly dies of hunger.[71] When the Argonauts came, they soon reached an agreement with him, to deliver him of the Harpies if he would show them how to reach their goal ; or Zetes and Kalais took pity on him, as he was their brother-in-law. In either case, they awaited the coming of the Harpies, and then rose into the air with drawn swords (for, as befits the children of a wind-god, they were winged), and chased the monsters until, in the usual form of the story, they came to the Strophades (which with a little good will can be taken to mean ' isles of turning or return '), where a divine messenger, Hermes or Iris, bade them go back and swore that Phineus should have no more trouble from the Harpies.[72] He then gave them an outline of their further adventures, and in particular, told them how to deal with the greatest obstacle, the Symplegades,—the Clashing Rocks. These stood at the entrance to the Pontos, and crashed together every now and again with irresistible force. He advised them, when they came near to this spot, to let loose a dove, which would fly between the rocks as they opened. If it was caught, they were to turn back ; but if it got through safely, they were to wait till the rocks opened again, and then row their hardest between them. They took his advice, and the Symplegades just clipped the tail-feathers of the dove. They then rowed between them, and got through with a little damage to the stern-works of the Argo. After this they had no adventures of any importance in the Pontos; but landing in the country of the Mariandynoi, whose king, Lykos, received them hospitably, they lost Idmon, one of the two seers who were of their company (the other was Mopsos; it is noteworthy that there is rather an overplus of prophets in this story, Phineus, Mopsos, Idmon and Orpheus all taking part in one way or another). He was killed by a boar while they were hunting; Tiphys the helmsman also died, of a disease; his place was taken by Ankaios, or Erginos.[73] Under his guidance they came to the Island of Ares, where the Stymphalian birds had taken refuge after Herakles had driven them from their native place; these they managed to frighten off by striking their shields. Here also they picked up the sons of Phrixos, who had set out from Kolchis to visit their father's native land, but had been shipwrecked. With this not unwelcome addition to their numbers, they pressed on and reached Kolchis safely.[74]

Now we pass into pure and simple *märchen*. Aietes had no mind to let the Fleece go (it is likely enough, if we had the earliest forms of the story in full, that the luck of his kingdom was contained in it, or at any rate that it was a powerfully magical object). After much bluster, he announced his terms; they might take the Fleece, if one of them would plough a large field with a pair of bronze bulls, the gift of Hephaistos to him, which breathed out fire, and would then sow it with some of the teeth of Kadmos' dragon, which Aietes had in his possession, and finally, would deal with the armed men who sprang up from the seed. Now Aietes had a second daughter, Medeia; like her father's sister Kirke, she was an enchantress, a priestess of Hekate. Hera persuaded Aphrodite to make her fall in love with Jason, which she did, through the agency of Eros; in Valerius Flaccus, she herself appears in the form of Kirke to finish the work of overcoming Medeia's scruples.[75] She therefore provided Jason with a wonderful ointment which made him and his armour proof against fire and all weapons for the space of a day. His own strength and skill enabled him to master and yoke the bulls and plough the field; the armed men he got rid of in the same way as Kadmos had, namely by throwing a stone among them to set them fighting. But Aietes suspected Medeia, and planned to set upon the heroes in the night and destroy them and their ship. Medeia therefore made her way secretly to them, and urged them to fly at once. On the way, she led them to the grove where the Fleece was, charmed the dragon, and showed them the Fleece itself.

Aietes discovered their flight, and either made after them or sent his son Apsyrtos in pursuit. Medeia, in the former version, had taken Apsyrtos with her (in this form of the story, he was a child) ; she now killed him, cut him up, and strewed his limbs in the way of her father, who stayed to pick them up and so lost the fugitives. In the latter, she beguiled Apsyrtos into an ambush, where he was set upon and killed by the Argonauts, thus discouraging his followers.[76] It is noteworthy that the tone of the story has quite altered, from the clean atmosphere of Homeric exploits to mean and treacherous magic and intrigue.

The object of the journey was now accomplished, and the return began. How this was achieved, is a subject on which ancient authorities differ widely, but their answers to the question fall into three main categories, neglecting the opinion of those who say they returned the way they came.

(1) The Argonauts went to the very verge of the earth, got into the stream of Ocean, and so sailed around until they somehow got into the Mediterranean again, and thus home to Thessaly.[77]

(2) They went up the Istros (Danube), as far as it would take them ; then carried their ship overland, got into the North Sea, presumably down the Rhine, and passed around the British Isles, down the coasts of France and Spain, and through the Straits of Gibraltar.[78]

(3) After going up the Istros, they passed overland into the Eridanos, a mysterious river made up of hazy notions of several European streams, including the Po, and so down to the Mediterranean.[79]

All three versions have this in common, that the Argonauts, wherever and however they reached the Mediterranean, touched at several places traditionally connected with the Minyai. A few of their adventures in this connexion are important enough to be told here.

After getting into the Tyrrhenian Sea, they landed at Aithalia (Elba), where they wiped off their sweat with pebbles from the beach ; ever since then, the pebbles have looked like human skin.[80]

Knowing that the wrath of Zeus pursued them for the murder of Apsyrtos (for the speaking prow of the Argo had informed them), they went to Aiaie, Kirke's island, and appealed to her, as an expert in all magic matters, to purify them, which she did.[81]

The Planktai, a doublet of the Symplegades, were encountered, but the unseen help of Thetis and her sister-Nereids steered them between these and the double danger of Skylla and Charybdis. Just before this, they had passed the Sirens, but Orpheus saved all but Butes from listening to their song, by playing on his lyre. Butes jumped overboard, but was rescued by Aphrodite.[82]

Wandering south, they were stranded in the Syrtis, and forced to carry the Argo overland till at last they came to Lake Tritonis. Here, as they made their way painfully out through the channels of the lake, befell the adventure with Triton, already described. During their overland journey, they came to the Gardens of the Hesperides.[83]

Getting at last nearer home, they touched at Crete. Here a bronze giant, Talos, prevented their landing. This monster was a survival of the Bronze race, or had been specially made by Hephaistos, and given by him, or by Zeus, to Europê, or Minos. He guarded the island by walking around it three times a day, and those whom he caught he burned to death, either by becoming exceedingly hot himself or by throwing them into a fire. But he had one weak spot. In one heel was the entrance to a vein, closed by a bronze pin, or a membrane; let that be opened, and he would bleed to death. Medeia, by her magic, sent him into something like a hypnotic trance, and he was soon dispatched by taking out the pin, or bursting the membrane.[84]

Returned to Iolkos, Medeia proceeded to take vengeance against Pelias. He was old, and she persuaded his daughters that she had a charm to make him young; to demonstrate it she cooked, in a cauldron of water impregnated with certain magic herbs, Jason's aged father Aison. He came forth a young man. She repeated the process with an old ram, who reappeared a tender he-lamb. Clearly, we have a doublet here, for either one of these experiments would have convinced the most sceptical, and in some accounts the ram only appears, Aison being by that time dead, whether by Pelias' machinations or otherwise. In any case, Pelias' daughters were convinced, and repeated the experiment with him; but this time Medeia was careful not to give them the right herbs, and Pelias regained neither youth nor life.[85] This was too much for the patience of Akastos, Pelias' son, who drove Jason and Medeia out of the country; they settled at Corinth, and there, after some years, Jason cast Medeia off and married Glauke, daughter of the local king, Kreon. Medeia sent the bride a robe and tiara smeared with a drug which burnt her and her father, who tried to rescue her, to death, and then escaped in a winged chariot. Her two children, Mermeros and Pheres, were killed either by herself (a story invented perhaps by Euripides, who certainly is the first to tell it) or by the Corinthians; in the latter legend, which is the Corinthian version, their vengeful ghosts destroyed the Corinthian children until

certain rites were instituted to appease them.[86]   Jason himself
had dedicated the Argo to Poseidon, at the Isthmos ; one day,
as he sat beneath it, a part of the woodwork fell upon him and
killed him.[87]   Medeia escaped to Athens, where we shall meet her
again in the story of Theseus.

Mention has already been made several times of Herakles, the
most famous of all Greek heroes, and the common property of the
entire race, although he may have been a Tirynthian and Thebes
claimed to be his native city ; the idea that he was specifically
Dorian is now exploded.[88]   His name (Glory of Hera ;   the
Germanic equivalent would be Frobert) shows that he was no
god, for no Greek god has a name compounded of another's ;
but it is likely enough that gods as well as other heroes have
been laid under contribution to form his complex legend.   Probably behind all the complexities there is, if we could come at it,
the figure of a real man, a baron of Tiryns, in, perhaps, Mycenaean
times, vassal of the greater king of Mycenae, and renowned as a
warrior and hunter of more than common courage and strength.
For some reason, he caught the popular imagination, and is
consistently represented as having just those virtues which the
generality of mankind most admires, strength, valour, good
nature, generosity, pity for the distressed, love of adventure, and
hardiness ;   with those vices which are most readily pardoned,
a hot temper, insatiable gluttony, and a lust as boundless as his
strength.   By stressing one side of his character, he becomes the
comic Herakles of the Attic stage, a sort of Ralph Roister Doister ;
by emphasizing the other, he is still more grotesquely transformed,
especially by the later Cynics and Stoics, into a strutting, ranting
moralist, who goes about looking for painful situations in which
to show his fortitude.   The most glaring examples of this are
to be found in Seneca's *Hercules Furens*, and in the *Hercules
Oetaeus*, a work somewhat after his style but too foolish and ill-
written even for him.

While properly associated with Tiryns, Herakles is claimed
by Thebes, where, according to the usual legend, he was born.
Elektryon, king of Mycenae, had a quarrel with the sons of
Pterelaos, who was the son of Taphios, son of Poseidon and
Hippothoe, a descendant of Pelops on her mother's side, and king
of the Teleboans.   In the fighting, all the sons of Elektryon save
one, Likymnios, and all the sons of Pterelaos except Eueres,
were killed ;   Elektryon, as Likymnios was still a child, handed
over his kingdom to Amphitryon, son of Alkaios, who was
betrothed to his daughter Alkmene.   But by an unfortunate
accident, Amphitryon killed Elektryon, and had therefore to leave

the country and take refuge in Thebes. Alkmene bore him no
malice, but insisted that he should avenge the quarrel of her father
and brothers before she would live with him. Amphitryon therefore asked Kreon, who was then king of Thebes, to give him an
army to attack the Teleboans ; Kreon consented, if Amphitryon
would first rid the country of a monstrous fox, which was fated
never to be caught by any pursuer. Amphitryon collected volun-
teers, to whom he promised a share of the booty expected from
the Teleboans. One of those who responded was Kephalos of
Athens, who brought with him the marvellous hound given to his
wife Prokris by Minos ; this was fated to catch whatever it chased.
The hunt began, and Zeus solved the riddle of the uncatchable
fox pursued by the invariably successful hound by turning both
into stone. Now began the campaign against the Teleboans,
in which the forces of Amphitryon were hampered by the immortality of king Pterelaos. This was a gift conferred upon him
by his ancestor Poseidon, and it depended upon a single golden
hair which grew in his head. His daughter Komaitho fell
desperately in love with Amphitryon, however, and pulled out the
fatal hair.[89] Now Pterelaos was killed and the island of Taphos,
where he lived, subjected, together with the other islands (the
Echinades) of the same group. Amphitryon put Komaitho to
death for her treachery, and returned in triumph to Thebes.

But meanwhile, the beauty of Alkmene had attracted Zeus.
Taking the form of Amphitryon, he visited her on the very night
of her husband's return, which he made three times the usual
length. Later in the night, the real Amphitryon came to her,
and she conceived twin children. One, Amphitryon's son,
Iphikles or Iphiklos, was an ordinary child, not destined to any
very distinguished career ; the other was Herakles. In this
story we have a very widespread belief, firstly that twins are
apt to be in some way remarkable, or that one of them is, and
secondly that one of the two is the child of a god or spirit of some
kind, not of the mother's mortal consort.[90]

Hera, who knew to what glory her husband's bastard was
destined, was furious and did everything in her power to kill or at
least hamper him ; to her machinations, in the story as we have
it, nearly all his misfortunes and trials are due. Before his birth,
she robbed him of his true inheritance ; for Zeus had meant him
to be lord of the surrounding peoples. But on the day when his
birth was expected, he mentioned this, and Hera tricked him into
an ambiguous oath, ' Verily, he that this day is born of a woman,
of the race that boasts my blood, shall be lord of all that dwell
around him.' Now Menippe, the wife of Sthenelos, was seven

months gone with child ; as her husband was of the blood of
Perseus, the son of Zeus and Danae, the conditions would be
fulfilled if she that day bore a son. Hera sent the Eileithyai to
delay the birth of Alkmene's children and bring Menippe's into the
world before his time. She bore Eurystheus, who thus got the
benefit of the oath of Zeus.[91]

Ovid has an amusing and obviously popular tale on this subject.
Eileithyia, to prevent Alkmene from being delivered, sat seven days
and nights with her hands clasped on her knees, a well-known magical
gesture to bind anything. But Alkmene had a clever waiting-maid,
Galanthis, who noticed the attitude of the goddess and recognized her
and her intentions. She ran hastily out from the house and cried to
Eileithyia, ' Give my mistress your congratulations ; she is safely
delivered.' Eileithyia, in astonishment, sprang up and raised her
hands ; at once the charm was undone, and Alkmene suddenly found
herself a happy mother. Galanthis, however, was seized by Eileithyia
and turned into a lizard, which still runs about houses.[92]

Hera then sent two serpents to attack Herakles and his brother
in their cradle ; Herakles clutched their necks in his hands and
choked them to death.[93]

Apollodoros records, from Pherkydes, a variant which may be a
piece of genuine tradition, or may be the result of some attempt to
rationalize. The serpents were not sent by Hera, but put into the
cradle by Amphitryon himself. When Herakles faced them and
Iphikles ran away, Amphitryon recognized that the former was the
child of Zeus.[94] The age of Herakles at the time is variously given ;
in Plautus he is just born, in Apollodoros he is eight months old.
The hero's infancy was uneventful after this ; his education was of
course traditionally entrusted to all the most celebrated experts.
Linos has already been mentioned as his music-master ; Eurytos of
Oichalia taught him to use the bow ; he was the grandson of Apollo,
and all the family were mighty archers, like their divine ancestor. In
one form of his legend, indeed, Eurytos was killed by Apollo because he
had the audacity to challenge him to a contest in shooting ; another
form of the tale we shall meet with later in this chapter.[95] Autolykos
taught him to wrestle ; so great a trickster (we shall hear more of
Autolykos in discussing Odysseus) was no doubt a past-master of all
the wiles of the ring. Amphitryon taught him to drive a chariot,
and his fencing-master was Polydeukes himself. After Linos' death,
Herakles, who escaped prosecution by pleading self-defence and quoted
a law of Rhadamanthys in support of his plea, was sent off to the cattle-
pastures by Amphitryon, where, according to Apollodoros, he grew to
a good height, six feet ; but Pindar [96] has an older tradition, that he was
a smallish man.

On Mt. Kithairon, at the age of eighteen, he killed a lion,

which was preying not only on the herds of Amphitryon but on those of Thespios, king and eponym of the town Thespiai. Thespios entertained him hospitably; on the way back from his visit and from the hunt of the lion, he fell in with messengers from Erginos, king of the Minyai of Orchomenos, coming to collect the tribute from Thebes. It was a fairly recent quarrel; Klymenos, king of the Minyai, had been fatally wounded by Perieres, the charioteer of Menoikeus, Kreon's father; being carried home to die, he left the blood-feud to his son, who after a successful campaign compromised by making the Thebans pay him tribute. Herakles cut off the noses and ears of the messengers, hung them around their necks, and told them they might take those to their king by way of tribute. Erginos naturally attacked Thebes at once, but Herakles, armed by Athena and backed by the Theban army, routed him and made the Orchomenians pay double tribute to the Thebans in future. Kreon rewarded Herakles by giving him his daughter Megara in marriage; his younger daughter married Iphikles, who was already the father of a son, Iolaos, by Automedusa daughter of Alkathus.[97]

Clearly we have here material of very different strata. Herakles outrageous conduct towards the messengers is disapproved by nobody save the sufferers and their countrymen; this has the flavour of a non-moral and probably old folktale, especially when we add an incident of his entertainment by Thespios. The latter had fifty daughters, and was desirous that some at least of them should bear children to his mighty guest. He therefore arranged that on every one of the fifty nights which Herakles passed with him, one of them should share his couch.[98] There is another version savouring yet more of folktale: Herakles enjoyed the favours of all fifty in one night,[99] or in seven nights; [100] or, one of the fifty would have nothing to do with him, and he therefore assigned her as a maiden priestess to his temple at Thespiai; [101] a transparent bit of aetiology,—possibly his priestess was originally supposed to be his wife, an idea by no means without parallel in the temple-ritual of numerous countries. The episode has no necessary connexion with the business of the lion of Kithairon; Diodoros tells it as a separate story. Most accounts say that all the daughters bore sons (the eldest and the youngest had each twin boys, according to some); later they or some of them colonized Sardinia.

Alkathus was a Peloponnesian, son of Pelops and Hippodameia. A fairly well-supported tale makes him, and not Herakles, the slayer of the lion. It had killed Euhippos, son of Megareus king of Megara, and the bereaved father acted as kings in folktales usually do, promising the hand of his daughter and the succession to his kingdom to whoever should kill the lion. Alkathus accepted, and became king of Megara, where, Pausanias says, he rebuilt the walls which had been destroyed by Minos.[102] A variant [103] is that he fell in with the lion after being obliged to leave Megara suddenly, because he had killed his brother Chrysippos. In any case, this Elean or Megarian hero seems out of the picture in a tale supposed to be Boiotian.

Herakles' nephew Iolaos proved a faithful comrade to him on many of his adventures. His own marriage had a horrible ending. After he had lived with Megara happily for some years and several children had been born to them, Hera again began to persecute him, this time by sending on him a fit of furious homicidal madness. In this state he imagined Megara and her children to be enemies, and killed them all. As to when this terrible thing happened, authorities differ ; what may perhaps be called the orthodox story, that in Apollodoros, says that it was the cause of his servitude to Eurystheus. Herakles went into voluntary exile ; Thespios performed on him the formal rites of purification demanded by Greek religion for any bloodshed ; but he was not satisfied, and went to Delphoi to seek advice. The prophetess for the first time called him Herakles, —he had previously been known as Alkeides, in commemoration of his reputed father's father,—and bade him go to Tiryns, there to serve Eurystheus for twelve years. If he performed the tasks Eurystheus should set him, he would be immortal. The Euripidean version, however, puts the madness after the performance of the last of the Twelve Labours.[104]

The death of the children (Apollodoros adds the burning, in the same fit of insanity, of two children of Iphikles ; in his version, Megara escaped and later married Iolaos) has this much foundation in fact, that there were at Thebes, in connexion with the festival called the Iolaeia, certain rites known or supposed to be commemorative of dead persons, and these were explained as being in honour of the children of Herakles ; Iolaos is a Theban hero, and his legendary connexion with Herakles may have something to do with the origin of the whole story. Some said that the children were killed, not by Herakles, but by certain strangers.[105] As to the chronological difficulty, it is a natural result of the accumulation of many legends from many sources upon Herakles.

Herakles married again, this time Deïaneira, daughter of Oineus of Kalydon ; for her he had to fight the river-god Acheloos. Acheloos had the power of taking various shapes, such as those of a bull and a serpent ; Herakles, however, was too much for him, and not only mastered him in wrestling but broke off one of his horns. The hero then departed, taking Deïaneira with him. On the way they came to a flooded river, the Euenos, which she could not cross ; a centaur, Nessos, offered to carry her, while Herakles shifted for himself. Herakles agreed, but Nessos tried to assault Deïaneira, for which Herakles promptly shot him. As he lay dying, he gave her the apparently friendly advice to take some of the blood from his wound and keep it safely, for if ever Herakles became indifferent to her, she could win back his love by smearing some of the blood on a garment and giving it him to wear. She therefore kept the supposed charm in a safe place. The marriage lasted for years, and Deïaneira bore Herakles several sons, the eldest being Hyllos, and a daughter, Makaria.[106]

Ovid has a characteristically Alexandrian piece of prettiness here ; Acheloos' broken horn was picked up by the Naiads, who filled it with fruits and flowers ; it thus became the horn of Plenty (*cornu Copiae*) so familiar from ancient and modern art alike. Pherekydes has a somewhat different version ; Herakles gave Acheloos his horn again, receiving in return the Horn of Amaltheia (Greek does not talk of a goddess called Plenty, being rather less fond of deified abstractions than Latin). Amaltheia had a bull's horn, which would fill itself with any sort of meat and drink its owner liked to ask for, in unlimited quantities.[107]

Quite early in the history of his legend some one, it is not known who, made a sort of canonical list of twelve exploits, supposed to have been performed in the service of Eurystheus, which are known as the ἄθλοι, a word generally rendered by *labores* in Latin, *labours* in English ; but both translations are rather inadequate.[108] The Greek name, though probably not the cycle, is as old as Homer, who also knows that Herakles served Eurystheus, who sent him his commands through his herald Kopreus, and that Athena many times helped him.[109] We are quite in the dark as to why this number in particular was chosen ; of course the older mythologists, who made Herakles into a solar hero, saw in it a reference to the twelve signs of the Zodiac ; but this idea is no better founded than the rest of the solar hypothesis. In general, this may be said : firstly, that the ' labours ' which seem to be the oldest take place, where indeed we should expect them to, in the northern Peloponnesos ; secondly, that the ulti-mate object of the series seems to have been the attainment of immortality, which is, in the tradition as we have it, won three times in a disguised form, first in the carrying off of the apples of the Hesperides, probably no other than the fruit of a Greek Tree of Life, second in the carrying away of Kerberos, which is apparently another form of Homer's story, how Herakles strove with and vanquished Hades himself (a Harrowing of Hell, in other words ; the incident is not an uncommon one in the lives of mythological heroes) ; and lastly, in the famous but comparatively late incident of the pyre on Mt. Oite.

Two other categories of exploits were drawn up by some fairly early author, perhaps Pherekydes ; these are the πράξεις, or Deeds, *i.e.*, the things (such as the war against Pylos) which Herakles did on his own account, without orders from anyone, and the πάρεργα, or Incidentals, the adventures into which he fell while performing the Labours. It will be convenient to follow this ancient classification, although it is largely artificial. I would again mention that many of the exploits had originally nothing whatever to do with Herakles, but were transferred to him from some less notable hero or half-forgotten god, on the principle of *habenti dabitur*. All manner of reasons are given why Eurystheus was Herakles' master, when admittedly he was not nearly so valiant or strong ; but that it was so is the nearly invariable tradition.[110] Combining it with what we gather from Homer, that Herakles was no underling, but a great lord with a palace of his own, we may, without being too fanciful, suppose, as has already been suggested, that the real Herakles was indeed a lord of Mycenaean times, but a vassal of the greater lord of Argos or of Mycenae.[111]

The Twelve Labours, then, in what is more or less their canonical order, are as follows.[112]

I. PELOPONNESIAN GROUP

1. *The Nemean Lion.* This creature was the offspring either of Orthros and Echidna, or of Selene, and was brought on the scene by Hera, for the usual reason, that she wished to trouble and endanger Herakles. It was an especially formidable beast, because it was invulnerable. Herakles therefore could of course make no impression on it with his bow or other weapons ; but his club served him in better stead. Having battered the lion, he closed with it and choked it in his arms. The next business was to skin it, which according to the Theokritean account he managed at length to do by using its own claws. Henceforth its skin was his invariable wear, if we may believe our literary sources ; it is anything but certain that artists of the earlier periods knew the hero as having either lion-skin or club.[113]

Plenty of fanciful details are to be found in various authors ; Apollodoros for instance says that Eurystheus was much alarmed when Herakles returned with the lion's skin on his shoulders, and forbade him in future to enter the city. For further security, the cowardly king used to crawl into a bronze pot which he had had buried in the earth, whenever Herakles came anywhere near with his latest capture, such as Kerberos.[114] Some ingenuity was wasted in determining where he cut the club; the rest of his armament was attributed to various deities, Hermes, according to Apollodoros, giving him a sword, Apollo a bow and arrows, Hephaistos a golden cuirass, Athena a mantle.[115] We need waste no time on these silly subtleties of grammarians, who needed the sage precept of Quintilian, that part of a scholar's business is not to know some things; a rather more respectable myth is that the lion became the constellation Leo.[116]

2. *The Hydra.* This was a serpent, the offspring of Typhon and Echidna, and lived in the swamps of Lerna. The name means simply ' water-snake ', but from quite early times (not, however, in Hesiod), the creature was represented as having numerous heads, anywhere from five to a hundred; nine is a favourite number. Most authors add that as fast as a head was cut off, another (or two more) grew up in its place. To make matters worse, Hera sent the Hydra an ally in the shape of a great crab, which however Herakles smashed under his foot. But, as a favourite proverb had it in later times, ' even Herakles could not fight two ', and as the crab had helped the Hydra he called in Iolaos to help him. The latter brought firebrands, and whenever Herakles cut off a head, Iolaos cauterized the stump, thus preventing any more growing up there. In the end the monster was killed. Herakles dipped his arrows in its blood, thus making any wound from them deadly.[117]

Again there are elaborations in plenty. The Hydra had one immortal head, which Herakles cut off and buried alive.[118] The crab (*cancer*) became the constellation so called.[119]

3. *The Erymanthian Boar.* This is perhaps the most uninteresting of all the adventures, although sixth-century vase-painters loved to show Herakles returning with his prey, while Eurystheus cowers in his bronze jar and peeps anxiously out at the beast. It was to be caught alive; Herakles therefore frightened it out of its lair by shouting, chased it into deep snow, and there netted it and so carried it off on his shoulders.[120]

4. *The Hind of Keryneia.* According to most accounts, this was sacred to Artemis; Euripides represents it as a dangerous creature and says that Herakles killed it, but that is apparently his own invention, certainly contrary to all other tradition.[121] Being sacred, it might not, of course, be hurt; but caught it might be. Herakles pursued it for a whole year, and finally ran it down, or came upon it while it slept, and made off with it.

Then Artemis met him, escorted by Apollo, and claimed her property. Herakles threw the blame on his employer, and was allowed to carry the hind back to Argos, where he let it go.[122]

The hind, despite her sex, contrived to have antlers, which were of gold ; her hooves were of bronze, according at least to Vergil.[123] As to where she led him in the long chase which ended in her capture, accounts differed ; roughly speaking, they varied from the ends of the Peloponnesos to the ends of the earth.[124]

5. *The Stymphalian Birds.* Stymphalos in Arkadia had a lake thickly wooded on its shores, which had become a perfect sanctuary for birds. These Herakles was commissioned to drive out. After some thought, he made a bronze rattle, or got one from Athena, of Hephaistos' manufacture, and with this frightened them out of their coverts ; he is generally represented as having then shot them. As to why anyone should want them shot, answers vary widely ; they were so numerous that they destroyed the crops (Diodoros ; but this sounds suspiciously like rationalizing); or they had feathers as sharp as arrows, which wounded those who came near ; or, they were man-eaters.[125]

6. *The Stables of Augeias.* Augeias, son of Helios and king of Elis, had, like his father, great herds of cattle. As their stables were never cleaned, the amount of dirt that had accumulated was enormous ; Herakles was set to cleanse them, which he did in a single day ; a common explanation of how he managed it was, that he turned the course of a river (Alpheios or some other, real or imaginary) through the stables.[126]

II. EXTRA-PELOPONNESIAN GROUP

7. *The Cretan Bull.* This, according to Akusilaos, was the one on which Europê arrived in the island (clearly, to him, her mount was not Zeus in disguise) ; most people said it was Pasiphae's bull. In any case Herakles caught it alive, showed it to Eurystheus, and then let it go ; it wandered about for some time, finally taking up its quarters at Marathon.[127]

8. *Horses of Diomedes.* This Diomedes was a son of Ares and Kyrene, and king of the Bistonians. His horses were accustomed to be fed with human flesh. Herakles gathered a volunteer force and set out to bring them to Eurystheus; or, according to the form of the story followed by Euripides and probably older, he went alone. Diomedes was either killed in battle, or else fed to his own steeds ; this latter procedure made them quite

tame, and they were safely brought to Argos, where Herakles dedicated them to Hera, as some say he had the bull [128]

In his army, if he had one, was a youth called Abderos ; the horses, which he was set to guard while the rest beat off an attempt to get them back on the part of Diomedes and his people, killed him, and the city of Abdera was founded in memory of him (or had already been founded by him before his death).[129]

9. *Girdle of the Amazon.* Hippolyte, queen of the Amazons, had a girdle which for some reason was a very desirable object. When one considers that the Amazons probably have no relation to any real people, but are inhabitants of that fairyland which stretches away from the borders of the known world, and that the girdle, or any other article of clothing commonly worn, retains a good deal of the personal qualities of its owner, it is obvious that such an article as this was a very natural thing for Eurystheus to want, and there is no need for such explanations as that of Apollodoros, that his daughter had a fancy to have it for an ornament, or even for his statement that Ares (the father of the Amazons) had given it her as a sign of her superiority over all other women. The story is connected with a relic which was shown in the temple of Hera at Argos in classical times as being the very girdle itself. Herakles set out, with or without an army, and defeated the Amazons, capturing Melanippe, their general ; the girdle paid the price of her freedom. Or, Hippolyte herself fell and the girdle was taken from her dead body.[130]

10. *Geryon.* This monster has already been described in Chapter II (p. 31). Living as he does in the farthest West, and having as his attendant the formidable dog Orthros or Orthos, he has more than a little likeness to Hades himself, particularly as Hades also has cattle in one form of the adventure with Kerberos, and Herakles throws their herdsman Menoites, sparing his life at Persephone's entreaty.[131] However, to the classical mythologists, he was a monster living somewhere towards the sunset, to reach whom Herakles had to take a very long journey. The oldest account is, that he sailed the stream of Okeanos in the golden cup of the Sun, which he got from Okeanos, or from Helios himself ; in either case, he drew his bow against the god, and forced him to give up the goblet.[132] He killed Orthros, the herdsman Eurytion, and finally Geryon himself, and put the cattle on board the cup, in which he sailed back. Later forms of the legend make his return a much harder business. Herakles, having got to the farthest west, set up a monument of

his presence there, the famous Pillars of Herakles, somewhere on the Straits of Gibraltar, although the ancient geographers were not agreed as to what or where exactly they were. Now he was obliged to make his way back through Spain, France, and Italy, in constant danger from robbers, who were tempted by his booty. In particular, the Ligyes (Ligurians) of Southern France made a very determined attack on him, somewhere near Arles. He spent all his arrows upon them, and as they still came on, prayed Zeus to help him ; the god sent him great plenty of stones (a waste, stony region in that neighbourhood was shown as the very spot where the miracle took place) and with these the hero beat off the Ligyes. Another version, quite early,[133] brings him to the neighbourhood of the Black Sea ; here he fell in with a monstrous woman, half a serpent, whom he asked if she had seen his horses (what he was doing with horses does not appear). She demanded his love in exchange for her information, and bore him three sons, Agathyrsos, Gelonos, and Skythes, of whom the youngest, Skythes, was able when he grew up to draw a bow which Herakles left behind, and put on a girdle of his. Their mother then drove away the other two ; Skythes became king of the land. He and his brothers are of course the eponyms or legendary ancestors of the Gelonoi, Aga-thyrsoi, and Scythians ; some native legend probably lies behind the Greek one. Or again, Herakles, after wandering through all Italy, got to Sicily, where Eryx, the legendary king of the mountain so called, a son of Aphrodite, challenged him to wrestle ; he won, and killed his opponent.[134] These are but samples of his adventures, connected of course with his wide-spread cult, particularly in Sicily and Southern Italy. Finally he reached home safely.

11. *Kerberos.* Here, more plainly than in any other adventure, we find Herakles doing as many heroes do, and harrying Hell. It was the most terrible of all his tasks, and he could not have accomplished it, but that Athena and Hermes guided and befriended him. The tale, which is as old as Homer, represents him simply as going down to the nether regions and bringing Kerberos back with him.[135] But Homer has heard of an older tale yet, in which Herakles fought with and wounded Hades in person, ' in the Gate, among the dead '.[136] Probably in the original story he set forth to conquer death and win immortality, and succeeded in doing so. But to later ages this was too incredible, as indeed one might expect it to become, seeing that the Greek idea of the might of the gods, and not least of Hades, rose far above any primitive level at quite an early period, and

8

reasons had to be found for such a prodigious venture. One fairly popular version is, that originally the Labours were to be but ten in number, but Eurystheus would not count the Hydra or the Stables of Augeias, because in the one case Herakles was helped by Iolaos, in the other he used the river. So he set him this task, which he no doubt hoped would make an end even of him. But Herakles made his way down, by the Hell-mouth at Tainaron (or elsewhere; there were of course local variants), and, according at least to an Orphic tradition, fright-ened Charon into taking him over the Styx, for which the god was put in chains for a year. He captured Kerberos, brought him up, showed him to Eurystheus, and then fetched him back again.[137]

There were numerous fantastic glosses to this story, the result of local sagas and the imagination of later poets; for instance, that the plant aconite sprang from the gall which Kerberos spewed,[138] or that he broke away from Herakles on the road from Mycenae and the Temple of Hera,[139] whence a spring in that neighbourhood was known as the Water of Freedom ($\dot{\epsilon}\lambda\epsilon\upsilon\theta\dot{\epsilon}\varrho\iota\upsilon\nu$ $\ddot{\upsilon}\delta\omega\varrho$) and freedmen used to drink of it; or that his terrible aspect produced sad effects on those who happened to see him.[140] Among other incidents, Herakles met the ghost of Meleagros, who told him of his own end, and, on Herakles offering to marry his sister, if he had one still alive, named Deïaneira.[141]

12. *The Hesperides.* Finally, Eurystheus sent Herakles to bring the golden apples of the Hesperides. We have already seen[142] how Herakles forced Nereus to show him the way; having arrived at or near the garden, he either slew the dragon,[143] or somehow managed to send it to sleep.[144] Another form of the story is, that he got Atlas to pluck the apples for him, and to enable him to do this, held up the sky for him meanwhile. This led to complications, however; Atlas either would not give up the apples, or would not resume his carrying of the sky, until Herakles, by force or fraud, made him do so.[145]

There is a story that the apples themselves went back to the garden, by the hand of Athena, since they were too holy to stay in the world.[146] This and other such tales are but embroideries of the original legend, which no doubt signified to begin with that Herakles won immortality,—the fruit of the Tree of Life,—by his exploit.

Parerga. These can be briefly told, for the most part; some have incidentally been told already. During the chase of the Boar, Herakles was received by the Centaur Pholos, who set roast meat before him, but hesitated to give him wine, since the wine-jar he had was the common property of the Centaurs. Hera-kles insisted, however, and the rest of the Centaurs arrived,

attracted by the smell, as soon as the jar was opened. A fierce
fight began, but Herakles soon killed or drove off his assailants.
One, Elatos, took refuge with Cheiron, who was accidentally
struck by an arrow which had gone through him. Cheiron could
not be healed of his wound, since the arrow was dipped in the
Hydra's venom, and was glad to give up his immortality to
Prometheus and die to be rid of his pain. Pholos himself got
his death-wound by curiously examining one of the arrows,
which by ill-luck he dropped on his own foot.[147] A minor encoun-
ter with a Centaur was the slaying of Eurytion ; this Centaur
had tried to violate the daughter of king Dexamenos ('The
Hospitable'), who had received him under his roof, and the
girl was rescued by Herakles, who in some accounts was in love
with her himself.[148] The story is variously localized. A comic
adventure was with the Kerkopes, ape-like but human creatures,
whose mother had warned them to beware the black-rumped
man. They tried to steal Herakles' weapons as he lay asleep,
but he awoke, caught them, and hung them upside-down from
a pole held across his shoulders. They thus got an excellent view
of his lower parts, and so amused him with their jokes at his
hairiness that he let them go. They came to a bad end, being
transformed into monkeys, or into stones, for trying to trick
Zeus. They also are variable in place and names.[149]

On various occasions, Herakles met and fought a number
of formidable persons, whom he overcame ; these include a
sea-monster, often called Triton, with whom the pediment of the
archaic temple of Athena at Athens, the Hekatompedon, represents him as wrestling ; Kyknos son of Ares, who robbed Apollo
of the victims for sacrifice that came to Delphoi ;[150] another
son of Ares, a full brother of Kyknos, called Lykaon, who challenged him to fight as he was on his way to the Hesperides ;[151]
Busiris (i.e., Per-Usire, House of Osiris, a city in the Delta), king
of Egypt, who used to sacrifice strangers to Zeus. He had been
advised to do this, in order to avert drought, by a seer, Phrasios
or Thrasios, whom he made the first victim. When he tried to
sacrifice Herakles, the latter made short work of him and his
servants.[152] A giant, Alkyoneus (not the one he killed in the
battle of the Gods and Giants) attacked him as he returned
from Erytheia by way of the Isthmus of Corinth ;[153] Herakles
struck the stone Alkyoneus threw at him with such force that it
flew back and killed the thrower.

Syleus (? 'the Robber') had Herakles for his servant, for
some reason, but regretted it, for Herakles' enormous strength
resulted in spoiling everything in his master's vineyard ; it is

the common story of the Strong Servant, Grimm 90, *The Young Giant*. Later, Syleus becomes a wicked man whom Herakles kills and gives his land to his good brother Dikaios (the Just).[154]

Praxeis. I deliberately omit a number of campaigns which Herakles is said by sundry authors to have undertaken, because they smack of rationalization, are often late in origin, and contain nothing characteristic; Herakles is represented as conquering a great part of the known world, founding numerous cities, and so forth, all stock features of the conception, especially in Hellenistic times, of how any great hero of saga must have behaved. Other adventures, however, have more flavour of real saga, and I give them briefly, in Apollodoros' order.[155]

Either before or after his marriage with Deïaneira, Herakles fell violently in love with Iole, daughter of Eurytos king of Oichalia. Her father and brothers, however, would not let him have her, and to make matters worse, Herakles in a fit of madness hurled one of them, Iphitos, from the walls of Tiryns, whither he had come to look for some lost cattle. He sought purification at the hands of Neleus, king of Pylos, who would not grant it him; for which reason he afterwards made an expedition against Pylos and killed Neleus and all his sons, save one, Nestor. The Delphic oracle bade him go into servitude for a year (or three years), although even this advice was not given until he had fought Apollo for his holy tripod, the fray being stopped by Zeus casting a thunderbolt between the combatants. Hermes accordingly sold him to Omphale, queen of Lydia, who set him to do women's work. Having completed his term of serfdom, he was freed from his guilt.[156]

Next, he set out against Troy. At an earlier date (generally it is put at the time of his abortive attempt to accompany the Argonauts) he had saved Troy from a sea-monster. King Laomedon had cheated Poseidon and Apollo of their pay for building the walls; Poseidon sent a huge sea-beast, which could be appeased only if Laomedon's daughter Hesione was given him to devour (this detail is not in the earliest accounts, and may have been added on the analogy of the story of Andromeda). Herakles undertook to slay the monster, and for a reward was to have Laomedon's marvellous horses. But again Laomedon cheated, after Herakles had performed his part, incidentally being swallowed by the beast and killing it from inside. Therefore Herakles, when opportunity offered, raised an army, conspicuous among whose members was Telamon, father of the greater Aias, captured the city, and gave Hesione to Telamon, to whom she bore Teukros.[157]

A similar expedition was that against Augeias, who had promised him part of his cattle for cleaning the stables. This was successful only after a hard struggle, for the twin sons of Molione, Eurytos and Kteatos, children of Poseidon, fought against him.[158] An equally furious fight took place against the sons of Hippokoon, ruler of Sparta, who had sided with the Pylians against him, and further had killed the son of his kinsman Likymnios in a quarrel over a dog. Here again he was successful in the end, but his brother Iphikles was killed.[159] Another campaign, undertaken in aid of Aigimios, king of the Dorians, against his neighbours the Lapithai, seems to represent an early effort of the Dorian race to make Herakles their peculiar hero, an attempt which has met with more success than it deserves in modern times.[160] Finally, he set out against and took Oichalia, and carried off Iole ; with this exploit his career ended tragically, in the story as we have it now, although in all probability this is no original part of the saga. Deïaneira heard of his love for Iole, and to win him back, tried Nessos' charm. But the Centaur's blood, mixed as it was with the poison of the Hydra, was deadly poison, and the robe on which she smeared it clung to Herakles' flesh and burned him unendurably. He therefore had himself conveyed to the summit of Mt. Oite, and set on a great pyre of wood ; this he induced Poias, the father of Philoktetes, to light, by promising him his bow and arrows. The mortal part of him was burned away ; the rest ascended to heaven, was married to Hebe, and at last was reconciled to Hera.[161] Such, in brief and with many omissions, is the traditional life and death of this most notable of heroes, the Greek Samson.

NOTES ON CHAPTER VIII, PART I

[1] See *The Mycenaean Origin of Greek Mythology* (Berkeley, Cal., 1932).

[2] In general, I follow here our most continuous account, Apollodoros, III, 2 foll. See also the relevant arts. in the classical dictionaries, and Preller-Robert, II, p. 346 foll. The best-known account of Europê and the bull is in Ovid, *Met.*, II, 843 foll. ; the oldest, apart from the passing mention in Homer, *Il.*, XIV, 321, that of Hesiod, frag. 30. See also Hyginus, *fab.*, 178. Her mother's name varies ; Hyginus calls her Argiope. No very striking divergencies occur in the story.

[3] Ovid, *Met.*, 236, cf. also *SA* VI, 14. Authorities differed as to whether it was his cousin on the father's side or his sister's son whom he killed.

[4] Apollod., III, 20 ; cf. Chapter X, p. 297.

[5] *Od.*, XIX, 178-9, a much-discussed passage, for which see Frazer, *G.B.*³, III, p. 58 foll. ; for the question whether ἐννέωρος means ' for eight ' or ' for nine years ', see the Homeric lexica, *s.u.*

[6] See Türk in Roscher, art. PASIPHAE.

[7] The most extraordinary part was the simulation by a young man of a woman in labour ; the local legend was that Ariadne landed there and died in childbed. See Plutarch, *Thes.*, 20 ; latest discussion, Nilsson, *M.M.R.*, p. 454.

[8] Fullest description in Sir A. Evans, *The Palace of Minos*.

[9] Most of the family are mere artificial links between the different races known to the Greeks ; among them are Belos (*i.e.*, Ba'al), Aigyptos and Danaos, whom we shall meet later, and other such obvious eponyms. We now pass to the Theban saga.

[10] Apollod., III, 24, says that a year in those days was eight of our years. This is an *oktaeteris*, the 8-year cycle by which the Greeks regulated their calendar (see the art. CALENDAR in any classical dictionary) ; we may perhaps compare Minos' eight-year tenure of office, above, note 5. The difficulty is that we have no real knowledge of how old the oktaeteris was.

[11] See any work on the history of the alphabet. The real difficulty is how much truth there may be in the assertion that Kadmos himself was a Phoenician, and incidentally the philological question of what his name means and to what language it belongs. One thing is certain, that Thebes is a Mycenaean foundation.

[12] P. 149 foll.

[13] Akusilaos, frag. 33 Jacoby ; from Hesiod, and paralleled also by Stesichoros, see his note, Vol. I, p. 382.

[14] Eurip., *Bacch.*, 337 foll. In all but the first story, it is Aktaion's hounds who kill him.

[15] Diod. Sic., IV, 81, 4, who also gives the second story. If we could be sure this was an old tale, we might say it was a relic of the non-virginal Artemis.

[16] See especially Ovid, *Met.*, III, 138 foll.; Nonnos, *Dionys.*, V, 287 foll.

[17] He is mentioned by Hesiod, *Theog.*, 978, and some later authors, including Apollod., III, 26 ; *ibid.*, 40, he marries Nykteis, daughter of Nykteus son of Chthonios (the Spartos, presumably), and begets Labdakos, the founder of the later dynasty. This provision of a descent in the male line from Kadmos is his sole *raison d'être* ; for the rest of the legend he is a mere encumbrance, who has to be got rid of somehow, either by the wrath of Dionysos, because he resembled Pentheus in his impiety (Apollod., *ibid.*), or by making Pentheus drive him out and seize the throne (Nonnos, V, 207 foll.). See Höfer in Roscher, art. POLYDOROS (1). The name Pinakos is supplied by the scholiast on Eurip., *Phoen.*, 8.

[18] The whole matter is well discussed in Roscher, art. KADMOS ; the metamorphosis is first mentioned in Eurip., *Bacch.*, 1330b foll. ; see also Ovid, *Metam.*, IV, 563 foll., who quite misses the point by making it the consequence of Kadmos' killing of the dragon of Ares ; Apollod., III, 39. Eurip., frag. 930 N², seems to have tried to bring the incident on the stage, probably in the lost *Kadmos*, see Nauck's note on the remains of that play.

[19] The *Antiope* of Euripides being lost, this story has to be put together from the outline of it in Hyginus (*fab.*, 8 ; in 7 he gives a rather different version), Apollod., III, 42–4, Pausanias, IX, 17, 6, who alone gives the tale of Antiope's madness, marriage and death, and some scattered mentions in other writers. Ovid (*Met.*, VI, 110) says that Zeus approached Antiope in the guise of a satyr ; Homer (*Od.*, XI, 260) says she was the daughter of the river Asopos.

20 Apollod., III, 44. The Argument to Sophokles, *Oed. Tyrannus*, cites the oracle alleged to have been given to Laios, which definitely makes this crime the reason for the curse on him.

21 See the passage of Pausanias cited in n. 19.

22 Cf. n. 20. The great authority for the story of Oidipus is of course Sophokles, so far as he does not follow peculiarly Attic versions ; a continuous account is given by Apollod., III, 48 foll., and later authorities are very numerous, *e.g.*, Seneca's *Oedipus*. See, besides the classical dictionaries, Preller-Robert, II, p. 876 foll.

23 This is the ancient etymology, right for once. The whole episode of the laming is so odd that it is not likely to have been invented to explain the name ; did Laïos want to prevent the child's ghost from walking ? For Polybos, see further Roscher, III, 2630.

24 Question and answer, the latter of which I have compressed in translating, are from the Argument to Sophokles, *Oed. Tyr.*

25 See Sir A. Evans in *Journ. Hell. Stud.*, XLV (1925), p. 27 foll.

26 *Od.*, XI, 271 foll. ; *Il.*, XXIII, 679.

27 Paus., IX, 5, 10–11. He adds that a picture at Plataiai by the painter Onasias showed Euryganeia looking on sadly at the combat between her sons. The *Oidipodeia* is a cyclic epic, whereof only a couple of fragments remain ; the other one (2, Allen) states that Haimon son of Kreon was among the victims of the Sphinx, a wide departure from the usual story, but found also in Apollod., III, 54, who has a certain amount in common with the *Oidipodeia*, so far as one can judge. According to schol., *Iliad*, IV, 376, Oidipus' second wife was called Astymedusa.

28 From the cyclic *Thebais*, frags. 2 and 3, Allen. Clearly the stories are doublets, clumsily combined by the poet. Oidipus' curse evidently was, ' Since they cannot dispose aright of their ancestral possessions, may they never dispose peaceably of the kingdom ', or ' Since they cannot rightly divide the meat, may they not divide the kingdom rightly '. A third tale (schol., *Il.*, IV, 376) is that Astymedusa charged Eteokles and Polyneikes (her stepsons in this version) with an attempt on her chastity, and therefore their father cursed them. The narrative now follows, in general, Apollod., III, 57 foll. ; Aeschylus, *Septem* ; Statius, *Thebais* ; Hyginus, *fab.*, 70 foll. Other authorities are quoted in the following notes.

29 Paus., IX, 5, 12.

30 Besides the fragments of Euripides' *Hypsipyle* (in Hunt, *Fragmenta tragica papyracea*, Oxford) and of his two plays on the subject of Alkmeon (N², p. 379 foll.), the chief authorities for this story are Apollod., III, 60–1 and 86 foll. ; Hyginus, *fab.*, 73 ; also numerous references in Statius.

31 Homer, *Il.*, IV, 383 foll., with the scholia ; Stat., *Theb.*, II, 482 foll.

32 Stat., *Theb.*, IV, 652 foll. ; for the other account see Eurip., *Hypsip.*, col. iv, 29 Hunt. Most authorities simply say the army wanted water.

33 Schol. Pind., *hypothesis Nemeorum*, 2 and 5 ; the interpretation is that of Krause, *Olympia* (Vienna, 1838), p. 40, n. 15.

34 Eurip., *Hypsip.*, 41 (64), 65.

35 For these child-gods, often represented as abandoned and constantly associated with serpents, see Nilsson, *M.M.R.*², p. 533 foll.

36 The reason for the variation is, that although the traditional number of seven held good for both champions and gates, no one knew the real ground-plan of prehistoric Thebes, obliterated as it was by the classical city, and there must have been many families eager to claim an ancestor who led a division of so famous an expedition.

[37] See Chapter III, p. 66.

[38] See *Class. Quart.*, XIX (1925), p. 148.

[39] See especially the *Supplices* of Euripides.

[40] Apollodoros, III, 79, doubtless from some Alexandrian poet or mythologist; Stat., *Theb.*, XII, 481 foll.

[41] See the fragments of Euripides' *Antigone*. They are not sufficient for the plot to be certainly reconstructed, and the address to Dionysos (fr. 177, N²) is doubtful, since *Antigone* is an easy mistake for *Antiope*. The story as given in Hyginus (*fab.* 72) is not said by him to be from Euripides, and he may be drawing on some later poet. See Nauck's notes, p. 411. In several accounts, e.g., in Statius, Argeia helps Antigone to bury Polyneikes.

[42] For the Epigonoi, see Apollod., III, 80–5 ; Hygin., *fab.*, 71. The names are Thersandros, son of Polyneikes, who was made king of the remains of Thebes; Alkmeon (and his brother Amphilochos, according to Apollodoros) ; Aigialeus ; Diomedes, son of Tydeus ; Promachos (Hyginus substitutes Tlesimenes, attested also by Pausanias, III, 12, 9), son of Parthenopaios ; Sthenelos, son of Kapaneus ; Polydoros, son of Hippomedon (the last according to Hyginus). Diomedes, Sthenelos, and the capture of Thebes go back to Homer, *Il.*, IV, 367, 401 foll., and doubtless the story has a kernel of fact. For the Catalogue of Ships, see T. W. Allen, *The Homeric Catalogue of Ships*, Oxford, 1921, *passim*.

[43] The chief surviving authorities are, besides the fragments of Euripides' two plays on the subject, Apollod., III, 86 foll., Hygin., *fab.*, 73, Paus., VIII, 24, 7 foll., confirmed on one point by the earlier testimony of Thucydides, II, 102, 4 (the new land). But much of the tradition is lost ; for example, we have not the cyclic epic *Alkmaionis*, which doubtless contained much that was interesting, nor any complete play of any dramatist on the subject. Euripides' *Alkmeon at Corinth* (cf. Apollod., III, 94–5) had a romantic plot suggestive of New Comedy. Alkmeon had by Manto, whom he met during his maddened wanderings, two children, Amphilochos and Teisiphone ; he left them with Kreon king of Corinth, whose wife later grew jealous of Teisiphone's beauty, and sold her into slavery. She was bought by her own father, who afterwards, on coming to Corinth to reclaim his children, somehow recognized her and also got back his son.

[44] See p. 153.

[45] See the art. Teiresias in Roscher (Buslepp) for more details. The chief authorities, besides Apollodoros, who quotes several of the older ones (III, 69 foll.), are Homer, *Od.*, X, 490–5 ; Hesiod, frag. 161–2 ; Kallimachos, *hymn.*, V, 57 foll. (from Pherekydes) ; Hygin., *fab.*, 75.

[46] See Chapter IV, p. 81.

[47] *Hymn. Homer.*, III, 172, perhaps the source of the tradition that Homer was blind. For the blindness of Demodokos, see *Od.*, VIII, 64.

[48] Eurip., *Phoen.*, 937 foll. ; see the whole scene, and cf. Stat., *Theb.*, X, 589 foll., 756 foll.

[49] See the articles in Roscher and in Pauly-Wissowa, and also Preller-Robert, II, 759 foll. An excellent handling of the whole story is that of Miss J. R. Bacon, *The Voyage of the Argonauts*, Methuen, 1925.

[50] Viz., that they were most of them descended from the daughters of Minyas, Apoll. Rhod., I, 230, which they were not in the lists we have.

[51] *Od.*, XII, 69–70. The chief surviving authorities after Homer

are Pindar, *Pyth.*, IV ; Apollonios Rhodios, *Argonautika*, with his immensely learned scholiast ; Valerius Flaccus, *Argonautica*, who, although based on Apollonios, often follows other traditions ; the ' Orphic ' *Argonautika* ; also several prose accounts, as Hyginus, *fab.*, 1–4, 12–27, *astron.*, II, 20 and 37 ; Apollod., I, 107 foll. ; the scholiast on Homer, *loc. cit.*, and others. Fragments of lost prose works, many of early date, dealing with the saga are to be found in abundance in schol. Apoll. Rhod. especially, also in the scholiast on Pindar. A number of plays were written on various parts of the story, but only Euripides' *Medea* survives entire.

[52] Phrixos only, Hyg., *fab.*, 2, Apollod., I, 81 ; both, Ovid, *Fast.*, III, 861. The text mainly follows the first two of these authorities, where they agree.

[53] Hygin., *fab.* 3. Another tale is, that Athamas sent Phrixos to get the ram, and Hera advised him and Helle to mount it, whereby they escaped being sacrificed (M1, 23) ; or Demodike, wife of Athamas' brother Kretheus, played Potiphar's wife to Phrixos' Joseph, Kretheus complained of him to Athamas, and he would have been executed but for the intervention of Nephele with the ram, Hyg., *astron.*, II, 20 ; or again, Helle, who in most accounts was drowned in the Hellespont, was saved by Poseidon, to whom she bore Paion, or Edonos (the mythical ancestors respectively of the Paiones and Edonians), *ibid.* The ram was not killed, but obligingly took off its own skin, *ibid.*

[54] So Hygin., *fab.*, 3, for example ; Hyg., *astr.*, II, 20, has another variant, viz., that Phrixos did not stay in Kolchis, but was brought home by Hermes.

[55] This is the usual situation, *e.g.*, in Pindar.

[56] For example, in the scholiast on Homer, quoted in note 51.

[57] So in Pindar, line 75 foll. See the schol., 133, and *cf.* Thuc., III, 22, 2, the men escaping from Plataiai were shod on the left foot only, ἀσφαλείας ἕνεκα τῆς πρὸς τὸν πηλόν. A third account is given by the scholiast just quoted ; Jason forded the Anauros barefoot, and then forgot to put on one of his sandals.

[58] Several accounts say that he was at work on a farm. The river is often called the Anauros ; but this, although really a proper name, is often used by later authors to mean ' torrent ', see Liddell and Scott[9], *s.u.*, hence it is not always sure whether they mean any particular river.

[59] See, for instance, Apoll. Rhod., III, 66 foll., cf. Chapter X, p. 291 and note.

[60] The genealogy is :—

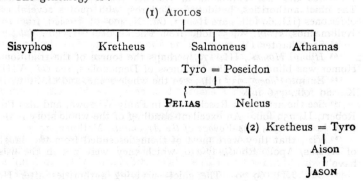

(1) AIOLOS

Sisyphos   Kretheus   Salmoneus   Athamas

Tyro = Poseidon

PELIAS   Neleus

(2) Kretheus = Tyro

Aison

JASON

[61] This is the version in Pindar, 157 foll., for example. But another version is, that Pelias asked Jason what ought to be done to be rid of a person by whom one's life was threatened. Jason answered, ' Send him to get the Golden Fleece ', and Pelias acted upon the hint ; so Apollod., I, 109.

[62] The chief sources for the list are Apoll. Rhod., I, 23 foll. ; Apollod., III, 111 foll. ; Hygin., fab., 14. The modern authorities quoted in note 49 give more details.

[63] See notes 32 foll. The chief authorities are Eurip., Hypsip., so far as it goes ; Apoll. Rhod., I, 609 foll. ; (in 622, Thoas is set afloat ' in a hollow chest ', again that persistent detail !) ; his scholiast ; Stat., Theb., V, 49 foll.

[64] Apoll. Rhod., I, 936 foll. For the Gegeneis, see Chapter III, p. 57.

[65] Apoll. Rhod., I, 1164 foll. ; more or less fully treated also by Theokritos, Id., XIII ; Propertius, I, 20 ; and of the later authors, Valerius Flaccus, III, 474 foll., and the Orphic Argonautika, 639 (642) foll. References and allusions are innumerable.

[66] See, for all these figures, the relevant articles in Roscher, also Frazer, G.B.³, VII, 216, 257, 264. The chief references for Bormos are Pollux, I, 55 ; Athenaios, XIV, 619 F foll. ; Hesychios, s.uu. Βῶρμος, Μαριανδυνὸς θρῆνος.

[67] See especially, for the first form of the story (Argive), Pausanias, I, 43, 7, cf. Konon, narrat., 19 ; for the second (Boiotian), Paus., IX, 29, 6–9 ; for the third, Theokr., Id., XXIV, 103 ; Apollod., II, 63. The oldest reference to the song is Homer, Il., XVIII, 569–71, where the scholiast gives more variants. αἴλινον is perhaps the Phoenician ai lanu, ' woe to us '.

[68] Lityerses, Sositheos, Daphnis, ap. Anon. in Westermann, Scriptores rer. mirab. Graec., p. 220 ; Pollux, II, 54. Maneros, Herodotos, II, 79, 2, 3.

[69] See Kretschmer, Glotta, XIV, p. 33 foll.

[70] Apoll. Rhod., II, 1 foll. ; Theokr., XXIII, 27 foll.

[71] Apoll. Rhod., II, 178 foll., and scholiast ; Val. Flacc., IV, 423 foll. ; Orph. Argonaut., 671 (674) foll. ; cf. Soph., Antig., 966 foll., with the scholia and the fragments of his three plays on this legend, Tympanistai and the first and second Phineus ; Hyginus, fab., 19 ; Apollod., I, 120 foll. Besides the variants already mentioned, these authors inform us, between them, that it was Zetes and Kalais, or their father Boreas, who blinded Phineus, to revenge Kleopatra ; that Asklepios or the Boreadai healed his children ; that his real crime was interfering with Perseus on his journey ; that Kleopatra accused her stepsons of assaulting her ; that Phineus (apparently) was not blind at all ; and almost every imaginable combination of two or more of the above motifs. See Preller-Robert, p. 810 foll. Phineus' second wife is most commonly called Eidothea, or Idaia.

[72] See also Chapter II, p. 29. Here again, various authors give different versions of what exactly became of the Harpies, where they went, etc.

[73] Apollon., II, 815 foll. ; Herodoros ap. schol. on II, 880.

[74] Apollon., II, 1030 foll.

[75] The best and most famous handling of the episode of Jason and Medeia is in Apollonios Rhodios, Books III and part of IV ; the incident of Aphrodite disguised as Kirke (Valerius Flaccus, VII, 210 foll.) is the subject of the famous picture by Titian absurdly called Sacred and Profane

Love by unlearned critics. The nude figure is Aphrodite ; tne draped woman in the foreground is Medeia ; the child playing in the background is Eros. The details have been somewhat altered by the painter, who likes to set his figures in a bright light ; in Valerius, the scene is Medeia's bedroom, at night. To the authorities already given must now be added Ovid, *Met.*, VII. A vase-painting (see Bacon, p. 24) shows a dragon (?) disgorging Jason, an unknown variant.

⁷⁶ Apollon., IV, 338 foll. ; for the story of Apsyrtos as a child, see, *e.g.*, Apollod., I, 133 ; cf. Chapter X, p. 292.

⁷⁷ This is Pindar's version, *Pyth.*, IV, 26 ; they land somewhere on the other side of Africa and then carry the ship for twelve days.

⁷⁸ So the Orphic Argonautika. It has been conjectured that Val. Flaccus, had he lived to finish his poem, would have used the same tradition, so as to bring in a reference to Agricola's exploits in Britain ; Mopsos, or a local Druid, could easily have been made to foretell his campaigns in a way complimentary to Domitian.

⁷⁹ Apollonios Rhodios, and most authors.

⁸⁰ *Ibid.*, IV, 654 foll.

⁸¹ *Ibid.*, IV, 557 foll.

⁸² *Ibid.*, IV, 842 foll. Peleus in Apollonios had already married Thetis ānd been deserted by her ; in Catullus (LXIV, 12 foll.) he saw her for the first time early in the voyage, coming with the other Nereids to look at the Argo.

⁸³ Cf. the passage of Pindar cited in note 77 ; Apoll. Rhod., IV, 1228 foll. ; a violent storm had driven them out of their way.

⁸⁴ *Ibid.*, 1637 foll. ; for Talos, see Apollod., I, 140–1 ; pseudo-Plato, *Minos*, 320 C (a feeble rationalization) ; schol. Plat., *Rep.*, 337 A ; schol. and Eustathios on *Od.*, XX, 302. Very little is left of Sophokles' *Daidalos*, in which Talos was mentioned (the schol. on Apoll. Rhod., IV, 1638, mentions a play of his called *Talos*, but this is probably his or the copyists' blunder for *Daidalos*) ; cf. Roscher, *s.u.*

⁸⁵ The tale is well known ; Ovid tells it (*Met.*, VII, 162 foll., with both Aison and the ram) and Apollod. (I, 143, 144 ; ram only). Alkestis was not present at the time, being already married to Admetos.

⁸⁶ Euripides, *Medea* ; Paus., II, 3, 6–11, who tells several other tales, (1) that Jason went to Korkyra after Pelias' death, and his elder son, Mermeros, was killed there by a lioness ; (2) that Medeia took her children as soon as they were born to the temple of Hera at Corinth, and there ' hid them away, thinking that they would be immortal ' ; but apparently they all died, and Jason left her when he found it out.

⁸⁷ Eurip., *Med.*, 1386–8.

⁸⁸ For Herakles, see especially Farnell, *Hero-Cults* p. 95 foll., and Preller-Robert, II, p. 422 foll., besides the relevant articles in Roscher and Pauly-Wissowa.

⁸⁹ The resemblance of this story to that of the Megarian Skylla, told in the next chapter, is obvious. It is still a common folktale, told, for example, of the several places known as Maiden Castle.

⁹⁰ The account in the text is from [Hesiod], *Scut. Her.*, 1 foll. ; Apollodoros, II, 54 foll., and represents the normal tradition. The authorities for the story of Herakles are so numerous, and variants so many, that it is not possible to give more than a selection in a work of this size. The tale of Amphitryon's exile seems an early device to bring Herakles from his native region, the Argolid, to Boiotia. The genealogy of his immediate relations is as follows :—

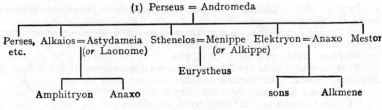

(1) Perseus = Andromeda

Perses, Alkaios=Astydameia Sthenelos=Menippe Elektryon=Anaxo Mestor
etc.   (or Laonome)   (or Alkippe)

                                    Eurystheus

        Amphitryon   Anaxo   sons   Alkmene

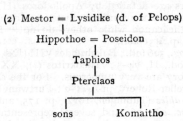

(2) Mestor = Lysidike (d. of Pelops)

Hippothoe = Poseidon

Taphios

Pterelaos

sons   Komaitho

91 Homer, *Il.*, XIX, 95 foll.

92 Ovid, *Metam.*, IX, 281 foll. ; cf. Paus., IX, 11, 3 ; Ant. Lib., 29.

93 A familiar story, best known perhaps from Pindar, *Nemeans*, I, 33 foll., Theokritos, *Id.*, 24, and Plautus' *Amphitruo*. The persistent hostility of Hera can hardly be part of the original story, to judge by Herakles' name ; good material, with interpretations with which I cannot agree, in A. B. Cook in *Class. Review*, XX (1906), p. 365 foll.

In dealing with this, Herakles' first feat of strength, it is proper to notice that throughout his career he shows decided affinity to a very popular hero of modern and medieval folktale, the *starker Hans* of German tradition, who is always prodigiously strong, but rather stupid.

94 Pherekydes, frag. 69 Jacoby = Apoll., II, 62 and schol. Pind., *Nem.*, I, 65.

95 *Odyssey*, VIII, 224 foll.

96 Cf. Chapter X, p. 293, and notes there.

97 Apollod., II, 65–70, who also provides Alkmene with another husband after the death of Amphitryon, namely Rhadamanthys.

98 Apollod., *ibid.*, 66 ; Diod. Sic., IV, 29, 3 foll. ; see further Höfer in Roscher, art. THESPIOS.

99 Paus., IX, 27, 7. This version is a great favourite with the Christian apologists, *e.g.*, Tatian, *c. Graecos*, 21 (p. 262 B, *edit. Benedict.*).

100 Herodoros *ap.* Athenaios, XIII, 556 F.

101 Pausan., *ibid.*, 6.

102 Pausan., I, 41, 3 foll.

103 Schol. Apoll. Rhod., I, 517 ; cf. Chapter X, p. 298. There are three other, unimportant, characters named Alkathus or Alkathoos ; see Bernhard in Roscher, *s.u.*

104 Apollod., 72 foll., 127 ; Euripides, *Herc. Furens*, *passim* ; the introduction to this play in Wilamowitz-Moellendorff's edition is one of the best-known discussions of the story of Herakles.

105 See Pindar, *Nem.*, III, 79 foll. (= IV, 61 foll.) and the scholiast there.

106 The chief accounts of this are Sophokles, *Trach.*, 9 foll., 555 foll. ; Ovid., *Met.*, IX, 1 foll.

107 Ovid., *loc. cit.*, 87–8 ; Apollodoros, II, 148 = Pherekydes, frag.

42 Jacoby. The motif is common, the best-known example perhaps being the Sangreal.

[108] Properly, an ἆθλος is something done for a prize of some kind, ἆθλον ; among other things, an athletic ' event '.

[109] *Iliad*, VIII, 362 foll. ; XV, 369.

[110] Apparently it is Iphikles who serves Eurystheus in the *Shield of Herakles*, 89 foll. ; H. there attributes his own toils to fate (δαίμων).

[111] See, for instance, *Od.*, XXI, 25 foll.

[112] The Labours are detailed by Apollodoros (II, 74 foll.). Besides many works of art, we have numerous lists in various authors, of whom some agree with the canon while others do not. For particulars, see Preller-Robert, II, p. 431 foll.

[113] Hesiod, *Theog.*, 326 foll. ; Bakchylides VIII (IX), 4 foll. ; Epimenides, fr. 2 Diels ; Apollod., II, 74–5 ; Theokritos (?), XXV, 201 foll. ; other mentions of the story are very numerous. For the dress and armament of Herakles, see Preller-Robert, pp. 441–2 ; Furtwängler in Roscher, *s.u.* ; B. Schweitzer, *Herakles* (Tübingen, 1922), p. 175, and Figs. 30 and foll.

[114] Apollod., *loc. cit.*, 76, and several representations in art.

[115] Apollod., II, 71 ; more refs. concerning the club in Preller-Robert, cited in n. 113.

[116] Hyginus, *poet. astron.*, II, 24 ; pseudo-Erat., 12 (the two agree almost word for word ; the Latin is derived from the source of the Greek).

[117] Hes., *Theog.*, 313 foll. ; it was the offspring of Typhon and Echidna ; Apollod., II, 77–80 ; more authorities in Preller-Robert, p. 444.

[118] Apollod., *loc. cit.*, 80.

[119] Pseudo-Erat., 11 ; Hygin., *poet. astron.*, II, 23.

[120] Hekataios, frag. 6 Jacoby ; Apollod., II, 83 foll.

[121] Eurip., *Herc. Fur.*, 375 foll. (one of the lists of the exploits of Herakles).

[122] Pindar, *Ol.*, III, 26 foll., with the schol., who names older authorities ; Apollod., II, 81–2.

[123] Pindar, *loc. cit.* ; Verg., *Aen.*, VI, 801–2. According to Pindar, Taÿgete dedicated the hind to Artemis ; Kallimachos (III, 98 foll.) says it was one of the first hinds Artemis hunted ; she caught four to draw her chariot, but Hera caused this one to escape, to make work for Herakles.

[124] See Preller-Robert, p. 451.

[125] Pausanias, VIII, 22, 3 foll., quoting Peisandros ; Apollodoros, II, 92–3 ; Diod. Sic., IV, 13, 2 ; cf. above, p. 202.

[126] Apollod., II, 88 foll. ; Theokr. (?) XXV ; Pindar had already heard of it, *Ol.*, X, 28–30, perhaps even Homer, *Il.*, II, 629 ; at least they mention incidents which in the ordinary story followed upon this.

[127] Apollod., II, 94–5, who quotes the earlier authorities.

[128] *Ibid.*, 96 foll. ; Eurip., *Alc.*, 482 foll. ; *Herc. Fur.*, 380 foll. ; Diod. Sic., IV, 15, 3 foll. A somewhat similar figure to Diomedes is Glaukos of Potniai in Boiotia, who was devoured by his own mares. See the frags. of Aesch., *Glaukos Potnieus*, with Nauck's notes.

[129] Apollod., *loc. cit.*, 97.

[130] Apollod., *ibid.*, 98 foll. ; Apollonios Rhodios, II, 966 foll. Allusions and variants are numerous.

[131] Apollod., II, 125 ; *ibid.*, 108, Menoites informs Geryon of Herakles' raid.

[132] Apollod., *ibid.*, 106 foll., a curious mixture of old and new forms of the tale, to which add Aesch., frag. 199 Nauck[2], whose note gives more refs. ; further details in Preller-Robert, II, p. 465 foll.

[133] Herodotos, IV, 8–10 ; this story puts Geryon's island in the neighbourhood of the Black Sea.

[134] Apollod., *loc. cit.*, 111 ; Eryx' father is there said to be Poseidon, but his paternal ancestry varies ; more refs. in Preller-Robert, *ibid.*, p. 479.

[135] Apollod., *ibid.*, 113 foll., and numerous other authorities, notably Eurip., *Herc. Fur.*, 610 foll., Seneca, *Herc. Fur.*, 662 foll.

[136] *Il.*, V, 395 foll. ; the common texts have, in 397, ἐν Πύλῳ ἐν νεκύεσσι βαλὼν κτε., but Aristarchos (see the scholiast *ad loc.*) rightly took πύλῳ as a common noun, ' gate ' (=πύλη) ; cf. Hades' Homeric epithet of πυλάρτης or Gate-warder.

[137] For the affair of Charon, see Verg., *Aen.*, VI, 392, with the note of Servius, and Norden's commentary.

[138] Herodoros *ap.* schol. Apoll. Rhod., II, 354.

[139] See Hesychios, *s.u.*

[140] Ovid, *Met.*, X, 65–7, says that some one, whom he does not name, was turned into stone at the sight of him.

[141] Bakchylides, V, 56 foll.

[142] Chapter II, p. 25.

[143] So, for instance, Eurip., *Herc. Fur.*, 398. Panyassis *ap.* Hyginus, *poet. astr.*, II, 6, says that Herakles and the dragon fought, and he or some later writer (it is not clear where the quotation from P. stops) makes Zeus interrupt the fight by turning both into constellations ; in pseudo-Erat., 3, the dragon is turned by Hera into the constellation Draco after having been killed. Schol., *Il.*, XI, 5, says that Emathion, son of Tithonos and Eos and brother of Memnon, tried to prevent Herakles taking the apples and was slain by him. Cf. Apollod., II, 119.

[144] So a number of vase-paintings, etc., for which see Preller-Robert, II, p. 492.

[145] Pherekydes *ap.* schol. Apoll. Rhod., IV, 1396 (see the whole note, and cf. Apollod., II, 120) ; Pausan., V, 18, 4 ; more refs. in Preller-Robert, *ibid.*, p. 494–5.

[146] Apollod., *loc. cit.*, 121. Pherekydes (*loc. cit.*) introduces the cup of the Sun into this adventure.

[147] Apollod., II, 83 foll. Pholos' misfortune is plainly a mere doublet of Cheiron's.

[148] Bakchylides, frag. 60 Bergk ; Apollod. II, 95 ; Hyginus, *fab.*, 31, 33 ; Diod. Sic., IV, 33, 1. She is named Mnesimache, Hippolyte or Deïaneira, and her father sometimes an Elean, sometimes an Achaian.

[149] Herodotos, VII, 216, where see commentators ; Suidas, *s.uu.* Εὐρύβατος, Κέρκωπες, μελαμπύγου τύχοις. It is clearly an old folk-tale, localized in Thessaly. A similar attack was made on him in Africa by pygmies, after his wrestling with Antaios, see Philostratos, *Imag.*, II, 22.

[150] ps.-Hesiod, *Scutum Herculis, passim.*

[151] Eurip., *Alc.*, 501–2 ; see Höfer in Roscher, III, 3341, 61 foll.

[152] Herodotus, II, 45 ; Isokrates, XI, 36 ; Kallimachos, frag. 44 Pfeiffer whence Ovid, *A.A.*, I, 647 foll., and several representations in art, see Preller-Robert, II, p. 517 foll.

[153] Schol. Pind., *Nem.*, IV, 43 ; cf. Chapter III, p. 58.

[154] See Euripides, frag. 687 N² foll., with Nauck's notes ; Apollod., II, 132 ; Konon, *narrat.*, 17. Two other comic stories relate how Herakles seized and ate a whole plough-ox or team of oxen, see Kallim., *hymn.*, III, 161 (Theiodamas king of the Dryopes), cf. Apoll. Rhod., I, 1211 foll., and schol. *ad loc.* ; Theiodamas made war on Herakles for the ox he had taken, and Herakles was obliged to arm even Deïaneira ; finally Theio-

damas was defeated and killed, and Herakles thus got his son Hylas ;
the other occasion was when he took the team of the peasant of Lindos,
Apollod., II, 118 ; see the commentators on the passage of Kallimachos.

[155] Apollod., II, 127 foll.

[156] Apollod., II, 127 foll. ; Soph., *Trach.*, 248 foll., where see Jebb.

[157] Homer, *Il.*, XX, 145 foll., with schol. ; cf. *Il.*, V, 265 foll. for the
horses ; V, 638 foll. (taking of Troy).   The scholiast mentioned, also the
relevant passage of Apollodoros (II, 103 foll.), together with *SdA* VIII,
157, are thought to go back to Hellanikos.

[158] Apollod., II. 139 foll. ;   more authorities in Preller-Robert, II,
p. 538 foll.   The Molionĕ, as they are generally called, are sometimes
simply twins, sometimes a double-bodied monster, a sort of Siamese twins.
See B. Schweitzer, *Herakles*, p. 17 foll., where, however, the argument
is often very fanciful.   Homer (*Il.*, II, 621, XI, 709 foll.) knows nothing
of their monstrous shape.

[159] Apollod., *ibid.*, 143 foll.

[160] *Ibid.*, 154 foll.

[161] See Sophokles, *Trachiniae, passim*, and commentators.   For the
death of Herakles, see Nilsson in *A.R.W.*, 1922, p. 310 foll. = *O.S.* I,
p. 348 foll.

CHAPTER VIII—PART II

TROY

Quegli è Omero poeta sovrano.
—DANTE, *Inferno*, IV, 88.

LEDA, daughter of Thestios king of Aitolia, and wife of Tyndareos king of Sparta, bore several children, of whom four are important in mythology, viz., Kastor, Polydeukes,—Pollux in Latin,—Klytaimestra, and Helen (Ἑλένη). In most accounts, though not in Homer, one at least of her sons was the child of Zeus; by all accounts Helen was his daughter. Beyond this, there is little agreement. Generally, Polydeukes is the son of Zeus, while his twin Kastor was begotten of Tyndareos. Helen in most accounts is hatched from an egg, laid either by Leda herself, whom Zeus visited in the form of a swan, or by Nemesis, in which case it was given to Leda. Variations are endless; in Homer, both the brothers are mortal; in the Homeric hymn addressed to them, both are immortal.[1] No less disagreement reigns among modern investigators as to the original nature of Kastor, Polydeukes, and Helen; beyond all doubt all three appear as fully human personages in epic, and beyond all doubt all three were worshipped as deities, the brothers (the Dioskuroi or sons of Zeus, as they are generally called after Homer's time), being patrons of mariners, to whom they appear in the form of what is now called St. Elmo's fire, and also being important deities at Sparta, while Helen seems to be an ancient tree-goddess, with a ritual not unlike that which we have found connected with Erigone. But whether we have deities degraded into heroes, or heroes elevated into deities, or a confusion between figures of saga and figures of cult, is a matter far from settled, and fortunately not important for our present purpose.[2]

Helen on occasion appears as St. Elmo's fire, but unlike her brothers, she is a bad sign.[3]

The Dioskuroi took part in sundry adventures, such as the Argonautic expedition ; but the one important adventure of their own is that which resulted in the death of Kastor. Leukippos (White-horse-man, *i.e.*, nobleman, person who can afford to keep fine horses for racing, etc. ; a dozen mythological nobodies have the same name), a descendant of Perseus, had two daughters, Hilaeira and Phoibe, who were betrothed to the two sons of Aphareus, Leukippos' brother. But Kastor and Polydeukes carried them off. Either for this reason, or as a result of a quarrel during a cattle-raid, the sons of Aphareus, Idas and Lynkeus, attacked them. The details of the ensuing fight are variously given ; but the end of it was that both the sons of Aphareus, and also Kastor, were killed. Polydeukes, who had always lived in the closest of unity with his twin, now prayed Zeus to let him share his own immortality with Kastor. Zeus consented, and so the twins either live together, one day in heaven and another in the House of Hades, or else they take it in turns to die, one being always in the underworld, the other out of it.[4]

Late writers identify the brothers with the constellation Gemini. The cult of the Twins was early brought to Rome, where Kastor is for some reason so much the more prominent that they are often spoken of loosely as the Castores. A minor adventure, alluded to in a fragment of Alkman, was a fight with the sons of Hippokoon, Herakles' opponents.[5]

Helen had a much more varied and adventurous career. Being by far the most beautiful of women, she was striven for by all manner of wooers. The first was Theseus, who carried her off to Aphidnai in Attica, when she was still but a child. Her brothers brought her back untouched, however, and captured Theseus' mother Aithra (the Athenians explained lamely that the hero was away at the time), who was given to Helen as an attendant and accompanied her to Troy.[6] Later, she was formally wooed by all the principal men of Greece, including Menelaos,—Agamemnon was already married to her sister Klytaimestra, but appeared to press his brother's claims. On the advice of Odysseus, who also was a suitor, but without much hope of success, Menelaos being the richest of them all, Helen was left free to choose whom she would, and the rest swore to respect her choice and stand by her husband in all need. She chose Menelaos, and for some years lived quietly with him, and bore a daughter Hermione. Then Paris appeared on the scene, favoured by Aphrodite, and induced Helen to run away with him.[7] Menelaos was absent and could not therefore interfere ;

but on his return, he and his brother roused all Greece (it is still remembered vaguely in Homer that Agamemnon was overlord of a great part of the country, in fact an emperor rather than a mere king), and a great expedition was raised against Troy.[8]

Stesichoros, who according to tradition was struck blind for speaking unmannerly of Helen in one of his poems, told in his famous Palinode a tale, apparently of his own invention, which fully vindicated her honour.   Paris carried her off by force, but they got no farther than Egypt, whose just king Proteus (apparently a rationalization of the sea-god) kept her safely till her husband should claim her.   Meanwhile a phantom of her accompanied Paris to Troy, to give occasion for the war, which Zeus had decided upon.   When Menelaos, on his way from Troy, got to Egypt, this phantasm vanished, and the real Helen accompanied him home.[9]

After elaborate preparations,[10] the fleet assembled at Aulis, where, as already told in Chapter V (p. 119), the incident of Iphigeneia took place.   Here also the Greeks saw a portent, interpreted for them by the seer Kalchas.   A serpent climbed into a tree wherein was a nest with eight young birds ; these it devoured, and then caught and ate the mother-bird, which was fluttering around.   It was then turned by Zeus into stone. The meaning of this was, that nine years should pass before the war came to an end, but Troy should fall in the tenth year.[11]

According to the post-Homeric account, all manner of delays befell the expedition ; two or three of these are important enough to be worth mention.   One is more or less Homeric, at least in outline.   The arrows of Herakles were necessary to the taking of Troy ; now these had descended from Poias (see p. 219) to his son Philoktetes.   He showed the Greeks the way to an island where was the shrine of the obscure deity Chryse, to whom they wished to sacrifice ; as the rite was going on, a serpent bit him in the foot, producing so loathsome a wound and causing him to utter in his spasms of pain such loud and ill-omened cries that they were obliged to set him ashore on Lemnos.   At last however Helenos, the Trojan seer, captured by the guile of Odysseus, declared that only by the arrows of Herakles could the city be taken ; Diomedes therefore (in Sophokles it is Neoptolemos, son of Achilles) and Odysseus went to Lemnos and induced him to come with them.   The two sons of Asklepios, Machaon and Podaleirios, were with the army ; the former contrived to heal the sore, and Philoktetes slew Paris and helped to win the campaign.[12]

Another delay is not in the Homeric tradition at all, but

is quite respectably old The fleet, on its way to Troy, somehow took a wrong direction, and landed in Mysia. The inhabitants, finding a strange army in their country, turned out in
force under their king Telephos, a son of Herakles, who distinguished himself in the battle, but was wounded by Achilles.
The wound would not heal, so, after the Greeks had gone away,
—for they had no serious quarrel with the Mysians,—Telephos
went to Delphoi and asked Apollo for advice. He was told,
' he that wounded shall also heal ', and therefore set out to
find Achilles. According to Euripides at any rate, he came
among the Greeks disguised as a beggar ; in one account, which
may or may not derive from him, he somehow got hold of the
baby Orestes and threatened to kill him if he were not relieved.
At all events, whether by persuasion or threats, he secured a
hearing ; Achilles protested that he knew no medicine, but it
was explained by Odysseus that the giver of the wound was
the spear itself. The scrapings of this were therefore applied,
and Telephos was healed.[13]

At length the fleet arrived before Troy, the ships were drawn
up on the beach, and the Greeks settled down to a long campaign
of attrition. A skirmish on landing caused them their first
serious loss ; Protesilaos, king or baron of part of the region of
Thessaly just opposite the southern end of Magnesia, was the
first to spring on shore, and was cut down by a Trojan, usually
said (but not by Homer) to have been Hektor. He had left at
home a young wife.[14]

Later authors elaborate this story, which Homer touches upon but
briefly. It was fated that the first Greek to leap ashore should fall,
and thus Protesilaos in a manner sacrificed himself for his comrades.
His wife was called Laodameia, and her story,—curiously enough, no
surviving Greek of the classical epoch mentions it, but it is familiar
from the Latins,—goes on to say that she was inconsolable for her
husband's death ; that the gods, in pity, let him return to her for three
hours ; and that, when he departed again, she did not survive him.
In the same battle Kyknos, an invulnerable son of Poseidon, was overcome and strangled by Achilles, whereat he turned into a swan
(κύκνος).[15]

The state of affairs at Troy itself was as follows. Paris, as
was natural, headed the war-party. He was the son of king
Priam and his chief wife Hekabe (Latin Hecuba). It had been
foretold to his father that he would be the ruin of the city, for
his mother had dreamed that she was delivered of a firebrand.
Therefore he was exposed on Mt. Ide (Doric and Latin Ida),
but was suckled by a she-bear, saved by shepherds and brought up

among them. From his valour he got the name Alexandros (practically = warrior, champion), and one day, descending to the city from the mountains, he so distinguished himself in sports that he was recognized as being no commoner, and thus regained his rank. While still among the shepherds, he had won the love of a nymph, Oinone, whom he deserted to go after Helen. Long after, when wounded by Philoktetes with one of the poisoned arrows of Herakles, he sought her out and craved for her help to cure his wound. She refused, but on learning that he was dead, remorsefully ended her own life.[16]

An obscure story states that Priam tried to elude the fates by putting to death, not Paris, but another child who was born on the same day, his illegitimate son by the wife of a citizen called Thymoites.[17]

Strong on the other side was Antenor, one of the principal elders of Troy, who on moral grounds disapproved of Paris' kidnapping of Helen, and urged that she and the wealth she had brought with her should be given back. A tradition as old as the Epic Cycle says that the Greeks recognized his virtues and fair-mindedness, and therefore spared him and such of his family as had survived the war, when Troy fell. He had been advised by them to hang a panther-skin outside his door, to indicate that his house was not to be sacked.[18]

From this there grew up a later account which made him out a most contemptible person, little better than a spy and a traitor in Greek pay. He, or his wife Theano the prophetess, betrayed the Palladion to the Greeks, and he opened the door of the Wooden Horse.[19]

The sympathies of Aineias were on the whole with the peace-party, and his own actions during the war, although correct and patriotic enough, were not especially distinguished. His house, the junior branch of the royal family,[20] had been cast into the shade by the ruling branch, and he is represented as feeling his position rather strongly. The foremost champion of Troy was one of the fifty sons whom Priam had had by various wives and concubines, Hektor, son of Hekabe. He is never represented as having much to do with diplomacy ; he is a chivalrous and most valiant warrior, a terror to the Greeks in combat, inferior only to Achilles, and an affectionate husband. His wife was Andromache, daughter of Eetion king of Thebe in the Troad, who, with his sons, was slain when Achilles took his town. Their son, Astyanax or Skamandrios, who was born during the war, did not long survive it, according to the post-Homeric account, being flung from the battlements by the victorious Greeks, who feared to leave any of Hektor's stock alive. Andromache herself became the slave-concubine of Neoptolemos, and after his death, according at least to the account followed by Euripides and others, wedded Helenos, who had taken refuge in Epeiros. She thus became the ancestress of the Molossian kings of later times.[21]

Most of the other sons of Priam are mere names ; they appear for a moment in a battle-scene, only to be killed or captured by one of the Greek champions. One of the youngest, Troilos, fell in a combat with Achilles early in the war. For some reason, he became rather prominent in later legend. No really important story, however, is connected with him.[22]

Of the two daughters of Priam who appear in legend, one, Kassandra, has already been mentioned (Chapter VI, p. 143). Her sister Polyxena appears in the post-Homeric tradition as a pathetic and noble figure. When Troy was taken, the ghost of Achilles claimed her as his share of the spoil ; she was therefore sacrificed at his tomb, or, to speak more correctly (for human sacrifice is a very rare phenomenon in Greece), she was put to death there in order to accompany her master to the other world.[23]

Hence, no doubt, springs the romantic story that Achilles was violently in love with her during his lifetime. This, in the later accounts, led to his death, for he was decoyed into an interview with her at the temple of Apollo Thymbraios, and there set upon and killed by Paris.[24]

Finally, Hekabe herself stands out very prominently in all versions of the Troy-saga, as a majestic but most unhappy figure. She sees her children slain one after another, and her husband cut down in the courtyard of his own palace. In the form of her story familiar in the classical (but not Homeric) tradition, she was apportioned as a slave to Odysseus. On the way back, the fleet touched at a point on the Thracian coast. Here she learned that her last son, Polydoros, who had been entrusted to Poly-mestor, king of that place, had been murdered by him for the sake of the treasure he had brought with him. She therefore decoyed Polymestor into her tent, pretending to have treasure hidden somewhere, and to know nothing of the boy's death. Her women meanwhile coaxed his children to come with them ; these were murdered before the eyes of their father, who was then blinded by the women with their brooch-pins. Finally, Hekabe herself was metamorphosed, turning into a bitch. As to what became of her after that, the stories differ ; but she died and was buried, and the spot called Kynos Sema (Dog's

Monument), between Abdera and Dardanos, was said to be named in memory of her.[25]

Various elaborations and rationalizings were current; she was called a dog because in her anger she howled and barked like one, or because she died a dog's death (by stoning), or the like. In dog-form she haunted Thrace for a great while, or she turned into a dog after she was stoned for being abusive, or in that shape she became one of Hekate's hell-hounds.[26] None of these tales is early.

Of the many Greek leaders, a few deserve especial mention. Agamemnon, son of Atreus and brother of Menelaos, appears, in accounts from Homer down, as a man of great prestige owing to his high position, rather than of outstanding personal merit, although he fights bravely enough; he is apt to be irresolute, and easily discouraged. Menelaos is somewhat eclipsed by his more eminent brother; as a warrior, he is not in the very first rank, although efficient; Achilles, Agamemnon, the two Aiantes, Diomedes, and, in the other camp, Hektor, outclass him.

Of these, the greater Aias (Latin Aiax), the son of Telamon, Herakles' old comrade, and commander of the little contingent from Salamis, is one of the most prominent figures of saga. Unlike some of the others, he is slow-witted, no speaker, but with a certain bluff common sense and unshakable courage. In the absence of Achilles, he is the most reliable champion of the invaders, especially good when things are looking most hopeless. With his courage go self-will and pride, the latter proving in the end his ruin. After the death of Achilles, his armour was claimed by both Aias and Odysseus, as the most notable of the surviving champions. The matter was tried before the assembled host, Athena presiding and the Trojan prisoners acting as evidence. On their testifying that they had been more harmed by Odysseus, the arms were awarded to him. Aias went mad with resentment, and in his madness slaughtered a number of sheep. which he supposed to be his enemies. On recovering his senses, he killed himself for grief and shame.[27]

The lesser Aias is the one hero for whom Homer ever shows any personal dislike. He is a splendid fighter, but violent and ill-mannered, and inferior in every way to his greater namesake. He is leader of the Lokrian contingent. After his crime against Kassandra, he departed for home and was shipwrecked on the way; swimming ashore, by the help of Poseidon, at the Gyrai Petrai, a range of cliffs near Naxos, he boasted that he had escaped despite the gods; whereat Poseidon smashed the rock on which he stood, and drowned him.[28]

Diomedes was the son of Polyneikes' old comrade Tydeus. He is prominent throughout the *Iliad*, both for his valour and also, especially from the tenth book onwards, for his frank and good advice to Agamemnon. Athena favours him, as she did his father, and by her he is emboldened to meet Ares and Aphrodite in battle, wounding both. Meeting Glaukos, one of the leaders of the Lykians, who fight on the side of Troy, he asks his name, and on finding that a hereditary friendship exists between them, proposes that they should avoid encountering each other in battle. In token of friendship they exchange armour; as Diomedes was wearing a plain bronze suit, while Glaukos had golden armour worth a hundred oxen, this gave rise to a favourite proverb for an unequal bargain, ' gold for bronze '.[29]

Diomedes survived the war, and returned safe home to Argos, or Kalydon. There, however, fresh trouble awaited him, in the post-Homeric story. Aphrodite was wroth with him for the wound he had given her, and Diomedes found that his wife Aigialeia had played him false. Apparently his own life was threatened, for he took refuge at the altar of Hera. Leaving Greece, he wandered through Libya and Iberia (Africa and Spain), till he reached Italy, where he was supposed to have founded Arpi, Canusium and Sipontum, and visited a number of places. In particular, the Islands of Diomedes, off the coast of Apulia, were said to be frequented by a particular kind of sea-birds, friendly to Greeks, but hostile to every one else, which were originally the comrades of Diomedes turned into bird shape. He was buried there, and the birds daily sprinkled his tomb with water. There and at several other places worship was paid to him, or a local deity was identified with him. Various tales were current as to the manner of his death or vanishing ; one, as old as Pindar, was that Athena made him immortal ; he married Hermione, adds the scholiast, and lives with the Dioskuroi.[30]

Of course, local legends were common. Argos claimed to possess his shield (there were many relics in the temple of Hera and other shrines, some, no doubt, really very old), and also the Palladion ; there was certainly an old image of Athena which was annually bathed, and the shield with it ; but Sparta also had the Palladion, and so had Athens, where Diomedes had left it with Demophon son of Theseus, or had landed there at night, when Demophon, mistaking his men for enemies, had taken it in the ensuing skirmish, and so forth.[31]

Still more prominent is Odysseus, king of Ithake, husband of Penelope and father of Telemachos. During the war, he was

prominent in every episode which required quick wits ; in battle,
he was formidable, but not one of the very foremost champions ;
when it is a question of casting lots to see who shall fight Hektor,
the Greeks pray that the lot may fall upon the greater Aias,
Diomedes, or Agamemnon (Achilles being absent), not on Odysseus, although he also has volunteered. Besides giving much
shrewd and good advice on many occasions, it was he who volunteered, among others, to go with Diomedes on the perilous night
expedition described in *Iliad* X, and was chosen ' because he can
use his wits exceeding well '.[32] He and Diomedes are constantly
represented, in Homer and after Homer, as acting in conjunction.
In particular, they made their way into Troy and stole the
Palladion together, the fatal image of Pallas Athena on the possession of which the luck of the city depended.[33] But Odysseus
was alone when he marked himself with weals, dressed as a beggar,
and, pretending to have deserted, entered Troy as a spy.[34]

After Homer, the character of Odysseus suffers a remarkable
degeneration. In the *Odyssey*, he is at times unscrupulous ; but
from the Cyclic epics on, and especially in Attic tragedy, he is a
most villainous double-dealer. His conduct in regard to Palamedes is especially vile, and he drags Diomedes down with him.
Palamedes, son of Nauplios, was as clever as Odysseus himself ;
he was credited with having invented several letters of the alphabet, together with other ingenuities. When the muster for the
war was forward, Odysseus pretended to be mad, so as to avoid
serving. He therefore yoked a horse (or an ass) and an ox to
his plough and proceeded to plough with them ; but Palamedes
put the infant Telemachos in the way, and noted that Odysseus
was sane enough to turn aside and avoid him ; or he drew his
sword against the child.[35] Odysseus was henceforth his enemy,
and found occasion to get him out of the way. He and Diomedes
drowned him while he was fishing ; or he forged a letter, supposed
to come from Priam, promising Palamedes gold if he would betray
the Greek camp, and, producing this before the host, bade them
search Palamedes' tent. The gold being found there (Odysseus
had taken care to hide it previously), Palamedes was found
guilty and stoned. Another version is, that Odysseus and Diomedes told him there was a treasure hidden down a well, and
flung stones upon him when he went down to look for it, thus
killing him ; but this is later than the others.[36]

One of the best-known characters in the whole cycle is Nestor,
and this is largely due to the loving, yet humorous drawing
of him in the *Iliad*. He is the surviving son of Neleus, and
king of Pylos (shown by late excavations to be a Mycenaean

site of considerable archaeological importance). He is much older than the rest, over sixty when the *Iliad* begins,[37] and no longer able to do much in the field, but highly honoured for his sage counsels and his somewhat long-winded, but interesting, reminiscences. He appears always as a peace-maker when the younger chiefs quarrel, and for the first half of the poem his advice is Agamemnon's chief guide ; after the failure of his scheme, the embassy of reconciliation to Achilles, he drops somewhat into the background, his place being taken in large measure by Diomedes, who has an old head on young shoulders. After the war, he reaches Pylos in safety, and appears in the *Odyssey* enjoying a dignified old age, still full of good advice and old stories, and having only one serious regret, the death in battle of his heroic son Antilochos, who was killed by Memnon while covering his father's retreat.[38]

But pre-eminent over all the rest is Achilles (properly Achilleus or Achileus), son of Peleus and Thetis, the strongest, swiftest, most valiant and most handsome of the whole army.

Of his birth something has been said in Chapter II ; a legend of which the earlier authors know nothing states that Thetis dipped him, while he was yet an infant, in the Styx, and thus made him proof against all manner of wounds, save in the heel by which she held him. A like invulnerability is claimed for the greater Aias, whom, while he was a baby, Herakles wrapped in the invulnerable skin of the Nemean lion, thus communicating its property to him. There was one spot which the skin did not touch, and through that, in the end, Aias thrust his own sword. In like manner Achilles, in the later versions of his story, died from an arrow-wound in the heel.[39]

Thetis knew that her son might either live a long and inglorious life, or go to Troy, cover himself with glory, and die young. Therefore she, or Peleus, hid him away, when the army was mustering, knowing that, as it was fated that Troy could not be taken without him, he would be asked to go, although he was not one of the wooers of Helen, having still, at that time, been under the care of Cheiron, by whom he, like Jason, was nurtured.[40] She therefore took him to the island of Skyros, where she dressed him as a girl, and left him at the court of king Lykomedes, lord of that island. Here he met and loved Deidameia, Lykomedes' daughter, who became by him the mother of a son, Pyrrhos (Red-head), afterwards nicknamed Neoptolemos (young warrior, new recruit) because he joined the army before Troy late in the war. But it was found out where Achilles was, and Odysseus and Diomedes went to Skyros. Here they contrived

to leave armour in the chambers of the women and he soon
betrayed his sex by the interest with which he handled it. He
therefore joined the fleet at Aulis.[41]

For the first nine years, after one or two fruitless embassies
to try and arrange a peaceful settlement, the war consisted of a
series of raids by the Greeks on the minor cities supporting
Troy, and on the hinterland generally. The fortress itself,
strongly garrisoned and supported by a considerable force of
Trojans and allies, was impregnable to the rudimentary siege-
operations of those days, but the campaign of attrition wore
down Priam's resources and stopped all possibility of increasing
them by trade.[42]　In the tenth year occurred the events which
form the subject of the *Iliad*. Agamemnon had had for his portion of the spoil Chryseis, daughter of Chryses, a priest of Apollo.
Much captivated by her beauty, he refused to let her father
ransom her ; the priest therefore besought his god to punish
the Achaioi, and a plague came upon the camp. Kalchas explained
the cause of the plague, and that it could be stopped only by
returning Chryseis without ransom. Agamemnon grudgingly
consented, but indemnified himself by seizing on Briseis, a slave-
girl belonging to Achilles, who was much attached to her. He
therefore withdrew from any further allegiance to Agamemnon,
and he and his contingent, the Thessalian Myrmidones, for some
time took no part in the fighting. Deprived thus of their foremost champion, the Greeks, despite the valour shown by Diomedes, Aias and others, were driven back on their camp and
compelled to fortify it with a wall.

Agamemnon, by the advice of Nestor, now sent to Achilles
an embassy, consisting of Aias of Salamis, Odysseus, and Phoinix
son of Amyntor, with instructions to offer the return of Briseis,
a huge honour-price, and, if the war should be brought to a
successful conclusion, marriage, without bride-price, to one of
the royal princesses, with seven cities for her dower. All three
urged him warmly to accept, in particular old Phoinix, who was
in some sense a client of his father Peleus. Phoinix, when a
young man, had incurred the anger of his father, by forming
a liaison with a slave-concubine of the latter's of whom his mother
was jealous. His father cursed him with childlessness, a curse
which was fulfilled ; Phoinix then, despite all efforts to prevent
him leaving, ran away and took refuge with Peleus, who was
kind to him and later gave him a barony. He had known and
tended Achilles from babyhood, and might be described as his
tutor. Even he, however, failed to overcome Achilles' bitter-
ness against Agamemnon, and the embassy departed.

It is to be noted that Achilles definitely put himself in the wrong by refusing such princely overtures ; there is thus a certain poetic justice in the heavy misfortune which befalls him afterwards in the loss of his best friend.

Phoinix' quarrel with his father was a peculiarly furious one. In a doubtfully genuine passage of Homer (*Il.*, IX, 458–61, rejected by Aristarchos), Phoinix has serious thoughts of killing the old man ; in a story which seems to be no earlier than Euripides (*Phoinix*, see the fragments in Nauck²), his father blinded him.

Next day, after vigorous resistance on the part of the Greeks, Hektor drove them back to the ships, and attacking the wall with several columns at once, contrived to force an entrance and set one of the ships on fire. But now Patrokles (or Patroklos), the favourite retainer of Achilles, got leave to go out wearing Achilles' armour and leading the Myrmidones. The Trojans, supposing that Achilles himself was upon them, retreated in disorder, but after a while Patroklos was killed, by the help of Apollo, and the Greeks in turn began to fall back. Achilles, on hearing of the death of his friend, went nearly mad, and appeared, unarmed, at the trench around the camp, where the sound of his war-cry made the Trojans give back and let the body of Patrokles be rescued. He now was anxious to fight at once ; Odysseus, however, insisted on the feud being healed in proper fashion, with payment of the compensation due to Achilles, and Thetis persuaded Hephaistos to make a new suit of armour for her son. Achilles next day utterly routed the Trojans, met and killed Hektor in single combat, and returned to camp, dragging the body behind his chariot. Funeral games were held over Patroklos, and Priam, coming secretly by night to Achilles, ransomed the body of his son. With his funeral the *Iliad* ends.

Probably in the actual campaign of which the saga is a more or less distorted reflection, and certainly in the saga itself, the Greeks were never able to cut the Trojan communications with their numerous allies in Thrace and in Asia. The steadiest and most loyal support was given by the strong Lykian contingent, led by Sarpedon, son of Zeus, and his kinsman Glaukos, of whom the latter has already been mentioned, the former was killed by Patroklos.[43] A formidable body of Thracians was brought to the Troad by Rhesos, the night before Hektor's final and nearly successful attempt on the camp ; but Odysseus and Diomedes, volunteering to go as scouts and see what the enemy were doing, caught a Trojan spy, Dolon, who had been persuaded with a promise of Achilles' immortal horses to bring word of the Greek movements, found out from him where Rhesos was, stole into his unguarded bivouac, and killed him and several of his followers, helped in their enterprise by Athena. Later tradition had it that if the horses of Rhesos, which the two adventurers carried off, had had time to feed on the pasture and drink the water of Troy, the city could never have been taken. Rhesos himself, being the son of one of the Muses, escaped the usual fate of men after his death, and became a kind of demi-god in Thrace, concerning whose origin and functions not a little difference of opinion prevails.[44] But still more noteworthy were two contingents which appeared on the scene after the death of Hektor.

The first of these was a body of Amazons, led by their queen Penthesileia, daughter of Ares. At once we notice a different tone from that of the Homeric story, which gives everywhere the impression of sticking relatively close to facts historical and geographical, although Homer handles details with the freedom of a great creative poet. The Amazons are outside his purview altogether, save as a vague and distant people with whom Priam once fought in his youth.[45] Penthesileia was as beautiful as she was valiant, and did much damage before she fell in battle with Achilles, who mourned over her after he had slain her. Hereupon Thersites took it upon himself to mock Achilles, who in a rage killed him. In Homer this low-born but glib-tongued demagogue, 'the uncomeliest man that came before Ilion', rails on the kings at the great council which follows the defection of Achilles ; and he is soundly beaten by Odysseus for his insolence. In the later tales, however, he is provided with a respectable pedigree and made a kinsman of Diomedes, who is highly displeased at his death ; an example of a sort of snobbishness in the later mythology, which tends to make every one royal if he is at all prominent.[46]

After Penthesileia came Memnon, son of Eos and Tithonos. He also distinguished himself against the Greeks, but like Penthesileia he fell before Achilles. His comrades, the Ethiopians. were turned into birds, who still fight around his tomb. He represents the far South, or East, as Penthesileia does the North ; the ends of the earth were drawn into the fray.[47]

Soon after this followed the death of Achilles himself, who was shot either by Paris, or by Apollo (disguised as Paris, in some accounts) ; his body was got out of the battle after a furious struggle, and magnificently buried, mourned, not only by all the Greeks, but by Thetis and her sister Nereids.[48] As to his fate after death, the early accounts vary from the later, and these from each other ; in Homer, he goes to the House of Hades like anyone else ; later it was said that he lived immortal, either on the island of Leuke, in the Euxine, or in the Elysian Fields, and by some that he was wedded to Helen.[49] Close upon his death followed the suicide of Aias son of Telamon, already mentioned. The Greeks now sent for Achilles' son, as without him Troy could not be taken, and after him, for Philoktetes, for a like reason. But still the city held out, and a stratagem was resorted to. Epeios, who was a skilled craftsman and helped by Athena, constructed an enormous wooden model of a horse, inside which a band of picked warriors was placed. The army then sailed away, leaving behind Sinon, who let himself be taken prisoner, professed himself a bitter enemy of the other Greeks, who had killed his friend and lord Palamedes and would have sacrificed him to secure a safe return, and pretended to reveal the secret of the horse ; it was an offering to Athena, purposely made too big to go through the gates, but if it could be brought in, the city would be impregnable. The Trojans for the most part believed him, although Laokoon, priest of Apollo, declared it was all a trick, and that the horse should be destroyed. He and his two sons were, however, killed by a pair of huge serpents which appeared swimming over the sea from Tenedos. The Trojans supposed this to be a punishment for his impiety, and hauled the horse inside the city, breaking down a part of the wall. Kassandra warned them in vain, and Helen walked around the horse, calling to the warriors inside in perfect imitation of the voices of their wives ; but Kassandra was not believed, and Menelaos, Diomedes and Odysseus restrained the others from answering Helen. That night little watch was kept ; the Greeks returned, the horse was opened, by Sinon or another, and the city was taken, after a sharp fight, in which Priam was killed by Neoptolemos, but Aineias and some others escaped ; his further adventures are told in Chapter XI.[50]

The returning fleet met with disasters, due to the wrath of Athena and the treacherous revenge of Nauplios, father of Palamedes. Athena raised a violent storm which scattered the fleet and wrecked many of the ships ; but a greater disaster awaited them off Cape Kaphareus in Euboia, where Nauplios decoyed them upon the rocks by showing false beacons. Several individual heroes escaped these disasters with varying results ; Nestor arrived safely at Pylos in a few days ; Neoptolemos, warned by Thetis, went home by land ; Odysseus went his own way, and his adventures form the subject of the *Odyssey*.[51]

After a frankly piratical raid upon a neighbouring people, the Kikones, who in the end beat him off with some loss, he was caught by a violent storm, which drove him to the land of the

Lotos-Eaters, situate, like most of the places Odysseus visits, in fairyland.[52] The natives received him hospitably, and gave his men lotos-fruit to eat ; the virtue of this was, that he who ate it forgot home and friends and desired only to live in Lotos-Land. Removing by force those who had succumbed to this magic, Odysseus sailed on, and came to the land of the Kyklopes. Most of his ships he left behind on an island a short distance away, but with his own crew he went exploring, entered the deserted cave of Polyphemos, one of the Kyklopes, and proceeded to steal provisions therefrom. Not content with this, he must needs await the arrival of Polyphemos himself, who promptly shut him and his companions into the cave, closing the door with a huge rock, and proceeded to cook two of the men for his supper. In the morning, he breakfasted in the same way, and Odysseus and the other survivors meditated revenge. To kill the giant as he slept was useless, for they could not move the rock ; but Odysseus prepared a sharp stake, and, when Polyphemos had supped on two more of his men, gave him a draught of very powerful wine which he had had from Maron, priest of Apollo, for sparing him and his household during the war. Having thus made him very drunk, he and his men heated the stake and blinded his one eye with it. Odysseus had told the giant that his name was Nobody (*Οὔτις*), so when the other Kyklopes came in response to his cries, and asked what ailed him, he replied, ' Nobody is killing me ', whereat they went away, supposing that he was merely ill. In the morning, Polyphemos opened the cave and let out his sheep and goats ; Odysseus and his men went with them, the men tied each between two ewes, and Odysseus clinging to the belly of a huge ram. Once in his ship, Odysseus shouted his real name to Polyphemos, and taunted him ; Polyphemos, after nearly smashing the ship with huge rocks, prayed to his father Poseidon not to let Odysseus reach home, or if he must do so, to make him arrive alone, in evil plight, very late, and find trouble awaiting him there.[53]

Leaving the Kyklopes, Odysseus came to the island of Aiolos, ruler of the winds, who lived there with his six sons, who were married to his six daughters.[54] He entertained Odysseus most hospitably, and as a parting present gave him, tied up in a bag, all the winds except the one which would blow him straight home. So they came safely to within sight of Ithake, when Odysseus, who had been at the helm all the while, fell asleep, and his men, thinking the bag contained treasure, opened it ; whereupon the winds rushed out and blew them to Aiolos' island, where they were refused any further help. Leaving him, they came to the country of the Laistrygonians, cannibal giants, who sank all the ships except Odysseus' own, and caught and devoured the crews. He and his own crew, however, managed to escape to the island of Kirke, Aiaia, where half the crew, going to spy out the land, were beguiled by the enchantress and turned into swine by a magic drink which she gave them. Then Odysseus went to their rescue, and on the way met Hermes, who gave him the herb moly ($\mu\tilde{\omega}\lambda\upsilon$), a powerful counter-charm. Armed with it, he was unaffected by Kirke's drugs, and so frightened her with his sword that she re-transformed his comrades and swore to do them and him no more harm. They lived together for a year, but at last he demanded to be told the way home. To his horror, he learned that he must go to the world of the dead, to learn his route from the ghost of Teiresias. By Kirke's instructions, he arrived safely at the House of Hades, met Teiresias and many other ghosts, including the spirit of his mother Antikleia, who had died during his absence, and learned how things stood at home. His wife was already besieged by wooers from all the neighbouring baronies, each anxious to marry her, not only for her great beauty, but to strengthen his claim to the supposedly vacant kingship, Telemachos being yet but a child. Returning to Kirke's island, he set out, passing a series of dangers of which she had forewarned him. Running between Skylla and Charybdis, he steered near the former, thus escaping with the loss of six men, whom the monster snatched out of the ship. He thus avoided the still worse risk of the Planktai, as he had already avoided that of the Sirens. The Seirenes were in form not unlike the Harpies, but without their loathsomeness and their powers of snatching their prey. Generally (but not in Homer) represented as birds with the heads of women, it is not at all impossible that they were originally, as Weicker has suggested, soul-birds, with the usual dangerous power of the dead to draw others to them. But their method was to sing enchantingly to all who passed their island, inviting them to land ; those who tried to do so, were wrecked on the rocks and drowned. Odysseus stopped the ears of his men with wax, and had himself bound to the mast, giving strict orders to tie him faster if he tried to get loose. He thus heard the song, which filled him with intense desire to join the singers, and at the same time neither he nor his crew was harmed.[55]

After passing Skylla, he came to Thrinakie, the island of the Sun, where occurred the adventure, already told, with the sacred herds. As a result of the men's impiety, Zeus, on their departure, wrecked the ship with a thunderbolt. Odysseus himself, after narrowly escaping death in Charybdis, floated on a piece of wreckage to the island of Kalypso, an Atlantid, who detained him seven years. But, although she offered to make him immortal, he would not forsake Penelope, so finally, by command of Zeus, brought by Hermes, she let him go and furnished him with materials and tools to make a large boat. On this he sailed away until within sight of Scherie, the land of the Phaiakes. Here Poseidon saw him, on his return from a banquet among the Ethiopians, which Zeus and Athena had taken advantage of to interfere on the hero's behalf. Raising a violent storm, he wrecked him once more ; however, Ino-Leukothea appeared and lent him her wimple, which saved him from drowning. After two days and nights in the water, he managed to land, and promptly crept into a thicket, where he slept, exhausted. In the morning, Nausikaa, daughter of Alkinoos, king of the Phaiakes, came down to the shore to wash the household's clothes ; Odysseus appealed to her and was shown the way to the palace, where he was kindly received, his tale listened to with great interest, and after being given rich gifts he was sent back to Ithake in one of the magical ships of the Phaiakes, which could go anywhere in a few hours. Poseidon had to content himself with turning the ship into stone on its return, as a hint, which was taken, that this convoying of all and sundry must cease.

Arrived at Ithake, Odysseus met Athena, who turned him into the semblance of an old beggar. In this form he soon introduced himself into his own hall, made himself known to Telemachos and to two thralls, Eumaios the swineherd and Philoitios the cowherd, who still were faithful to him, and interviewed Penelope. She was by this time at her wits' end. For a while she had kept her many wooers at bay by pretending that before remarrying she must finish a great winding-sheet which she was weaving against the death of Laertes, Odysseus' father. This she secretly unravelled every night, until she was betrayed by one of her maids and forced to finish it. The supposed beggar won her confidence by exactly describing Odysseus to her, and approved her scheme to tell the wooers that she would marry whichever of them could string her husband's bow and perform a certain feat of archery with it. Next day the trial took place. When all had failed, Odysseus asked, as if in jest, to be allowed to try. He succeeded at once, performed the feat prescribed, and then shot down Antinoos, chief of the wooers. A furious struggle followed, in which Odysseus, his two faithful thralls, and Telemachos succeeded in killing all their opponents. Next day Odysseus made himself known to his aged father, and the blood-feud which was at once begun by the kin of the slain was stopped by the intervention of Athena.

As to what happened after that, accounts differ so widely (for here the *Odyssey* ends) that it is hopeless to give them all in a book of this size. The points of agreement are, firstly, that Odysseus appeased Poseidon by going inland till he met a man who mistook the oar he carried for a winnowing-fan, and there founding a shrine to the god ; and that he met his end in a skirmish in which he was shot by Telegonos, his son by Kalypso or Kirke, who had set out to look for him and did not recognize him. A sort of ending is huddled on to the story by making Telegonos marry Penelope, and Telemachos Kirke.[56]

Agamemnon arrived home safely, to be met with murder and treachery. His family had been accursed ever since the days of their ancestor Tantalos, whose son Pelops won his desires by treachery and violence. Oinomaos, king of Pisa, had a fair daughter Hippodameia, whose hand might be won on certain conditions. The suitor was to take her into his chariot and drive away with her ; Oinomaos was to follow, and spear the suitor if he could catch him. Twelve adventurers had perished in this manner, when Pelops arrived on the scene and bribed Myrtilos (in some accounts, with a promise of Hippodameia's favours) to take out the linch-pin of his master's chariot-wheel and put in a dummy of wax. Oinomaos was thus thrown and killed ; but Pelops avoided his obligations by drowning Myrtilos. The blood-guilt brought evil upon his two sons, Atreus and Thyestes. Thyestes seduced his brother's wife Aërope, and stole a marvellous golden ram which the gods had given him, and which was the pledge of sovranty over Mycenae. Atreus banished his brother, but afterwards pretended to be reconciled and recalled him. Having got him thus in his power, he set before him a dish made of the flesh of Thyestes' own children. On learning what had befallen him, Thyestes invoked a horrible curse on his brother, and departed. He now learned that he might raise up an avenger by a union with his own daughter, Pelopia. There was born a son, Aigisthos, who carried on the feud. In Agamemnon's absence, he seduced Klytaimestra, already enraged against her husband by the sacrifice of Iphigeneia ; greeting Agamemnon with pretended fondness, she and her paramour set upon and killed him, and with him, Kassandra. It was to revenge this that Orestes killed his mother and Aigisthos.[57]

Menelaos escaped from the great storm with some portion of his fleet, and reached Egypt. Here (apart from the business

9

of Helen, already narrated) he had a curious adventure. Setting out from the mainland, he found himself becalmed on the island (now long a part of the coast, owing to the silt carried down by the Nile) of Pharos, until he and his men were almost starved and even reduced to catching and eating fish, the very last resort for an Achaian. A sea-nymph, Eidothea, took pity on him, and advised him to lie in wait for her father Proteus, herdsman of the sea, when he came out of the water at noon to sleep among his herds of sea-monsters. She disguised Menelaos and some of his men in fresh seal-skins, counteracting their vile odour with ambrosia. When the moment came they fell upon Proteus, who turned into all manner of shapes, including water and a tree, but was held fast through them all, and at last told Menelaos that he was stayed because he had forgotten to offer sacrifice to the gods before leaving Egypt, and must go back and do so ; he also gave him much information as to the fate of the other chieftains. After some further wanderings Menelaos at length reached home, in possession of much wealth gathered on the way, and just in time for the funeral of Aigisthos and Klytaimestra.[58]

NOTES TO CHAPTER VIII—PART II

[1] Homer, *Il.*, III, 236 foll. (*Od.*, XI, 300, is strongly suspected of being an interpolation) ; *hymn. Homer.*, XVII (earliest mention in a surviving work of Kastor and Polydeukes as sons of Zeus, but *cf.* Hesiod, frag. 91). The schol. H. on *Od.*, *loc. cit.*, says it is a ' later ' idea ; schol. V, *ibid.*, says Polydeukes was Zeus' son, Kastor Tyndareos'. For Helen's birth, see the *Kypria*, frag. 7 Allen (Nemesis lays the egg) ; cf. Chapter II, p. 23 ; Kratinos *ap.* Athenaios, IX, 373 E (the egg given to Leda to hatch) ; Eurip., *Helena*, 17 foll. (Leda visited by the swan) ; *SdA* III, 328 (Leda lays the egg). In the last passage, Helen and the Dioskuroi are all born from the one egg ; M1, 204 (p. 64, 28 Bode), Leda lays two eggs, from one of which Polydeukes and Kastor are born, from the other Helen and Klytaimestra ; cf. Horace, *Sat.*, II, 1, 26, *A.P.*, 147. In all authors Helen is daughter of Zeus, Klytaimestra of Tyndareos ; Hesiod, frag. 92, says Helen was daughter of Zeus and an Okeanid, θυγατρὸς Ὠκεανοῦ καὶ Διός (so the MSS. of the source, Schol. Pind., *Nem.*, X, 150, see Rzach's note). See p. 253.

See in general for the contents of this chapter, Preller-Robert, III, ii ; also the relevant arts. in Roscher and Pauly-Wissowa.

[2] See for the controversy, Farnell, *Hero-Cults*, Chapter VIII and p. 323 foll. Dioskuroi as St. Elmo's fire, see, *e.g.*, Pliny, *N.H.*, II, 101 (single flame is Helen, and a bad sign ; double flame is Kastor and Polydeukes, and drives the bad one away).

[3] See last note ; but Eurip., *Orest.*, 1637, says she is a saviour of mariners.

[4] Pindar, *Nem.*, X, 55 foll., with schol., and commentators ; here

both brothers are always together ; but in Verg., *Aen.*, VI, 121, apparently, certainly in Servius, *ad loc.*, Lucian, *dial. mort.*, I, *init.*, Kastor is in Hades one day, Polydeukes the next.

⁶ Pseudo-Eratosthenes, 10, and Hyginus, *poet. astron.*, II, 22 ; Wissowa, *R.K.R.*, p. 268 foll. ; Alkman, frags. 15 and 16, 1 Bergk = frag. 1 with notes, Diehl. They seem to have been fighting as allies of Herakles.

⁶ See especially Plutarch, *Theseus*, 31 foll.

⁷ Hesiod, frag. 94 ; Isokrates, X, 40 (who makes the oath the wooers' own idea), Eurip., *Iphig. in Aul.*, 55 foll. (a manifest interpolation, but not a very late one ; the author makes it Tyndareos' suggestion) ; Apollod., III, 132, and Hyginus, *fab.*, 78, who name Odysseus. It is superfluous to give references for Paris' seduction of Helen, since every author from Homer down who tells the story at all mentions it, but Hesiod, frag. 93, with Stesichoros, frag. 35, gives a reason for Helen's conduct ; Tyndareos once forgot Aphrodite at a sacrifice, and by way of revenge she made all his daughters light.

⁸ The main authority is now the *Iliad*, supplemented by the fragments of the Cycle, with details from later authors. The expedition is usually said to have consisted of 1,000 ships (*e.g.* Verg., *Aen.*, II, 198), but the numbers in the Homeric catalogue (for the historical value of which see Allen, 1921, *passim*, which also gives other and later lists) amount to 1186. Strictly speaking, Troy (Τροίη, Τροία) is the region, the city (Hissarlik ?) is Ilios, Ilion, or Pergamon (Pergama) ; but the city, after Homer, is often called Troia.

⁹ Stesichoros, frag. 26 Bergk ; add to the references in his note Herodotos, II, 112 foll. ; Euripides, *Helena, passim.*

¹⁰ They lasted ten years, according to *Iliad*, XXIV, 765 (a manifest interpolation), Schol. *Il.*, IX, 668, Dictys, II, 9 foll., and others.

¹¹ *Iliad*, II, 303 foll.

¹² *Ibid.*, 718 foll., and then a multiplicity of authors, through Sophokles' *Philoctetes* (where see Jebb's introduction for more details and variants) down to Dictys, II, 14. Poias is sometimes a shepherd, sometimes a king, and it is sometimes he, sometimes Philoktetes, who lights the pyre and is given the bow and arrows.

¹³ See the summary of the *Kypria* (Proclus' *Chrestomathia*, in Allen, *Homeri Opera*, Vol. V, p. 104), and the fragments of Euripides' *Telephos*, with Nauck's notes. Sundry later authors (as Dictys, II, 1 foll.) elaborate the story in various ways.

¹⁴ *Iliad*, II, 698 foll. ; the schol. on 701 says that Aineias, Achates (Vergil's *fidus Achates*) and Euphorbos, as well as Hektor, were named as the slayer by various authorities.

¹⁵ Catullus, LXVIII, 75 (73) foll. ; Ovid, *Heroid.*, 13, and commentators on both ; Hygin., *fab.*, 103, 104. Kyknos, *Kypria* ap. Proclus, p. 105 Allen, and many later authors ; Ovid, *Met.*, XII, 71 foll.

¹⁶ See the fragments of Euripides' *Alexandros* ; Apollod., III, 148 foll. ; Hygin., *fab.*, 91. For Oinone, see Parthenios 4, Konon 23 ; Ovid, *Her.*, V ; Quintus Smyrnaeus, X, 259 foll. (whence Tennyson had the story).

¹⁷ SA II, 32, citing Euphorion.

¹⁸ See Homer, *Il.*, VII, 347 foll. ; Pausanias, X, 26, 8 and 27, 3 (painting by Polygnotos of the sack of Troy, at Delphoi). *Ibid.*, 27, 2, he cites the *Little Iliad* (frag. 16, Allen) to the effect that Agenor was killed in the sack by Neoptolemos.

¹⁹ For instance, Dictys, IV, 22 ; V, 1, 4, 8 ; Lykophron, 340 foll.,

with the commentary of Tzetzes; and several other late authors, whose material would seem to be of Alexandrian date.

[20] The pedigree is as follows, according to Homer, *Il.*, XX, 213 foll. :—

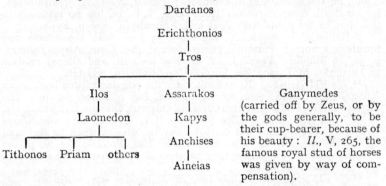

Dardanos
|
Erichthonios
|
Tros

Ilos — Assarakos — Ganymedes

Ilos
|
Laomedon

Tithonos Priam others

Assarakos
|
Kapys
|
Anchises
|
Aineias

Ganymedes (carried off by Zeus, or by the gods generally, to be their cup-bearer, because of his beauty : *Il.*, V, 265, the famous royal stud of horses was given by way of compensation).

Later authorities add that Zeus loved Elektra, one of the Pleiads, who bore two sons, Dardanos and Eetion (not of course Andromache's father, but identified with Iasion, Demeter's lover) and a daughter Harmonia, Kadmos' wife ; see Preller-Robert, II, p. 391 and notes ; the usual form of the story is due to Hellanikos, frags. 23, 24, 135 Jacoby. Dardanos went across to the Troad on a raft, for there were then no ships, or floated there on an inflated hide, at the time of the Deluge, Lykophron, 73 foll., where see schol. ; he married the daughter of the local king, Teukros (possibly the old Anatolian god Tarku, Ramsay, *Asianic Elements*, p. 47), and succeeded him. On the other hand, Priam is so often called Δαρδανίδης, which by all Homeric analogy should mean ‘son (or grandson) of Dardanos’, not merely ‘descendant of D.’, that probably a shorter pedigree was also known to Homer.

[21] Apart from the *Iliad*, see especially Eurip., *Troades*, 704 foll. ; *Andromache*, 1 foll., 1243 foll.

[22] The story of Troilus and Cressida is wholly medieval.

[23] The story dates from the *Iliu Persis* (see Allen, *Homeri opera*, V, p. 108) ; its best-known handling is in Euripides, *Hec.*, 218 foll.

[24] *E.g.*, Dictys, IV, 10 foll.

[25] Again Euripides' *Hecuba* is the best-known account. In the *Iliad* (XX, 407 foll. ; XXII, 46 foll.), Polydoros is son of Laothoe, and is slain in battle by Achilles.

[26] Plautus, *Menaech.*, 714 foll. ; Tzetzes on Lykophron, 315, 1176 ; Ovid, *Met.*, XIII, 565 foll.

[27] After *Od.*, XI, 543 foll., where see schol., and the *Little Iliad* (Allen, *Hom. op.*, V, p. 106). The best-known account of the contest for the arms is Ovid, *Met.*, XIII, 1 foll. ; of the death of Aias, Sophokles' *Aiax*.

[28] *Od.*, IV, 499 foll. ; cf. *Il.*, II, 527 foll. (inferiority to Aias Telamonios), XXIII, 473 foll. (he answers Idomeneus ‘shamefully’, *i.e.*, with blatant and unprovoked rudeness), 774 foll. (he sulks and is laughed at on losing a race ; Antilochos, in sharp contrast, makes a good-natured joke over coming in third). For Aias, and the relations between the name of his father Oileus and the name of the city, Ilios or Wilios, see Farnell, *Hero-Cults*, p. 293 foll.

[29] *Il.*, VI, 119 foll. ; see, in general, this and the preceding book.

[30] Aigialeia, *Il.*, V, 412 foll., with schol. (she was the youngest daughter of Adrastos, and therefore Diomedes' aunt) ; Lykophron, 592 foll., with Tzetzes' note ; Vergil, *Aen.*, XI, 269 foll., with Servius ; Strabo, VI, 3, 9 foll., for the adventures of Diomedes ; Pindar, *Nem.*, X, 7, with schol., for his death or apotheosis. (Hor., *carm.*, I, 6, 15, has no reference to this, but to his fights with Ares and Aphrodite.) See p. 253.

[31] Kallimachos, *hymn.*, V, especially 35 foll., with the scholia and Spanheim's notes ; Plutarch, *quaest. Graec.*, 48 ; Clem. Alex., *protrept.*, p. 36, 16 Stählin ; Paus., I, 28, 9. For his cult, and alleged relation to Diomedes of Thrace, see Farnell, *Hero-Cults*, p. 289 foll.

[32] *Il.*, VII, 179–80 ; X, 218 foll. ; for the position of this book as an integral part of the poem, see A. Shewan, *Lay of Dolon, passim*. The name of Odysseus is also written Olysseus, Odyseus, Olyseus, Lat.Vlixes, etc.

[33] *Iliu Persis*, frag. 1 Allen (= Dion. Hal., I, 68, 2 foll.), which says that the real Palladion was carried away by Aineias when he fled, and the Greeks got only an imitation ; *Little Iliad*, Proclus, Vol. V, p. 107 of Allen's Homer, which says they got the real Palladion ; very numerous references in later works.

[34] *Od.*, IV, 242 foll. ; *Little Iliad, ibid.*, besides later works.

[35] *Kypria*, p. 103 Allen ; Hygin., *fab.*, 95 ; Lykphron, 815 foll., with Tzetzes, *ad loc.* ; SA II, 81, who says that Odysseus sowed salt. A lost tragedy of Sophokles, Ὀδυσσεὺς Μαινόμενος, dealt with this subject.

[36] To the references in the above note, and the fragments of Euripides' *Palamedes*, add *Kypria*, frag. 21 Allen ; Hyg., *fab.*, 105 ; Dictys, II, 15, who says Agamemnon was privy to the plot, according to some. There are many minor variants of this and the preceding incident. Dictys also gives an elaborate account of Palamedes' services to the army, I, 4–6, 16, 19, etc.

[37] He had lived two generations (2 × 30 years), *Il.*, I, 250, by the time of the war. So the schol. on the passage, rightly. Hence, by the time the *Iliad* opens, he was about 70. Ovid, *Met.*, XII, 187–8, absurdly makes him live three centuries instead of three generations.

[38] *Od.*, III, 111–2 ; IV, 187–8 ; Pindar, *Pyth.*, VI, 28 foll., with schol. ; Quintus Smyrnaeus, II, 244 foll. The story was told in the cyclic *Aithiopis* (Allen, *Hom. Op.*, V, p. 106).

[39] *Iliad, passim ; Aithiopis*, fragments and summary of Proclus ; Statius, *Achilleis*. Invulnerability of Aias, see Pindar, *Isth.*, V (VI), 35 foll., whence the story seems to have started through a misinterpretation, see commentators *ad loc.* ; cf. Philostr., *heroic.*, 13, 3 ; argum. Soph., *Aiax* (p. 6 of Jebb's ed. of the *Aiax*) ; Lykophron, 457, with Tzetzes, *ad loc.* For Achilles being dipped in the Styx, see, *e.g.*, Stat., *Achill.*, I, 134, II, 269 ; Hyg., *fab.*, 107 ; SA VI, 57. Cf. Quintus Smyrnaeus, III, 60 foll.

[40] Hesiod, frag. 96, 49 foll. ; later references to Achilles' education by Cheiron are innumerable.

[41] Schol., *Il.*, IX, 668, says this is a later form of the story ; in Homer (*ibid.*), Achilles has conquered Skyros ; for the details, see Schol. B. on *Il.*, XIX, 326 ; D. adds that the tale is found παρὰ τοῖς κυκλικοῖς (' in poets of the Epic Cycle ' or ' in common authors ' ?) ; Sophokles, frags. of the *Skyrioi* or *Skyriai* (too small to show how he handled the story) and several later authors, as Apollod., III, 174 ; Ovid, *Met.*, XIII, 162 foll. ; Stat., *Achill.*, I, 20 foll.

[42] This is merely hinted at in the *Iliad*, in the recurring references to the great pre-war wealth of Troy. The story now follows the *Iliad*.

[43] *Il.*, XVI, 477 foll. Glaukos was afterwards killed by the greater Aias, see Quint. Smyrn., III, 277 foll.

[44] See *Iliad*, X, ·and [Euripides], *Rhesos*; cf. Farnell, *Hero-Cults*, p. 289.

[45] *Il.*, III, 189.

[46] See the fragments of the cyclic *Amazonis*; the fullest account in later writers is Quintus Smyrnaeus, I, 18 foll., who generally follows good early tradition. References are common, and it was a favourite subject in art, like all stories of the Amazons. The genealogy of Thersites, for whom see *Il.*, II, 212 foll., is thus given by Quint. Smyrn., I, 770 foll.

Agrios *brother of* Oineus

| | |
Thersites   Tydeus
|
Diomedes.

They were therefore first cousins once removed.

[47] See Quint. Smyrn., II; the story goes back to the *Aithiopis*. Cf. Ovid, *Met.*, XIII, 576 foll.

[48] *Il.*, XIX, 416–17; XXI, 277–8; XXII, 359–60; Soph., *Philoct.*, 332 foll., where see Jebb's note for more refs.; Hyg., *fab.*, 107; SA VI, 57 (a rationalizing account); Quint. Smyrn., III, 60 foll.

[49] Homer, *Od.*, XI, 467 foll.; *Kypria*, Proclus, p. 106, Allen; Alkaios, frag. 14 Diehl (48*b*, Bergk); Pindar, *Nem.*, IV, 49; Eurip., *Androm.*, 1259 foll.; also several later passages. Marriage with Helen, Philostr., *Heroic.*, 20, 32 foll., possibly suggested by Lykophron, 272 foll., which however says that his posthumous bride was Medeia. See further Farnell, *Hero-Cults*, pp. 285 foll., 409.

[50] Epeios and the Wooden Horse, first in *Od.*, VIII, 492 foll., IV, 271 foll., XI, 523 foll., then in many authors. It is quite conceivably a confused reminiscence of some Oriental siege-engine. So, in antiquity, Pliny, *N.H.*, VII, 202; Paus., I, 23, 8 and others.· Sinon, first in the *Iliu Persis*, best known from Verg., *Aen.*, II, 57 foll. The enormous number of conditions which had to be fulfilled before Troy could be taken seem to reflect the wonder, in a time of very rudimentary ideas of siege-tactics, that so strong a place ever fell at all.

[51] The story of the Returns of the Heroes (Νόστοι) is sketched by Proteus, *Od.*, IV, 492 foll., cf. III, 130 foll.; it was told in full in the *Nostoi* of the Epic Cycle. For the storm, see especially Aesch., *Agam.*, 648 foll., Verg., *Aen.*, I, 39 foll.

[52] I entirely agree with Eratosthenes (*ap.* Strabo, I, 2, 14), that 'Homer neither knew these matters (the geography of the Western Mediterranean) nor meant to make Odysseus' wanderings take place in known regions'. For the counter-view, see, in antiquity, Strabo himself; in modern times, Victor Bérard (see p. 37 n. 4).

[53] Besides *Od.*, IX, 106 foll., see Euripides, *Cyclops*.

[54] *Od.*, X, 1 foll., where no one is in the least shocked at the family arrangements. Perhaps it is from this that (as in Euripides' lost *Aiolos*, see the fragments in Nauck; Ovid, *Heroid.*, XI) the tale arose concerning another Aiolos that one of his sons, Makareus, had an incestuous passion for his sister Kanake.

[55] For Weicker's views, see his work *Der Seelenvogel* (see Bibliography). Later legends had it that the Seirenes drowned themselves in vexation when Odysseus escaped them, and that one of them, Parthenope, came

ashore at the site of Naples, which was originally named after her. See Lykophron, 712 foll., with the notes of Tzetzes. Her sisters, Leukosia and Ligeia, were also washed ashore, and all had cults both separately and in common.

⁵⁶ The story was told in the Cyclic *Telegonia*, for which see Allen, *Hom. Op.*, V, pp. 109, 143 foll.

⁵⁷ Besides Chapter IV, p. 86, and notes there, see Pindar, *Ol.*, I, 69 foll., with scholiast, which gives, among other particulars, a list of the unsuccessful suitors ; for the rest of the story of the Pelopidai, see especially the following plays : Aeschylus, *Agamemnon, Choephoroe, Eumenides* ; Sophokles, *Electra* ; Euripides, *Orestes, Electra* ; Seneca, *Thyestes, Agamemnon.* Continuous prose narratives, Apollod., *Epit.*, 2, 3 foll. ; Hyginus, *fab.*, 83 foll. In the tragedians, but not in Homer, Orestes is helped throughout by his sister Elektra, who ultimately marries his friend Pylades.

⁵⁸ See *Od.*, IV, 351 foll. Vergil introduces Proteus again in *Georg.*, IV, 387 foll.

ADDITIONAL NOTE A (see Note 1)

For an interesting discussion of the cults of the Dioskuroi and Helen, see F. Chapoutier, *Les Dioscures au service d'une déesse*, Paris 1935.

ADDITIONAL NOTE B (see Note 30)

The birds are Great Shearwaters (*Puffinus Kuhli*), and part of the story, that they sprinkle the tomb of Diomedes with water, is based on their habits. See D'A. W. Thompson, *Glossary of Greek Birds* ² (Oxford 1936), pp. 88–91.

ADDITIONAL NOTE C (see p. 245)

Skylla and Charybdis were later located in the Straits of Messina, which really have dangerous whirlpools (good popular account in *National Geographic Magazine*, Vol. CIV (1953), pp. 579–618).

CHAPTER IX

THE LEGENDS OF GREEK LANDS

Quacunque enim ingredimur, in aliqua historia uestigium ponimus.
—CICERO, *de finibus*, V, 5.

For walk where we will, we tread upon some story.

EVERY spot in Greece and in the Greek colonies had its local legend. Of these, many became so famous that they have been already considered, without regard to geographical order ; but there remain many more, less well known because no great writer had handled them, or because the notable works in which they were treated have perished, or unimportant to the mythologist because they give no more than the genealogy of the local families, or the name of some imaginary hero supposed to have stood godfather to a neighbouring town. In dealing with the rest, I begin with the extreme north of the Greek world and pass southwards, afterwards sketching the mythology of the colonies.

Thrace is not Greece, but must be mentioned here, not only on account of Rhesos, with whom we dealt in the last chapter, but far more because of Orpheus. It is fortunately not necessary to take up space here with the many problems arising in con-nexion with this mysterious figure, as, whether or not he was in any sense historical, and if he was one or many. We are discus-sing, not so much the reputed founder of the Orphic sects and the apocryphal author of a mass of religious and magical litera-ture, as the legendary musician, husband of Eurydike.

Orpheus, then, is said to have been the son of one of the Muses, Kalliope being often named. His father is variously given, being sometimes a local king, Oiagros, sometimes Apollo. He was a devoted follower of Dionysos, as became a good Thracian, an adept in magic and in all manner of wisdom (the later the tale is told, the more various are his accomplishments), but in particular, so marvellous a musician that not only men but beasts and the very trees followed him to listen, while the rivers ceased to flow in response to his melodies. His instrument was the lyre, Apollo's chosen vehicle. Wherever he went, he introduced the cult of Dionysos.

He loved and married the Dryad Eurydike (the name simply means 'princess' or 'queen', literally 'widely-judging'; I can see no kind of reason for supposing that she was, as some would make her out, a goddess of the underworld), but their married life was short. Aristaios tried to force his attentions upon her, and in running away from him she trod on a snake, by the bite of which she died. Orpheus determined to rescue her, and so descended to the realm of Hades, where he so charmed all the shades, and Hades himself, with his music that his petition was granted; Eurydike might return with him, on condition that he did not look back at her until they reached the upper world. But he broke the condition; not hearing her footsteps behind him, as they came near the world of the living, he looked back, and she disappeared.[1]

Here we have a very old tale, known apparently from Thrace to North America, of the man who went to the other world to fetch his wife and (usually) lost her after all his efforts because he broke some tabu. To regard it as a late addition to the legend of Orpheus because it happens not to be mentioned by any very early author is most illogical. It is not a Greek story, so why should the Greeks tell it of Orpheus if it had not always formed part of his history?[2]

Bereft finally of Eurydike, Orpheus was inconsolable. He became a solitary, or at least shunned the companionship of all women. At last the women of Thrace, in great wrath at his neglect of them, fell upon him in the course of a Dionysiac orgy and tore him in pieces. His head, flung into the river Hebros, floated out to sea, and finally came ashore at the island of Lesbos, where it would seem that an oracle of Orpheus existed in later times.[3]

All manner of fanciful details gathered around this part of the tale. Orpheus, wanting nothing more to do with women, was the originator of homosexual passion; the women were marked with tatuing, as a punishment and sign of infamy by their husbands, and that is why all Thracian women are tatued; the lyre was turned into the constellation Lyra, or it was buried with the head, or it was dedicated in a temple of Apollo, and a thief who made off with it was torn to pieces by dogs for his impiety. The tearing in pieces of Orpheus may quite possibly have a germ of truth in it, the ritual tearing (and devouring?) of an incarnation of Dionysos; the head which speaks or sings (as Orpheus' does in some versions) after it is severed, is familiar enough in folktales.[4]

Passing over the local legends of Macedonia as not being Greek, we come to Thessaly, a very ancient and fruitful source of mythology, containing, among other very old centres of legend, Mt. Olympos itself, probably the original Olympos, although it is not the only one, and a landmark on the route of the Hellenic invaders from the north. And as these invaders naturally made for the two great plains of Northern and Central Greece, Thessaly and Boiotia, rather than for the hilly districts between, these two regions are connected in mythology and have many tales in common.

To Thessaly belongs Ixion, a hero whose parentage is variously given,[5] and whose adventures are curious. Marrying Dia, daughter of Eïoneus the son of Magnes (*i.e.*, Coast-man, the son of the eponym of Magnesia ; his daughter is apparently the eponym of the city Dion), he promised a large bride-price, but his father-in-law when he came to fetch it fell into a pit of burning coals prepared for him by Ixion. As this was very near to murdering a blood-relation, if indeed they were not actual blood-kin, and no one had ever done such a thing before, no one would purify Ixion until at last he took refuge with Zeus, who consented to purify him. With most base ingratitude, Ixion tried to seduce Hera ; she complained to Zeus, who formed a double of her, Nephele, out of a cloud (as the name imports) ; and by Nephele, Ixion became the father of the first Centaur, or of the race of Centaurs (properly Kentauroi ; the meaning of the name is very doubtful). Ixion was bound to a burning wheel, which revolves for ever, in the air or (later) in the underworld.[6] But his progeny continued, and were as rough and impious as their father. In shape they were part man, part horse, either a complete man with the barrel and hind legs of a horse springing from the small of his back, or a horse with the body of a man from the waist up where the horse's head and neck should be ; the former is the earlier shape. Their encounters with Herakles have already been described ; their great opponents were the Lapithai, whose chief was also connected with Ixion, Perithoos (' the very swift '), son of Zeus and Dia. The other outstanding Lapith was Kaineus, originally a girl, Kainis. But, being raped by Poseidon and told she might have what she liked as a reward, Kainis asked to be turned into a man, that no such thing might again befall her, and in addition, to be made invulnerable. Being thus transformed, Kaineus was noted, in some stories, for his impiety, for he would worship nothing but his own spear, probably a trace of some local aniconic cult. He also had some quarrel with Apollo. One day the Lapiths were holding high festival, on account of the marriage of

Perithoos with Hippodameia (not the daughter of Oinomaos ; the name, literally ' female tamer of horses ', means no more than ' high-born lady '), or of the birth of a child, Polypoites, to the pair. They invited the Centaurs, who tried to carry off their women, especially Hippodameia. A furious fight ensued, ending in the rout of the Centaurs. Kaineus met his end in the battle ; being invulnerable, he was driven into the earth by the Centaurs' blows. [7]

There is no need whatever to take the Lapithai as anything but a real people of northern Thessaly, the Centaurs as other than wild hill-folk, credited by their neighbours with monstrous shape (compare our own tradition that Kentish men have tails), or Ixion as a sun-god or other meteorological phenomenon.

In order to understand the Boiotian stories, and their connexion with those already told, it is well to begin with a genealogy of the children of Hellen, the ancestor of the Hellenes or Greeks, as it was understood in later times,[8] remembering that it contains much that is artificial, together with a certain amount of real tradition. In the days of Deukalion the son of Prometheus, Zeus was wroth at the iniquities of the men of those times, the Bronze race, and destroyed them with a great flood. Prometheus warned his son, who made an ark for himself and his wife Pyrrha. When the waters subsided, they found themselves on Parnassos, and were advised, either by the oracle of Ge-Themis or by a special message from Zeus, to throw ' the bones of their mother ' over their shoulders ; guessing that the stones of Mother Earth were meant, they tried the experiment, and the stones cast by Deukalion became men, those thrown by Pyrrha, women. Hellen, the eldest son of this Greek Noah and his wife, had three sons, Doros, Xuthos, and Aiolos, the ancestors of the Aiolic, Ionic and Dorian Greeks. The genealogy continues :—

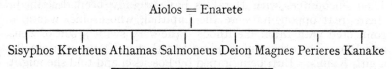

Aiolos = Enarete

Sisyphos Kretheus Athamas Salmoneus Deion Magnes Perieres Kanake

and Alkyone Peisidike Kalyke Perimede

Several of these we have met before. Alkyone married Keyx son of the Morning Star, and they were changed into birds, she into a halcyon, he into another sea-fowl called *keyx*, because of their impiety (they called themselves Zeus and Hera) or because he was drowned at sea and she mourned for him so piteously that the gods released her.[9] A very artificial genealogy makes Kanake the grandmother of Iphimedeia, the mother of Otos and Ephialtes.[10] Kalyke and her husband Aethlios had a son Endymion, the handsomest of men, who was beloved by Selene. He, either by his own wish, granted by Zeus, or by contrivance of Selene or for some other reason, was cast into perpetual sleep.[11] He had, but not by Selene, a son Aitolos, eponym of Aitolia, who in turn became the father of a progeny as shadowy as himself; among his descendants was Marpessa, the beloved of Apollo (Chapter VI, p. 142). A great-great-grandson of his was Oineus king of Kalydon, of whom the following famous story is told. By forgetting to sacrifice to her, he incurred the wrath of Artemis, who therefore sent a great boar which ravaged his country Kalydon. His son Meleagros collected a band of chosen heroes to do battle with this creature,—the tale is almost as famous as that of the Argonauts, although it so happens that no very important work describing it has come down to us. After much trouble and the loss of some of their number, they succeeded in killing the boar, the honour of 'first spear' going to no man, but to the virgin huntress Atalante, of whom more will be said presently. Meleagros loved Atalante, and insisted on giving her the spoils of the boar ; his mother's brothers, the sons of Thestios, tried to take them from her, and Meleagros, so the story usually runs, killed them. Thereupon his mother Althaia took vengeance on her son for the death of her blood-kin. When Meleagros was born, the Moirai appeared in the birth-room, and declared that the child should live until the brand which then lay on the fire should burn to ashes. Althaia snatched it off and kept it preciously ; but now she flung it again into the fire, and as it burned, Meleagros drooped and died.[12] At his funeral, the women who mourned for him were turned into birds (μελεαγρίδες, guineafowl).

Thus far the common story ; but of this fairy-tale there is no trace in Homer. He knows of the boar-hunt, and that a quarrel somehow arose over the spoils, but it was between the Kalydonians and their neighbours the Kuretes. Meleagros after a while quarrelled with his mother Althaia, who cursed him, 'being exceeding grieved over the slaying of her brother', presumably by Meleagros in battle ; he then withdrew from the war, and the Kuretes pressed the Kalydonians hard. He remained proof against entreaties and offers, until at last his wife Kleopatra (daughter of Idas and Marpessa) besought him to go forth to fight, and he consented. He had died some time before the Trojan War, but Homer does not say how.[13]

As to Atalante, most accounts tell of two heroines of that name—one an Arkadian, daughter of Iasos (Iasios, Iasion) son of Lykurgos of Tegea, and Klymene daughter of Minyas; the other a Boiotian, daughter of Schoineus. In fact, the two are probably one, another by-form of Artemis, like those discussed in Chapter V. She was an Amazonian heroine, a great huntress and full of courage, who is mentioned by a few authorities as taking part, not only in the Kalydonian boar-hunt, but in the Argonautic expedition. The central feature of most versions of her saga is, however, the foot-race. She had been exposed in infancy by her father, who wanted a son, not a daughter, but a she-bear nurtured her. When she grew up and found her parents again, her father would have had her marry ; but she refused to wed any man who would not race with her, to wed her if he won and be put to death if he lost. Finally a lover, Hippomenes or Meilanion, appeared on the scene, who was favoured by Aphrodite. By her advice, he took with him three apples of the Hesperides, and dropped or threw these in her way at judicious intervals ; as she stopped to pick them up, he gained, and so won the race. Another version is that he merely joined in her hunts until, by the intervention of Aphrodite, her heart was softened and she yielded to him. By most accounts their son was Parthenopaios ; but there are two versions according to which they profaned with their passion a sacred place of Zeus or Kybele, and by way of punishment were turned into lions.[14]

Athamas has already been spoken of in connexion with the Argonautic saga ; connected with the same story is the family of his brother Salmoneus, who had a daughter Tyro, beloved of Poseidon. The story is as old as Homer (or some very early interpolator of his), how she loved the river Enipeus and often wandered along its banks ; how Poseidon disguised himself as the river-god and visited her, making a great wave curl over them both ; and how he then revealed himself, and how at the end of her time she bore twins, Pelias and Neleus, whom we have already heard of.[15] The latter had a daughter Pero, who was wooed by Bias, the son of her father's half-brother Pheres. Neleus made it a condition of the match that he should receive as bride-price the cattle of Iphiklos, which were carefully guarded against robbers. Now Bias had a brother Melampus, a notable seer, who had received the gift of understanding the speech of beasts and birds ; for on the killing by his servants of a pair of snakes, he had burned their bodies as if they were human and protected their young, who in return one day licked his ears, after which he could understand the speech of all creatures, and particularly of birds, who are far better prophets than men. He undertook to get the cattle for his brother, but was caught and imprisoned by Iphiklos' men, and abode in prison for a year. At the end of that time, by overhearing the gossip of some wood-worms, he learned that the building was about to fall, and foretold this mishap ; whereupon Phylakos, father of Iphiklos, promised him the cattle and his freedom if he would discover what made Iphiklos childless. This he was able to do, and so returned in triumph, and Bias married Pero.[16]

Geographically, Peleus, father of Achilles and husband of Thetis, belongs in this region ; his name would seem to signify ' man of Pelion ', and he is king of Phthia. His father, however, is Aiakos of Aigina, and Telamon, father of the greater Aias, is generally his brother. There is a connexion, real or mythological, between Aigina and Thessaly, as is exemplified by the following story. Aiakos was the most pious of men, and well beloved of his father Zeus ; yet all his people died of a great plague. He therefore besought Zeus to have pity on his forlorn state, and the god in answer to his prayer turned a number of ants into human beings, thus repopulating Aiakos' deserted realm. Now the people over whom Peleus ruled were the Myrmidones, and this was traditionally derived from μύρμηξ, an ant.[17]

A fairly wide-spread story gives Peleus another brother Phokos (' Seal-man '), and gives a reason why he did not live in Aigina. He and Telamon killed Phokos, accidentally or on purpose, and Aiakos banished them both. Telamon went to Salamis, Peleus to Thessaly.[18]

However Peleus got to Phthia, the following story is told of him, besides the adventures we have already heard. He had killed some one, and taken refuge from the consequent blood-feud in the court of Akastos, the son of Pelias, who purified him. Now Akastos had a wife, the granddaughter of Kretheus, by name Hippolyte, who fell in love with Peleus. Followed much the same incidents as those familiar from the Hebrew tale of Joseph and the wife of Potiphar. Akastos believed his wife's story, and contrived to leave Peleus asleep on Mt. Pelion, having first hidden his wonderful sword, which Hephaistos had given him. Cheiron, however, came to the rescue and gave him his sword back, wherewith he easily defeated all wild beasts and monsters that beset him, and in reward for his chastity, Zeus favoured his match with Thetis.[19]

A variant, going back to Pherekydes, says that Akastos' wife was called Astydameia, adds some details of a romantic kind, and ends by making Peleus capture Iolkos, cut Astydameia to pieces, and

march his army between the portions of her body, a procedure reminiscent of a Macedonian rite of purification for an army.[20]

The legends of Boiotia have practically all been told.   It
remains only to say that running through most of the genealogies
come the names of Minyas and his descendants.   He is connected
with Orchomenos, a site once important, in the days of the
Minoan-Mycenaean culture, but only a memory in classical times.
Therefore there are next to no stories connected with him, and
his genealogy is a mass of confusions and contradictions.   The
tale of his daughters and their resistance to Dionysos was told in
Chapter VI (p. 153) ;   the only other legend of any account concerns his daughter Klymene.   This much-married lady [21] was
beloved by the Sun, to whom she bore Phaethon.   When the
boy grew up, he was taunted with not having a father, and applied
to his mother for information.   She assured him that he was the
son of none other than the Sun-god, and he set out to find his
father.   After long wanderings he reached the far East where the
Sun's palace is.   Here he was received and recognized by Helios,
who invited him to choose what gift he liked.   He asked to be
allowed to drive the chariot of the sun for one day.   Helios protested vainly, and Phaethon next day mounted the car and
essayed to guide the immortal horses.   But he was quite unequal
to the task, his team bolted with him, and the earth was in danger
of being burned up.   At last Zeus, at the appeal of Ge, slew
Phaethon with a thunderbolt, and Helios resumed charge of the
chariot.   Phaethon fell into the Eridanos, and his sisters wept
for him till they turned into trees from which distils the gum
known to us as amber.[22]   Phaethon had a passionate admirer, one
Kyknos (not the son of Ares whom Herakles slew, nor yet Achilles'
opponent), who in grief for him turned into the bird, the swan,
which bears his name.[23]

Attica had probably no more legends, and those of no greater
interest, than any other territory, but the eloquence of Athenian
writers, and the comparatively good preservation of their literature, have made them far better known.   We have already spoken
of some of them ;   the others are now to be told.

Side by side with the serpent-shaped Erichthonios is Kekrops,
who was born from the ground and was snake-formed where his
legs should have been.[24]   Save for the affair of his daughters, no
important story is told of him ;   he is rather a venerable ancestor,
a sort of Adam, than a subject of legend.

It is not true, as has been asserted *ad nauseam*, that a legend represented him as the inventor of marriage.   That is merely a conjecture

of Klearchos of Soloi, a pupil of Aristotle, who suggested that perhaps Kekrops was fabled to be twy-formed because he was the first to substitute for promiscuity a permanent union of the different natures cf man and woman The 'invention' is nothing but a fourth- or third-century rationalization of the legend.[25] Kekrops being a sort of Adam, who could there have been before him to marry or live unmarried ?

Erechtheus, who is often identified with Erichthonios, has a fairly good claim to be nothing but a local form of Poseidon, with whom he certainly is connected in some way. But in legend, he is rather the enemy, not exactly of Poseidon himself, but of his children and worshippers, and is befriended by that god's great rival Athena. Born from the earth, like Kekrops and Erichthonios, and nurtured by Athena, his principal exploit was the war against the Eleusinians and their ally Eumolpos, who strangely enough is represented as a Thracian, a statement so curious that one suspects the clan of the Eumolpidai, his alleged descendants, of really having northern blood. He was a son of Poseidon and Chione daughter of Boreas, and made war upon Athens. Erechtheus, who consulted Delphoi about the matter, was told that he must sacrifice one of his daughters to secure victory. He informed his wife Praxithea (daughter of the river-god Kephisos), who readily consented ; after the sacrifice was performed, the armies joined battle, and the Eleusinians were defeated, Eumolpos being killed by Erechtheus. Poseidon, however, in wrath caused the death of Erechtheus and all his house.[26]

Somewhere in this vague and inconsistent succession of kings comes Pandion, variously stated to be Erichthonios' successor or the grandson of Erechtheus. He had two daughters, Philomela and Prokne. The latter married Tereus king of Thrace, who had been her father's ally in a war with Labdakos of Thebes, and was a son of Ares. But Tereus saw Philomela, fell violently in love with her, and seduced or raped her. Then, lest Prokne should know of it, he cut out Philomela's tongue and hid her away She, however, managed to embroider an account of her woes on a piece of needle-work and to send it to her sister ; the latter, in revenge, killed her own son Itys, and served him up at a banquet to his father. Tereus, on discovering what had happened, pursued Prokne and Philomela to kill them ; but he was turned into a hoopoe, and the women respectively into a nightingale and a swallow.[27]

So the story is told by all Greek authors ; the Latins make Philomela the nightingale, Prokne the swallow; but clearly the

Greek account is better, for it explains why the nightingale always sings mournfully (she is lamenting her child), and why the swallow chatters (she has no tongue, and keeps trying to tell her story). The son is not infrequently called Itylos.[28] See p. 340B.

Oreithyia is usually daughter of Erechtheus, once or twice of Pandion. She was snatched away by Boreas (the North Wind), as she played by the banks of the Ilissos, or on the Areiopagos, and became his wife. She was the mother, as already stated, of Zetes and Kalais, and of several other children, whose names are variously given.[29]

The legends are in all cases quite clear and tolerably consistent in their telling ; but, save for the central figure in each case, the names vary greatly, persons being represented as belonging now to this generation or family, now to that. The conclusion seems inevitable that the Attic traditions contain much myth and *märchen*, especially the latter, which cares little for names, and not much true saga, which regularly keeps the names religiously.

Prokris is again usually daughter of Erechtheus, sometimes of Kekrops. Of her and her husband Kephalos (that Kephalos who was loved by Eos and had the hound from which no beast could escape, see Chapter II, p. 36, and Chapter VIII—I, p. 206) a pretty and romantic story is told. Kephalos, who had a spear or dart which could not miss, was an ardent hunter, and so often absent that Prokris became jealous and lay in wait for him. Tired and hot with hunting, he called on the evening breeze (*aura* in both Greek and Latin) to come and cool him. Imagining that Aura was the name of some woman, Prokris started ; Kephalos, hearing the bushes rustle, flung his inevitable dart and mortally wounded her.[30]

But as to their relations otherwise, accounts differ. In Ovid, Prokris is a most faithful wife ; her husband gravely offends her by trying, in disguise, to shake her constancy, and the magical hound, presumably the spear also, was given her by Artemis. The other version is that she got them from Minos, in return for healing his disease (see Chapter X, p. 300), and also for yielding to his solicitations.[31]

King Pandion,—Apollodoros, who distinguishes two of that name, makes him out to be the later one, Erechtheus' grandson,— was driven out of his kingdom by the sons of Metion (here conceivably we have a faint echo of some real quarrel for the kingship) and took refuge in Megara, where four sons were born to him, Aigeus, Pallas, Nisos and Lykos. After his death these reconquered Attica, of which Aigeus became king, not greatly to the content of his brothers. He was without children, and on consulting Delphoi was given a mysterious-sounding oracle, the interpretation of which was that he was to touch no woman until he returned home. However, the wording puzzled him, and he went to consult Pittheus, king of Troizen and son of Pelops. Pittheus saw what was meant, made Aigeus drunk, and introduced him to his daughter Aithra. So runs the common story, but almost as common is the tale that Poseidon was Aithra's lover. The probable solution is that Aigeus, the eponym of the Aegean Sea, is none other than a local form of Poseidon himself. At all events, Aigeus left behind him at Troizen a sword and a pair of sandals, which he put under a great rock, and bade Aithra send him the son he was confident that she would bear, as soon as he was old enough to shift the rock and get these tokens of his father.[32]

A child was born, and named Theseus. On reaching young manhood, he fulfilled his father's behest, but refused to take the easy sea route to Athens, insisting on going by land, because that offered more prospect of adventures. Hence he met and conquered the brigand Periphetes, surnamed Korynetes or the Club-man, near Epidauros; he took his club and henceforth used it (one of the many traits in his legend manifestly imitated from Herakles). Next came the turn of Sinis, surnamed Pityokamptes, or Pine-bender, because he used to tie those whom he caught to two pine-trees, bent to the ground, and let them fly up, tearing the victim in two. Theseus gave him the same death. After staying to hunt and kill the Grey Sow of Krommyon, he entered the Megarid, where he met another brigand, Skeiron, who used to compel passers-by to wash his feet, and as they did so, kick them into the sea. Flinging him from a cliff, he next encountered, at Eleusis, a formidable wrestler, one Kerkyon of Arkadia, whom also he overcame and killed. Next, as he approached Athens, he met Damastes, otherwise Prokrustes (the Stretcher), whose notion of humour was to lay all comers on a bed and then lop them or rack them out to make them fit it. Theseus meted out the same measure to him, and without further adventures arrived in Athens.

Here Medeia, who had taken refuge with Aigeus, prepared a cup of poison for him, pointing him out to Aigeus as a likely pretender to the throne. But Aigeus recognized his son in the nick of time and dashed the poison away; Medeia took refuge in flight, and her son Medos became the eponym of the Medes, after murdering, with the aid of his mother, Perses son of Helios.[33]

Athens was just then in a state of turmoil, as Pallas and his strong sons were plotting against Aigeus. Theseus, however, met and overthrew them. He next hunted and caught the Mara-

thonian bull (the one Herakles had brought from Crete—another
contact between the two heroes) and sacrificed it to Apollo.[34] Now
came a more serious and dangerous contest. Minos had reduced
Athens to the position of a tributary state, under hard terms.
His son Androgeos had been murdered in Attica, and he prepared
an expedition against it and its ally Megara. The latter state he
overcame under circumstances very like those under which
Amphitryon overcame Pterelaos (Chapter VIII—I, p. 206).
Nisos, king of Megara, had a purple lock of hair, and so long as he
kept it on his head, the city could not fall. But his daughter
Skylla was bribed by or fell desperately in love with Minos, whom
she saw from the walls, and contrived to cut off the fatal lock,
which she brought him as a love-gift. When the city fell, Minos
refused to have anything to do with such a traitress. She leaped
into the sea, and clung to the stern-post of his ship as he sailed
away ; she was turned into a sort of bird called *keiris* or *kirris*
(unidentified), her father into a sea-eagle, which pursues it.[35]

Athens made terms with Minos ; a yearly tribute of seven
youths and seven maidens was to be sent, whom he shut up in the
Labyrinth, to lose their way and die of hunger, or be killed and
eaten by the Minotaur. Theseus volunteered to be one of the
number. On the way to Crete, Minos insulted one of the virgins,
and Theseus interfered. Minos bragged of his sonship to Zeus,
who in response to his prayer thundered out of a clear sky.
Theseus, to counter this, jumped overboard at Minos' challenge
and brought back, by the help of Amphitrite, a gold ring which
Minos threw overboard.[36] Reaching Crete, he met Ariadne,
daughter of Minos, who fell in love with him and provided him
with a clue of thread by the help of which he could find his way
out of the Labyrinth ; he met and killed the Minotaur, found his
way back by following the clue, which he had fastened near the
entrance, and sailed away in safety, taking with him his fellow-
victims and Ariadne. Why Minos did not pursue was a question
which exercised some of the ancients.[37] In any case, Theseus got
safely away, and sailed as far as Dia (Naxos), where, according to
the usual form of the story, he treacherously left Ariadne behind ;
one reference, however, makes it clear that in the original form
of the tale he forgot her, presumably owing to some charm, or the
breaking of some tabu ; it is a *märchen* of the Master-Maid type.[38]
Deserted, Ariadne was found by Dionysos, who wedded her.

The constellation Corona is identified with the garland or wreath
which Dionysos gave his bride.[39] It is fairly clear that Ariadne is
originally a goddess, not a heroine ; the fairy-tale and the romantic

love-story have been superimposed upon her real nature, that of a
mother-goddess (see Chapter VIII—I, p. 184, and note 7).   A number
of rites observed in historical Athens were popularly supposed to
commemorate incidents in this adventure.

Theseus, on starting, had promised that if he returned safely
he would change the black sails of the ship which bore the human
tribute for white ones.   But he forgot to do this, and Aigeus,
seeing the black-sailed vessel approach, naturally thought that
his son had perished, and so flung himself into the sea and was
drowned.[40]   Theseus was now king, and instituted reforms, the
most notable being the *synoikismos*, or union of the scattered
Attic communities into one political centre, Athens.   Here we
touch sober history ; such a union certainly did take place, and
likely enough as the result of the constructive policy of some early
statesman or statesmen, not by mere spontaneous development.
He soon had to face a serious war ; the Amazons (provoked, in
some accounts, by Theseus, who had joined in Herakles' campaign
against them) invaded Attica, but were defeated, and their leader,
Hippolyte or Antiope, became his wife.[41]   They had a son
Hippolytos, who is the chief figure of a tragic story.
After the death of the lad's mother, Theseus married again,
this time Ariadne's sister Phaidra.   She fell passionately in love
with her stepson, and in the absence of Theseus, at last let him
know of her affection.   He repulsed her, and she hanged herself,
first writing a letter incriminating him.   Theseus, returning, read
the letter and cursed his son ; now Poseidon had granted him
three wishes, and the curse was one of them.   Hippolytos, therefore, as he drove away from his father, who had banished him, was
met by a huge sea-monster which frightened his horses ; they
bolted, threw him from the chariot, and dragged him to death.
Too late, Theseus perceived his error.[42]

Theseus was credited, like Herakles, with several amatory adventures, for example, with the daughters of all or most of the brigands
whom he killed on his way to Athens.   This is but one of the many
resemblances between the legends of the two heroes, largely due, no
doubt, to deliberate imitation by Attic saga-men of the better known
tale.

No further important adventures remain, save those already
mentioned in other contexts.   Theseus is represented as having
been the constant friend of Herakles, whom he sheltered after the
killing of Megara and her children.   In the end, he left Athens in
consequence of rebellions against him, took refuge in Skyros, and
was there murdered by Lykomedes, or died by accident.   He

was succeeded, according to one tradition, by Menestheus son
of Peteos, who had led the revolt against him ; Menestheus, who
in the Homeric Catalogue of the Ships leads the Athenian contingent, is represented as having been in turn succeeded by the
sons of Theseus, Demophon and Akamas. Of these, or rather
of the former, two tales are told. According to one, when the
orphaned children of Herakles were pursued by Eurystheus, they
and Iolaos, together with Alkmene, took refuge at Marathon ;
Demophon received them, but found that he could not hope to
resist Eurystheus unless a virgin were sacrificed to secure victory.
Makaria daughter of Herakles offered herself, Iolaos miraculously
became young again in the battle, and the enemy were routed,
Eurystheus being killed by Iolaos in the battle or captured and
afterwards put to death at the bidding of Alkmene.[43]

The subsequent adventures of the children of Herakles form
an important saga, that of the Return of the Herakleidai, the
mythological form of the Dorian Invasion, by which the Achaian
civilization was brought to an end and the population of historical
Greece given its final form. The outline of it is as follows.
Hyllos, the eldest son of Herakles, consulted Delphoi to know
when he and his brethren might reclaim their father's inheritance,
—i.e., Tiryns, but, by the Dorian extension of the claim, the whole
Peloponnesos. Apollo bade him await ' the third fruit ' ; supposing this to mean the third harvest, he attacked the Isthmos
three years later. The Peloponnesians met him, and at his own
proposal the matter was decided by a duel between him and
Echemos, leader of the Tegean contingent, chosen as the bravest
champion of the defenders. Hyllos was killed and his host,
according to agreement, retired, pledged to make no further
attempt for a hundred years. At the expiration of that time,
Temenos, great-grandson or great-great-grandson of Herakles,
again questioned Apollo and got the same rejoinder. On asking
for an explanation, he was told that Hyllos ought to have understood that ' third fruit ' meant ' third generation '. That time
having been now reached, Temenos and the rest of the Herakleidai
again made ready their host, and after sundry further delays,
crossed at the other end of the Gulf of Corinth (near Patrai, the
modern Patras), taking, by advice of the oracle, the ' three-eyed
one ' as their leader ; this turned out to be an exile from Aitolia,
one Oxylos son of Andraimon, who when they met him was riding
a one-eyed horse, or driving a one-eyed mule. Under his directions they entered the Peloponnesos, met the defenders under
Tisamenos son of Orestes, and defeated them. They then cast lots
for the three great divisions of the conquered territory, Argos,

Lakedaimon, Messene. Of the three chief Herakleidai of that time, Aristodemos was lately dead, but his two sons Prokles and Eurysthenes represented him. They won Lakedaimon; Temenos got Argos, and Kresphontes Messene.[44]

The sons of Aristodemos founded the two royal houses of historical Sparta ; but Kresphontes was killed in an insurrection headed by Polyphontes, who was also a Herakleid. Two of Kresphontes' sons died with him, but the third, Aipytos, was smuggled out of the country by his mother, Merope, who was forced to marry Polyphontes, and reared by her father Kypselos king of Arkadia. On reaching manhood, he returned secretly (or openly ; the story varies), killed Polyphontes, and regained the throne of his father. Temenos, like his brother, came to an untimely end, for he favoured his son-in-law Deïphontes at the expense of his sons ; the latter therefore contrived his death. The throne, however, was given to Deïphontes by right of his wife Hyrnetho.[45] After this the tale of the Herakleidai passes insensibly out of mythology into more or less dependable history.

But to return to Attica, that country claimed to be the motherland of the Ionian settlements in Asia Minor, and told the following tale in connexion therewith. Erechtheus had a daughter Kreusa (i.e., ' queen ', ' princess ') who was loved by Apollo. To him she bore a son, whom she exposed for fear of her father's anger. Hermes rescued the child and carried him to Delphoi, where he was brought up as a temple-servant. Years afterwards, Xuthos, an ally of Erechtheus who had married Kreusa, came to Delphoi with her to ask for offspring. Apollo bade him welcome as his son the first person he met on going (ἰών) out of the temple. He met his wife's child, and named him Ion from the circumstances of the meeting. Kreusa, supposing the boy to be a bastard child of her husband and that her own infant had long ago perished, tried to kill him ; being caught in the act, she took refuge at an altar, and there a recognition took place ; by divine revelation from Athena all was explained and mother and son returned to Athens with the supposed father. So at least Euripides tells the story ; Ion prospered, and had four sons, the eponyms of the four Ionic tribes, the Geleontes, Hopletes, Argades and Aigikores.[46] Here we have a mythological background for the event which followed on the Dorian invasion, the exodus of a considerable number of the inhabitants of Greece to colonize Ionia and the islands.

Daidalos, as already mentioned, was an Athenian ; Sokrates, in jest or in earnest, claimed descent from him. He would appear to have been a sort of patron saint of craftsmen (Sokrates himself was a sculptor, as his father had been before him). He was the son of Metion (' Knowledgeable man ') and descended from the craftsman's god Hephaistos. After his arrival in Crete, he found that Minos would not let him go again ; he therefore got hold of wax and feathers, and made wings for himself and his son Ikaros. With these they succeeded in flying away, but Ikaros, flying too near the sun, melted his wings, fell into the sea near Crete, and was drowned ; that portion of the sea was afterwards known by his name. Daidalos escaped to Sicily, or Italy, and Minos, following him to the west, met his end in Sicily, for the local king Kokalos set his three daughters to bathe him, and they drowned him in hot water. [47]

Finally, just on the border-line between mythology and history, may be mentioned the tale of Kodros the last king of Attica. In his day the Peloponnesians invaded the country ; learning from the oracle of Delphoi that that side should be victorious whose king fell, he disguised himself as a peasant and contrived to provoke some of the enemy's soldiers into killing him in a quarrel. The invaders retired discomfited, and the Athenians decided to have no more kings, as a tribute to Kodros' incomparable patriotism. [48]

Of Megara there is really almost nothing to say. The tale of Nisos has been told ; the few other traditions recorded in Pausanias [49] suggest that they had next to no tales of their own, but sought to form some connexion with those of other people ; they claimed, for instance, that Alkmene was buried in their territory ; they paid honours to Pandion of Athens (the Athenians said that Megara had been left to him by the native king Pylas) ; they had a tomb of Hippolyte the Amazon.

Corinth again is not rich in legends of a purely local kind ; rather are there Corinthian versions of one or two sagas ; for instance, the connexion of Medeia with their city seems to be the work of Corinthian saga-men or writers of epic or chronicle. The founder of the city, Korinthos son of Zeus, was a person whom no one not a Corinthian believed in, and his very name a synonym for a piece of tiresome nonsense. [50] The name of the city is pre-Hellenic, Korinthos having the same suffix as labyrinthos, Hyakinthos, and other old names, and the first syllable meaning nothing in Greek ; traditionally, however, there had been a yet older name, Ephyra, said locally to be the name of a daughter of Okeanos who had been the first to live there. The Isthmos was sacred to Poseidon, who had disputed with Helios for it ; Briareos had decided the quarrel in his favour, but given Helios the Akrokorinthos, a height rising above the city, which still has remains of pre-Hellenic times, imperfectly explored. On the Isthmos also the body of Ino's child Melikertes had come ashore, and he was honoured in the great Isthmian Games and identified with the minor deity Palaimon, as already mentioned.[51]

Corinth claimed as its own the hero Sisyphos, whose punishment in Hell and whose outwitting of Death are told elsewhere (Chapter IV, p. 81 ; X, p. 294). His pedigree has already been given ; from Homer down he is the most cunning of mankind, generally in later times spoken of as a great rascal, but occasionally praised for his wisdom. In origin he is probably that non-moral figure of folktale, the Master Thief. He is generally king of Corinth, but of his kingly deeds we hear little. Most of the stories concerning him bring him into contact with the two other masters of trickery, Odysseus and his maternal grandfather Autolykos. The former is commonly said, in post-Homeric accounts, to have been Sisyphos' son ; Antikleia, Autolykos' daughter and Odysseus' mother, somehow met with him before she married Laertes, the father of Odysseus in Homer.[52] The latter had a wit-contest with Sisyphos. His father Hermes had given him the power of always escaping capture when he stole, and further, of altering the appearance of what he had taken, making a black beast into a white one, for instance. But Sisyphos, perceiving that his herds diminished and those of Autolykos increased, marked his beasts on the under-side of their hooves, and so was able to track them.[53]

Sisyphos had a son Glaukos, who in turn became the father of Bellerophon (Bellerophontes in Homer). Malten has made it very probable that this hero, who fights a monster of Oriental type, is the father of a line of Lykian princes, and whose adven-tures are connected with Asiatic place-names, is originally no Greek ; however, he was adopted as early as Homer's day. He lived for a while with Proitos king of Argos ; but the latter's wife, Anteia, or, as she is usually called after Homer, Stheneboia, behaved towards him exactly as Akastos' wife did towards Peleus. Proitos, in a jealous rage, sent him to Iobates king of Lykia, bearing a letter which directed that he should be put to death. The king therefore sent him first to fight the Chimaira, a fire-breathing monster who was shaped like a lion in front, a dragon behind, and a goat (*chimaira* ; hence her name) in the middle. He killed her, and was then sent to do battle, first with the Solymoi, a formidable tribe of those parts, next with the Amazons. As he survived both campaigns, a last attempt was made on his life, by setting a band of chosen warriors to lie in wait for him. As, however, he killed them all, Iobates realized that he was something more than an ordinary mortal, and gave him his daughter and half his kingdom. His daughter Laodameia became by Zeus the mother of Sarpedon, and his son Hippolochos was father of Glaukos, the second in command of the Lykians at Troy. Then misfortune fell on him, two of his children perished, —Isandros in battle against the Solymoi, Laodameia by the shafts of Artemis,—and he ' wandered alone on the Aleïan plain (*i.e.*, Plain of Wandering), eating his heart out, shunning the path of men'.[54]

Thus far Homer. Later authors add that Bellerophon mastered the winged horse Pegasos which had sprung from the head of Medusa (Chapter II, p. 30). He was enabled to do this by means of a wonderful bridle which Athena brought him in a dream, while he still lived in Corinth. It was by the help of Pegasos that he was able to defeat the Chimaira ; in one account, he used him to wreak vengeance on Anteia, whom he induced to ride with him, and then flung off from a great height. His fall was caused by an attempt to fly up to heaven, in which he was thrown, escaping alive, but lamed.[55]

Coming now to Argos, we find a long series of sagas, beginning in the most ancient times. Phoroneus, according to their tradition, was the first of men, and his daughter was the first of women, Niobe, who also was the first earthly love of Zeus. Or, when men had ceased to be all of one language and Hermes had given them their several speeches, Zeus feared that they might become too unruly, and sent Phoroneus to be the first king and judge of the earth. Niobe's son was Argos, originally not the same as Argos Panoptes, but often confused with him. As father of Phoroneus is named the river-god Inachos ; the reason why neither Inachos or any other Argive river has any water in a dry summer, and the land is proverbially ' thirsty ' from Homer down, is that Phoroneus was appointed judge between Poseidon and Hera as to which should have the country, and decided for the latter, whereat Poseidon dried up their waters in wrath.[56]

At some time sufficiently vague and ancient, just after the subjection of the Titans, Inachos, who was then king of the land, had a fair daughter Io (said to have been priestess of Hera, and conceivably nothing but a local form or title of that goddess herself), whom Zeus loved. But the jealousy of Hera was aroused, and Zeus turned Io into a heifer to disguise her. Hera asked for the heifer, and Zeus could not refuse her without betraying himself. Hera then set Argos Panoptes, who had eyes all over his body, to watch her. Hermes contrived to beguile Argos into sleeping, and so slew him ; Hera then sent a worse plague, a

gad-fly which maddened Io and drove her on long wanderings
till at last she reached Egypt. Here she bore a son Epaphos
(interpreted by the Greeks to mean ' he of the touch ', explained
by a story that Zeus made Io pregnant by merely touching her
with his hand), and, her sanity recovered, she was henceforth
worshipped by the Egyptians as Isis.[57]

Epaphos became father of Libye (*i.e.*, Northern Africa) and
she the mother of Belos, who had several sons, or at any rate two,
Danaos and Aigyptos. Of these the latter had fifty sons, the
former fifty daughters. As the brothers quarrelled, Danaos, who
was the weaker, was obliged to leave the country, and took refuge
in Argos from his nephews, who pursued after, being desirous of
wedding their cousins. This was of course the natural thing for
them to do, by Greek law, for a girl with no brothers, an ἐπίκληρος
or encumbrance on the estate, as Attic law called her, was by a
universal custom married to her next of kin. Only the hate of
Danaos stood in the way, and he was obliged to yield to so reasonable a demand. However, he directed his daughters to kill each
her husband on the wedding night. Only one, Hypermestra or
Hypermnestra, disobeyed ; her husband Lynkeus escaped, but
as to what happened to him afterwards, and what became of
Hypermestra, accounts differ.[58] One daughter, Amymone, was
rescued from a satyr by Poseidon, who became her lover himself ;
their son was Nauplios, eponym of Nauplia (not the father of
Palamedes). A spring, called after her name, arose from a stroke
of Poseidon's trident.[59]

Proitos, Bellerophon's host, had a twin brother Akrisios, with
whom he strove even before they were born, who banished him
from Argos, and whom he in turn banished, with the help of
Iobates.[60] This Akrisios had a daughter Danae, of whom it was
prophesied that she should bear a son who should kill his grandfather. Therefore Akrisios shut her up in a tower or chamber of
bronze, that none might come near her. But Zeus loved her,
and visited her in the form of a shower of gold. In due time she
bore a son, Perseus. Akrisios therefore put her and her infant
afloat in a chest ; this was carried by the waves to the island of
Seriphos, where Diktys, brother of Polydektes king of the island,
found them and gave them shelter and nurture. The boy grew
to young manhood ; meanwhile Polydektes had fallen in love with
Danae, who did not return his affection. Her son was formidable
enough to make any open violence dangerous ; therefore Polydektes, when for some reason he collected gifts from the nobles of
the island, managed to extract from him an undertaking to fetch
the head of the Gorgon Medusa as his offering. He hoped thus to

get rid of him once and for all ; but the gods favoured Perseus. Athena also counselled him as to his course.   By her advice, he made his way to the Graiai, and by stealing their one eye from them forced from them directions for finding the Gorgons ; from some nymphs he got the Cap of Darkness (῎Αϊδος κυνῆ), the winged Shoes of Swiftness and a wallet (κίβισις) in which to carry his booty.   Arrived at the Gorgons' habitation, he found them asleep, and flying close to Medusa, but with his back turned towards her, he looked at her image reflected in his shield and was thus guided to cut off her head.   With this in his wallet, he escaped from the two other Gorgons, who could follow him only by sound, as his cap made him invisible.   On the way home, passing a certain place on the coast (Joppa, according to some) he saw a virgin of wonderful beauty chained to a rock.   This was Andromeda, daughter of Kepheus king of the Ethiopians and his wife Kassiepeia or Kassiopeia, who had offended the sea-goddesses by saying that she was more beautiful than they.   Therefore Poseidon had sent a sea-monster which could not be appeased but by sacrifice of the offending queen's daughter.   Perseus, who had fallen in love with Andromeda at first sight, then and there offered to kill the monster if he might marry her.   The parents consented, Perseus after a furious battle killed the monster (or turned it to stone by showing it the Gorgon's head), and married Andromeda, but not without having to fight and overcome a strong force led by a former suitor, Phineus.   He spent a year with his parents-in-law, and finally departed, leaving his first-born son to be heir of Kepheus, who had no sons.   Sailing with Andromeda to Seriphos, he found his mother sitting a suppliant at an altar, where Polydektes kept her surrounded until she should either yield or die of hunger (her person was of course inviolable so long as she remained thus in sanctuary ; but it was no sacrilege to prevent any food reaching her).   With the help of the head, Perseus soon rescued her, and leaving Polydektes and his supporters turned to stone and putting the kingship in the hands of Diktys, he went on with his wife to Argos.   Here he found that Akrisios had gone to the Pelasgiotis, to escape him ; following him, he accidentally fulfilled the prophecy by casting a diskos at some sports, which hit Akrisios on the head.   Leaving the scene of his unintentional shedding of kindred blood, he retired to Asia, where his son Perses became the ruler of the Persians, named after him.[61]

Orestes, after the death of his mother and his own release from the Erinyes, and after the rescue of Iphigeneia, appears in one more episode, more discreditable to himself, at least as the Attic tragedians told the story.   He was betrothed to his cousin

Hermione, daughter of Menelaos and Helen ; but she married
Neoptolemos instead, and went to his kingdom in Epeiros.
Therefore, Orestes treacherously set upon Neoptolemos at Delphoi, murdered him, and proceeded to carry off Hermione. The
fate of his son Tisamenos or Teisamenos has already been mentioned.[62]

Having thus brought the fortunes of Agamemnon's family to a
conclusion, I now give a genealogy of the house. Omitting various
collaterals, it runs as follows :—Zeus—Tantalos (king of Sipylon in
Asia Minor)—Pelops and Niobe—Atreus and Thyestes, whereof the
latter's story has been already told—Agamemnon and Menelaos, sons
of Atreus, and in some accounts, Anaxibia, who married Strophios
king of Phokis and became the mother of Pylades—Agamemnon then
married Klytaimestra and had issue Orestes, Elektra, Chrysothemis,
Iphianassa, from whom Iphigeneia is sometimes distinguished (as by
Sophokles), sometimes identified, not mentioned at all in Homer :
Menelaos had, besides Hermione, two sons, Megapenthes and Niko-
stratos, both illegitimate. The tradition is constant in representing Pelops as a foreigner (which he probably was, *i.e.*, he represents
the coming of this house to Greece from Asia Minor, where we know
from Hittite evidence that an Achaian kingdom existed in the thir-
teenth century B.C.), but inconstant in sometimes inserting, somewhere
in the genealogy, a certain Pleisthenes, sometimes omitting him
altogether.[63] Agamemnon and Menelaos are in the oldest tradition
respectively kings of Argos (or Mycenae) and Sparta, but this varies
somewhat in later authors.

The rest of the Peloponnesos really has but little in the way
of legends, so far at least as our information goes ; no doubt many
interesting local traditions have been lost. I mention a few which
seem worth recording in a manual such as this.

Conflicting legends arose concerning the foundation of the
great games at Olympia. Generally it was said that Herakles
was their author ; he had instituted the ceremony, and in particular the great sacrifice to Zeus which formed its central feature,
as a thank-offering after his victory over Augeias. But other
founders were named here and there, as Pelops, Endymion
(who is frequently said to have been king of Elis, although his
eternal sleep, at all events in connexion with the love of Selene,
is regularly put in Latmos), and, in a silly and obviously late
and artificial story, a Daktyl called Herakles, shortly after the
birth of Zeus.[64]

Sundry temple-legends are scattered about the peninsula ;
for example, near Patrai was a shrine of Artemis Triklaria (Her
of the three estates or allotments), of which it was alleged that in
former times human sacrifice was used there, and a romantic story

was told to account for it.   Komaitho, priestess of the temple (who was supposed to remain virgin till she was of age to marry, when she was removed from her office), fell violently in love with Melanippos, a young man of beauty as remarkable as her own. Their families opposed their union, so they met secretly in the temple.   Artemis avenged this profanation by sending plague and famine on the land, which was ended by the sacrifice of the lovers, and by a yearly sacrifice of a boy and a girl, the most beautiful that could be found.   This continued until Eurypylos brought the mysterious chest from Troy which has already been mentioned.[65]

Arkadia had several weird legends.   At Mantineia there was a shrine of Poseidon which might not be entered.   One Aipytos the son of Hippothus cut the thread which barred out intruders and went in ; whereat there came a great wave from the interior of the shrine and blinded him for the rest of his life.[66]   At Tegea there was a cult of Ares open only to women ; whatever the reason may have been for this, the local explanation was that once the Spartans attacked the city and were pressing it hard, when the women, armed with what weapons they could find, valiantly attacked the invaders, led by a certain Marpessa, surnamed the Sow, and utterly routed them, capturing their king Charillos.[67]   At Tegea also was an ancient goddess, the Kneeling Auge, Αὔγη ἐν γόνασιν, concerning whom the local story ran that she was loved by Herakles ; that her father Aleos sent her to be drowned ; and that on the way to the sea she bore her child, Telephos.   The usual story was that she bore the child secretly, exposed him on Mt. Parthenion, where a hind suckled him, and was afterwards set adrift with him in a chest, which grounded on the coast of Asia Minor ; whence in due time Telephos became king of Mysia, as has already been told.[68] The Arkadians also claimed, even more vigorously than the Athenians, that they were the original inhabitants of the country, indeed that they had been there since before the moon was created ; consequently it is not surprising that they told of an ancestor, Pelasgos, who was born from the earth.[69]   But it would take too long to give even a list of these venerable ancestors, scattered up and down the country, whose whole story is that they lived in early times and that some noble or royal family is descended from them.   Oibalos of Sparta may serve as an example ; his name appears to be good Spartan, and his history is simply that he was one of the members of the ancient royal family which was there before the Dorians came ; hence poets anxious to display their learning occasionally call anyone connected with Sparta Oibalides, or descendant of Oibalos ; Ovid even uses the word of inhabitants of Sparta's colony Tarentum.[70]

In the islands a certain number of legends survive, although some are obscure and late. The story of Tenes, eponym of Tenedos, may serve for a specimen of the way in which tales went on being made and elaborated in later times into an artificial mythology of which, probably, the people at large knew little or nothing. Tenes was the son of Kyknos, a king of Kolonai on the mainland. His wicked stepmother Philonome tried to seduce him, and failing, accused him as Phaidra did Hippolytos. She induced a flute-player to bear false witness against him, and Kyknos, believing the story, set Tenes and his sister Hemithea adrift in a chest, which drifted to the island Leukophrys, whose inhabitants made Tenes king and named their island after him. Now Kyknos, discovering the deceit, punished the guilty parties, and sailed to Tenedos to be reconciled to his children. But Tenes cut his boat adrift from the moorings with an axe and sent him away. Later, Tenes was killed in defending Hemithea against Achilles, who remembered too late that Thetis had warned him not to kill Tenes. Consequently, no flute-player is admitted in the rites of the heroized Tenes, no one may mention Achilles in connexion with them, and ' the blow of Tenes ' is a proverb for a rash act. The tale is of course made up to explain the tabus and the proverb ; but our evidence goes no further back than the time of Aristotle, and may with considerable probability be taken to imply that the invention is a late patching together of themes from older and better stories.[71] Similar reasons justify the omission, in a book like this, of several other late legends.

Delos, the holy island of Apollo, possessed a picturesque figure enough in the priest-king Anios. He is the son of Rhoio (Pome-granate-girl), daughter of Staphylos (Grape-cluster-man) and granddaughter of Dionysos. Being with child by Apollo, she, like so many other heroines, was set adrift by her father in a chest. Coming ashore in Euboia (or according to some, in Delos itself) she bore Anios, whom she named because of the trouble and pain (ἀνία) she had endured. But his divine father befriended the boy, taught him divination, and prospered him. He had three daughters, Oino, Spermo, and Elaïs (i.e., Wine-girl, Seed-girl, and Olive-girl), who could, by the grace of Dionysos, produce wine, corn and oil at will ; whereby they were able to supply Agamemnon's army before Troy.[72]

This story is so quaint as to suggest that it is genuinely popular ; from Keos comes a very pretty romance which, at least in its developed form, is rather a literary product. Akontios, a young man of respect-able but not rich parents, loved a high-born maiden Kydippe. He threw her an apple, one day when they met at a festival, having written upon it, ' I swear to Artemis to marry none but Akontios '. She picked the fruit up (apples were a very common love-gift, but she did not, apparently, realize this) and innocently read the words, pro-nouncing them aloud, as was the usual ancient custom in reading. She thus irrevocably bound herself by the vow, and whenever her parents tried to marry her to anyone else, she fell desperately ill until the match was broken off. At last the true reason of her infirmities was found out, and Akontios won her.[73]

Rhodes, the Sun's island, had a fairly copious mythology. It goes without saying that Rhodos or Rhode, the female eponym of the island, was supposed to have been his consort ; under the former name, she became the mother of seven sons, one of whom, Kerkaphos, was afterwards the father of Ialysos, Kamiros and Lindos, from whom the three principal towns took their names.[74] A later hero, and an unfortunate one, was Althaimenes, a sort of Oidipus, of whom it was foretold that he should kill his father, Katreus king of Crete. He therefore left his native country and came to Rhodes. There he became the slayer of his sister, Apemosyne, who had accompanied him and whom he killed with a kick, because she had been seduced by Hermes and he would not believe her story. After all, he fulfilled the prophecy, for Katreus, endeavouring in his old age to see his son, was mistaken for a brigand and killed by Althaimenes in the ensuing fight. On discovering the truth, Althaimenes retired from human society and was at length, by his own prayer, swallowed up in the earth ; afterwards he was honoured as a hero.[75]

Passing to the mainland of Asia, we find here and there a few stories, other than those already told, worth mentioning ; one or two more are related in the next chapter. The foundations of the various Greek cities were of course recorded in local traditions, but most of these were more or less historical, and the others, so far as they have come down to us, generally consist merely of the bald statement that such a person founded such a town ; for example, that Branchidai, the famous oracle of Apollo near Miletos, was founded by Branchos son of Apollo. Such state-ments are often of great importance to the historian or the student of Greek and Asianic religion, but they are hardly the concern of the mythologist, since they involve no stories. Still less is he concerned with most of the traditions of the cities in Sicily and Magna Graecia ; a glance at the opening chapters of the sixth book of Thucydides' history will show their nature :

'In the fifth year after the foundation of Syracuse, Thukles and the Chalkidians set out from Naxos, made war on the Sikels and drove them out, and founded Leontinoi'; 'When Troy fell, certain of the Trojans escaped the Achaians, sailed to Sicily, settled alongside of the Sikels, and were in general called Elymoi ; their cities are Eryx and Egesta.' But the following are less jejune legends.

Pyramos and Thisbe were near neighbours in Babylon. They loved each other, but their parents would not hear of their marrying. However, by talking through a chink in the party-wall between the two houses, they contrived to make an appointment at the tomb of Ninos, outside the city. Thither they went by night. Thisbe, arriving first, was frightened by a lioness, which worried the cloak that she dropped in her flight, thereby staining it with blood, for she had just come from a kill. Pyramos arrived later, found the cloak, supposed the beast had eaten her, and killed himself. Later, Thisbe returned, found him dead, and killed herself with his sword. Their blood flowed on the roots of a mulberry-tree, and henceforth its fruit, which had formerly been white, was red.[76]

It is noteworthy that Ovid introduces this story as one not well known. Where he got it is unknown, and hardly any allusions to it are found elsewhere. Both the lovers have the names of rivers, and quite conceivably the tale was originally one of the loves of river-deities.

A certain instance of the loves of rivers is the story of Alpheios and Arethusa. The latter was a spring at Syracuse, and also one in Elis ; such doublets of names between the mother-country and the over-seas settlement are in no way surprising. The story went that Alpheios, the river of Elis, loved Arethusa and followed her. She was beloved by Artemis, who changed her into a stream of water and gave her power to flow under the sea to Sicily. But Alpheios followed, also under the sea, and the two were joined on Sicilian ground.[77]

Not many tales are told of Sicilian gods and heroes, so far as our records go. Taras (Tarentum) had a romantic story ; its founder Phalanthos was told at Delphoi that he should find a city when he was rained on from a clear sky. He wandered in vain for years, but one day as he lay with his head in his wife's lap, she wept over him and her tears fell in his face. Now her name was Aithra (Clear Sky) and he recognized the fulfilment of the prophecy, took courage, captured Taras from its barbarian inhabitants, and founded a Greek city there.[78] Kroton (Cortona) claimed Herakles as its originator ; while he was returning from the conquest of Geryon, the good old hero Kroton received him hospitably, but a robber, Lakinios by name, tried to steal the oxen, and in the scuffle Herakles accidentally killed his host. He buried him honourably, and foretold that in time to come a famous city should stand on that spot.[79] Siris was said to have been founded by Trojans, who brought with them a statue of Athena, a sort of Palladion. In later times, the Ionians took their city, and killed certain of them who took refuge in the temple. Rather than see such impiety, the statue closed its eyes, and closed they remained.[80] The same city claimed to have witnessed the death of Kalchas, a rather audacious transference of a story which by rights seems to belong to Klaros, near Kolophon in Asia Minor. But Italy and Sicily were full of such transferences, the adventures of Odysseus in particular being localized there; Kirke, for example, gave her name to the promontory of Circeï, the Laistrygonians were supposed to have lived at or near Formiae, and so forth. The tale of Kalchas runs as follows. After the Trojan War, Kalchas one day met Mopsos, and proceeded to a contest of seer-craft with him,—a somewhat risky thing to do, since it had been foretold to him that if he met a better seer than himself, he would die. He asked Mopsos how many green figs there were on a tree which grew near; Mopsos answered that there were ten thousand, and that they would just fill a bushel, with one over. This proved to be correct, and Kalchas died.[81]

Finally, the little town of Temesa had a remarkable ghost of its own, the so-called ' hero '. Odysseus landed there, and one of his men violated a girl, for which the inhabitants stoned him to death. Thereupon all manner of misfortunes befell them, and Delphoi advised them to honour him as a hero, build him a shrine, and yearly to present him with the fairest of their maidens. This proved effective, and the custom was kept up until one Euthymos, a famous boxer of quite historical times, arrived in the place, saw the intended victim, and offered, if she would marry him, to save her. She agreed, and he met the ghost and so drubbed it that it left the country and plunged into the sea, never to return.[82]

NOTES ON CHAPTER IX

[1] For full references to Orpheus, see the relevant articles in the classical encyclopaedias. Only a few are given here. Mother, Kalliope, Verg., *Ecl.*, IV, 57, and most authors; Polymnia, ' some people ' *ap.* schol. Apoll. Rhod., I, 23. Father, Oiagros, Plato, *Symposium*, 179d,

10

and most authorities; Apollo, Ovid, *Amores*, III, 9, 21 foll., and a few others. Power of his music, Horace, *carm.*, I, 12, 7, and countless other passages. Eurydike, her death and Orpheus' journey to recover her, see especially Verg., *Georg.*, IV, 456 foll.

² See Rose in *Aberystwyth Studies*, IV, p. 21, and add Frazer, *Belief*, III, p. 235.

³ Fullest description, Ovid, *Met.*, XI, 1 foll.

⁴ Phanokles, frag. 1, Powell; Hygin., *poet. astr.*, II, 7; pseudo-Erat., 24; Lucian, *adu. indoct.*, 11–12.

⁵ Antion is his father in Aeschylus, Phlegyas in Euripides, Peision in Pherekydes, schol. Pind., *Pyth.*, II, 39.

⁶ Pindar, *Pyth.*, II, 21 foll., with schol.; Aesch., frags. of *Ixion* and *Perrhaibides*, with Nauck's notes, and the schol. of Pindar; more refs. in Preller-Robert, II, p. 12 foll. Add Rose in *Folk-Lore*, XXII (1911), p. 285.

⁷ Homer, *Il.*, XIV, 317 foll. (an interpolation, but a fairly early one); Pindar, frag. 167 (Bergk); Apoll. Rhod., I, 57 foll. and schol.; Hom., *Od.*, XXI, 295 foll., says a single Centaur, Eurytion, began the quarrel by misbehaving himself in Peirithoos' house when drunk; for the great fight see *Il.*, I, 262 foll., II, 742 foll.; ps.-Hesiod, *Scutum Herculis*, 178 foll.; perhaps the best-known account is Ovid, *Met.*, XII, 182 foll. It was also a favourite subject in art (*e.g.*, the metopes of the Parthenon).

⁸ What follows is largely from Apollod., I, 47 foll. For the flood-legend, cf. also Ovid, *Met.*, I, 260 foll., and for such tales in general, Frazer, *F.O.T.*, I, 104 foll. According to Ovid, the immediate cause was the wickedness of the Arkadian king Lykaon, who, like Tantalos, killed his own son and served up his flesh to Zeus at a banquet.

⁹ Apollod., I, 52; Ovid, *Met.*, XI, 270 foll., who tells also the story of Keyx' brother Daidalion: his daughter Chione was loved of both Hermes and Apollo, and bore twins to the two gods, Autolykos son of Hermes and Philammon son of Apollo. But she boasted that she was more beautiful than Artemis, for which the goddess shot her; Daidalion in his grief leaped from the top of Parnassos, whereat Apollo saved his life by turning him into a falcon.

¹⁰ The genealogy is:

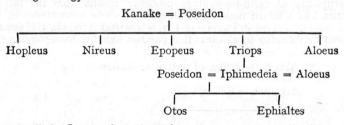

Kanake = Poseidon

Hopleus — Nireus — Epopeus — Triops — Aloeus

Poseidon = Iphimedeia = Aloeus

Otos — Ephialtes

¹¹ Apollod., I, 56; but there is no agreement as to the reason for Endymion's sleep (a punishment for desiring Hera, Epimenides *ap.* schol. Apoll. Rhod., IV, 57, where a dozen other accounts are given, from various authors from Hesiod to the Alexandrians). See further, v. Sybel in Roscher, *s.u.*

¹² Apollod., I, 64 foll.; Ovid, *Met.*, 273 foll.; Oineus had another son, Toxeus, whom he killed for jumping over the ditch (presumably, of the city Oineus ruled over; possibly the germ of the tale of Romulus

and Remus, Chapter XI, p. 314). Another Toxeus was one of Meleagros' uncles.

[13] Homer, *Il.*, IX, 527 foll., cf. II, 642.

[14] Hesiod, frag. 21b (Boiotian, Schoineus addresses a suitor, the race and the apples mentioned) ; Ovid, *Met.*, X, 560 foll. (perhaps the best-known account ; daughter of Schoineus, incident of the race with Hippomenes, pollution of shrine of Great Mother) ; Theognis, 1287 foll. ; Propertius, I, 1, 9 foll. ; Apollod., III, 105 foll. For more references and details, see Schirmer in Roscher, *s.u.*

[15] Homer, *Od.*, XI, 235 foll., cf. Chapter X, p. 288.

[16] Homer, *Od.*, XV, 225 foll. (who clearly knew a form of the story rather different from that given above) ; Apollod., I, 96 foll.

[17] Ovid, *Met.*, VII, 523 foll. Aiakos was son of Zeus and the nymph Aigina after whom the island was supposed to be named.

[18] Ovid, *Met.*, XI, 266 foll. ; but the story is as old as the *Alkmaionis* (frag. 1, Kinkel). For references, see Roscher, III, 1829, 26 foll.

[19] Hesiod, frag. 79 ; Pindar, *Nem.*, IV, 54 foll., with schol. ; Aristophanes, *Clouds*, 1063, with schol. ; schol. Apoll. Rhod., I, 224 ; these differ from each other in small details. Other variants of the tale of Potiphar's wife in Greek are, Phaidra and Hippolytos, Bellerophon and Stheneboia, Eunomos and Ochna (Plut., *quaest. Graec.*, 40), while Antheus and Kleoboia (or Philaichme) is something like it, Parthenios, 14 ; but this story was invented by Agathon, Arist., *Poetics*, 1451[b] 20 foll.

[20] Apollod., III, 163 foll. For the proof that this comes from Pherekydes, and more passages to the same effect, see Preller-Robert, II, p. 72 n. 3.

[21] She is variously mated to Phylakos, Kephalos, and Iasos (father of Atalante), see Stoll in Roscher, *s.u.* Another Klymene, also said to be mother of Phaethon, is an Okeanid ; in so vague a pedigree as that of the Minyai, it is not well to be certain that they are separate at all.

[22] See especially the fragments of Euripides, *Phaethon*, and Ovid, *Metam.*, I, 750–II, 366.

[23] Ovid, *ibid.*, 367 foll.

[24] His shape is mentioned in many passages, *e.g.*, Eurip., *Ion.*, 1163–4, Apollod., III, 177, which also mentions his birth from the ground. The multiplicity of earth-born kings probably results from the fact that Attica had a mixed population, all claiming to be autochthonous. The succession, as given in Pausanias, I, 2, 6 (contrast Apollod., III, 177 foll.), shows by its many breaks that it is patched together from varying traditions.

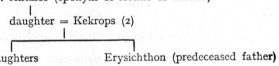

1. Aktaios (eponym of Attike or Aktike)
   |
   daughter = Kekrops (2)
        |
   ┌─────────────────────────┐
   daughters   Erysichthon (predeceased father)

3. Kranaos (another eponym)
   |
   Atthis (again an eponym) and other daughters.

4. Amphiktyon (son-in-law of Kranaos ; usurps throne).

5. Erichthonios (no relation ; usurps).

[25] Klearchos *ap.* Athenaios. XIII, p. 555 D, cf. Justin, *hist. Phil.*

epit., II, 6, 7. See Wilamowitz-Moellendorff in *Class. Rev.*, 1906, p. 446b ;
Preller-Robert, II, p. 137, n. 3, who cites a number of other rationalizations
equally silly.

²⁶ See especially the fragments of Euripides, *Erechtheus*, and Lykurgos,
in Leocratem, 98 foll. Cf. Apollod., III, 201 foll.

²⁷ Soph., *Electr.*, 127, cf. Aesch., *Agam.*, 1140 foll. ; Apollod., III.,
193 foll. ; Ovid, *Met.*, VI, 424 foll.

²⁸ The story of the nightingale, her sister, and the child of one or
other of them seems to have been very widespread ; there is, for instance,
a very similar tale quoted from Boios by Antoninus Liberalis (11), wherein
the injured wife is Aedon (Nightingale), her sister Chelidonis (Swallow-
girl) and the husband Polytechnos (Many-crafted ; he was not a king
but a carpenter). See Addenda.

²⁹ Plato, *Phaedr.*, 229 B foll., and many later passages, as Apollod.,
III, 199, who gives her children as Kleopatra, Chione, Zetes and Kalais ;
this Kleopatra was the wife of Phineus.

³⁰ Ovid, *Met.*, VII, 794 foll.

³¹ Ovid, *ibid.*, 690 foll. ; Apollod., III, 197 foll.

³² Apollod., III, 206 foll. ; Plut., *Theseus*, 3 foll., a work which is our
best-informed authority, in the absence of many of the earlier accounts,
for the Theseus-saga. For Aigeus = Poseidon, see Farnell, *Hero-Cults*,
pp. 86, 337. Theseus is probably a man, not a god.

³³ Plutarch, *op. cit.*, 6 foll. ; Hyginus, *fab.*, 27.

³⁴ Plut., *op. cit.*, 13–14. The fragmentary *Hekale* of Kallimachos
deals with Theseus' reception, on his way to capture the bull, by an old
woman of that name, and with her death and subsequent cult.

³⁵ Aesch., *Choeph.*, 613 foll. (no metamorphosis ; Hermes intervenes
in some way) ; [Vergil], *Ciris* ; Ovid, *Met.*, VIII, 6 foll. ; Hyginus,
fab., 198, who says Skylla was changed in *piscem* cirim quem uocant,
hodieque si ea auis (the sea-eagle) eum piscem natantem conspexerit,
mittit se in aquam raptumque unguibus dilaniat. Cf. D'Arcy W. Thompson, *Class. Quart.*, XIX (1925), p. 155 foll., on the question of identification.

³⁶ Bakchylides, XVI, *passim* ; Hyginus, *poet. astron.*, II, 5.

³⁷ See on the whole matter Plut., *op. cit.*, 19, who gives some quaint
rationalizations.

³⁸ Plut., *ibid.*, 20 foll. ; for the forgetfulness, cf. Theokr., II, 45,
with the schol. The most famous literary descriptions surviving are
Catullus, 64, 52 foll., Ovid, *Heroid.*, X.

³⁹ Hyginus, *poet. astr.*, II, 5 ; [Eratosthenes], 5.

⁴⁰ Plut. and Catull., *loc. cit.*

⁴¹ Plut., *op. cit.*, 24 foll. ; the war with the Amazons is a favourite
Athenian boast, *e.g.*, Herodotos, IX, 27, 4. Numerous older authorities,
as Pindar and the author of the epic *Theseis*, are cited by Plutarch. An
obscure tale states that Antiope was killed by Theseus, see Seneca, *Phaedr.*,
927.

⁴² See especially, for this story, the *Hippolytus* of Euripides, the
Phaedra (or *Hippolytus*) of Seneca, Ovid, *Met.*, XV, 492 foll. (cf. Chapter
VI, p. 140, and note 13), and *Heroid.*, IV.

⁴³ Death of Theseus, Plut., *op. cit.*, 32 foll., mixed up with a rationalizing account of his sojourn in Hades. Children of Herakles, see especially Eurip., *Heraclidae*, but references in other authors (as Herod., IX,
27, 2) are very numerous. Demophon is notable chiefly as an inconstant
lover ; having won the heart of the Thracian princess Phyllis he departed

for Athens, promising to return soon ; as he never came back, she hanged herself. See especially Ovid, *Heroid.*, II.

⁴⁴ Herod., IX, 26, 2 foll. ; Pausanias, I, 41, 2, cf. VIII, 5, 1 ; III, 1, 6 ; V, 3, 5 foll. ; Apollod., II, 169 foll.

⁴⁵ Kresphontes, Apollod., II, 180 ; Paus., IV, 3, 3 foll. ; Hyginus, *fab.*, 137, which seems to give the plot of Euripides' lost *Kresphontes* ; the son (named, not Aipytos, but Kresphontes or Telephontes) comes to Polyphontes, pretending to be his own slayer ; Merope is on the point of killing him as he sleeps when he is made known to her by an old retainer ; by her help Polyphontes is deceived and killed. The plot is familiar in English from Matthew Arnold's *Merope.* See also the fragments of Euripides' play, with Nauck's notes. Temenos, Apollod., II, 179 ; Paus., II, 19, 1 ; 28, 3–7. Of Euripides' plays *Temenidai* and *Temenos* not enough remains for the plot to be intelligible.

⁴⁶ The *Ion* of Euripides is the only important surviving source for this legend.

⁴⁷ Cf. Chapter VIII—I, p. 183. Daidalos' parentage, Plato, *Ion*, 533 A ; his descent from Hephaistos and Sokrates' descent from him, *Alcib.*, I, 121 A ; *Meno*, 97 D, describes his statues, which could move of themselves (like Hephaistos' works), a legend for which various rationalizations were found. Detention in Crete, Xenoph., *memorab. Soc.*, IV, 2, 33 ; Ovid, *ars amat.*, II, 21 foll. ; *Met.*, VIII, 183 foll., and many other passages, which also describe the flight. The reason for the detention is sometimes desire to use his skill, sometimes revenge for his having helped Pasiphae. Pursuit, death of Minos, Herod., VII, 170 ; Apollod., *epit.*, I, 12 foll. ; Athenaios, I, 10 E.

⁴⁸ Velleius Paterculus, I, 2 ; Justin, *epit. Trogi*, II, 6, 16–21, who has a slight variant ; the Dorians were to win if they did not kill the king of Athens. Cf. Horace, *carm.*, III, 19, 1–2. The son of Kodros is said to have founded Miletos, Herod., IX, 97, and several other passages.

⁴⁹ Paus., I, 39, 4 foll.

⁵⁰ Paus., II, 1, 1, cf. Pindar, *Nem.*, VII, 105 ; Aristoph., *Ranae*, 439 ; and schol. on both. Pindar's scholiast gives among others the following explanation ; Διὸς Κόρινθος means ' Zeus' Corinth ', not Korinthos son of Zeus ' ; for Aletes was assured by Zeus at Dodona that he could become king of Corinth if he were given a clod of Corinthian earth. He therefore went there and begged bread of a churlish fellow who gave him a clod instead ; subsequently he was able to become master of the city, and so called it ' Zeus' Corinth ', because Zeus had given it him. The story is an illustration of what the Middle Ages called *traditio per terram*, see Nilsson in *Arch. f. Religionswissenschaft*, XX (1920) p. 232 foll. (= *O.S.* I, p. 330 foll.), citing parallels in Plutarch, *quaest. Graec.*, 13, 22 ; Suetonius, *Vespas.*, 5 (add Augustine, *de serm. in mont.*, I, 50), Herod., VIII, 137, 4–5.

⁵¹ Paus., II, 1, 1 foll., citing the Corinthian poet Eumelos. For Palaimon-Melikertes, cf. Chapter VI, p. 151.

⁵² Above, pp. 245–6 ; Homer, *Il.*, VI, 153–4 ; Aesch., frag. 175 N² ; Soph., *Ai.*, 190, with the schol. there, and several other tragic passages ; Suidas, *s.u.* Σίσυφος.

⁵³ Hygin., *fab.*, 201 ; Polyainos, *strateg.*, VI, 52.

⁵⁴ Malten in *Jahrbuch d. k. d. archäolog. Instituts*, xxxx ; Hom., *Il.*, VI, 155 foll.

⁵⁵ Hesiod, *Theog.*, 325 ; Pindar, *Olymp.*, XIII, 63 foll., with schol., who among other particulars states that Bellerophon was really the son

of Poseidon, perhaps a mere blunder, see v. Christ's note on v. 69, but cf. Hesiod, fr. 245 ; schol. on Homer, *loc. cit.* ; Eurip., frags. of the lost *Stheneboia* and *Bellerophontes* ; Hygin., *fab.*, 57 ; *poet. astr.*, II, 18, cf. pseudo-Erat., 18 (the constellation Equus is Pegasos, but some say it is Cheiron's daughter Hippe) ; Apollod., II, 24 foll. Pegasos is commonly said to have produced the spring Hippokrene (' Horse's spring ') by a stamp ; the metaphor of a poet riding him is modern. His name has nothing to do with πηγή.

⁵⁶ Pausan., II, 15, 5 foll. ; Apollod., **II**, 1 foll. ; Hygin., *fab.*, 143 ; Plato, *Tim.*, 22 A. Phoroneus had two sons, Kar the eponym of the Karians, of some importance in the local genealogies, and Apis, not the Egyptian sacred bull, but the eponym of Apia, said to be the old name of the Peloponnesos (see Homer, *Il.*, I, 270, and schol. A there).

⁵⁷ Aesch., *Suppl.*, 291 foll. (where Hera, not Zeus, transforms Io), *P.V.*, 561 foll. ; Ovid, *Met.*, I, 583 foll. ; he says (722) that Hera, when Argos was killed, set his eyes in the tail of her peacock ; Apollod., II, 5 foll., who says that Hera caused the Kuretes to steal Epaphos away, whereat Zeus killed them and Io wandered over Syria in search of her son, whom she finally found at Byblos. The genealogies of all this family are crowded with names clearly intended to connect the principal nations of the eastern Mediterranean, and their legends not infrequently contain incidents of a like kind.

⁵⁸ Aesch., *Suppl.*, *passim* ; Apollod., II, 11 foll. ; Hyg., *fab.*, 168, 170. See further the relevant arts. in Roscher (DANAIDEN, DANAOS, etc.).

⁵⁹ Apollod., II, 14 ; Hyg., *fab.*, 169. The persistent connexion of the Danaides with water makes it not unlikely that they are in reality fountain-nymphs. A quaint continuation of the legend in several authorities is that Danaos offered his daughters as prizes in a foot-race and so found new husbands for them all. Hypermestra is generally said to have been imprisoned by her father, but ultimately rescued—by Lynkeus or by intercession of Aphrodite—and reunited to her husband.

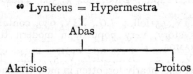

⁶⁰ Lynkeus = Hypermestra

Abas

Akrisios   Proitos

See Apollod., II, 24 foll. Finally Akrisios became king of Argos, Proitos of Tiryns.

⁶¹ Apollod., *ibid.*, 34 foll. ; Hygin., *fab.*, 63, 64 ; Ovid, *Met.*, IV, 610 foll. ; schol. Apoll. Rhod., IV, 1091, 1515 (from Pherekydes) ; we have no early accounts preserved entire, but cf. [Hesiod], *Scutum*, 216 foll. ; Pindar, *Pyth.*, XII ; Simonides, frag. 13 Diehl ; Eurip., fragments of *Andromeda*. See also chapter II, p. 36 foll.

⁶² See especially Euripides, *Andromache*.

⁶³ For the Hittite evidence, see Forrer in *Mitteilungen d. deutschen Orientgesellschaft*, 63 (Mar. 1924), since summarized and commented on by many writers, e.g., P. Giles in *Year's Work*, 1925.

⁶⁴ See Pindar, *Olymp.*, X, 22 foll. ; the other traditions, good and bad alike, are conveniently collected in Pausanias, V, 7, 6 foll.

⁶⁵ Paus, VII, 19, 2 foll. Cf. Chapter VI, p. 153.

⁶⁷ Paus, VIII, 5, 5 ; 10, 3.

67 *Ibid.*, VIII, 48, 4, 5.

68 *Ibid.*, VIII, 4, 9, citing Hekataios ; 48, 7, which gives the local story, and remarks that she was identified with Eileithyia. For the significance of her attitude, see Ploss-Bartels, *Das Weib*[8], par. 321 foll.

A version perhaps deriving from Sophokles' *Mysoi* (see Pearson ii, p. 70) makes Teuthras king of Mysia adopt Auge and marry her to Telephos, who had become his ally. They discovered their relationship by a miracle, at the last moment (Hygin., *fab.* 100; Aelian *N.A.* iii, 47).

69 For instance, Hesiod, frag. 43 ; a later genealogy (Akusilaos, frag. 25 Jacoby) says he was son of Zeus and Niobe daughter of Phoroneus.

70 For the various traditions concerning Oibalos, see Roscher, *s.u.* ; the reference to Ovid is *Fast.*, III, 230, *Oebaliae matres* (woman of Tarentum).

71 For authorities and criticism, see Halliday in *Class. Quart.*, XXI (1927), p. 37 foll.

72 Lykophron, 570 foll., with the scholiast ; Diod. Sic., V, 62 ; SdA III, 80 ; Ovid., *Met.*, XIII, 632 foll., adds that when Agamemnon tried to make the girls prisoners, they prayed for help to Dionysos and were turned into birds—Servius specifies doves, and says that for that reason no dove may be hurt on Delos.

73 See especially Kallimachos, frags. 67–75 Pfeiffer ; Ovid, *Heroid.*, XX, XXI. Keos is also the scene of the story of Kyparissos, a pretty boy beloved by Apollo or Seilenos (? Silvanus in the Latin authorities) or Zephyros : he grieved so deeply over the accidental death of a pet stag that he turned into the tree (cypress) which bears his name : Ovid, *Met.*, X, 106 foll. ; S and SdA III, 64, 680 (which also gives a different version), G. I, 20 ; P.G. I, 20 ; Nonnos, XI, 364.

74 Rhodos, Pindar, *Ol.*, VII, 14, 71 foll., with the schol. ; Rhode, Apollod., I, 28 ; he calls her daughter of Poseidon, Pindar says Rhodos was daughter of Aphrodite ; but usually Rhode (instead of Klymene) was the mother of Phaethon and his sisters, *e.g.*, schol. Hom., *Od.*, XVII, 208 ; she is daughter of the river-god Asopos. See Höfer in Roscher, *s.u.*

75 Apollod., III, 12 foll. ; Diod. Sic., V, 59. These two authors differ in some details.

76 Ovid, *Met.*, IV, 55 foll. ; *I.G.*, XIV, 930, contains one of the few references to this story, very popular in modern times. See further Roscher, *s.u.* PYRAMOS.

77 Pausanias, V, 7, 2 ; Ovid, *Met.*, V, 577 foll. This is the famous story ; but an older one, nearly forgotten in modern times, is that Alpheios loved Artemis, see, *e.g.*, Telesilla, frag. 1 Bergk.

78 Paus., X, 10, 6–8 ; see further, Giannelli, p. 1 foll.

79 Ovid, *Met.*, XV, 12 foll. ; more authorities, Giannelli, p. 154 foll.

80 Lykophron, 984 foll. ; Strabo, VI, 1, 14 ; Justin, *epit. Trog.*, XX, 2, 3 foll. See Giannelli, p. 103 foll.

81 Hes., frag. 155 (Klaros) ; Lykophron, 978 foll., and Tzetzes, *ad loc.*

82 Paus., VI, 6, 7 foll.

CHAPTER X

MÄRCHEN IN GREECE AND ITALY

Sed ego te narrationibus lepidis anilibusque fabulis protinus auocabo.
—APPULEIUS, *Metam.*, IV, 27.

But I will straightway divert you with pleasant old wives' tales.

TO avoid all misunderstandings, I state here that in the present chapter I have simply collected a number of stories which seem to be indubitably of the *märchen*-type, having no serious claim to be called either myth or saga. I offer no opinion as to their relations to the modern European and other stories to which I compare them; for a brief but excellent discussion of that, see Halliday, *Greek and Roman Folklore*, Chapter III, to which, and to his private criticisms and suggestions, any merit this chapter may have is mostly due. For purposes of comparison I have used the list of folk-tale themes by Mr. Jacobs, which appears as Appendix C of the *Handbook of Folk-lore*, imperfect and sketchy though it is, because it is the only one conveniently accessible in English. To each title I have added the number and name of the story in the best-known of all European collections, that of the brothers Grimm,[1] which best illustrates the type in question, and a reference to the discussion of the matter in the best-known commentary, Bolte-Polivka. Other works, however, have been freely drawn upon.

1. *Cupid and Psyche type.* G. 88 (*The singing, hopping lark*; much the same story as *Beauty and the Beast*); a fragment also in G. 137 (*The Three Black Princesses*). See B.P. II, 266; III, 114.

A certain king had three daughters, the youngest of whom, by name Psyche, was so lovely that she was adored as Venus herself. The goddess became jealous, and sent Cupid to make Psyche fall in love with some unsightly wretch. But he fell in love with her himself, and persuaded Apollo to tell her father that she must be dressed as a bride and abandoned on the top of a mountain. Thence, by the agency of the West Wind, he had her transferred to a fairy palace built in a hidden valley, and here he visited her, but always in the dark. After a time, she begged to be allowed to bring her sisters to see her, and this he reluctantly granted. On the first visit, they became madly jealous, and on a second visit they discovered that she had never seen her mysterious husband. Coming again, they assured her that he was a cannibal monster, and gave her a lantern to discover him and a sharp knife to kill him. Waiting till he slept, Psyche turned the light on him, and was awe-struck by his beauty. But a drop of oil falling on him awoke him, and he left her, upbraiding her disobedience. She set out to look for him, contriving to avenge herself on her sisters. After many adventures, she came to the dwelling of Venus, who received her harshly and set her to perform impossible tasks,—first to sort out a mingled heap of various grains, then to fetch water from an inaccessible fountain, finally to go down to Hades and fetch a supply of beauty from Persephone. The first tasks were accomplished by the unexpected help of ants and an eagle ; the third, by following the good advice given by a tower from which she was minded to throw herself in despair, was nearly completed when, having almost returned to the upper world, she had a curiosity to examine the supposed casket of beauty which she carried. It contained, however, not beauty but a deathly sleep, which at once overcame her. Now Cupid interfered in person, having at last won the consent of Iuppiter to the marriage, and she was revived and united to him.[2]

Appuleius appears to have started this story with the notion of making it an allegory ; the names of the principal characters suggest the human Soul (Psyche) and the divine Love which is so prominent in Platonic philosophy. But it would appear that he soon forgot his didactic purpose, and went on to tell this loveliest of fairy-tales for its own sake. It is the only folk-tale told as such by any classical writer. The essentials, as the parallels from other sources show us, are as follows : a mortal marries a supernatural being, from whom he or she is parted by disobedience to some command. There, in some versions, the tale ends[3] ; in other stories, the separated lovers are reunited as a result of the mortal's wandering in search of the super-natural mate, and performing a series of apparently impossible tasks ; a theme which recurs in No. 27 (Jason, or Mastermaid). In Greece we have the first part of the story (which also resembles Jacobs' No. 2, ' Melusina ') in the legend of Peleus and

Thetis, already told in Chapter II. Otherwise, however, the story is not common in Greece.

No. 4 (Penelope) has, as the name implies, been told in telling the story of Odysseus' return. It is merely to be noted that it is a *märchen*, not a saga, although Odysseus himself is a figure of saga and appears as such in the *Iliad*. The central theme (as in Scott's *Noble Moringer*, for instance) is that of the husband who returns just in time to prevent his wife, who supposes him dead, marrying some one else ; as a subsidiary theme it occurs, for example, in Grimm 92, *The King of the Golden Mountain*.[4]

Nos. 6 and 7 (*Punchkin* and *Samson*) contain an element found in Greek legend, the life-token or external soul. We have met with this in the story of Meleagros, in its later form (see Chapter IX, p. 258 ; Phrynichos, who won the tragic prize for the first time in 512 B.C., seems to have been the earliest to use this version of the story).[5]

No. 8 (*Herakles*) is the story of the garment of Nessos. The idea of a burning robe, which is not an essential part of the story, seems to have struck the Greek fancy, witness its re-currence in the tale of Medeia and Glauke (Chapter VIII—I, p. 204).

No. 14 (*Rea Silvia*, which would be more appropriately called *Tyro*) is a story widespread in the classical areas.[6] A mother abandons or exposes her new-born child or children (in the latter case usually twin boys). A beast suckles them, they are rescued, and in time they are recognized, restored to their (generally royal) rank, and often rescue their mother from some imminent danger. Tyro is perhaps the best-known example, for Romulus and Remus are not genuine mythology.[7] In the post-Homeric form of her story, her twins Pelias and Neleus were suckled when she exposed them, the former by a mare, the latter by a bitch. Pelias' face was trodden upon by a pasturing horse, making it discoloured (πέλιος), hence his name. Growing up, they rescued their mother from the persecution of her stepmother Sidero (' Iron-woman ', *i.e.*, hard-hearted [8]), whom Pelias killed as she sought refuge in the temple of Hera.

If we could believe the rubbishy author of the *Lesser Parallels* falsely ascribed to Plutarch, there was an Arkadian story very like Romulus and Remus, which might well have been its source ; but that egregious person is so perfectly capable of inventing story and authority alike that no reliance can be placed upon his unsupported word.[9] In his tale, for what it is worth, the parts of Rea Silvia, Mars, Romulus and Remus are played by Phylonome, daughter of Nyktimos, Ares, and Phylonome's twin boys, while the wolf and the shepherd also appear, and the Erymanthos replaces the Tiber.

Numerous other children are said to have been suckled by beasts, on being exposed by their parents : Aigisthos by a goat ; [10] Phylakides and Philandros, sons of Apollo and a Cretan nymph Akakallis,[11] also by a goat ; while another goat was the foster-mother of Asklepios, in one version of the legend.[12] A cow tended Aiolos and Boiotos, sons of Melanippe by Poseidon[13] ; a doe gave her milk to Telephos ;[14] another version of the tale of Aka-kallis and Apollo makes her the mother of Miletos, the eponym of the city so called, and states that he was tended and fed by she-wolves.[15] Atalante,[16] daughter of Iasion, being exposed by her father, who wanted a son, was found by a she-bear robbed of her cubs, who nursed her. Hippothoos, son of Poseidon and Alope,[17] found a foster-mother in a mare when he was exposed, which happened not once, but twice ; one late version of the story states that Antilochos, son of Nestor,[18] was exposed in infancy and suckled by a bitch, while coins of Kydonia in Crete show the same animal (or, less likely, a she-wolf) performing the same service for a child who is probably Kydon, the obscure founder of this obscure town,[19] whose parentage is variously given. He also grew up to found a city. A better-known tale of the same kind is that of Iamos,[20] founder of the prophetic clan of the Iamidai, whom his mother Euadne bore to Apollo : ' with a sore heart she left him on the ground ; but two grey-eyed serpents tended him, by the will of the gods, and nurtured him with the harmless venom of bees. . . . In reeds and thick brambles was he hidden, his tender body bathed in the sheen of gilly-flowers, yellow and bright red.' And so in due course he was found by his grandfather, who had been instructed by Apollo.

It is not surprising, therefore, that the Greeks credited the heroes and deities of other countries with a similar adventure. Cyrus the Great [21] was fostered by a bitch or cow when exposed by his grandfather ; a euhemerizing tale of Kybele makes her the daughter of a mortal king, Maion, by his wife Dindyme ; being, like Atalante, exposed because she was not a boy, she was suckled by panthers and other wild creatures, until ultimately found by a shepherd.[22] Attis, her cult-partner, had a like experience in babyhood.[23] His mother Nana was made pregnant by putting a pomegranate into her bosom ; her child was exposed, and this time, it would seem, no female animal suckled him, but a he-goat somehow contrived to tend him. How much of this curious story is Greek and how much barbarian is not a question which can be discussed in this book ; Pausanias, who tells it, says it is a native tale from Pessinus in Phrygia. Finally, to pass to the other end of the ancient world, Justin[24] has preserved to us a legend of Habis, grandson of Gargoris king of Tartessos. The king, on hearing that his daughter had borne a bastard son, made several attempts to destroy the child, but again and again he was spared by the beasts and suckled by them. Ultimately he grew up and became the culture-hero of his people.

That Paris was nurtured by a she-bear has been mentioned in telling the tale of Troy, and the story of the nursing of Zeus has been discussed in treating of the legends of that deity. A less likely nurse is a gull or swan ; yet Lykophron alludes to Kyknos, son of Poseidon, as ' the gull's nursling ', and the author of the scholia on him tells the story in full. Kyknos' mother, Skamandrodike, concealed the birth and exposed her child near the seashore. There, according to the account which Lykophron got from some unknown source, it would appear that the gulls brought him some kind of food ; his scholiast says a swan was seen hovering over him ; in either case, the attention of fishermen was attracted to him by the bird or birds, and he was rescued, and, in what would appear to be the more popular version, named Kyknos (Swan) because a swan had tended him.[25]

It is not therefore surprising that this tale was told, in flattery or perhaps, by simple people, in sincerity, of great men of comparatively late date. The dynasty of the Ptolemies in Egypt was founded by the reputed son of Lagos, a Macedonian noble, and of his wife Arsinoe. Lagos is said to have suspected the child to be none of his and to have exposed him, whereat, according to ' a tale that has got about from Macedonia ', an eagle came to the rescue, sheltered the child from rain and sun by spreading its wings above him, kept off other birds, and fed the infant with its own blood.[26]

No. 15, *The Juniper Tree* (G. 47), has no exact parallel in Greek. In this, a stepmother kills her stepchild, who thereupon is turned into a tree and then into a bird, in which form he brings about the death of the stepmother. But the separate elements of the tale are all there. For jealous stepmothers we need recollect only the story of Ino and Themisto (Chapter VI, p. 151) ; metamorphoses of all sorts are very common ; and the revelation and punishment of a murder by some unlooked-for means (a theme which recurs, for example, in G. 115, *The Bright Sun brings it to Light*) is to be found in the well-known story of the Cranes of Ibykos.[27] Ibykos is a perfectly historical figure, a lyric poet of about 550 B.C., some few fragments of whose works have come down to us. According to the story, he was set upon and murdered by certain ruffians, and in dying, called on a passing flock of cranes to see justice done. Some time afterwards the murderers were sitting in a theatre when a flock of cranes passed, whereat one whispered to another ' There go Ibykos' avengers '. He was overheard and the murder came to light. A similar tale is told by Plutarch of one Bessos, a parricide, who amazed his guests by killing a nest of young swallows, explaining that they were accusing him of killing his father; suspicion being thus aroused, inquiry was made and Bessos found guilty and punished.[28] In Grimm, the murdered child is unwittingly eaten by his father; we may compare the tale of Tereus and Prokne.[29]

Although Type 16 (*Holle*, G. 24) is not Greek, it contains a theme (*Courteous and Discourteous*) which is. As mentioned in Chapter VIII, p. 198, Jason wins Hera's favour by his kindness to her when she is disguised as a poor old woman. In the story as we have it, she hates Pelias because he forgot to sacrifice to her; I conjecture that in the original tale she appeared in disguise to him also, and was rudely repulsed.[30]

Type 17 (*Catskin, Allerleirauh*, G. 65) again is not Greek; but one detail, the girl who is disguised in a garment made of the skins of beasts, reminds one of the madman in Horace who fancies that a beast (a lamb) is his daughter; in one variant of the modern story the girl actually turns into a lamb. Incest between father and daughter, again, is a not uncommon feature of Greek stories (*e.g.*, Thyestes and Pelopia), and on an attempt at this the whole plot of the modern *märchen* turns.[31]

Theme 21 (*Beauty and the Beast*), in some variants, as G. 88, often combines with the *Home-comer's Vow*, and this at least is good Greek. For example, Idomeneus, the Cretan leader at Troy, was caught in a storm on his way home, and vowed to sacrifice the first thing that met him, if he returned safe. This proved to be his own son; on his attempting to fulfil, or actually fulfilling, his vow, he was driven into exile.[32] Not dissimilar are the stories in which the Devil helps to build a bridge, on condition that the first living thing that crosses shall be his; he is befooled by making a dog or other beast cross first. A story of this kind is told of Alexander the Great. An oracle bade him sacrifice the first living thing which he met as he left the city; this proved to be an ass-driver, who saved his life by pointing out that the ass, not he, met Alexander first.[33]

No. 20 (*Cinderella*) again has a detail which we may parallel from Greek, the famous episode of the slipper. Much the same story is told of the famous courtesan Rhodopis, a contemporary of Sappho (about 600 B.C.), and an inhabitant of Egypt.[34]   As she was bathing one day, an eagle snatched up one of her slippers and flew away with it, finally dropping it in the lap of the then Pharaoh, Psamtik, as he was dispensing justice.   He was so impressed by the beauty of the slipper and the strange way in which it had come to him that he ordered the owner to be sought out, and having found her, married her.   The story is of course fabulous, and an interesting illustration of the way in which *märchen* are told of real people.

Nos. 25 (*Flight from Witchcraft*) and 27 (*Jason*, or as I prefer to call it, *Mastermaid*), represented by G. 51 (*Foundling*), 56 (*Dearest Roland*), 186 (*The True Bride*) and a host of others, are best illustrated by the Argonautic saga, which contains all the principal *Mastermaid* episodes except the final reunion of the lovers, albeit some are in a disguised form.   Jason, as already narrated (Chapter VIII, p. 202), performs the seemingly impossible tasks set him by Aietes with the help of Medeia's magic. On their departure, in some versions of the story, Medeia persuades her brother Apsyrtos to come with her, and when the pursuit grows hot, cuts him in pieces, which she flings behind her.   Aietes, stopping to pick up the remains of his son, is thus delayed,[35] and Jason and Medeia escape.   This grim story has for its counterpart the very pretty one of Atalante's race.[36]

It is, however, characteristic of the Greek way of telling a story that *Mastermaid* becomes unrecognizable, or nearly so, by the dropping of the magical motif.   Thus, Jason neither forgets Medeia by magic nor is reconciled to her again ; Theseus is, in most versions of the tale, simply faithless to Ariadne (see Chapter IX, note 38).

Possibly Theme 26 (*Bertha* ; G. 89, *The Goosegirl*), in which the maid passes as her mistress by changing clothes with her, finds an echo in the story told by Herodotos of how the Pharaoh Amasis passed off a daughter of his predecessor Apries as his own daughter, when Kambyses demanded her,[37] and even in the apologue of St. Chrysostom, that if we had power over the beauty of the body, as we have over that of the soul, we should probably spend our time adorning the maid (the body) instead of the mistress.[38]   Again in Grimm's version and some others, the faithless maid forces her mistress to swear not to reveal the secret to any person, and the oath is evaded by telling it to a stove, while the king listens at the stove-pipe.   This somewhat suggests the story of Midas' barber.[39]

No. 31 (*Sleeping Beauty* ; G. 50, *Briar Rose* ; Perrault, *La belle au bois dormant*) contains the theme of the neglected fairy whose spite makes all the mischief. As gods in Greek often play much the same part as fairies in modern Europe, we may compare the neglect of Pelias to sacrifice to Hera, of Oineus to sacrifice to Artemis, and of the gods themselves to invite Eris. In like manner, Perithus forgot to invite Ares to his wedding-feast, in one version of the story, and Ares stirred up the Centaurs to attack the Lapiths in consequence.[40] Like fairies again, the gods will not directly counter one another's actions.[41] A further parallel to the plot of the *Sleeping Beauty* is to be found, not only in the sleep of Endymion (Chapter IX, p. 258), but in the long sleep of the semi-historical Epimenides of Crete.[42]

No. 32, *The Bride Wager* (G. 22, *The Riddle*), has a sort of parallel in the story of Bias, Melampus, and Pero (Chapter IX, p. 259) ; a romantic tale of the winning of a bride is that of the wooing of Agariste, daughter of Kleisthenes of Sikyon. Here there is no riddle to guess, as there generally is in the modern stories, but the bride's father invites eligible suitors from all over Greece, entertains them for a year, and makes trial of their skill, bodily and mental. Hippokleides of Corinth, after being prime favourite, spoils his chances by an exhibition of dancing which goes beyond all bounds of propriety. This is patently an Oriental motif, the Jataka of the Dancing Peacock; finally Megakles of Athens wins her.[43]

As regards No. 33 (*Jack and the Beanstalk*), 34 (*Journey to Hell*), 49 (*Man obtains power over Beasts*), we may regard the modern stories as a degeneration of something not unlike sundry Greek ones. The modern heroes climb up or down into some sort of fairyland (or, less commonly, as in G. 3, *Mary's Child*, attain the Christian heaven for a while), or get hold of a charm for making beasts obey them ; the ancient heroes attain heaven or harrow hell ; the ancient beast-charmer is Orpheus.[44]

Nos. 35 (*Jack the Giant Killer*) and 43 (*Valiant Tailor*) have this much in common, that some of the most popular Greek heroes, as Odysseus and Herakles, are quite small men, at least as compared with the giants they conquer.[45] Odysseus again appears in the oldest literary form we have of Type 36 (*Polyphemus*; G. 191a, *The Robber and his Sons*).[46]

Type 37, *Magical Conflict*, is not exactly paralleled in Greek ; but we may compare the various flights in which one person tries to escape from another by changing shape, the combat of Herakles with Acheloos, and the struggles of Peleus and Menelaos with Thetis and Proteus respectively.[47] As these concern sea-creatures, it is worth noting that water is as wonderful a thing in Greek folk-belief as in our own. Pausanias knows of a spring near Patrai which makes those cattle which drink of it bring forth only male calves[48] ; the Water of Life is represented by a spring in Kilikia which can revive dead birds that fall into it[49] ; Iphimedeia pours water into her bosom and is visited by Poseidon ; it may be doubted whether the anthropomorphic god was in the original tale[50] ; Persephone and Artemis alike, in Ovid, pour water over those whose shape they would change.[51] A related theme is that in which a boy or girl learns the art of shape-changing and is then sold under various forms (horse, cow, etc.), always changing back into human form and running away. This is exactly the method by which Mestra, daughter of Ery-sichthon, supplied her father's wants after he was cursed by Demeter.[52]

Type 38 is *The Devil Outwitted* (cf. G. 100, *The Devil's Sooty Brother*). Greece knew no devil, but Sisyphos outwits Death, as follows. Zeus, being wroth with him for betraying his intrigue with Aigina, sent Death to fetch him. Sisyphos somehow deceived Death and bound him ; released by Ares, Death tried again with more success, but Sisyphos lived long enough to direct his wife Merope to cast out his body unburied. Hades, on hearing of such impiety, allowed him to go back to earth until he should have punished Merope. Once alive again, he care-fully refrained from doing any such thing, and so apparently lived on till he died of sheer old age.[53]

Type 40, *Prophecy Fulfilled*, is abundantly illustrated in Greek ; I need only mention Paris, Perseus, Oidipus, Jason, and Althai-menes. Type 44 (*William Tell*) somewhat resembles the stories told of the Cretan archer Alkon. He did not indeed shoot an apple off his son's head, but he shot rings off various people's heads without hurting them, and when his sleeping child was seized by a snake, he killed the snake without harming the child.[54]

Type 46 (*Gelert*) appears in Greek in the oldest known form. A certain nobleman of Phokis had fears for the safety of his baby son and therefore hid him in a vessel of some kind ; visit-ing the spot one day, he found a great serpent coiled around the vessel, and flinging his spear he killed both it and the baby. Too late he learned that the serpent had come to keep off a prowling wolf. In the Welsh tale the serpent is replaced by the faithful hound Gelert, and Prince Llewelyn's child is not hurt ; but in both a place is named after the misjudged beast (Ophiteia, *i.e.*, Snaketown ; Beddgelert, *i.e.*, Gelert's grave).[55]

Types 47 (*Grateful Beasts*), 48 (*Beast, Bird, Fish*) and G. 71 (*Six go through all the World*) form a group which has interesting

developments in Greek lore. They are, in my opinion, fundamentally the same story. In the first two, the hero does certain
beasts a kindness, as in G. 60, *The Two Brothers,* and in return
is helped by them, each in its own way, a fish bringing him lost
treasure from the water, a bird some object on an inaccessible
hill, and the like ; or they simply help him in a more or less
human way, stealing for him, rescuing him from drowning, and
so forth, as in G. 104a (*The Faithful Beasts*), B.P. II, 451. This
I take to be a transitional form of the story. In the third story,
the hero gets about him, not beasts, but men, each of whom
has some peculiar gift (enormous appetite, insensibility to heat,
prodigious speed). By their help he accomplishes all manner
of impossible feats. If now we examine the list of the Argonauts,
as given, for instance, by Apollonios Rhodios, we find several not
dissimilar figures.[56] His catalogue begins with Orpheus, the
wonderful musician and seer, later we find Tiphys the skilful
pilot, Kastor the great horseman and Polydeukes his brother,
the mighty boxer, Lynkeus, whose eyes are so keen that he
can see through the earth, Periklymenos, who when he fights
may wish for what he likes from Poseidon, Euphemos, who
is so swift that he can run along the tops of the waves without
wetting his feet, Zetes and Kalais, who can fly, besides Argos
the skilled craftsman, who builds the Argo. It is to be noted that
in the forms of the story which we possess, little use is made
of these men's powers, apart from the services of Argos and
Tiphys. In particular, not one of them helps Jason in his tasks
at Kolchis, Medeia doing it all. It seems therefore likely that
in an earlier version of the story, now lost, these ' specialized '
heroes, as we may call them, helped Jason. That they were replaced by Medeia is easily accounted for, both by the picturesque-
ness of the heroine herself, and by the overwhelming popularity
of the Homeric poems with their wholly human and non-magical
heroes. In like manner, the champions of the Arthurian cycle,
who in the Welsh tales have many magical traits, are in Malory
normal medieval knights, and no enchanters. Yet even in the
Argonautic story as we have it (see Chapter VIII, p. 201) the
specialized heroes play some part here and there, as in the episode
of the Harpies.

No. 54 is the famous *Singing Bone* (G. 28), well known in
English from the fine ballad of *Binnorie.* Even more widely
known, from Goethe's use of it in the prison scene in *Faust,*
is G. 47 (*Juniper Tree*). The general idea is the same. An
unnatural murder is committed and the body of the victim disposed of. Either a musical instrument is made of some part of

the corpse (a bone made into a flute or a harp strung with the hair) or the dead person turns into a bird. The music, or the bird's song, then reveals the crime. What stories the peasants in antiquity told on this theme we do not know ; but that they told some is highly probable, for this fantastic tale has passed into an episode in Vergil's *Aeneid*. Aeneas, wanting wood for a sacrifice, begins to pull cornel-bushes from a mound. To his horror, they bleed, and a voice issuing from the mound tells him that the speaker is his kinsman Polydoros, foully murdered and buried there ; the bushes have sprung from the lances with which he was transfixed.[57]

As regards 56 (*Tom Thumb* ; G. 37, *Thumbthick*, and 45, *Thumbkin on his Travels*), we may compare, besides a number of jokes which may not be of popular origin at all, the legend of the Pygmies, who from Homer onward are represented as a very small people, yearly attacked by migrating cranes. Possibly such persons as the Kerkopes may have a similar origin, viz., in all probability, a confused rumour of the real pygmy tribes of Africa.[58]

No. 59 (Frog-Prince ; G. 1, *Frogking or Iron Henry*) turns on the transformation of a prince into a frog. As Petronius has the phrase, *amicus uester qui fuit rana nunc est rex* (your friend who once was frog is now king), we may reasonably suppose that some such tale existed in antiquity.[59]

A *märchen* is usually a combination of several motifs, each of which may, and often does, recur in some other story. I note the following (besides some other more distant and perhaps fanciful resemblances) which seem to be common to Greek and later folklore.

(1) A person (or animal), swallowed by a monster of some sort, afterwards emerges alive and unhurt. This occurs, for instance, in G. 5 (*Wolf and Kids*). We may instance, besides the tale of Kronos and his children, and the adventures of Herakles (Chapter VIII, p. 218) and Jason (*ibid.*, note 75), Horace's mention of the lamia or female monster which swallows a child only to disgorge it unhurt.[60]

(2) The trick by which Hop-o'-my-Thumb saves his own life and that of his brothers at the expense of the ogre's daughters recurs in the story of Ino and Themisto (Chapter VI, p. 151) In the same legend, Ino intrigues against Phrixos and Helle in the time-honoured fashion of stepmothers. It is less obvious why an uncle (as in *Babes in the Wood*) should be frequently wicked, or a father-in-law (as in the Welsh story of *Kulhwch and Olwen*), so commonly a disagreeable character ; but here

again we find parallels in the Argonautic saga in the persons of Pelias and Aietes.

(3) The magical plant which can restore the dead to life is not unknown to Greek *märchen*. Against G. 16 (*The Three Snake-leaves*) we may set the tale of Polyidos the seer. Glaukos, son of Minos of Crete, fell into a vat of honey and was drowned. Polyidos having found out by divination where he was, Minos bade him restore the child to life. This was less unreasonable than it seemed, for the Kuretes had assured him that whoever could find out the aptest simile for a tri-coloured cow which he possessed could both find the lost child and hand him back alive ; Polyidos had compared the beast to the fruit of the dog-rose.[61] So the seer was shut up with the corpse of the child, and presently saw a serpent approach it. On his killing the snake, another came, looked at the body, went away and returned with a herb, with which it restored its dead mate to life. Polyidos took the hint and used the same herb on Glaukos, with satisfactory results.[62]

(4) There is a very common European story, represented by G. 17, *The White Snake*, in which the hero comes somehow into contact with a serpent (either by eating it or by its touching him or spitting into his mouth), and as a result, can understand the language of beasts. This is good Greek.[63] Melampus the great seer saved the young brood of a pair of snakes which his servants had killed, and burned the bodies of the old ones. The young serpents one day, when they were full grown, licked his ears, thus giving him power to understand the speech of birds. A similar thing befell Helenos and Kassandra in childhood.

(5) Alongside the many modern stories of riddles (as G. 22, *The Riddle*), we may set, not only the tale of Oidipus and the Sphinx, but the romance of Apollonius of Tyre, which, while medieval in the Latin epitome that now survives, seems to go back to classical sources. The plot is that of the pseudo-Shakespearian *Pericles*.[64]

(6) Killing in play. G. 22a, *How Children played at Slaughtering*, which seems ultimately to go back to a popular story, although only literary forms are now known, is to all intents and purposes found in Aelian ; the children of a priest play at sacrifices, and really kill the pretended victim (one of themselves). Aelian, but not Grimm, has the sequel that their mother in a rage killed the survivor and was therefore put to death by their father.[65]

(7) The argument used alike by characters in Sophokles and Herodotos,[66] that a brother or sister should be saved rather

than a husband, wife or child, because these are not irreplaceable, is known to be a very ancient Oriental theme. It persists in modern folktales.

(8) Passing over some comic fragments and a passage in Petronius[67] which are somewhat reminiscent of the Land of Cocaigne, where pigs run about ready roasted, but of whose popular origin we have no proof, it is to be noted that the theme of the Sword of Damokles, a popular moral tale in antiquity,[68] recurs in a modern *märchen*. Dionysios, tyrant of Syracuse, invited him to a magnificent banquet, in the middle of which Damokles suddenly noticed that a sword was hanging over his head, suspended by a single hair. This, he was told, was an emblem of the life of his host, in continual fear of revolt or assassination. Exactly the same motif occurs in a variant of G. 39, 2 given by B.P. I, 366, save that the sword is replaced by a millstone. The rest of the tale is quite different, the entertainers being dwarfs, not tyrants, and the guest a servant-girl.

(9) The dragon's tongues form a common enough incident in various stories ; the hero kills a dragon or other monster, usually many-headed, and afterwards proves that he, and not some rival, has done so by producing the beast's tongues, which he has cut out and kept. It was in this way that Alkathus,[69] son of Pelops, proved himself to be the slayer of the Kithaironian lion, which had been troubling the people of Megara. Peleus in the same way proved himself the best huntsman during his stay with Akastos.

(10) Of the many stories of metamorphosis, ancient and modern, one of the commonest in our folklore is that of the deserted lover who turns into a flower. Examples will be found in B.P. I, 502–3, who cite numerous instances in illustration of the occurrence of such an incident in G. 56 (*Dearest Roland*). Such, according to Ovid, was the fate of Klytie, once loved by the Sungod, who from long and vain gazing on the sun, finally turned into a sunflower.[70]

(11) A not infrequent motif is that of the pool or spring of wine, of which very good examples will be found in B.-P. II, 85 (in a variant of G. 71) and III, 95, cf. 106 ; the story commented on is G. 136, *Iron Hans*. It will be remembered that King Midas (Chapter VI, p. 157) caught the prophetic Seilenos by mixing wine with the waters of a spring from which he drank, and that in the Latin imitation of the story (Chapter XI, p. 318), Numa caught Faunus and Picus in the same way.

(12) This work does not deal with fables, but some fables contain obvious bits of folktales ; an example is the theme of

the fattened thief, who cannot crawl back through the hole he has crawled in by in order to steal the food with which he bulges. In the best-known version of the story the thief, in defiance of zoology, is a young fox,[71] which has crept into a corn-basket, and is advised by a weasel to starve until thin enough to get out. It is to be noted that in stories of the type of G. 73 (*The Wolf and the Fox*), the wolf is continually getting into trouble in the same way. See B.P. II, 109, 110, for variants; it is occasionally the fox who is thus in difficulties.

(13) In G. 87 (*The Poor Man and the Rich Man*), God disguises himself as a homeless tramp, and asks hospitality from a rich man, who denies it him, then from his poor neighbour, who treats him well. God gives him in return three wishes, which he uses wisely. The rich man also contrives to obtain three wishes, which he misuses absurdly. The latter theme is especially common, notably in the famous French tale of *Les trois souhaits*. In Greek, on the one hand, we find once more that what is elsewhere a *märchen* has risen to a more dignified plane; the tragic story of Theseus and his wishes (see Chapter IX, p. 266) has already been told, likewise the curious story of Midas and the golden touch (Chapter VI, p. 164). But the motif also exists simply as a funny story, pressed into the service of fable. Phaedrus tells how Hermes was poorly lodged by two women, a courtesan and the mother of a baby. He gave them a wish apiece; the latter wished that her son might speedily become bearded, and the baby straightway grew a beard; the former, that she might draw after her whatever she touched, with the result that she drew her own nose to a prodigious length in trying to blow it. As to the first part of Grimm's tale, while it is to be noted that Phaedrus' story also begins with hospitality shown to a god, a close parallel is furnished by the well-known story of Baucis and Philemon, in Ovid. Zeus and Hermes, visiting mankind in disguise, were repulsed by the rich, but kindly entertained by a poor old couple, Baucis and Philemon, whom therefore they saved from the deluge that overwhelmed the rest of the district, and gave them a wish. They asked to be made priest and priestess of the gods, into a temple of whom their house had suddenly been changed, and to die at the same time. Years after they were simultaneously changed into trees. As this story is found in a classical author, I give it; but Professor Calder thinks it not unlikely that it really is, what it purports to be, Levantine.[72]

(14) In tales of the type of G. 10 (*The Jew in the Thorns*) the hero gets possession of a bow or gun which never misses its mark and a fiddle or other instrument which sets every one danc-

ing when it plays. The former suggests the story of Kephalos (Chapter IX, p. 263), while the latter reminds one, not only of Orpheus and Amphion, but of Areion also. This famous musician (a historical person), beset by the crew of the ship he sailed on, who intended to murder him for the money he had just earned in a ' tour ' of Italy, begged leave to sing a last song. This done, he leaped overboard, and was carried safely to the Peloponnesos, by a dolphin, which had come to listen to his music. On the arrival of the would-be murderers, he handed them over to Periandros, tyrant of Corinth, for punishment.[73]

(15) Metamorphoses in antiquity include turning into an ass, or back again, after eating a plant of some kind or the like ; this is found also in modern folktales, as G. 122.[74]

(16) The skilful craftsman in G. 124 (*The Three Brothers*), who can shave a hare as it runs, is paralleled by the sharp fellow in Petronius who could cut a hawk's claws as it flew.[75]

(17) The cauldron used by Medeia for rejuvenating Aison (Chapter VIII, p. 204) has its parallel in G. 147, *The Man who was smelted Young*.[76]

(18) Little but successful men have already been discussed ; an example of the successful, or at least ambitious, little bird, is to be found in G. 171. The wren, who in this tale claims to be king of birds, is called ' king ' not only in English and German (Kinglet, *Zaunkönig*), but also in Greek (βασιλίσκος), while Plutarch has an Aesopic fable not unlike Grimm's story.[77]

(19) Dick Whittington's cat, and the other cats of folktale who make a fortune for their owners when brought into a catless region overrun with mice or rats, are really not unlike the story in Plutarch of the man who made a ' corner ' in water. Aphrodite bade him take aboard water and nothing else (he was a merchant), and sail at once from Cyprus. Obeying her, he found himself in the midst of a becalmed fleet, sold his cargo at his own price, and came back rich.[78]

(20) Minos, by the evil magic of Pasiphae, was so wrought upon that his touch was poison to any woman save herself, until Prokris cured him.[79] The like tale is told of Mahmud Khan of Cambay, who was brought up on poisons, and it is really only the even better-known story of the Poison Maiden, with the sexes reversed.

(21) The Pharaoh ' Rampsinitos ' (Rameses III ?) had a great treasury built, says Herodotos ; but the builder left a loose stone in the wall, through which his two sons used to creep in and steal. The king, seeing his treasures vanish, set traps and caught one of the thieves. His brother, at his urgent request,

cut off his head and took it away, thus preventing recognition, and saving him from torture. To this there are Oriental parallels enough ; but it is noteworthy that it exists as a Greek story pure and simple, told of two semi-divine figures, Trophonios and his brother, or half-brother, Agamedes. The treasury was that of Hyrieus, or of Augeias king of Elis ; Agamedes was caught, and Trophonios beheaded him.[80]

(22) While Rameses III is barely recognizable in Herodotos, and Trophonios and Agamedes are figures of mythology, there is no doubt of the historicity of M. Atilius Regulus, who served as a general in the First Punic War. He was defeated and captured by the Carthaginians in 255 B.C., and according to the Roman version of the story, was sent by his captors to Rome to arrange an exchange or ransom of prisoners. Having advised the Senate to do no such thing, he returned to Carthage, in fulfilment of his obligation. Popular ingenuity exhausted itself in grisly conjectures as to what the Carthaginians then did to him ; one of the many stories is that he was put into a vessel full of spikes pointing inwards. Now this is a form of torture said to have been inflicted at one time or another on a number of people, and it does not seem reasonable to suppose that all stories of this kind are due to reminiscences of the classical tale, which in this form is not particularly well known. We may therefore hold it to be popular, both in antiquity and in modern times.[81]

NOTES TO CHAPTER X

[1] See general bibliography, and add Stemplinger in *Neue Jahrbücher*, 1922, p. 378 foll. The reader should be careful to use a complete Grimm. as many of the English copies for the use of children are mere selections, Bolte-Polivka supply the text of several tales, omitted in the edition of 1857, from which the ordinary German editions are taken.

[2] Appuleius, *Metamorphoses* (= *Golden Ass*), IV, 28–VI, 24. The edition of L. C. Purser (London, 1910) contains a good summary of earlier work, besides giving the editor's own very sane conclusions. See also MacCulloch, Chapter XII ; Lang, *Custom and Myth*, p. 64 foll. For Peleus and Thetis, add to the references in Chapter II, notes 52 and 53, Sophokles, frag. 155 N[2], 151 P ; Apoll. Rhod., IV, 865 foll., and schol. on 816 ; Lykophron, 178, and Tzetzes, *ad loc.* ; Apollod., III, 171 ; see further, B.P., II, p. 68 ; Frazer, *Apollodorus*, Vol. II, p. 311 ; J. J. Jones in *Aberystwyth Studies*, V, p. 77. See p. 304.

[3] As in the story of Peleus and Thetis, see last note, and many modern tales.

[4] See Nilsson, *Hist. Gk. Rel.*, p. 38.

[5] Phrynichos, frag. 6 N[2].

[6] See, for a useful although not always critical list, E. S. McCartney, *Greek and Roman Lore of Animal-nursed Infants* (Papers of the Michigan

Academy of Science, Arts and Letters, IV, 1924), p. 15 foll.; parallels, *ibid.*, p. 16, note 2.

[7] Apollod., I, 90 foll.; schol. Hom., *Il.*, X, 334; Aelian, *V.H.*, XII, 42.

[8] A cruel person has an 'iron' heart from Homer onwards.

[9] Pseudo-Plutarch, *Parall. Min.*, 36.

[10] Hygin., *fab.*, 87, 88, 252; Aelian, *V.H.*, XII, 42; his name could be taken to mean 'goat-man' (αἴξ, a goat).

[11] Paus., X, 16, 5.

[12] *Ibid.*, II, 26, 3–5.

[13] See the fragments of Euripides' two tragedies on Melanippe, with Nauck's notes.

[14] First, it would seem, in Soph., frag. 86 N², 89 P.; see the notes of both editors. For later refs., see Schmidt in Roscher, V, col. 277 foll.

[15] Anton. Lib., 30.

[16] Aelian, *V.H.*, XIII, 1.

[17] Hyg., *fab.*, 187, cf. 252, and Ael., *V.H.*, XII, 42.

[18] Hyg., *fab.*, 252.

[19] See Roscher, *s.u.* KYDON.

[20] Pindar, *Ol.*, III, 44 foll.

[21] Herodotos I, 122, 3; Justin, *epit. Pomp. Trog.*, I, 4, 10; XIV, 4, 12; cf. Aelian, *V.H.*, XII, 42.

[22] Diod. Sic., III, 52, 1.

[23] Pausan., VII, 17, 10–11.

[24] *Epit. Trog.*, XLIV, 4, 1–11.

[25] Lykophron, 237, and Tzetzes *ad loc.*

[26] Suidas, *s.u.* Λάγος.

[27] Plutarch, *de garrul.*, 509 F.

[28] Plut., *de sera numin. uind.*, 553 F.

[29] Cf. Cosquin, 1886, I, 4, 13; Dawkins, p. 274; B.-P., II, p. 316.

[30] Apoll. Rhod., I, 14.

[31] B.P., I, p. 304; Hor., *Sat.*, II, 3, 214.

[32] S.A., III, 121; cf. Eurip., *I.T.*, 20; Pausan., IX, 33, 4; pseudo-Plutarch, *de fluuiis*, 9, 1.

[33] Valer. Max., VII, 3, *ext.* 1.

[34] Strabo, XVII, 1, 33; Aelian, *V.H.*, XIII, 33 (draws on Strabo or his source); Oriental variants, Cosquin 1922, p. 30 foll.

[35] For one allusion among many to this, see Cicero, *de imp. Cn. Pomp.*, 22.

[36] See Chapter IX, p. 259.

[37] Herod., III, 1 foll.

[38] Chrysost., *ad Theodorum*, I, 20 B.

[39] Chapter VI, p. 145.

[40] See SA VII, 304; cf., *e.g.*, Chapter VIII, p. 198; Chapter VIII, ii, note 7.

[41] See Eurip., *Hippol.*, 1328.

[42] Pliny, *N.H.*, VII, 175; more references in Grote, II, p. 456; Bouché-Leclercq, *Hist. de la divination*, II, p. 99.

[43] Herod., VI, 126 foll.; see Warren in *Hermes*, XXIX (1894), p. 476 foll., and Macan, 1895, II, p. 304.

[44] Several tales originally dealing with exploits like that of Herakles will be found in Welsh tradition; see, *e.g.*, Gwynn Jones in *Aberystwyth Studies*, VIII, p. 37 foll.

[45] See Homer, *Od.*, IX, 515; Pindar, *Isthm.*, III, 20.

[46] See Chapter VIII, ii, p. 244 ; compare B.P., III, p. 369 ; Frazer, *Apollodorus*, II, p. 404 foll.; see page 304

[47] See Chapter II, p. 26 ; VIII—II, p. 248 ; for flights, cf. Chapter IX, p. 278 (Arethusa and Alpheios) ; Nemesis and Zeus (*Kypria*, frag. 7 Allen) ; Aigina and Zeus (schol. A on Hom., *Il.*, I, 180) ; Mestra (Ovid, *Met.*, VIII, 855).

[48] Paus., VII, 22, 11.

[49] Pseudo-Arist., *de mirabilibus*, 29.

[50] Apollod., I, 53.

[51] Ovid, *Met.*, V, 543 ; III, 189.

[52] Cf. Chapter IV, p. 95 ; Hesiod, frag. 112b ; Lykophron, 1393, with Tzetzes, *ad loc.* ; Ovid, *Met.*, VIII, 871 foll. ; Palaiphatos, *de incred.*, 25 (24) ; Anton. Lib., 17. Cf. *Folk-Lore*, XXII, p. 461 ; Bompas, *Folklore of the Santal Parganas*, p. 136.

[53] Pherekydes, frag. 119 Jacoby ; see Willisch in Roscher, IV, col. 961.

[54] SPhB V, 11.

[55] Paus., X, 33, 9–10 ; see page 304.

[56] Apoll. Rhod., I, 23, 105, 146, 153, 156, 179, 211.

[57] Verg., *Aen.*, III, 19 foll.

[58] Homer, *Il.*, III, 6 foll. ; many refs. in later authors, e.g., Juvenal, III, 167, and the geographers, as Strabo, I, 2, 28 ; XVII, 2, 1 ; Mela, III, 81 (Parthey) ; Pliny, *N.H.*, IV, 44. See Tyson, *Philological Essay concerning the Pygmies of the Ancients* (suggesting that they were apes), London, Nutt, 1894 (re-issue, originally pub. 1699), with the valuable introduction by Andrew Lang.

[59] Petronius, 77, 6.

[60] Horace, *ars poet.*, 340. One would like to know the stories of *The Lamia's Tower* and *The Sun's Comb* alluded to by Tertullian (*aduers. Valent.*, 3).

[61] Apollod., III, 17 foll. ; Hygin., *fab.*, 136 ; cf. Pliny, *N.H.*, XXV, 14 ; *Etymol. Mag.*, *s.u.* ; for parallels, B.P., I, 128.

[62] Apollod., I, 96 foll.

[63] Schol., Hom., *Il.*, VII, 44 ; for more refs., see Engelmann in Roscher, II, col. 975.

[64] The riddle runs : scelere uehor, maternam carnem uescor, quaero fratrem meum, meae matris filium, uxoris meae uirum, nec inuenio.

[65] Aelian, *V.H.*, XIII, 2.

[66] Herod., III, 119, where see commentators ; Soph., *Antig.*, 904 foll., a passage regarded as spurious by some, but rightly retained in the text by Pearson. See Pischel in *Hermes*, XXVIII (1893), p. 465 foll.

[67] As Krates, frags. 14 and 15 Kock ; Telekleides, frag. 1 ; Pherekrates, frags. 108, 130 ; Aristophanes, frag. 508 ; Nikophon, frag. 13 ; Metagenes, frag. 6 ; Petronius, 45, 4.

[68] Cicero, *Tusc. disp.*, V, 61 ; Horace, *carm.*, III, 1, 17 ; Persius, *sat.*, III, 40 ; Plutarch, *de sera num. uind.*, 554 D.

[69] Dieuchidas *ap.* schol. Apoll. Rhod., I, 517 ; Apollod., III, 166.

[70] Ovid, *Met.*, IV, 256 foll.

[71] Horace, *Epp.*, I, 7, 29, where see commentators.

[72] Phaedrus, *append. fab.*, 3 ; Avianus, *fab.*, 22 ; Ovid, *Met.*, VIII, 618 foll., see Calder in *Discovery*, III (1922), p. 207; cf. page 304.

[73] Herod., I, 23–24 ; Ovid, *Fast.*, II, 79 foll. ; Plutarch, *sept. sap. conu.*, 160 E foll. ; Aelian, *N.A.*, XII, 45 ; and several others.

[74] Appuleius, *Metamorphoses, passim* ; Lucian, *Lucius* ; Augustine, *ciuit. Dei*, XVIII, 18.

[75] Petron., 45, 9, where see Friedländer.

[76] See further the notes of B.P. on the story.

[77] Pseudo-Arist., *hist. anim.*, IX, 615ª 19 ; Plut., *praec. ger. reip.*, 806 E ; Pliny, *N.H.*, X, 203.

[78] Plut., *quaest. Graec.*, 54.

[79] Apollod., III, 197 ; Anton. Lib., 41, 4–5 ; cf. Chapter IX, p. 263.

[80] Herod., II, 121, see commentators there ; add B.P., III, p. 395 ; *Telegonia*, epitome of Proclus (Vol. I, p. 57, Kinkel, p. 109 Allen) ; Pausanias, IX, 37, 3 ; Charax, *Hellenika*, frag. 5 (6) Jacoby (= schol. Arist., *Nubes*, 508).

[81] See B.P., I, p. 108–9 ; add G. 89 and 135 ; Cassius Dio, frag. 43, 29 (Vol. I, p. 170, Melber = Zonaras, VIII, 15, Vol. II, p. 216 Dindorf); cf. Cicero, *in Pisonem*, 43.

Additional to Note 46 : see J. Qvigstad, *Lappiske Eventyr og Sagn* (Oslo 1928), II, pp. 448–9.

Additional to Note 55 : the story of Beddgelert seems to be modern (E. Jones, 1794) ; see Jacobs, *Celtic Fairy Tales*, p. 262 foll.

Additional to Note 72 : for Baucis and Philemon, see now Fontenrose in *Univ. of Calif. Publications*, XIII, 4 (1945), pp. 93–120.

Additional to Note 2 : for an elaborate study of the story, see Jan-Öjvind Swahn, *The Tale of Cupid and Psyche*, Lund, 1955.

CHAPTER XI

ITALIAN PSEUDO-MYTHOLOGY

Quae ante conditam condendamue urbem poeticis magis decora fabulis quam incorruptis rerum gestarum monumentis traduntur.
—LIVY, *praefatio*, 6.

Traditions of times before Rome was founded or thought of, better suited to the fancies of a poet than to the scrupulous veracity of the historian.

THE earliest historians of Rome lived in the time of the Second Punic War. Hence, since the written materials which are known or reasonably supposed to have existed when Roman historiography began were few and scanty in the extreme,[1] our knowledge of the early history of the country must perforce depend on what the earlier Greek writers have to tell us, which is not much,[2] on the evidence of archaeology, which is most useful as far as it goes, but sorely needs a commentary, and on such traditions as Italian historians have preserved for us. The mythologist is concerned with these alone ; and he must share the disgust of the historian when he realizes that the overwhelming majority of them are not genuine popular native traditions at all, but comparatively late, artificial tales, put together either by Greeks or under Greek influence.

That there were no native Italian traditions is a proposition incredible in itself and directly contradicted by at least one scrap of evidence, the often-quoted statement of the elder Cato that ballads used to be sung at feasts in which the famous deeds of old days were related.[3] The contents of these Niebuhr imagined we might reconstruct from the accounts preserved to us in Livy and other writers concerning Romulus, Titus Tatius, and other figures of Roman legend ; but unfortunately, ever since Schwegler's critique of the older historian's theory, it has been generally recognized by all competent scholars who have examined the question that we are in no such fortunate position.[4] The existing traditions, for the most part, utterly lack all the characteristics of genuine popular fancy, whether dealing with myth or saga, and the Greek materials show all too plainly through the Italian covering. For the most part, the stories are a dry, pragmatical narrative of alleged facts, somewhat after the manner of a chronicle, and a little analysis shows that almost every incident is either an anticipation of some later real event, a bit of aetiology, or a borrowing ready-made of a Greek tale. At best, we can suppose that here and there a real fragment of popular Italian imagination has furnished part of the material, and here also we must be on our guard ; for the story may be indeed a popular one, but due to popular Greek fancy, not that of any Italian people.

In particular, this is true of the tales concerning the gods. Most of these can be rejected at once ; they are stories actually found in Greek authors or occur (as in Vergil) as episodes in poems on Greek models. Italian gods were vague personalities, with definite and limited functions, and are not thought of as marrying, having children, forming connexions of love or friendship with mortals, or doing any of the things which Greek imagination ascribed to the Olympians.[5] The borrowing was due partly to the wide appeal of the picturesque Greek anthropomorphism, partly to the very popular and early theory that all nations worshipped much the same gods, although the names might vary.[6] Less easy for us to grasp is the craze for supplying all nations with legends on the Greek pattern, and the incredible levity with which the later Greeks neglected the genuine local tales in favour of the products of their own fancy. Thus, in Egypt, the abundant mythology concerning Osiris is overlaid in some writers with an artificial legend copied from that of Dionysos ;[7] the Gauls are provided with an ancestor, the son of the sea-nymph Galateia ;[8] and even the Jews' traditions were replaced, for Greek readers, with an account of the departure from Egypt in which the authors of the book of Exodus would have recognized but little.[9] Unlike Egypt and Judaea, Italy had probably not reduced her traditions to writing, and in any case, the admiration for the learning of Greece and the docility with which her historical methods, especially the worst of them, were copied, were equalled only by the contempt felt by the old-fashioned Roman for the practical abilities of those degenerate Greeks whom he knew.

Some legends, which deal with the supposed founding by Greeks, or Trojans, of sundry Italian towns, have already been mentioned[10] : but the story of the foundation of Rome deserves separate treatment.

Aineias, in the *Iliad*, is rescued from imminent danger by Poseidon, usually unfriendly to Troy, who gives as his reason the fact that that hero is destined to be the future ruler of the Trojans ; and there was indeed a local legend in the Troad according to which a noble house was descended from him.[11] But it was not to be expected that so eminent a figure of epic tradition should be left unclaimed by the Italiote Greeks. Hence, possibly as early as Stesichoros, a tale was current according to which he sailed from Troy after the siege and, like his compatriot Antenor, went to some place in Italy, probably Kyme (Cumae).[12] Later, a series of shrines of Aphrodite were pointed out as having been founded by Aineias in his wanderings, which took him around the Peloponnesos to Epeiros, and so to Sicily and Italy, where he finally landed at Laurentum.[13]

It is noteworthy that of all the authors cited for this story not one is early. It is clearly a tissue of local temple-legends and other traditions put together by Hellenistic writers, and therefore not worth examining in detail in a work like this. The earliest author who distinctly stated that Rome was founded by Aineias was Timaios, but the tale soon won credence in Rome, where it seems to have been an article of faith, at least for diplomatic purposes, by the end of the First Punic War.[14] The earliest Roman writer to mention it, so far as surviving works go, is Cato the Elder.[15]

The developed tale, as Vergil tells it in the Aeneid, is as follows. Aeneas,—it is convenient to give his name its Latin form in dealing with this more or less Latinized story,—survived the fall of Troy, either fighting his way out, or somehow slipping through the Greek army, or simply allowed to go, whether because he had opposed the war (in one version he had betrayed Troy to them [16]), or through the admiration which his piety and valour excited among them. He then set sail, to find a new land wherein to settle with the surviving Trojans who followed him. After spending a short time in Thrace, he went to Delos, where he was bidden by the oracle to go to the land of his forefathers. Remembering that Dardanos, the ancestor of the Trojan royal family, came from Crete, he proceeded to that island. But pestilence broke out among his following, and his family gods, appearing in a vision, told him that Dardanos' original home was Italy, to which therefore he must go. Sailing from Crete, he arrived in Epeiros, where he found Helenos established as king, after the death of Neoptolemos, and married to Andromache. From him he received further particulars of his future adventures. He was to look for a place where he should see a white sow with thirty farrow. On his way to this place, which was somewhere on the farther coast of Italy, he was to visit the Sibyl at Cumae, who would tell him more. He had already, on the way to Epeiros, fallen in with the Harpies on the Stro- phades, and their chief, Kelaino, had told him that he should never found a city until hunger had made him and his men eat the very plates off which they fed. After a few minor adven- tures, he arrived in Sicily, where his kinsman Akestes received him hospitably. Here Anchises died. Next year he left Sicily, and now Vergil introduces an episode which is no part of the orthodox tradition, but possibly borrowed from Naevius or Varro.[17] A sudden storm, sent by Iuno, drives Aeneas upon the coast of Africa, near the site of Carthage. Here he and his men are hospitably received by Dido, or Elissa, foundress of Carthage, whom Venus causes to fall violently in love with Aeneas. When, after a stay of some months, he is at last warned by Iuppiter that he must go on his way, she in despair at his depar- ture kills herself. He now returns to Sicily, celebrates funeral games in honour of the anniversary of his father's death, and loses part of his fleet, which is set on fire by the women in his following, incited thereto by Iuno. With the remaining vessels and the best of his followers (the older and weaker have been left behind, under the protection of Akestes, to found a city in Sicily), he arrives at Cumae, where the Sibyl foretells his future struggles and triumph, but refers him to yet another authority, the beatified spirit of his own father. Under her guidance he penetrates to the lower world, gaining admittance by showing the famous golden bough, which it has been revealed to him where to find by doves sent by his mother to guide him to it. Anchises gives him a forecast of Roman history down to the accession of Augustus, and he returns to the upper world much cheered. Landing at the future site of Laurentum, he finds the sow and her farrow, and as he and his followers eat, they use flat cakes of bread for dishes, afterwards eating them and so fulfilling the Harpy's prophecy. He now enters into friendly relations with Latinus, the king of that part of Italy, who has been warned by an oracle to give his daughter in marriage to a foreigner. Turnus, prince of the Rutuli, claims to be the man of destiny, as he is partly of non-Italian origin, but Latinus favours Aeneas. A chance quarrel breaks out, and Aeneas finds him- self confronted with a confederation of the Rutuli, the Latins, and the following of Mezentius, the exiled tyrant of Caere. He however secures allies, the Etruscans under Tarchon, who have been warned to expect success against Mezentius only if a foreigner leads them, and Euandros, king of the Arkadian colony on the future site of Rome. After fierce fighting he is victorious, kills Turnus in single combat (Vergil's poem ends here) and proceeds to marry Lavinia, Latinus' daughter, after making a treaty of peace very favourable to the conquered Latins, who are to retain their name and customs, but accept from Aeneas the gods and sacred rites which he brings with him.[18]

In passing it may be mentioned that Dido seems to have been introduced into classical literature by Timaios. Her name appears to be Phoenician, and is perhaps that of a goddess. Her sister Anna has an obviously Semitic name (Hannah, ' the gracious one ') and is quite likely a goddess, not a woman ; compare the names Hannibal, Hanno, etc. Dido's other name, Elis(s)a, is plainly Semitic, and that of her husband, Sichaios or Sicharbas, is perhaps *zchar-ba'al*, ' Baal remembers '. The story referred to in *Aeneid*, I, 368, is a not unfamiliar folk-tale. Dido and her followers beg to be sold as much land as a bull's hide will surround ; they then cut the hide into very thin strips and so secure enough to build a citadel upon. Its application to this particular instance depends on the resemblance between the place-name Byrsa (' citadel ') at Carthage and the Greek βύρσα, a hide.[19]

Anna reappears in Ovid.[20] After various adventures and wanderings she arrives in Italy, where Aeneas meets her and commends her to the care of Lavinia. But the latter is jealous and plots against her. Warned by the ghost of Dido, she flies and is carried off and hidden by the river-god Numicius. Ovid clearly wished to connect her with the Italian (mostly Roman) goddess Anna Perenna, with whom of course she has nothing to do. Whether she is connected with the obscure deity Anna to whom a dedication has been found in Sicily,[21] does not appear. Silius Italicus copies Ovid, to whom the story of Anna's adventures is probably due.[22]

Aeneas's landing at Laurentum and founding of Lavinium are due to certain facts and theories of Italian cult. The two little towns Lavinium or Laurolavinium and Lanuvium were from very ancient times an important religious centre for Latium,[23] especially the former, where in historical times Roman magistrates used to perform certain ancient and traditional rites in honour of Vesta and the Penates. There can be little or no doubt that originally Vesta was simply the deity of the king's hearth, and the *di penates*, those guarding his storeroom. But in time these homely little deities acquired more importance, and as the *Vesta publica* and *Penates publici*, they incorporated in some sort the luck of the state or confederation. Furthermore, the speculations of mythologists connected the *penates publici* of Rome, on the one hand with the cults of Lavinium, on the other with the Samothracian divinities. Now between Troy and Samothrace there existed a traditional connexion. What then was more natural, for a late mythologizer, than to make a pious Trojan hero bring to Italy the cult of the Samothracian gods, that is, of the Penates ? [24]

The portent of the sow is perhaps a genuine local tradition, at least in its origin, for Varro says that the sow's body, preserved in brine, was still shown at Lavinium. [25] If we could be sure that this relic was really old, *i.e.*, older than the acceptance (by about the second century B.C.) of the tale of Aeneas' wanderings, and furthermore, if we could believe with any confidence that a word for a sow, *troia* [26], existed in early Latin, we should have an obvious starting-point for the saga ; but unhappily, we cannot be sure that the word is not very much later than the saga, and certainly the testimonies to the existence of the sow and of places in Italy called Troy are all later. [27] The number of the farrow, thirty, corresponds a little too closely to the traditional number of the cities in the Latin League to escape the suspicion of being a *uaticinium ex euentu*. As to the eating of the tables, it has been repeatedly suggested that this is to be connected with certain *mensae paniceae* used in Roman ritual. [28]

King Latinus is a figure as old as Hesiod ; in Vergil, he has a curiously artificial genealogy, Saturnus—Picus—Faunus and Marica—Latinus. All these are minor Italian deities, the most important being Saturnus (cf. *supra*, p. 43). Picus is the sacred woodpecker, the bird of Mars ; Faunus is, or the Fauni are, a sort of fairies, around whom gathered a little cult and a certain amount of picturesque superstition ; Marica is a local water-nymph. Among such vague figures Euhemerism raged unchecked, and most of them were converted into early kings of the Italian tribes. Since there was no foundation for the story either in history or in any real tradition, nearly every author remodelled it to suit himself ; thus Latinus is sometimes the friend of Aeneas, sometimes his more or less determined enemy ; Rome is founded now by his descendants, now by those of Aeneas (the marriage of the Trojan hero to Lavinia gets over this difficulty) ; sometimes Turnus appears as a party to the combat with the Trojans, sometimes he does not ; in some accounts Latinus is killed in the war, in others he survives ; and the causes of the quarrel are of the most various kind. [29]

Of the other participants in the war, Mezentius and Turnus appear for the first time in Cato, [30] according to whom Turnus was Latinus' ally against Aeneas, Latinus was killed, and Turnus sought the aid of Mezentius ; Aeneas and Turnus both hav-

ing perished, Ascanius, Aeneas' son, and Mezentius decided the
issue by a single combat in which the latter was killed. That
Mezentius, who appears as king of Caere in older authors, should
be exiled from his kingdom on account of his cruelty, is apparently
Vergil's own invention.[31] Camilla, the Amazonian heroine of
the latter half of the poem, who falls in battle against the Trojans,
cannot be proved to have any other origin than the poet's imagination, with details of course introduced from older descriptions
of Penthesileia or other such warrior-maids.[32]

Euandros (Evander), although as artificial a figure as any
of the rest, is at least not uninteresting as showing the growth
of these pseudo-sagas. He is an Arkadian, arrived at the head
of a small party of his countrymen at the place where Rome
was afterwards to stand. We can clearly see why this should
be so. In the first place, there was at Rome an ancient festival,
the Lupercalia, for which, as usual, an explanation was sought
in Greek ritual. The only parallel that occurred to the minds
of Roman and Greek theorists was the Arkadian Lykaia, which
had a name suggestive of wolves, like the Lupercalia, and was
connected with Pan, as the Lupercalia were connected, or supposed to be connected, with Faunus. Add to this the convic-
tion that there was a strong Greek element in Rome, and the
conclusion was patent ; Rome had been visited at some time by
colonists from Arkadia. If further proof were required, the
name of the Palatine Mount suggested, to the easily satisfied
etymologists of those days, the Arkadian hero Pallas and the
Arkadian town Pallanteion. Perhaps the name Euandros
itself was invented to meet the necessities of the theory. It
has been suggested that, as it could be taken to mean 'Good-
man', it is a sort of translation of Faunus ('the Favourable
one'). If it is pure invention, I should rather take it as meaning
'Strong-man', a not inappropriate name for the earliest settler
of a city whose name suggested the Greek ῥώμη (strength).[33]

Thus the many resemblances between Latin and Greek which
they rightly perceived, and the many more which fanciful etymologies suggested, were to be attributed to the coming of Greek-
speaking Arkadians, who had brought with them the rites of
Pan and the (Chalkidian) Greek alphabet which the Romans
used, and we use after them. Aeneas and his Trojans accounted
neatly for the fact that the Romans manifestly were not wholly
Greek in speech or ways, and that they had the supposedly Trojan
cult of the Penates. It remained only to construct a genealogy
which should bring in the Greek and the non-Greek elements,
and of such there was no lack. Latinus had had a wife or a

11

sister called Rhome, or Aeneas a son named Rhomos, and after
him or her the city, founded by Aeneas or by contemporaries
of his, had been named.[34] For, to those versed in the lore of
Greek mythological historians, it was evident that, as Corinth
was named after Korinthos, Chaironeia after the hero Chairon,
the Chaonians of Epeiros after Chaon, and Italy itself after the
prehistoric king Italos, so Rome must have been founded by,
or named after, some one called Rhomos, or Rhome, or,—here the
native Roman antiquaries added their contribution,—Romulus,
a word which simply means ' Roman ', and is derived from *Roma*
as *Siculus*, a Sicilian, from *Sicilia*. It was not until an attempt
was made to introduce dates that a difficulty arose.

Aeneas was a quite datable person, for it was a received
doctrine, as a result of Alexandrian researches into genealogy,
that Troy fell about the year 1190 B.C. of our reckoning ; while
the Roman chronologers[35] had worked out the date of their
city's foundation as being somewhere in the eighth century B.C. ;
the now traditional date, 753, was by no means universally
accepted, especially at first. But on this date, or anywhere
near it, Aeneas could not possibly have founded Rome, for he
came between four and five hundred years too early. The gap
had somehow to be filled up. The method adopted to fill it
satisfied another requirement. Alba Longa, on the Alban Mount,
had been, according to a tradition apparently long established,[36]
the head-centre of the Latin League, the ancient confederacy
of which Rome later became the chief. It was therefore plausible
(and perhaps historically correct as well) to suppose that Rome
was a colony of Alba. Hence a list of Alban kings, of whom
hardly more than the names need be mentioned.

The usual list, given by Livy and Dionysios, is as follows.
After Aeneas' death, which occurred in the third year after his
arrival, his son Ascanius became king, and after thirty years
founded Alba Longa, as the population of Lavinium was growing
too large and required an outlet. This Ascanius is variously
stated to have been the son of Aeneas by Kreusa (this is Vergil's
account), or by Lavinia. In the former account, he had a half-
brother, called Silvius because Lavinia, fearing for the safety of
her child, took refuge in the woods after Aeneas' death and there
bore his posthumous son. In other accounts, Silvius is the son
of Ascanius. After Silvius came a line of kings, father succeed-
ing son without disturbance, thus : Aeneas Silvius, Latinus
Silvius, Alba, Kapetos (or Epytos, or Atys), Kapys, Kalpetos
or Capetus, Tiberinus (after whom the Tiber, formerly called
Albula, was named, because he was drowned in it), Agrippa,

Amulius (or Romulus), Aventinus, Proca, and Amulius. There
are other and shorter lists.[37]

The name Silvius is probably the result of the earlier figure
of Rea Silvia. Aeneas, Latinus, Kapys and Kalpetos are all
names borrowed, with or without some slight change, from other
and older parts of the tradition ; Romulus is an anticipation
of his better-known descendant, Tiberinus and Aventinus are
formed from the names of places. Agrippa may owe his origin
to a desire to compliment Augustus' great minister. No time
need be spent over these artificial phantoms, to whom not even
Vergil[38] could undertake to give any semblance of life and reality.

The last name of this line rises a little way out of the ghostly
obscurity of the rest. Amulius, according to the story, was not
the rightful king, but had driven from the throne his virtuous
brother Numitor, whose sons he had killed. Numitor had a
daughter, Rea Silvia, otherwise known as Ilia (the latter, probably, because she was originally Aeneas' daughter, as she still
is in Ennius [39] ; the origin of the former name is doubtful, but the
resemblance to the name of the goddess Rhea is perhaps no
accident [40]). Amulius made her a Vestal virgin, that she might
have no offspring ; but fate was against him, and Mars got her
with twin children. When these were born, Amulius either
drowned the mother (who thereupon became a river-goddess,
and wife of the river-god Tiber [41]) or imprisoned or beheaded or
got rid of her in some manner ; the children were flung into the
Tiber. But the river was in flood, and the children, who were
in a small vessel of some kind, drifted ashore unharmed, near
the foot of the Palatine. Here a she-wolf heard them crying,
and leaving her den in the Lupercal, suckled them. A woodpecker (Mars' bird) also attended them,[42] bringing them food in
its bill. Thus strangely nursed they lay for some time, until
the herdsman of the royal cattle, Faustulus, noticed them and
took them home, where his wife, Acca Larentia, brought them
up. Their high lineage appeared, however, in their valour and
enterprise, and soon they rose to a position of eminence among
the country lads, some of whom they gathered about them into
a sort of retinue. One day, a quarrel having broken out with
Numitor's shepherds, Remus, the younger twin, was captured
and taken to Alba, where he was handed over to Numitor for
judgement. Faustulus, in desperation, told Romulus, the elder
twin, all that he knew or guessed, and the latter hurried to Alba
to rescue his brother. Numitor meanwhile, struck by the noble
appearance of Remus, was making inquiries, and when Romulus
came on the scene, recognition soon followed. The grandfather

and grandsons plotted together ; Amulius was assailed and killed, and the kingdom restored to Numitor.[43]   The twins then decided not to remain in Alba, but to found a new settlement at the place where they had been saved from death.   The question therefore arose which of them should be king of it.   The gods must be asked whether Romulus or Remus should be king, and consequently, whether the new foundation should be called Roma or Remora.   Romulus took up his station on the Palatine to look for an omen from the flight of birds, one of the commonest Italian forms of divination ; Remus in like manner went to the Aventine, a little way down stream.   After a long wait Remus saw six vultures, one of the most important of birds in augury ; but shortly after that, Romulus saw twelve, and was adjudged the victor.[44]

Romulus now proceeded to build a town on the Palatine, of which hill, apparently, he took formal possession by hurling his lance at it from the Aventine, a truly heroic throw, for the shortest distance from one hill to the other is some 250 yards.   A cornel tree, sprung from the lance, which had taken root on the Palatine, was shown in later days.[45]   Remus contemptuously jumped over the new-made walls, for which he was slain by Romulus, or by one of his followers.   Being now sole and undisputed sovereign of the little community, Romulus provided himself with more followers by opening, on the Capitol, a sanctuary (asylum—the word is pure Greek and has no Italian equivalent), to which landless and outcast men soon flocked from all parts.   But a new difficulty arose ; the neighbouring states rejected with scorn all offers of intermarriage, and the Romans themselves had no women.   In order to get wives for his men, therefore, Romulus invited several neighbouring peoples, in particular the Sabines, to witness circus-games which he and his men were celebrating, and to bring with them their wives and children.   In the midst of the games, the Romans seized and carried off all the unmarried girls.   War ensued ; the smaller states were easily defeated, but the Sabines, under their king, Titus Tatius, were less readily disposed of.   They attacked Rome, and laid siege to the Capitol, which served as an outpost. Tarpeia, the daughter of its commandant, promised to betray the citadel to them in return for what they wore on their left arms, meaning their gold arm-rings.   They fulfilled their promise, in disgust at her treachery, by crushing her under their shields.[46] However, the Capitol was theirs, and using it as a base, they attacked the Palatine, whose garrison met them in the Forum, then a marshy and undrained strip of land.   At first the Romans had the worst of it, when Romulus vowed a temple to Iuppiter Stator (' Stayer of Flight ') and the Sabines in their turn began to give back. As both sides rallied for a last effort, the kidnapped women, many of them by this time mothers and carrying their infants in their arms, rushed in between the armies, begging their husbands and fathers to make peace. This appeal was effective ; the Sabines moved to Rome, where they took up their quarters on the Capitol ; Romulus and Titus Tatius ruled together until the latter was killed in a private quarrel. Finally, Romulus himself, while reviewing his host, disappeared in a sudden and violent thunderstorm, and subsequently appeared in a glorified shape to a citizen, one Iulius Proculus, to say that he was now a god, and to be worshipped under the name of Quirinus.

It was only to be expected that a story so full of marvels should be rationalized. According to various theorists of antiquity, the Twins were not begotten by Mars, but by Amulius, who had disguised himself as the god to ruin his niece ; [47] the boys were not exposed, but taken care of by Numitor, who gave them a good education in the town of Gabii, where Romulus learned his excellent knowledge of augury ; [48] or, they were exposed, but found by Faustulus, whose wife, being an immoral woman, was nicknamed *lupa* (prostitute), hence the fable of the she-wolf (*lupa*) which suckled them. Romulus did not vanish in a thunderstorm, but was secretly killed by the envious senators, who regarded him as a tyrant, and who took advantage of the sudden tempest to tear him in pieces, which they hid.[49] This rubbish need not trouble us long.

If, however, we apply the more sober canons of modern criticism, it is at once obvious that we have to do with an aetiological myth, given its present shape by some one (or more probably, by a series of persons) well acquainted with Rome, its topography and ancient ritual. The place where the Twins were washed ashore was marked by the Lupercal, a cave associated with the Lupercalia, and by a venerable fig-tree, known as the Ficus Ruminalis or Fig of Suckling ; in Italy, as elsewhere, the milky juice of the fig appears to have been much esteemed as a fertility-charm, and branches of figs were used in the ancient ritual of the Nonae Caprotinae.[50] The charitable Faustulus and his wife are two well-known deities, Faunus or Faustulus and Acca Larentia ; the she-wolf is the sacred beast of Mars, as is also the woodpecker. As to the famous rape of the Sabines, Roman marriage involved a pretence of seizing and carrying off the bride (' marriage by capture '),[51] and certain old customs affecting women were regarded as honours done to them, by way of consolation for the violence they had suffered.[52] The death of Remus illustrates the sanctity of the city wall by an outstanding instance ; brother must not spare brother if he is guilty of impiety towards it.[53] The Sabines serve to account for the real existence of a strong Sabine (Osco-Sabellian) element in the population of Rome,[54] and incidentally for the almost forgotten ritual which went on somewhere on or near the Capitol, at what was supposed to be a grave and was probably the shrine of an ancient goddess, Tarpeia.[55] The supposition that Romulus had partners in his rule, first his brother and then Titus Tatius, was clearly intended to throw light on the fact that nearly all Roman magistrates, from the consuls down, numbered either two or a multiple of two. Finally, the hero's deification cleared up another difficulty—the existence, alongside of Mars, of another warlike deity, Quirinus.

But we have still to ask whether this is Italian aetiology, or whether we have to deal with Greek ideas applied to local material. To begin at the beginning, the statement that Mars was the father of the children is most suspicious ; all our evidence goes to prove that Italian deities were not supposed to beget children either upon each other or on mortal women ; the one folktale likely to be Italian in which anything of the kind happens is one in which no god plays any original part. Then, the whole legend of the exposure and miraculous deliverance of the twins is very Greek in atmosphere ; even if it be urged that stories of this kind are world-wide, and that we may have to do with a native tale somewhat Hellenized, it is suspicious that the boys should be twins, since twins are particularly apt to be founders of cities in Greek legend.[56] The transformation of Romulus into a god, and the interpretation of Tarpeia as a dead woman, not a goddess, are thoroughly Greek, for hero-cult is a Greek and not a Roman characteristic.[57] The reducing of Faustulus and Acca Larentia to human rank is a piece of Greek Euhemerism, and the rest of the legend is so like Greek aetiological myths, especially the later ones, that we become suspicious of it even where we are not able, as we often are, to produce close Greek parallels to details of the story.[58] We may, therefore, safely dismiss at least the bulk of this famous tale as being a foreign invention, and therefore relatively late.

It is, however, at least in part, absolutely fairly early ; in the year 295 B.C. two magistrates, Gnaeus Ogulnius and Quintus Ogulnius, curule aediles, raised a considerable amount of money from fines inflicted on usurers. With this they performed several public works ; among others they either erected an image of the she-wolf with the twins or else added images of the twins to an existing statue of a she-wolf.[59] At the beginning of the third century B.C., therefore, some legend was current which concerned children and a protecting she-wolf ; and it seems but natural to suppose that it was the tale of Romulus and Remus. But in 295 B.C., Greek influence was no new thing in Rome ; the Sibylline Books, which meant the cult of Apollo, had long been in the possession of the Roman government, and the first *lectisternium*, or exposal to public adoration, in Greek fashion, of statues of the gods reclining at table, had taken place more than a hundred years before, in 399 ; [60] hence if the Ogulnii believed a Greek tale, that is no more to be wondered at than that Shakespeare used Italian novels for his plots.

The reigns of the remaining six kings (the number seven, being the sacred number of Apollo, is in itself suspicious) are chiefly filled with pseudo-historical incidents,—wars, treaties, laws and so forth,—which become somewhat more credible as we reach the last three, the Etruscan dynasty of the Tarquins, which in all probability had a real existence, although the details of its rise and fall are patently fictitious. The few events which savour of the marvellous, or seem to have, somehow, an origin in popular imagination, are now to be discussed.

The second king, Numa Pompilius the Sabine, has at least a good Italian name, which may well be Sabine in origin. In him we find a very familiar figure of folklore, the inventor or originator of customs, and so far as that goes, he might be a product of Italian popular imagination. However, this sort of culture-hero is so very common in Greece that in so Hellenized an atmosphere it is more likely that his exploits are nothing but a Greek or Greek-taught explanation of Roman phenomena. He is said to have kept the peace throughout his long reign, and to have originated the greater part of the ceremonies of the Roman state religion. As to the source of his inspiration, three tales are told, all or some of which are often found together. The most obviously Greek is that he was a disciple of Pythagoras, some of the Pythagorean ' symbols ' or tabus resembling Roman ritual prescriptions and thus no doubt giving rise to the story. However, as Numa was supposed, in the received chronology, to have lived long before Pythagoras was born,[61] this tale was generally rejected in later times. A second story, and by far the most popular, was that he had a divine wife or counsellor, the nymph Egeria,[62] whom he used to meet by night outside the Porta Capena (the southern gate of historical Rome, leading to the Appian Way), in the grove of the Camenae. Conceivably, this may be genuine Italian, for there is nothing peculiar to Greece, or to any other country, in the idea that a man renowned for his wisdom got advice and help from some deity. Naturally later rationalizers busied themselves with the story, and declared that it was a clever invention of Numa's to lend weight to his decrees. The third tale, as we have it, concerns only one of Numa's ordinances, the *procuratio* or expiatory ritual to be adopted when anything is struck by lightning. It is to the effect that Egeria advised him to catch Faunus and Picus, two fairy-like woodland gods, and ask their help. He did so, by leaving wine near a spring from which they commonly drank, and so obliged them to show him how to summon Iuppiter him-, self. The god proceeded to name the materials of which the expiatory sacrifice was to be composed. He demanded a head ; here Numa interrupted him with the words, ' of garlic '. Iuppiter continued, ' Human——' and again Numa intervened with ' Hair ' ; the god tried again, and demanded ' the life——', ' of a sprat ', interrupted Numa ; Iuppiter was amused, and consented to have his warning thunderbolts expiated at this cheap rate.[63]   The first part of this story is simply Midas and Seilenos ;[64] the second has all the flavour of a genuine folktale, full of the rough humour and plays upon words which we find in the earliest extant Roman comedies ; it may well be native, and it may even be that the original characters were Numa and Iuppiter. The origin is obvious ; it is an aetiological story, intended to explain why such curious materials as garlic, hair, and live sprats were used in this rite. In substance it may well be correct ; the thunder is induced to spare mankind by being given something like a man, namely a living creature, associated with a *caput* (=head, whether of an animal or of garlic ; also life, personality) and with an actual part (the hair) of a human being.

Iuppiter, by a further act of his grace, caused to fall from heaven a mysterious shield, *ancile*. Numa, fearing lest this treasure be stolen (for it was revealed to him that it was a *pignus imperii*, or pledge of sovranty, the mascot or luck of the State, in other words), employed a skilled smith, one Mamurius, to counterfeit it eleven times over. Hence there were in future twelve sacred shields, which were used by the Salii, a very ancient college of priests, for their sacred war-dances.[65]   This Mamurius stipulated that for his pains he should have his name included in the hymn of the Salii.[66]   A story, preserved only in late authors whom we have here no means of checking, adds, that either to do him honour (Servius) or in commemoration of a quarrel in which he was driven out of the city (Lydus), the following ceremonial was yearly performed ; a man dressed in skins was driven out with rods, and he was called Mamurius. Here we have, in all probability, the wide-spread rite of driving out Winter, or Death, or one of the many forms which the worn-out vegetation-spirit assumes, as is demonstrated at length in the *Golden Bough* ; but whether or not the rite is old at Rome, and consequently whether the stories about Mamurius were made up to account for it, or his name introduced later into the ritual (as, for instance, that of Judas has been introduced into many European festival customs of this kind, and that of Guy Fawkes into the well-known English popular ritual of November 5) we cannot tell. Certain it is that the words *mamuri ueturi*, whatever they may mean, occurred in the hymn of the Salii.[67] As to the shields, we know that they were of a shape characteristic of the Bronze Age, viz., something like the Arabic figure 8. No doubt those preserved at Rome were of very respectable anti-quity, and they may have been originally imported ; either of these circumstances would be reason enough for supposing them to be divine.

The next reign, that of Tullus Hostilius, is marked by one famous legend.[68] It was agreed that a war between Rome and Alba should be decided by a fight between chosen champions ; whichever state's representatives lost should become the subjects of the other. The Romans were represented by triplets, the Horatii, and the Albans also by triplets, the Curiatii. After a long and doubtful combat the latter were all killed, while one of the Horatii survived. On returning home, he was met at the gate by his sister, who had been betrothed to one of the Curi-atii. On seeing her brother wearing a garment she had her-self made for her betrothed, she wailed ; for which lack of pat-riotism her brother killed her then and there. He was accused of murder before two judges appointed by the king, condemned, but allowed to appeal to the people, who acquitted him. He was then ordered to purify himself from the ritual taint of homi-cide, which he did by passing with veiled head under a beam, fixed across one of the narrow streets of the town. Here we have, beyond reasonable doubt, an artificial combination of several bits of aetiology. A group of five ancient tombs lay not far from Rome in the direction of Alba ; the story of the fight of six champions and the death of five of them would furnish this monument with the necessary legend. Another tomb stood near the Porta Capena ; Horatius' unfortunate sister provided it with a named occupant. A prototype was wanted for that fun-damental feature of Roman criminal jurisprudence, the trial on appeal before the people. Horatius furnished an ideal ' hard case ', in which the sovran prerogative of mercy might be exercised, and attention paid to mitigating circumstances. Finally, it would seem that there really existed a beam called the *tigillum sororium*, and near by, an altar of Iuno Sororia ; both these names were naturally, though wrongly, explained by a reference to a sister (*soror*) ; [69] the ritual connected with them was in the hands of the clan of the Horatii, and either was or might be taken to be purificatory ; the supposition of an ancient atonement for blood-guilt accounted for all this satisfactorily. We have, then, a most ingenious legend, plainly the work of some antiquarian who possessed not only good information but considerable imaginative ability. Of a folktale there is no trace.

Tullus finally ended his life in an ill-judged attempt to stay a pestilence by certain mysterious rites to Iuppiter Elicius, the god whom Numa had successfully evoked under the same title. A thunderbolt destroyed him and his house. [70] Clearly this is a moral tale, of a sort familiar among all peoples who believe in magico-religious rites of an esoteric kind ; he met his end by meddling with matters which were not for laymen. I see no need to conclude from this that Roman kings were supposed to have specially close relations to deity, but rather the contrary.

Coming down to the Etruscan dynasty,—for the fourth king, Ancus Marcius, is of no interest for our purpose,—we find several legends, most of which cluster around the sixth king, Servius Tullius. It would seem that we have here a certain amount of real popular tradition ; he is consistently represented as a mild and well-beloved ruler, having the interests of the common people at heart ; and he was identified in antiquity with an Etruscan hero, Mastarna, who to judge from the little Etruscan evidence we have was a man of many and romantic adventures. [71]

His birth was portentous. There suddenly appeared in the hearth-fire of the palace a shape like that of the male organ of generation. A slave-woman, Ocrisia or Ocresia, recently taken prisoner at the capture of the city of Corniculum, where her husband had been of the royal blood, was the first to see this wonder, and reported it to the king (Tarquinius Priscus), who after taking counsel with his queen, Tanaquil, and other experts in divination, left Ocrisia alone, dressed like a bride, with the hearth-fire. She conceived in some mysterious manner, and in due time bore the future king, Servius Tullius. We need have no hesitation in recognizing here a genuine folktale, for we find it again, in a different setting, in the Vergilian commentator Servius. At the site of the town of Praeneste, a girl was sitting before a fire when a spark fell into her bosom ; she conceived, and bore a notable hero, who founded Praeneste, after a series of adventures, culminating in the appearance of a supernatural fire which surrounded him.   In like manner, Servius' divine parentage was recognized when one day, as he slept, a fire played harmlessly around his head. [72]

The royal couple, perceiving that Servius was no common slave-child, [73] gave him every care and attention, and in due time he, and not the king's sons, succeeded to the throne.   Here he was helped, like Numa, by a divine consort, the goddess Fortuna, or perhaps we ought rather to say Nortia, an Etruscan goddess who was often identified with her. [74]   A natural consequence of this (or rather, one of the factors which led to the invention of this particular tale) was that many of the older shrines of Fortuna, whose cult, although not native Roman, became very popular with the lower classes especially, were supposed to be foundations of this king.   At last, however, his own daughter Tullia, who had married one of the sons of Tarquinius, plotted against him with her husband ; Servius was killed, and as his body lay in one of the streets, Tullia drove her carriage over it, thus giving the place the name of Vicus Sceleratus, or Street of Sin. [75]

The last king, Tarquinius Superbus, need not detain us long. It is of no interest to the mythologist as such that he is said to have oppressed the people (hence his title, practically=the Tyrant), and the story of his taking of Gabii [76] is merely an adaptation of two well-known episodes in Herodotos.   His fall is coupled, indeed, with one of the most famous tales in the world, that of Lucretia, but this is at once so familiar from its immortal treatment by Shakespeare and so divorced from anything genuinely ancient Roman or Italian, that it need not be told here. [77]

Two republican stories deserve attention.   The first is that of Genucius Cipus.   He was a praetor, and as he went forth to war, suddenly horns grew upon his head.   On consulting a diviner, he was assured that he would become king on his return to the city.   Rather than destroy the Republican constitution, he went into exile.   The grateful state put up, in commemoration of this self-sacrifice, a bronze effigy of a horned head over the gate by which he went out.   Here we have an unusually elaborate bit of aetiologizing ; behind this story there is apparently nothing but the effigy of a horned human head, a type not uncommon in Etruscan art.   Why it came to be called Genucius Cipus we do not know ; the use of horns to signify power is not uncommon in antiquity. [78]

More famous is the fine story of Marcus Curtius.   In the midst of the Forum there suddenly appeared a great chasm, and the diviners stated that it would never close until that in Rome which was of most worth was used to fill it. Curtius, perceiving what was meant, mounted his horse and plunged in ; at this sacrifice of a valiant patriot, the chiefest treasure of Rome, the chasm closed. Its traces formed in after-times the *lacus Curtius*, a depression of no great size in the Forum, no doubt a remnant of the days when it was little better than a swamp. For those who found this tale too romantic, there was another ; in the fight between Romulus and the Sabines, one of the latter, a chieftain called Mettius Curtius, was bogged at that point and rescued with some difficulty.[79]

Reversing the general plan of this book, I now proceed to consider the tales told of Italian gods. The crop of non-Greek stories is but scanty, and among those only one or two can claim to be in any way native and popular.

Of Ianus, the god or spirit of the doorway,[80] few stories are told, because he had no Greek equivalent and therefore no ready-made mythology. Ovid has indeed one quaint tale concerning him which starts from his double face. When shown in human form at all, Ianus is simply a two-faced head, either by itself, or, in later art, awkwardly fitted upon a body. Therefore, he can see behind him. There was a nymph, Carna by name, who had beguiled many eager suitors by bidding them go before her into a cave, and then running away from them once their backs were turned. This scheme, naturally, failed with Ianus, who then gave her, in return for her favours, the power to chase away certain nocturnal vampire-like creatures known as *striges*, a gift which she put to good use in saving from their attacks the infant son of Proca, presumably the Alban king of that name.[81] The story is certainly the invention of Ovid himself, or some one not much earlier, as is shown by the confusion of Carna (really a very obscure deity who had a festival on June 1) with a cult-associate of Ianus, the spirit of the door-hinge (*cardo*), Cardea.

When the Sabines made their attack on the Capitol, as a result of Tarpeia's treachery, Ianus came to the aid of the Romans, assisted by the local fountain-nymphs, and barred the assailants' way with a sudden outburst of boiling water. The story would seem to go back, in part at any rate, to Varro, and to have for its *raison d'être* two place-names, the *porta Ianalis* or Gate of Ianus, which was always open, and the Lautolae (washing-places), near the double arch or *ianus* in the Forum (not far from the present Arch of Septimius Severus), where, it was said, there had once been hot springs. It is a not improbable suggestion[82] that,

since Latin commonly speaks of ' closing ' or ' opening ' a fountain or other supply of water, Ianus may really have been thought
of occasionally as associated with water-deities.   It is in this
capacity that Ovid represents him as being, by the obscure goddess Venilia, the father of the nymph Canens.[83]

As might be expected, Ianus was euhemerized into an early king
of the region around Rome, or a benevolent foreigner who for some
reason came to Italy in very ancient times and taught the inhabitants
agriculture, among other things.   Thus humanized, he is often brought
into relations with the euhemerized Saturn, to whom in some variants
he shows kindness and hospitality.[84]

Iuppiter seems to touch the Aeneas-saga at one point in a
way which left its impression on something more than literature.
There was a cult of Iuppiter Indiges on the river Numicius, and
the story appears to have gained some credence that this was no
other than Aeneas, who had disappeared there after a battle and
henceforth received divine honours.[85]   Another vagary of identification is rather amusing, from the amount of nonsense that
has been written about it.   A few late Greek authors gravely
inform us that Picus, of whom we shall speak presently, ' is
also called Zeus '.   It is not worth while to weary the reader
with a list of the card-castles which have been built on this
slenderest of foundations ; the origin of the blunder has been
acutely pointed out by Principal Halliday.[86]   Vergil, in the
Aeneid, gives Latinus the pedigree Saturn—Picus—Faunus,
which he doubtless got from an earlier author ; some sciolist
appears to have got hold of this genealogy and gravely to have
concluded that if Picus was the son of Saturn, and Saturn the
Latin name of Kronos, Picus must be the Latin name of Zeus,
since he did not appear to be either Poseidon or Hades.

With Iuppiter, in Graeco-Roman cult and in hellenizing
mythology, but not in pure Italian cult, Iuno is connected.   Of
her, Ovid has a very pretty tale, which probably represents
his own fanciful working over of some folk-story.   Iuno (*i.e.*,
Hera ; the whole setting of the tale is, as Preller-Jordan rightly
say, Greek) was very angry at the birth of Athena without
mother.   Determining to work a parallel miracle herself, she
met Flora and told her of her plight ; Flora gave her a certain
magical flower, the touch of which made her pregnant, and in
due time Mars was born.[87]   That there was some tale in Italy
of a wonderful flower which could make a barren woman conceive, we may well believe, although even that is not necessary,
for it may equally well be Greek ; but for the rest, the story

depends on a few facts of cult, namely, that Iuno's festival, the Matronalia, was on the first of March (Mars' month), and that, being a goddess of the life of women, she might easily be imagined to be a mother herself, if she was conceived as having human form at all. Add to this the Greek genealogy which makes Hera mother of Ares, and the tale of her production of Hephaistos without father, and the rough material for the story is complete. Flora is the goddess of flowering or blossoming plants (*flos, florere*).

Of Mars there is told a curious tale which has been ingeniously handled by Usener. Mars, says Ovid, was enamoured of Minerva, and begged Anna Perenna to act as go-between. She put him off as long as possible, and finally told him that Minerva consented. But on unveiling his bride, Mars discovered that she was not Minerva, but hideous old Anna, and the gods had a hearty laugh at his discomfiture.

That there is, lurking somewhere in this story, a popular element, no folklorist doubts. The disguising of someone else as the bride is one of the commonest of European wedding-customs, whatever its ultimate origin may be, and so it is suggested that in the original story Mars went on with his wooing and ultimately won Minerva, or, much more likely, Nerio, who is known to have been his cult-partner and is sometimes identified with Minerva.[88] This is a quite intelligible legend to have grown out of a perfectly well-known spring-rite, the sacred marriage.[89]

But on closer examination this appears quite untenable. In the first place, we have no sort of proof that any Roman deity is thought of as marrying at all;[90] if we suppose this difficulty got over, we have no reason whatever, outside the details given by Ovid and plainly depending on his own fancy, for supposing that Anna Perenna, or any other deity, was thought of as being old and decrepit; and finally, there is not an atom of evidence that she was in any way associated with Mars in cult. The story can be easily explained; Ovid, or some one before him, finding the festival of Anna the year goddess (*annus*) on the fifteenth day of Mars' month (*i.e.*, the first full moon of the year, which began on March 1 originally), amused himself by bringing these two deities somehow into conjunction. The material was very likely furnished by the author's knowledge of some popular custom or folktale (not necessarily Italian) and all he did was to apply the incidents to Mars, Nerio-Minerva, and Anna Perenna, instead of to named or unnamed human beings.

Hercules is a foreigner, and to some extent brought his mythology with him, for Italy seems to have been full of tales concerning his wanderings on the eventful journey back from Spain ; some have been treated elsewhere, for they are obviously pure Greek.[91] But one or two stories are possibly native, although we have no proof that they are popular, and they do not seem to correspond to anything in native ritual. Apart from the fact that his numerous children included Pallas, son of Euandros' daughter,[92] after whom the Palatine was named, and Latinus, there is the famous tale of his fight with Cacus. As Hercules rested on the future site of Rome, this brigand or monster, who lived in a cave on the Aventine, or in some other retired spot, took a fancy to some of the cattle of Geryon which Hercules had brought back with him, and proceeded to carry them off. Dragging them tail-foremost to his cave, he hid them there, only to be betrayed by their lowing when Hercules finally began to move off with the rest and the stolen beasts answered the bellowing of their mates. Hercules then attacked him, forced his way into the cave, killed him, and got back the cattle. Before leaving Rome, Hercules gave directions for his own worship there, and also introduced into the old and savage rite of human sacrifice (that of the Argei) the humane modification that in future puppets, not real human victims, were to be used. Needless to say, among the numerous founders of Rome are certain followers of his whom he left behind there.[93] It is also needless to mention that Cacus appears in a more or less rationalized form, according to the taste of the author who tells the story.

It is of some interest to note that in all probability Cacus is a very old Roman deity. He is said, in some variants, to have had a sister Caca who in later times was worshipped in a way reminiscent of the cult of Vesta ;[94] and although his cave is said to have been on the Aventine, the Palatine preserves a memorial of him in the ancient Scalae Caci, or staircase of Cacus, cut into the rock. It is far from unlikely that the primeval settlement on the Palatine worshipped a pair of fire-deities, Cacus and Caca, god and goddess of the communal hearth, as Vesta in later times was of that of Rome.

Of Vesta herself several stories of miracles are reported. Thus, when the Vestal Aemilia found herself under grave suspicion of impiety because the holy fire of the goddess, for which she was responsible, but which had been under the charge of a novice, had gone out, she appealed to Vesta to prove her innocence, and therewith flung a strip of her linen robe on the cold ashes, which immediately caught fire. Another Vestal, Tuccia, was accused of unchastity, and cleared herself by carrying water in a sieve from the Tiber.[95] But miracles of this kind (ἐπιφάνειαι, ἀρεταί) are hardly mythology ; they continued to be told of the various gods, much as they are still told at the shrines of popular saints. More interesting are the stories clustering around the *penus Vestae*, a sort of cupboard in her round shrine in the Forum, in which were kept several very holy objects, and which no man⁹⁶ might ever approach. One of these holy things was said to be the Palladium itself, brought there by Aeneas' follower Nautes, who had had it from Diomedes.⁹⁷ So sacred was it that even the pious *pontifex maximus*, Lucius Caecilius Metellus, when in the year 241 B.C. he made his way into the *penus* during a fire to rescue it and the other relics, paid for his involuntary sacrilege with his eyesight. Of Vesta herself, Ovid gives us a feeble attempt at a legend ; Priapos one day found her asleep, and would have molested her, but that his ass brayed and woke her up, since when the ass has been Vesta's chosen favourite among beasts. It is superfluous to comment on the taste of an author who associates with so ancient a goddess a deity who did not reach even Greece, to say nothing of Rome, until the Macedonian period.⁹⁸

The Penates had their legend of a miracle, apart from the story that they were originally fetched by Aeneas from Troy. On an attempt being made to transfer their ancient and very holy images from their original site at Lavinium to Alba Longa or to Rome, they vanished and were found again in their old places,⁹⁹ where finally they were allowed to remain without further molestation.

Fortuna has already been mentioned in connexion with Servius Tullius. There was an ancient statue of her at Rome which for some reason, perhaps to prevent its holiness from dissipating, was kept veiled. The popular explanation, or what seems to be such, was that the goddess was ashamed of her favours to a mortal, and so kept her veil over her face.¹⁰⁰

A very ancient cult, much influenced in later times by the Greek ritual of Damia, imported from Tarentum, was that of the Bona Dea. In her worship no man might be present, no myrtle might be used, and also no wine ; or at least, if wine were present it must be referred to as milk and the vessel which contained it called a honey-jar. Of these tabus, which although interesting are nothing out of the way in an ancient cult of a fertility-power, the following explanation is given in various authors ; the Bona Dea was the wife, or the daughter, of Faunus, and renowned for her chastity. Her father (in the second version of the story) conceived an unholy passion for her and tried to gain her compliance by making her drunk. As she was still stubborn, he beat her with myrtle-rods ; finally, he changed himself into a serpent and in that form accomplished his desires. In the first version, the Bona Dea of her own accord drank too much, for which her husband beat her to death. Hence wine and myrtle are avoided in her ritual, and in commemoration of her chastity, no man may be present. It is a feeble bit of late aetiology, behind which may lurk two facts, that the name of the goddess was Fauna, and that a serpent had something to do with her ceremonial, although the second point is far from certain, since a divine lover who disguises himself as a snake is a familiar detail of Greek legend.

Hercules, according to another tale, came across women who were worshipping the Bona Dea and asked them for a drink, which was refused, as no man might have any part in the offerings of the goddess. He thereupon decreed that no woman might have any part in his ritual at the Ara Maxima in Rome.[101]

The above stories of the Bona Dea suppose her, in the usual euhemeristic fashion, to have been a woman deified after her death. In like manner another ancient and obscure goddess, Acca Larentia, or Larentina, is humanized in a late and artificial story, which has effectually obscured her real nature, except that we may suppose her to be likewise connected with fertility, vegetable or animal. A certain man, the sacristan of a temple of Hercules, amused himself by throwing dice, one throw for himself and one for the god. The stake, if he lost, was to be a good dinner and the company of a pretty courtesan. Hercules, who among other things was a god of luck according to Roman ideas, naturally won, and the loser sent for one Acca Larentia to spend the night in the temple. The god made his presence known to her and told her, when she left in the morning, to make friends with the first man she met. This person turned out to be very wealthy, and when he died he left his property to Acca, who in turn bequeathed it to the State ; in gratitude for this, she was made a goddess. As Rome, until Greek influence made itself felt, knew nothing of the worship of individual dead persons (hero-cult), it needs no elaborate proof that this story is a late and artificial creation.[102]

Of much the same kind are the numerous assertions that the goddess Carmentis, or Carmenta, was the mother of Euandros, and a prophetess ; this last assertion may rest on nothing better than an absurd derivation of her name from *carens mente*, referring to her inspired frenzies, or from *carmen*, which among other things may mean an oracle.

Still worse is the legend of the Dea Tacita, which apparently is pure invention on the part of Ovid. This obscure goddess, a deity of the under-world, is probably the same as Larunda ; the latter, for some reason which we cannot now guess, was considered in Ovid's time to be the mother of the Lares, with whom it is very doubtful if she had originally anything to do. Ovid finds or invents a form Lara of her name, and declares that originally she was called Lala (chatterer),—another Greek etymology. This Lala insisted on blurting out all she knew about the designs of Iuppiter on Iuturna (fresh proof, if any were needed, that the story is very late), whereat the god in great wrath deprived her of the power of speech, and sent Mercurius (*i.e.*, Hermes Psychopompos) to convey her to the lower world. On the way, Hermes took advantage of her inability to call for help, and thus she became the mother of the Lares.[103]

Picus, the sacred woodpecker, apparently never was, properly speaking, a god ; but as the bird of Mars, he enjoyed a good deal of respect. Hence it occurred to some fairly early euhemerizer to turn him into a prehistoric king. There remained the problem of how he came by his bird-form, and an answer was found in the malign activities of Kirke, who was located on the promontory called after her (Circeii). As Ovid tells the story, he was happily wedded to a nymph, Canens (the Singer), and repulsed Kirke when she wooed him. In revenge, she turned him into a woodpecker, and his queen, after long and vain search for him, faded away, like Echo, into a bodiless voice, at the place which afterwards was called Canens after her. The tale is not wholly Ovid's own invention, although the picturesque figure of Canens may be ; elsewhere Picus is represented as married to Kirke herself, or to Pomona.[104]

Pomona, the goddess of *poma* (fruit, especially tree-fruit, such as apples or pears) is likewise the heroine of a love-story, told by Ovid. She was coy, although her beauty caused all manner of deities to pay court to her. At last Vertumnus, taking advantage of his power to change (*uertere*) himself into all manner of shapes, assumed the form of an old woman. In this disguise, he pled his own cause so eloquently that when he resumed his proper shape, Pomona was quite ready to listen to him. This is the kind of tale which anyone coming after the great Alexandrians could tell, if he had invention enough ; it is a love-story in which the characters are labelled with the names of gods, and nothing more. The functions of Vertumnus are obscure, but it is certain that he has nothing to do, in cult or in popular belief, with Pomona.[105]

NOTES ON CHAPTER XI

1 See especially Schwegler; Pais 1913 and 1926, *passim*; Homo, Introduction. Much of the material of this chapter is from the first two of these and from Preller-Jordan.

2 The first Greek writer to do more than barely mention Rome is Aristotle; the earliest historians to give any connected and full account of Roman matters were Hieronymos of Kardia and Timaios, both in the third century B.C. See Dion. Hal., I, 72, Schwegler, p. 6 foll.

3 Cato, Origines, VII, frag. 12, Jordan (= Cicero, *Brutus*, 75, *Tusc. disput.*, IV, 3).

4 Schwegler, p. 53 foll., where references to Niebuhr are given.

5 For the character of Italian *numina*, see Wissowa, *R.K.R.*, p. 23 foll.; Warde Fowler 1908, index, *s.u. Deities*; 1911, *passim*; cf. Rose, *Rom. Quest.*, Chapter IV, *P.C.I.*, Chapter III. See p. 334.

6 See Rose, *Rom. Quest.*, p. 53.

7 See Diod. Sic., I, 13, 4 foll.

8 See the passages cited in Chapter III, note 55.

9 Josephus, *contra Apionem*, especially I, 34, II, 2; Strabo, XVI, 2, 35 foll.; Tacitus, *Hist.*, V, 2 foll. (who clearly draws upon Apion).

10 See Chapter IX, p. 278.

11 Homer, *Il.*, XX, 307–8; νῦν δὲ δὴ Αἰνείαο βίη Τρώεσσι Ϝανάξει | καὶ παίδων παῖδες τοί κεν μετόπισθε γένωνται. See Strabo, XIII, 1, 53, who mentions that some were so complaisant as to alter Τρώεσσι to πάντεσσι, in allusion to the Romans. Cf. Vergil, *Aen.*, III, 97.

12 See K. O. Müller, *Die Dorier* (1824), I, p. 222.

13 See Dion. Hal., I, 48 foll. Cf. Farnell, *C.G.S.*, II, p. 638 foll., 738; *Hero-Cults*, p. 55. There were sundry other accounts of the wanderings of Aineias, see especially Dion. Hal., *loc. cit.*

14 See Justin, *Hist. Philip. Epit.*, XXVIII, 1, 6, cf. Dion. Hal. I, 51, 2 (in both passages, diplomatic relations entered into on the strength of an alleged friendship of the other state to Aeneas, or non-participation in the Trojan War).

15 Origines, frag. 8 foll., Jordan.

16 Menekrates of Xanthos *ap.* Dion. Hal., I, 47, 3. The various ramifications of the story of Aeneas, other than those given in Chapter VIII, may be consulted conveniently in Nettleship, *Vergilii Opera*, ed. Conington, fourth ed., Vol. II, p. xlv foll.; Schwegler, *op. cit.*, I, p. 279 foll., besides Klausen, *Aeneas und die Penaten*, which is the great storehouse of facts and of the older theories.

17 The evidence for Naevius having originated or suggested the story rests upon one passage, *Bellum Punicum*, I, frag. 24 (Nonius, p. 335, 2, 474, 7 M) *blande et docte percontat, Aeneas quo pacto | Troiam urbem liquisset*, which makes it clear that the poem contained an episode in which some one, perhaps Aeneas, was asked, perhaps by Dido, about the fall of Troy. The evidence for Varro is much stronger. According to SdA IV, 682, and V, 4, he said that Anna, and not Dido, died for love of Aeneas; which shows that he was acquainted with the story of the visit to Carthage in some form.

18 The above account is mainly from the *Aeneid*. The chief source, outside of Vergil, now surviving is Dion. Hal., I, 45 foll.; for further particulars, see the works cited in note 16, and the relevant articles in Roscher.

[19] See Roscher, art. DIDO.

[20] *Fast.*, III, 545 foll.

[21] See *Not. degli Scavi*, XVII (1920), p. 328 ; *Y.W.*, 1922, **p. 53.**
Anna Perenna will be discussed later in this chapter.

[22] Sil. Ital., *Punica*, VIII, 49 foll. Silius ventures on one small correction or alteration of Ovid, by making Anna, on leaving Africa, go to
Kyrene instead of Malta.

[23] Relevant passages conveniently collected in Wissowa, *R.K.R.*, p.
164, and notes.

[24] The best discussion of this matter, first handled at length in modern
times by Klausen, is in Wissowa, *Ges. Abh.*, p. 95 foll. (= *Hermes*, XXII,
p. 29 foll.).

[25] Varro, *de re rustica*, II, 4, 18.

[26] See du Cange, *Glossarium ad scriptores mediae et infimae Latinitatis*,
s.u. troga, troia ; Walde, *s.u. troja*. It seems to be the source of mod. Fr.
truie, but its own origin apparently cannot be traced back to classical
times. One of its probable cognates is Welsh *twrch* (boar) ; it might
conceivably be a Gaulish word therefore.

[27] The earliest are Cato, *Origines*, I, frag. 8 ; Livy I, 1, 4 ; Festus,
p. 504, 12 Lindsay (from Verrius Flaccus, presumably). SdA IX, 9
mentions it as a tradition (traditur), but gives no authority.

[28] See SA I, 736 ; III, 257 ; VII, 111 ; for comment, see Schwegler,
op. cit., I, 324.

[29] See for instance Cato, *Origines*, I, frag. 9 foll. ; Livy, I, 1, 5 foll.;
Dion. Hal., I, 57, 1 foll.

[30] *Orig.*, I, frag. 10 Jordan.

[31] Elsewhere he appears as an Etruscan leader, cruel to his enemies,
but not to his own subjects.

[32] Wissowa in Roscher, art. CAMILLA, suggests that Vergil is using
some local legend. I doubt this.

[33] For the legend of Euandros, see, besides Roscher, *s.u.*, Schwegler,
op. cit., I, 350 foll., 443 ; the chief ancient accounts are the *Aeneid*, Book
VIII, with the ancient commentaries thereupon, and Dion. Hal., I, 31
foll. The fixed points are (1) the Lupercalia and their alleged identity
with the Lykaia, (2) the relationship of Euandros to Carmentis-Carmenta.
That the name of Rome means ' strength ' is asserted, for instance, by
Solinus, I, 1, who also says that its pre-Euandrian name was Valentia.
This idea seems due to Ateius Capito, see SdA I, 273 (p. 102, 15, Thilo-
Hagen).

[34] These accounts will mostly be found in Festus, p. 326 foll. Lindsay ;
for complete account and analysis, see Schwegler, I, p. 400 foll.

[35] For some criticism of their materials, see Cicero, *Brutus*, 62 ; Livy,
VIII, 40, 4.

[36] If it was not an ancient (and probably true) tradition, it is hard to
see why it was so persistent in historical times, when there was nothing
on the Alban Mount but the temple of Iuppiter Latiaris. Hitherto, no
remains of any considerable settlement of early date have been found
there ; for an ingenious explanation of this, see Homo, p. 72.

[37] The chief lists are : Livy, I, 3 ; Dion. Hal., I, 70 foll. ; and somewhat earlier than either, Diod. Sic., VII, frags. 3 foll. For the others,
see Pais, 1913, I, p. 265 ; complete proof of the late and utterly worthless
character of the tradition had already been given by Schwegler, I, p. 337 foll.

[38] If we may trust Servius (on Verg., *Ecl.*, VI, 5), Vergil had thoughts
in his early days of attempting the subject, but soon gave it up.

[39] Ennius, *Annales*, I, 37 Vahlen.

[40] See Schwegler, I, pp. 339, 429 ; for various etymologies see Lorentz in Roscher, IV, 64, 18 foll.

[41] As such she appears, for instance, in Horace, *carm.*, I, 2, 17, where see the commentators for more examples. A variant makes the Anio her husband, see SA I 273.

[42] For the woodpecker, see Plut., *Q.R.*, 21, *Romul.* 4, *de fort. Roman.*, 320 D.

[43] The principal authorities for this tale are Livy, I, 4 foll. ; Dion. Hal., I, 76 foll., and Plutarch's Life of Romulus. The earliest surviving account is that of Ennius, see the fragments of *Annales*, I, in Vahlen's, Müller's, or Miss Steuart's ed. For criticism see, besides the authorities already cited, the admirable article ROMULUS (J. B. Carter) in Roscher.

[44] Livy, I, 7, 1 ; Dion. Hal., I, 86, 3–4, who adds that Romulus cheated ; Florus, I, 1, 6. The place on the Aventine where Remus took his auspices was called Remoria, Festus, pp. 344, 345 Lindsay, Dion. Hal., *ibid.*, 2 ; many versions of the story, as Ovid, *Fast.*, IV, 817, Plut., *Romul.*, 9, first version (he goes on to give the one told by Dion. Hal.), say nothing of the priority of Remus' vultures. The name Remus seems to be derived from Remoria. See p. 334.

[45] Schwegler, I, 395.

[46] Livy, I, 11, 6 foll. ; Dion. Hal., II, 37, 2 foll. ; for full citations and discussion, see Pais, 1906, p. 96 foll. ; Höfer in Roscher, V, 111.

[47] Dion. Hal., I, 77, 1.

[48] *Ibid.*, I, 84, 5 ; see Schwegler, I, 399, and for the rationalizing stories in general, *ibid.*, 396 foll.

[49] Livy, I, 16, 4, and many other passages ; see for full references, Schwegler, *op. cit.*, I, 534. The explanation given in Frazer, *G.B.*[3], IX, 258, while ingenious, labours under the difficulty, not only of finding such customs as he describes in ancient Italy at all, but of trying to find ritual meanings in what is almost certainly a mere rationalization.

[50] See Warde Fowler, 1908, p. 176 foll. ; Wissowa, *R.K.R.*, p. 184.

[51] See Rose, *Rom. Quest.*, p. 103 foll., and for full references, Rossbach, p. 328 foll.

[52] See Rose, *Rom. Quest.*, pp. 133, 157, 183, 205.

[53] See *op. cit.*, pp. 131, 181. There is a Greek legend which perhaps originated this one : see Plut., *quaest. Graec.*, 37, cf. Apollod., I, 64.

[54] This is recognized and variously accounted for by all modern writers on Rome ; see, for some remarks on the question, *J.R.S.*, XII (1922), p. 109 foll.

[55] See the authorities cited in note 6.

[56] See Eitrem, *Beiträge zur Religionsgeschichte* (Kristiania 1915), p. 152 foll.

[57] See Rose, *Le culte des héros et les dieux Mânes*, in *Actes du congrès international d'histoire des religions tenu à Paris en octobre* 1923, II, p. 138 foll.

[58] See for instance notes 49, 56, 59.

[59] Livy, X, 23, 12 ; for comment, see J. Carcopino, *La louve du Capitole* (Paris 1925), p. 20 foll.

[60] Livy, V, 13, 6.

[61] See Livy, I, 18, 2.

[62] Livy, I, 21, 3. The chief sources for the life of Numa are, besides Livy, I, 18 foll., Dion. Hal., I, 62 foll., and Plutarch's *Numa*. For more authorities and excellent discussion, see Buchmann.

[63] See Valerius Antias *ap.* Arnobius, *aduersus gentes*, V, 1, p. 173

Reifferscheid (= Annales, II, frag. 6, Peter) ; Ovid, *Fast.*, III, 291 foll. For Ovid's untrustworthiness, see Wissowa, *Ges. Abh.*, p. 136, and in general the whole of the article, *Römische Sagen*, from which this reference is taken.

[64] See Chapter VI, p. 157. This is the interpretation of Preller-Jordan, I, 375 ; Wissowa, *R.K.R.*, p. 212, *Ges. Abh.*, p. 137, and Buchmann, p. 54, would rather derive it from Menelaos' adventure with Proteus, *Odyss.*, IV, 351 foll.

[65] For the Salii, see Wissowa, *R.K.R.*, p. 555 foll. ; Rose, *P.C.I.*, 95 foll. ; Deubner in Chantepie de la Saussaye, II, p. 447. (I would note here that Deubner's views and mine, which agree, were reached independently.)

[66] Ovid, *Fast.*, III, 383 foll. For other references, see the passage already cited from Wissowa in note 63.

[67] See Iohannes Lydus, *de mensibus*, IV, 49 (p. 105 Wuensch). Cf. SA VII, 188 ; Minucius Felix, *Octauius*, 22, 8 (24, 3). See, in general, Frazer, *G.B.*[3], IX, p. 229 foll., who gives fuller references.

[68] See Livy, I, 24 foll. ; Dion. Hal., III, 15 foll.

[69] Probably Iuno Sororia is Iuno of Growth or adolescence. See *Mnemosyne*, N.S. liii (1925), p. 413.

[70] Livy, *ibid.*, 31, 8.

[71] See *oratio Claudii* (C.I.L., xiii, 1668 ; Dessau, *Inscr. Lat. Sel.* 212 ; Furneaux, *Annals of Tacitus*, II, p. 210), 16 foll. ; Müller-Deecke, *Etrusker*, I, 110. See p. 334.

[72] Dion. Hal., IV, 2 ; Ovid, *Fast.*, VI, 621 foll. ; cf. Plut., *Romul.*, 2, who gives the story in a different context ; SA VII, 678 ; Pliny, *nat. hist.*, XXXVI, 204 ; Warde Fowler, 1916, p. 58 ; Rose, in *Mnemosyne*, N.S., liii (1925), p. 410 foll., *P.C.I.*, p. 80. For Servius Tullius in general, see, besides Dion. Hal., *loc. cit.*, Livy, I, 39 foll.

[73] As his name, Servius, means etymologically ' slave's son ' if it is a Latin word at all, naturally a story of how he came to be so lowly born must grow up in some way.

[74] See Müller-Deecke, *op. cit.*, II, p. 58 ; Plut., Q.R., 36, 74 ; Ovid, *Fast.*, VI, 563 foll.

[75] See Livy, I, 48, 7 ; see, for an ingenious explanation, Pais, 1913, p. 506.

[76] Livy, I, 53, 4 foll. ; see Herodotos, III, 153, 2 foll., V, 92ζ, 2.

[77] The most moving ancient account is in Livy, I, 57 foll.

[78] Valerius Maximus, V, 6, 3 ; Ovid, *Metam.*, XV, 565 foll. ; see Wissowa, *Ges. Abh.*, p. 134 and refs. there.

[79] Varro, *de ling. Lat.*, V, 148–150 ; Livy, I, 12, 10, VII, 6 ; Val. Max., V, 6, 2 ; Dion. Hal., II, 42, 5–6. A third story, cited by Varro, is much more prosaic ; the place is called lacus Curtius because it was struck by lightning and therefore fenced in, according to the usual ritual, when a certain Curtius was consul.

[80] An attempt has repeatedly been made to connect him with Diana, through a supposed original form Dianus. But (1) this is philologically unlikely, for the name Dianus, although it exists, is late, whereas on this theory it should be early ; (2) the facts of cult and the history of Italian religion are against it, for the functions of Ianus and Diana have nothing to do with each other, and Ianus is a native Roman deity, which Diana is not ; (3) it fails to explain the undoubted connexion between Ianus and the door (*ianua*).

[81] See Ovid, *Fast.*, VI, 101 foll. ; Wissowa, *op. cit.*, p. 138–40, and refs. there.

[82] See Stoll, Roscher, II, col. 41 ; Ov., *Fast.*, I, 259 foll., *Met.*, XIV, 7:5 foll. ; Macrob., I, 9, 17, cf. Varro, LL, V, 156.

[83] *Metam.*, XIV, 333–4. Where Arnobius (*aduers. nat.*, III, 29) got his account of Ianus, *Caelo atque Hecata procreatum . . . patrem Fonti, Vulturni generum, Iuturnae maritum*, seems not to be known, but it is manifestly late, syncretistic, and worthless.

[84] For instance, Plut., Q.R., 22 ; Varro (?) *ap.* August., *de ciuit. Dei*, VII, 4 ; more references in Stoll, *op. cit.*, cols. 22 foll.

[85] See especially Livy, I, 2, 6 ; Dion. Hal., I, 64, 4–5, who adds that some said it was Anchises, not Aeneas, and that the shrine consisted of ' a small mound, with a very fine grove about it '. Cf. Verg., *Aen.*, XII, 794, with the commentators ancient and modern ; Ovid, *Met.*, XIV, 581 foll. ; Anon., *de orig. gent. Rom.*, 14, 2 foll. For full references see Schwegler, I, p. 287, n. 21 ; Preller-Jordan, I, 94, II, 142.

[86] Halliday in *C.R.*, XXXVI (1922), p. 110 foll. The earliest mention of this absurdity is Diod. Sic., VI, fr. 5 ; for later authors see Halliday, p. 112, n. 4. Arnobius *adu. nat.*, II, 71, contents himself with making Picus brother of Iuppiter. The original author of the pedigree was some euhemerizer, possibly Ennius.

[87] Ovid, *Fast.*, V, 231 foll. Paulus, *epit. Fest.*, p. 86, 17 Lindsay, says Mars is called Gradiuus *quia gramine sit ortus*, which may refer to some such tale. See Preller-Jordan, I, p. 341.

[88] Ovid, *Fast.*, III, 677 foll. See Usener in *Rhein. Mus.*, N.F., XXX, p. 182 foll. ; Warde Fowler, 1908, pp. 52–3 ; Wissowa, *R.K.R.*, p. 147, *Ges. Abh.*, p. 167.

[89] Bailey, *P. Ouidi Nasonis Fastorum liber III*, Oxford, 1921, p. 39.

[90] See, in answer to the attempts to prove the contrary made by Frazer and others, Rose, *Rom. Quest.*, p. 81.

[91] The idea, found in both ancient and modern writers (as Propertius, IV, 9, 71, where see Butler's note ; Varro, LL, V, 66 ; Preller-Jordan, II, p. 281) that he is in some way identical with the native god Semo Sancus Dius Fidius, is now generally given up and seems to have little to recommend it. See p. 334.

[92] Dion. Hal., I, 43, 1.

[93] See especially Dion. Hal., I, 39 foll. ; Verg., *Aen.*, VIII, 185 foll., with the notes of Servius ; Propertius, IV, 9. For the Argei, see for example Dion. Hal., I, 38, 2, and for the likeliest explanation of the real origin of the rite, Frazer, *Journ. of Philol.*, XIV (1885), p. 156, with whom I am now disposed to agree, rather than with the solution adopted in *Rom. Quest.*, p. 98. See also Birt in *Rhein. Mus.*, 1926, p. 124 foll.

[94] See SA VIII, 190. Thilo and Hagen's text of this note follows the reading of most MSS. and of M1, 153, which copies the passage, in saying of Caca, *sacellum meruit in quo ei per uirgines Vestales sacrificabatur* ; but the *codex Floriacensis* gives instead, *in quo ei peruigili igni sicut Vestae*, etc., which is strongly preferred by Wissowa in Roscher, VI, col. 241, 35.

[95] See Dion. Hal., II, 68, 3 foll.

[96] Not even the Pontifex Maximus, see Wissowa, *op. cit.*, col. 251, 11 foll., which also gives an account of the misadventure of Metellus.

[97] References in Preller-Jordan, I, p. 299, n. 1 ; behind this tale seems to lie the fact that the family of the Nautii, who claimed descent from (or rather, had invented as their ancestor) this Nautes, had an especial connexion with the (originally non-Roman) cult of Minerva.

[98] Ovid, *Fast.*, VI, 313 foll. ; *ibid.*, I, 391 foll., tells the same tale, but with the nymph Lotis in place of Vesta.

[99] See Dion Hal., I, 67, 1–2 ; SA III, 12, which also mentions yet another miracle of Vesta ; a chaste maid who slept in her temple at Lavinium was unharmed by a stroke of lightning which killed an unchaste girl sleeping by her. Presumably, both were Vestals.

[100] Ovid, *Fast.*, VI, 563 foll. ; part of the story is also in Plut., Q.R., 36, *de fort. Roman.*, 322 F.

[101] For the Bona Dea as wife of Faunus, see Lactantius, *inst. diuin.*, I, 22 ; Arnob., *aduers. nat.*, V, 18 ; Plut., Q.R., 20. The first two cite as their authorities Varro and Sextus Clodius, and give the name of the goddess as Fauna (? reading uncertain) Fatua ; she is Faunus' daughter in Macrob., I, 12, 24–25 ; Tertull., *ad nat.*, II, 9 ; SdA VIII, 314. Hercules and the Bona Dea, Propert., IV, 9, 21 foll. ; Macrob., I, 12, 28. For a convenient summary of the known facts about her, see Peter in Roscher, *s.u.*

[102] See, for the legend, Plutarch, Q.R., 35 ; variants and references to the chief modern literature in Rose, *Rom. Quest.*, p. 185.

[103] Ovid, *Fast.*, II, 581 foll. ; excellent comment in Wissowa, *Ges. Abh.*, p. 149.

[104] Ovid, *Metam.*, XIV, 320 foll., see Wissowa in Roscher, I, col. 850 foll. ; other versions of the legend, Verg., *Aen.*, VII, 189, with the note of Servius ; Valerius Flaccus, VII, 232 ; Plut., Q.R., 21, cf. Rose, *Rom. Quest.*, p. 178, Halliday, art. quoted in note 86.

[105] See Ovid, *Metam.*, XIV, 623 foll.

ADDITIONAL NOTE A (see Note 5)

Cf. also H. Wagenvoort, *Roman Dynamism* (Oxford 1948), Chap. III ; H. J. Rose, *Ancient Roman Religion* (London 1949), Chap. I.

ADDITIONAL NOTE B (see Note 44)

For this, see Samuel Ball Platner and Thomas Ashby, *A Topographical Dictionary of Ancient Rome* (London 1929), p. 447 and refs.

ADDITIONAL NOTE C (see Note 71).

See also Philippe Fabia, *La table claudienne de Lyon* (Lyon, 1929).

ADDITIONAL NOTE D (see Note 91)

The fullest account of the legends and cult of Hercules is J. Bayet, *Les origines de l'Hercule romain* (Paris 1926).

BIBLIOGRAPHY

A. CLASSICAL AUTHORS

A few editions and abbreviations are given here ; the remaining quotations are self-explanatory

A. See Servius.

Abel. See Orphica.

Aesop. *Aesopi fabulae*, recensuit Aemilius Chambry. Paris, Les Belles Lettres, 1925 (only complete edition).

Apollod. *Apollodori Bibliotheca*, edidit Richardus Wagner (Mythographi Graeci, Vol. I). Lipsiae (Teubner), 1894. Cited by the continuous sections, not by chapter, section and sub-section.

Hyginus. *Hygini Fabulae*, ed. H. J. Rose, Lugduni Batauorum apud A. W. Sijthoff, n.d.

Jacoby. *Die Fragmente der griechischen Historiker*. Von Felix Jacoby. Berlin, 1923.

Jordan   *M. Catonis praeter librum de re rustica quae exstant.* Henricus Jordan recensuit et prolegomena scripsit. Lipsiae, 1860.

Kern. See Orphica.

Kock. *Comicorum Atticorum fragmenta*, edidit Theodorus Kock. Leipzig, 1880–8 (3 vols.).

M1, M2, M3. *Scriptores rerum mythicarum Latini tres, Romae nuper reperti.* . . . Integriores edidit. . . . Dr. Georgius Henricus Bode. Cellis, 1834 (2 vols.).

Macan, 18 95. *Herodotus, the Fourth, Fifth and Sixth Books.* R. W. Macan. London, 1895.

N². *Tragicorum Graecorum Fragmenta.* Recensuit Augustus Nauck. Editio secunda, Leipzig, Teubner, 1889.

Orphica. *Orphica* ; recensuit Eugenius Abel. Accedunt Procli Hymni, Hymni magici, Hymnus in Isim alique eius modi carmina. Lipsiae et Pragae, 1885 (' Abel '). *Orphicorum Fragmenta*, collegit Otto Kern. Berolini, 1922 (' Kern ' or ' Kern, 1922 ').

P. *The Fragments of Sophocles* ; edited with additional notes from the papers of Sir R. C. Jebb and Dr. W. G. Headlam by A. C. Pearson. Cambridge, 1917 ; 3 vols.

Peter. *Historicorum Romanorum fragmenta.* Collegit disposuit recensuit Hermannus Peter. Lipsiae, 1883.

Ph. See Servius.

Powell. *Collectanea Alexandrina : reliquiae minores Poetarum Graecorum aetatis Ptolemaicae.* Edidit Iohannes U. Powell. Oxonii, 1925.
Pr. See Servius.
RP[8]. *Historia Philosophiae Graecae.* Testimonia auctorum conlegerunt notisque instruxerunt H. Ritter et L. Preller. Editio octaua, quam curauit Eduardus Wellmann. Gothae, 1898.
Rzach. *Hesiodi carmina :* recensuit Aloisius Rzach : editio tertia. Teubner, 1913 (editio minor).
Servius. *Seruii Grammatici qui feruntur in Vergilii carmina commentarii.* Recensuerunt Georgius Thilo et Hermannus Hagen. Lipsiae in aedibus B. G. Teubneri. Vol. I, 1881 ; Vol. II, 1884 ; Vol. III, i, 1887 ; ii (by Hagen alone), *Appendix Seruiana,* ceteros praeter Seruium et scholia Bernensia Vergilii commentatores continens, 1902.
Cited thus : A(nonymi breuis expositio) ; Ph(ilargyrii grammatici explanatio) ; Pr(obi qui dicitur commentarius) ; S(eruius) ; Sd, Seruius Danielis, or Seruius auctus ; V(eronensia scholia) ; followed in all cases by A(eneid), B(ucolics), or G(eorgics), and the number of the line.
V. See Servius.

B. MODERN WORKS

The following is a list of books which the author found particularly useful. Some recently published works have been added since the author's death.

Allen 1921. T. W. Allen, *The Homeric Catalogue of Ships.* Oxford 1921.
Berger 1904. Prof. Dr. E. H. Berger, *Mythische Kosmographie der Griechen,* Supplement zu Roschers Lexikon. Leipzig, 1904.
Bonney. T. H. Bonney, *Volcanoes.* London, 1912.
Bouché-Leclercq. A. Bouché-Leclercq, *Histoire de la Divination dans l'antiquité.* Paris, 1879–82 (4 vols.).
Buchmann. G. Buchmann, *De Numae regis Romanorum fabula.* Dissertatio inauguralis, Lipsiae, 1912.
Carcopino. J. Carcopino, *La louve du Capitole.* Paris, 1925.
Chantepie de la Saussaye. *Lehrbuch der Religionsgeschichte, begründet von Chantepie de la Saussaye.* Vierte, vollständig neubearbeitete Auflage . . . herausgegeben von Alfred Bertholet und Edvard Lehmann. Tübingen, 1925 (2 vols.).
Cook. Arthur Bernard Cook, *Zeus : a Study in Ancient Religion.* Cambridge, Vol. I, 1914 ; Vol. II, 1925; Vol. III, 1940.
Cosquin 1886. Emanuel Cosquin, *Contes populaires de Lorraine.* Paris, n.d. (preface dated 1886), 2 vols.
Cosquin 1922. Emanuel Cosquin, *Les Contes indiens et l'Occident.* Paris, 1922.
Cosquin, E.F. Emanuel Cosquin, *Études folkloriques.* Paris, 1922.

Daremberg-Saglio. *Dictionnaire des antiquités grecques et romaines, d'après les textes et les monuments* . . . ouvrage redigé . . . sous la direction de MM. Ch. Daremberg et Edm. Saglio. Paris, 1877-1919.

Dawkins. R. M. Dawkins, *Modern Greek in Asia Minor* . . . *with a chapter on the subject-matter of the folk-tales*, by W. R. Halliday. Cambridge, 1916.

Decharme. P. Decharme, *Mythologie de la Grèce antique.* Cinquième édition ; Paris, n.d. (a reprint of the revised edition of 1884).

Farnell, *C.G.S.* Lewis Richard Farnell, *The Cults of the Greek States.* Oxford, 1896-1909 (5 vols.).

Farnell, *Hero-Cults.* Lewis Richard Farnell, *Greek Hero-Cults and Ideas of Immortality.* The Gifford Lectures delivered in the University of St. Andrews in the year 1920. Oxford, 1921.

Fontenrose. Joseph E. Fontenrose, *Python ; a study of Delphic Myth.* Berkeley and London, 1959

Frazer, *T.E.* Sir J. G. Frazer, *Totemism and Exogamy ; a Treatise on certain early forms of Superstition and Society.* London, 1909 (4 vols.).

Frazer, *G.B.*[3]. Sir J. G. Frazer, *The Golden Bough ; a Study in Magic and Religion.* London, 1911-15 (12 vols.).

Frazer, *F.O.T.* Sir J. G. Frazer, *Folk-Lore in the Old Testament ; Studies in Comparative Religion, Legend and Law.* London, 1919 (3 vols.).

Frazer, *Belief.* Sir J. G. Frazer, *The Belief in Immortality and the Worship of the Dead.* London, Vol. I, 1913 ; Vol. II, 1922 ; Vol. III, 1924.

Frazer, *W.N.* Sir J. G. Frazer, *The Worship of Nature.* Vol. I, London, 1926.

van Gennep 1910. A. van Gennep, *La Formation des Legendes.* Paris, 1910.

Gianelli. Giulio Gianelli, *Culti e miti della magna Grecia.* Firenze, 1924.

Grant. Michael Grant ; *Myths of the Greeks and Romans.* [London] 1962.

Grote. George Grote, *A History of Greece from the Earliest Period to the close of the generation contemporary with Alexander the Great.* New edition, London, 1903 (10 vols.). The first part of this work deals principally with the myths and sagas.

Gruppe, *G.M.R.* Otto Gruppe, *Griechische Mythologie und Religions-geschichte.* Munich, 1906 (2 vols. = I. Müller, *Handbuch der klassischen Altertumswissenschaft,* V, 2, i and ii).

Gruppe 1921. Otto Gruppe, *Geschichte der klassischen Mythologie und Religionsgeschichte.* Supplement zu Roschers Lexikon. Leipzig, 1921.

Guthrie. William K. C. Guthrie : *The Religion and Mythology of the Greeks* (Cambridge Ancient History, 2nd ed. Vol. II, Ch. XL, 1961).

Harrison, *Proleg.* Jane Ellen Harrison, *Prolegomena to the Study of Greek Religion.* Cambridge, 1903.

Harrison, *Themis*[2]. Jane Ellen Harrison, *Themis : a Study of the Social Origins of Greek Religion*. Second edition revised. Cambridge, 1927.

Herter. Hans Herter, *De dis Atticis Priapi similibus*. Bonnae, 1926.

Homo. Leon Homo, *Primitive Italy and the Beginnings of Roman Imperialism*. London, 1927.

Kern, 1926. Vol. I of Otto Kern, *Die Religion der Griechen*, 3 vols. Berlin, 1926–38.

Latte. Kurt Latte : *Römische Religionsgeschichte* (Handbuch der Altertumswissenschaft). Munchen, 1960.

MacCulloch. J. A. MacCulloch, *The Childhood of Fiction : a Study of Folk Tales and Primitive Thought*. London, 1905.

A. Mommsen. August Mommsen, *Feste der Stadt Athen im Altertum :* Umbearbeitung der 1864 erschienenen Heortologie. Leipzig, 1898.

Murray 1925. Gilbert A. Murray, *Five Stages of Greek Religion*. Oxford, 1925.

Nilsson, *Feste*. M. P. Nilsson, *Griechische Feste von religiöser Bedeutung, mit Ausschluss der attischen*. Leipzig, 1906.

Nilsson, *Hist. Gk. Rel.* M. P. Nilsson, *A History of Greek Religion*. Translated from the Swedish by F. J. Fielden, with a preface by Sir James G. Frazer. Oxford, 1925.

Nilsson, *M.M.R.*[2] M. P. Nilsson, *The Minoan-Mycenaean Religion and its Survival in Greek Religion*. Ed. 2, Lund, 1950.

Nilsson, *GgR.* M. P. Nilsson, *Geschichte der griechischen Religion*, 2 vols. Munich, 1955 (ed. 2, I[2]), 1955.

Nilsson, *O.S.* M. P. Nilsson, *Opuscula Selecta*, 2 vols., Lund, 1951, 1952.

Nock 1926. *Sallustius, Concerning the Gods and the Universe*. Edited with Prolegomena and Translation by Arthur Darby Nock. Cambridge, 1926.

Pais 1906. Ettore Pais, *Ancient Legends of Roman History*. London, 1906.

Pais 1913. Ettore Pais, *Storia critica di Roma durante i primi cinque secoli*. Vol. I, parte prima : Le Fonte, l'età mitica. Rome, 1913.

Pais 1926. Ettore Pais, *Histoire romaine*. Tome premier, fasc. i. Paris, 1926.

Page. Denys L. Page, *History and the Homeric Iliad*. 1960.

Parkes. Henry B. Parkes, *Gods and Men*. London, 1960.

Pauly-Wissowa. *Paulys Realencyclopädie der classischen Altertumswissenschaft*. Neue Bearbeitung begonnen von Georg Wissowa (etc.). Stuttgart, 1894–

Pfister. Friedrich Pfister : *Greek Gods and Heroes*. London, 1961.

Preller-Jordan. L. Preller, *Römische Mythologie*. Dritte Auflage, von H. Jordan. Berlin, 1881–3 (2 vols.).

Preller-Robert. L. Preller, *Griechische Mythologie*. Vierte Auflage bearbeitet von Carl Robert. Berlin, 1894—

Reinach, *C.M.R.* S. Reinach, *Cultes, Mythes et Religions.* Paris, 1908–23 (5 vols. ; first ed. of Vol. I in 1905).

Rohde. Erwin Rohde, *Psyche : Seelencult und Unsterblichkeitsglaube der Griechen.* Vierte Auflage. Tübingen, 1907 (2 vols.).

Roscher. *Ausführliches Lexikon der griechischen und römischen Mythologie* . . . herausgegeben von W. H. Roscher. Leipzig, 1884–1937.

Rose, *Rom. Quest.* H. J. Rose, *The Roman Questions of Plutarch.* A new translation with introductory essays and a running commentary. Oxford, 1924.

Rose, *P.C.G.* H. J. Rose, *Primitive Culture in Greece.* London (Methuen), 1925.

Rose, *P.C.I.* H. J. Rose, *Primitive Culture in Italy.* London (Methuen), 1926.

Rossbach. August Rossbach, *Untersuchungen über die römische Ehe.* Stuttgart, 1853.

Schwegler. A. Schwegler, *Römische Geschichte.* Vol. I ; Römische Geschichte im Zeitalter der Könige. Tübingen, 1853.

de Waele. F. J. M. de Waele, *The Magic Staff or Rod in Graeco-Italian Antiquity.* The Hague, 1927.

Walde. Alois Walde, *Lateinisches etymologisches Wörterbuch.* Heidelberg, 1906.

Warde Fowler 1908. W. Warde Fowler, *Roman Festivals of the Republic.* London, 1908.

Warde Fowler 1911. W. Warde Fowler, *The Religious Experience of the Roman People.* London, 1911.

Warde Fowler 1916. W. Warde Fowler, *Virgil's Gathering of the Clans.* Oxford, 1916.

Warde Fowler 1918. W. Warde Fowler, *Aeneas at the Site of Rome.* Oxford, 1918.

Warde Fowler 1919. W. Warde Fowler, *The Death of Turnus.* Oxford, 1918.

Warde Fowler 1920. W. Warde Fowler, *Roman Essays and Interpretations.* Oxford, 1920.

Wide-Nilsson. A. Gercke and E. Norden, *Einleitung in die Altertumswissenschaft,* II, 4 : Griechische und römische Religion, von S. Wide und M. P. Nilsson. Leipzig und Berlin, 1922.

Wissowa, *R.K.R.* Georg Wissowa, *Religion und Kultus der Römer.* Zweite Auflage. München, 1912. (= Müller, *Handbuch,* V, 4, 2ᵉ Auflage).

Wissowa, *Ges. Abh.* Georg Wissowa, *Gesammelte Abhandlungen zur römischen Religions- und Stadtgeschichte.* München, 1904.

ADDENDA

Page 38, note 24. For some account of the ramifications of this myth in various ages and countries, see K. Marot, *Die Trennung von Himmel und Erde*, in *Acta Ant. Hung.*, I (Budapest 1951), pp. 35–63.

Pages 43 and 69, *n*. 2. Hesiod goes on to say that there succeeded a Silver Age, much inferior to the Golden. The men of that time took a hundred years to grow up, and finally were destroyed by Zeus because they were unjust and impious. Then came the Bronze Age, when everything was made of bronze, even the houses, ' and black iron there was none '. These men were violent and destroyed each other, and that was the end of them, whereas those of the former ages had become daimones after death. Next came the Heroic Age, which was much better ; that was the time of the Theban and Trojan Wars. Finally came the present, or Iron Age, which is very vile, and will grow worse.

Page 110. Strabo, X, 3, 19, says that the Korybantes (see p. 170) were said, at Prasiai in Rhodes, to be the children of Helios and Athena ; but the Athena there meant is a local Rhodian goddess, identified with but not originally the same as the Greek Athena.

Page 161, note 25. The earliest allusion to the story of Midas and the asses' ears seems to be Aristophanes, *Plut.*, 287, where see the scholiast.

Page 162, note 45. A more successful attempt to connect Herakles with Palaimon is made by Wilamowitz-Möllendorff, *Glaube der Hellenen*, I, pp. 217–18, who points out that a Ἡρακλῆς Παλαίμων is mentioned in *I.G.* VII, 2874. The ' wrestler ' is not there a sea-god, but a local deity of the neighbourhood of Lake Kopais in Boiotia, and was not unnaturally absorbed into the greater personality of Herakles, possibly at a date later than that of Diphilos, the comedian on whom Plautus draws for the *Rudens*.

Page 173. A pretty tale of a Dryad, which may or may not be of popular origin, is preserved in a fragment of the historian Charon of Lampsakos (*ap.* schol. Apoll. Rhod., II, 477, supplemented by schol. Theokr. III, 13). A certain Rhoikos of Knidos, being for some reason in Nineveh, saw an oak in danger of falling and bade his slaves prop it up. Its Dryad appeared to him, thanked him for saving her life, and offered him anything he liked to ask. He asked for her favours, which she promised him, and said that a bee should come to tell him when to visit her. But when it came, Rhoikos was in the middle of a game of draughts, and spoke to it rudely ; whereat the offended Dryad blinded him.

Page 177. To the animals sacred to gods add the vulture, which is the bird of Ares, according to Cornutus, p. 41, 15, Lang. A long list is given by Eustathios on the *Iliad*, p. 86, 40 foll., for comment on which see C. Reinhardt, *de Graecorum theologia capita duo* (Berlin, Weidmann, 1910), p. 90 foll.

Page 180, note 36. Incomparably the best work on Priapos is Hans

Herter, *De Priapo*, Töpelmann, Giessen, 1932 (*Religionsgeschichtliche Versuche und Vorarbeiten*, Vol. XXIII).

Page 183, end. For the rite of spitting and consequent loss of power by Glaukos, cf. Westermarck, *Ritual and Belief in Morocco*, I, p. 93, where a man is warned not to spit into anyone's mouth lest he should lose his *baraka*, or power.

Page 188. For the Sphinx, see further C. Robert, *Oidipus*, chapter II. There is reason to believe that in an early form of the story (preserved by no author, but found in art) the Sphinx was killed in a fight by Oidipus ; in this form of the legend there may have been no riddle.

Page 193. The only parallel to Euadne's action is in Quintus Smyrnaeus, *Posthomerica*, X, 464–7, where Oinone (see p. 234) throws herself on the funeral pyre of Paris. But as Quintus himself (*ibid.*, 479–82) compares her act to Euadne's, he may very well be inventing the story. See E. Rohde, *Der griechische Roman*, pp. 119–20, note 1.

Page 211. The Nemean lion was not invulnerable in the earliest form of the tale, see O. Berthold, *Die Unverwundbarkeit* (Giessen, Töpelmann, in the series *Religionsgeschichtliche Versuche und Vorarbeiten*), pp. 2–5.

Page 231 and Chapter XI. The Dioskuroi were reputed to help men elsewhere than in storms. The most famous of their many appearances on land was the affair of the Sagra, about 560 B.C. The inhabitants of Lokris in Italy, being at war with their neighbours of Kroton, sought aid from Sparta, which refused, but said they might have the Dioskuroi. These (perhaps in the form of images or other cult-symbols) they accepted. With an army of 15,000 men they met 130,000 Krotoniates at the river Sagra, and won a complete victory, in the course of which two young men on white horses, wearing the red cloaks of Spartan warriors, were seen on the Lokrian wings. That same day the news of the victory was miraculously brought to Sparta and elsewhere in Greece, thus giving rise to the proverb ' truer than what happened at the Sagra '. Rome claimed to have been similarly favoured, the Dioskuroi fighting against the Latins at Lake Regillus and afterwards carrying the news to Rome, while much later, in the Third Macedonian War, they announced the capture of King Perses long before the official dispatches could reach Italy. See Cicero, *de nat. deor.*, II, 6, and III, 11, 13 ; Diodorus Siculus, VIII, frag. 32 (= *excerpta Vaticana*, p. 13, 14) ; Justin, *Hist. Phil. epit.*, XX, 3 ; Suidas, *s. u.* ἀληθέστερα τῶν ἐπὶ Σάγρᾳ ; Dion. Hal., *Antiquit.*, VI, 13, 1–3 ; Plutarch, *Aemil. Paul.*, 25.

Page 247. It is noteworthy that Myrtilos, or Myrsilos as he is sometimes called, has a Hittite name. Mursil was king of the Hittites about 1350–1310 B.C. (Hall in *Journ. Hell. Stud.*, XXIX, p. 19 foll.).

Chapter IX. A pretty local legend is that of Pygmalion king of Cyprus. He fell in love with a beautiful statue (Ovid, who tells the story best, says he made it himself ; the other authorities say it was a statue of Aphrodite, but do not mention who made it). He prayed to the goddess to give him a wife resembling the statue ; she did better and made the statue itself live ; Pygmalion promptly married it, or her, and she bore him a son Paphos, after whom Aphrodite's island of Paphos was named. See Ovid, *Met.*, X, 243 foll. ; Clem. Alex., *Protr.*, p. 51 Pott., Arnobius, *aduers. nat.*, VI, 22, both citing Philostephanos' *Kypriaka*, but neither mentioning the miracle. Why some modern writers call the woman Galatea is one of the lesser mysteries of mythology ; no ancient gives her any name.

Page 257. There is another Greek Noah, Ogygos, said to have been a very ancient king of Thebes (this clearly disagrees with the ordinary legends of Kadmos, Amphion and Zethos, and the rest). A few authors, as Varro *ap.* Augustine, *de ciuit. Dei*, xxi. 8, Nonnos III, 204 foll., say that in his days there was a great deluge ; but Deukalion is far better known, and Ogygos little more than a name.

Page 262. Homer half-tells another tale of Itylos and his mother, *Odyssey*, XIX, 518. The nightingale is a daughter of Pandareos (cf. p. 28), and weeps for her son Itylos, child of Zethos the king, whom she slew unwittingly. The scholiasts call her Aedon and say that she was envious of Niobe (wife of Zethos' brother Amphion) for her many children, and plotted to kill them at night ; but by a misunderstanding, her own child slept in the wrong bed, and so was killed by her. Then she mourned until the gods turned her into a nightingale.

Page 271. Argos claimed to be the first place to which fire was brought from heaven, and, in proof of it, showed a holy fire in the market-place, see schol. Soph., *Elektra*, 4, 6.

Page 275. The story of Komaitho is certainly not old and quite possibly a literary invention of novelistic type ; see Wilamowitz-Möllendorff, *Glaube der Hellenen*, I, 384.

Near Pylos in Triphylia a story was told of a certain Minthe, *i.e.*, mint, who was the mistress of Hades, whereupon Persephone in jealousy turned her into the plant which bears her name (Strabo, VIII, 3, 14 ; Ovid, *Metam.*, X, 728–30).

Chapter X. The story of *Swan-Maiden* (No. 3 in Jacobs' list) does not exist in Greek as we have it ; but the following tale, quoted from Varro by the scholiast on Statius, *Theb.*, VIII, 198, is a little like it. A certain Patron had taken a lost child, by name Smikros, a descendant of Apollo, into his household. One day Smikros and the other servants caught a swan, which they wrapped in a garment and gave to Patron. On being uncovered, it proved to have turned into a woman, who told Patron to make an especial favourite of Smikros. This he did, finally marrying him to his own daughter ; from this union was born Branchos, who founded the oracular shrine of Branchidai.

The wide-spread tale of how Old Age came into the world is found in Nikandros, *Theriaka*, 343 foll., who says it is an ὠγύγιος μῦθος, or very ancient legend, as it may well be. Zeus sent a load of youth to mankind, who put it all on the back of an ass. He, being thirsty, went to a spring to drink, but found a snake there. The snake asked for his load as the price of the water, and the ass consented ; hence a snake can cast his skin and grow young again, but man grows inevitably old. See Frazer, *Folk-Lore of the Old Testament*, I, p. 66 foll.

Page 329, note 16. For the historical basis of the legend of Aineias, see L. Malten in *Archiv für Religionswissenschaft*, Vol. XXIX (1931), p. 23 foll.

Page 127. This explanation of the origin of Venus is disputed by R. Schilling, *La religion romaine de Vénus* (Paris, 1954), who however bases his views on an etymology of the name Venus which has been strongly criticized by Ernout in *Rev. de Phil.* for 1956.

Page 262. One late Greek, the rhetorician Himerios, sides with the Roman regarding the bird-forms of Prokne and Philomela, *Orat.* LXXIV (XXIV), 5.

INDEXES

(Names are given (1) in the form in which they appear in this book, with indications of the pronunciation; (2) in Greek letters, if they have a Greek form; (3) in their Latin form, if that differs substantially from the Greek. Readers unacquainted with the ancient languages are asked to note that in Greek, *ai, eu, oi* are diphthongs, pronounced approximately as in English *aisle, euphony, boil*, unless the contrary is indicated, but *ae, oe*, are always two separate syllables; in Latin words *ae, oe*, are diphthongs.)

A. Mythological Names, Greek and Latin, including Fabulous Places

Abdē'rŏs, *Ἀβδηρος*, 214

Ac-, see also Ak-

Acca Larentia, 313 foll., 327

Achā'tēs, *Ἀχάτης*, 249 n. 14

Ă'chĕrōn, *Ἀχέρων*, 88, 100 n. 62

Achĭ'llēs, *Ἀχιλ(λ)εύς*, 13, 26, 80, 198, **233** foll., 260, 276; armour of, 236; in Hades, 88; and Helen, 243; invulnerability, 239

Ădmē'tŏs, *Ἄδμητος*, 140, 148

Ădō'nĭs, *Ἄδωνις*, 124, 157

Ădrā'stŏs, *Ἄδραστος*, s. of Tă'lăŏs, 67, 190 foll.

Ăē'dōn, *Ἀηδών*, 282 n. 28, 340

Ăē'llō, *Ἀελλώ*, 28, see Harpies

Aesculapius, 139, see Asklepios

Ăĕ'rŏpē. *Ἀερόπη*, 247.

Ăĕ'thlĭŏs, *Ἀέθλιος*, 258

Ăgămē'dēs, *Ἀγαμήδης*, 301

Ăgămĕ'mnōn, *Ἀγαμέμνων*, 119, 143, 231, 247, 276; genealogy of, 274

Ăgăpē'nōr. *Ἀγαπήνωρ*, 194

Ăgăthy̆'rsŏs, *Ἀγάθυρσος*, 215

Ăgaū'ē, *Ἀγαύη*, 152, 185

Ăgdĭ'stĭs, *Ἄγδιστις*, 170

Ăgē'nōr, *Ἀγήνωρ*, 149, 183-4

Ăglaū'rŏs, *Ἄγλαυρος*, 110–11, 158

Ă'grĭŏs, *Ἄγριος*, 57

Āī'ă, *Aἶα*, 197, 201

Āīāī'ă or ——ē, *Aἰαίη, Aeaea*, 203, 245

ae, for ai in Latin forms

Āī'ăkŏs, *Aἰακός, Aeacus*, 66, 84, **260**

Āī'ās, *Aἶας, Aiax*, (1) s. of Telamon, 198, **236** foll.; invulnerable, 239; (2) s. of Oileus, 142, **236** foll.

Āīē'tēs, *Aἰήτης*, 33, 197, 202, 292, 297

Āīgāī'ōn, *Aἰγαίων, Aegaeon*, see Briareos

Āī'geūs, *Aἰγεύς, Aegeus*, 263 ff.

Āīgĭăl'ēī ă, *Aἰγιάλεια*, 237

Āīgĭ'ălēus, *Aἰγιαλεύς*, 194, 196

Āīgĭ'mĭŏs, *Aἰγίμιος*, 219

Āīgĭ'nă, *Aἴγινα*, 281 n. 17, 294

Āī'gīpān, *Aἰγίπαν*, 59

Āīgĭ'sthŏs, *Aἴγισθος, Aegisthus*, 85, 247, 289

Āī'glē, *Aἴγλη*, 23; see Hesperides

Āīgy̆'ptŏs, *Aἴγυπτος, Aegyptus*, 220 n. 9, 272

Āīnēī'ās, *Aἰνείας, Aenē'as*, 125, 127, 153, **234** foll., 249 n. 14, 296, **307** foll.

343

[1] Γαλινθιάς in Anton. Lib. 29.

[1] Shakespeare did *not* pronounce it Hypērīon; it is not his fault if his readers cannot scan.

¹ Perhaps a mistake of Ovid's, see Roscher II, 1386, 2 ; not in Greek.

[1] The form Phaeton is a mere blunder, with no ancient authority.

[1] Schol., Od. X, 2, perhaps corrupt.

---

[1] But usually pronounced in English to rime with 'seen us.
[2] Rimes with 'deuce', not with 'see us'.

crab, ally of Hydra, 212 ; becomes constellation, *ibid.*

Crete, *Κρήτη, Crēta*, 46, 48, 61, 94, 113, 117, 137, 167, 171, **182** foll., 191, 265, 277, 293, 297, 307 ; bull of, 213, 265

cross-roads, 121

crow, legend of, 140

Cū'māē, *Κύμη*, 98 n. 48, 138, 307, 308

Cȳ'prŭs, *Κύπρος*, 122, 127, 300

Cyrus the Great, 289

DĂI'DĂLĂ, the, *Δαίδαλα*, 104

Dā'möklēs, *Δαμοκλῆς*, 298

Dancing Peacock, Jataka of, 293

Dē'lŏs, *Δῆλος*, 95, 114, 115, 120, 135, 159 n. 3, 276, 307

Dĕ'lphōī, *Δελφοί, Delphi*, 86, 135, 137, 184, 187, 194, 196, 197, 209, 218, 233, 262, 263, 267, 268, 269, 278, 279 ; oracle, legends of, 159 n. 8 ; called Pytho, 136

Devil, no Greek, 78, 294 ; as bridge-builder, 291

Di'ŏn, *Δῖον, Dium*, 256

dīthȳrámbŏs, *διθύραμβος*, 150

Dōdō'nă, *Δωδώνη*, 53, 175, 198

Dōlĭ'ŏnĕs, *Δολίονες*, 199

dolphins, legends of, 155, 300

Dorian Invasion, 267, 275

Dōrians, *Δωριῆς*, 205, 219

Dōriŏn, *Δώριον, Dorium*, 174

Dyaus, 47

E, DELPHIC, 137

Ĕchĭ'nădĕs, *Ἐχινάδες*, 206

Egypt, *Αἴγυπτος, Aegyptus*, 232, 247, 272, 306

Ĕlĕu'sĭs, *Ἐλευσίς*, 92, 95, 262, 264

Ē'lĭs, *Ἧλις*, 52, 157, 209, 278, 301

Ēpēī'rŏs, *Ἤπειρος, Ēpī'rŭs*, 235, 274, 307

Ĕpīmĕ'nīdĕs, *Ἐπιμενίδης*, 139, 293

Ĕrȳmánthŏs, *Ἐρύμανθος*, river, 289; boar of, 212

Ethiopians, *Αἴθιοπες, Aethi'ŏpĕs*, 242, 273

Ēubōī'ă, *Εὔβοια, Euboēa*, 103, 104, 276

Euē'nŏs, *Εὔηνος*, 142, 209

Euhemerism, 5 foll. ; in Italy, 310, 323, 327

Euthy'mŏs, *Εὔθυμος*, 279

Exodus, 175, 306

FĪcVs RŬMĬNĀLIS, 315

' fifty ', meaning of, 41 n. 86

Fórmiae, 279

Fŏrum, 314, 322

France, 215

GĂ'BĬĪ, 321

Gallicia, 89

Games ; Olympian, 167, 274 ; Pythian, 137 ; Isthmian, 270 ; Nemean, 191

Gelert, 294

geography, Greek, 18

God, folk-tale concerning, 299 ; gods, Greek, association with beasts, 176–7 ; characteristics of, 176 ; flight of, from Typhon, 59 ; and Giants, 57, 117 ; in Homer, 19 ; identifications of, with foreign deities, 59 ; and Titans, 22 ; the Twelve, 164 n. 68, 181 ; gods as demons, 62 ; gods, Italian, 306

Golden Bough, 308

Greeks, attitude of, towards gods, 148 ; towards burial, 192 ; beliefs concerning birds, 105 ; eschatological ideas, inconsistency of, 88 ; local legends of, Chapter IX *passim* ; racial composition of, 18

HEARTH, cult of, 167 ; see Hestia, Vesta

Hĕ'kătē's Island, *Ἐκάτης νῆσος*, 28

Hĕ'lĭkōn, *Ἑλικών*, 63, 174

Hellespont, *Ἑλλήσποντος*, 197

(H)énna, *Ἔννα, Ἔννα*, 91, 94

Hĕrmĭ'ŏnē, *Ἑρμιόνη* (town), 105

Hĭppŏklēī'dēs, *Ἱπποκλείδης, Hippocli'des*, 293

Hĭppŏkrē'nē, *Ἱπποκρήνη*, 284 n. 55

Hittites, 274